VIETNAM AND BEYOND

Vietnam and Beyond

Tim O'Brien and the Power of Storytelling

Stefania Ciocia

LIVERPOOL UNIVERSITY PRESS

First published 2012 by
Liverpool University Press
4 Cambridge Street
Liverpool
L69 7ZU

This paperback version published 2014

British Library Cataloguing-in-Publication data
A British Library CIP record is available

ISBN 978-1-84631-820-7 cased
     978-1-78138-004-8 paperback

Typeset by XL Publishing Services, Exmouth
Printed and bound in the UK by CPI Group (UK) Ltd, Croydon CR0 4YY

Contents

Acknowledgements

I would like to thank Thomas Docherty, Rod Edmond, Páraic Finnerty, Abdulrazak Gurnah, Giorgio Mariani and Andrew Palmer for their feedback and support in the various stages of development of this project.

I am particularly grateful to Keith Carabine, whose incisive comments on my manuscript have been invaluable. I cannot thank him enough for his advice and generous encouragement.

Sections of Chapter 1 and Chapter 5 first appeared as 'Conradian Echoes in Vietnam War Literature: Tim O'Brien's Rewriting of *Heart of Darkness* in "Sweetheart of the Song Tra Bong"' in *Symbiosis: A Journal of Anglo-American Literary Relations*, 11.1 (2007), pp. 3–30, and are reprinted here by kind permission of the journal. My thanks go to Chris Gair and the reviewers of *Symbiosis* for this early demonstration of interest in my work on O'Brien.

This book is dedicated to Amedeo and Marilena, my parents.

List of Abbreviations

The editions of Tim O'Brien's works cited parenthetically in the text are abbreviated as follows:

GAC *Going After Cacciato* (London: Flamingo, 1988)
IID *If I Die in a Combat Zone* (London: Harper Perennial, 2006)
JJ *July, July* (London: Flamingo, 2002)
LW *In the Lake of the Woods* (London: Flamingo, 1995)
NA *The Nuclear Age* (London: Collins, 1986)
NL *Northern Lights* (London: Flamingo, 1998)
TL *Tomcat in Love* (London: Flamingo, 2000)
TTC *The Things They Carried* (London: Flamingo, 1991)

Introduction

In March 2010, Houghton Mifflin Harcourt brought out the twentieth anniversary edition of the Pulitzer Prize and National Book Critics Circle Award finalist *The Things They Carried*, marking with this decision the book's status as Tim O'Brien's most accomplished and significant work – a remarkable compliment indeed, if one thinks that his earlier *Going After Cacciato* had won the National Book Award in 1979. With its publication some six months before President Obama declared the end of the war in Iraq and set July 2011 as the deadline for the beginning of the withdrawal of American troops from Afghanistan, the twentieth anniversary edition of this seminal text about the war in Vietnam has rekindled comparisons between the conflict in the Southeast Asian peninsula, and the more recent American military interventions in the Middle East. Echoing O'Brien's epistemological insecurity of two decades ago, Joseph Peschel declares that 'the only certainty is overwhelming ambiguity', regardless of one's stance on 'the moral and political validity of the wars in Iraq and Afghanistan'.[1] On his part, having drawn his own explicit comparison between these conflicts and Vietnam, O'Brien focuses on the human and emotional cost of warfare, on the soldiers as well as their families and, by extension, on society as a whole:

> Obviously there are differences [between now and then], chief among them the absence of the draft. But there are enough similarities. These are wars in which there are no uniforms, no front, no rear. Who's the enemy? What do you shoot back at? Whom do you trust? At the bottom, all wars are the same because they involve death and maiming and wounding, and grieving mothers, fathers, sons and daughters.[2]

1 Joseph Peschel, 'Tim O'Brien's *The Things They Carried*, released in 20th anniversary edition, renews war's ambiguity', in Steven Levingston, 'Political Bookworm. Where Tomorrow's Must-read Political Books Are Discovered Today', *The Washington Post*, 24 March 2010, http://voices.washingtonpost.com/political-bookworm/2010/03/tim_obriens_the_things_they_ca.html (accessed 25 November 2010).
2 Tim O'Brien, quoted in Susan Hodara, 'Asking the Whole Country to Embrace a War Story', *The New York Times*, 29 January 2010, http://www.nytimes.com/2010/01/31/nyregion/31bookwe.html (accessed 25 November 2010).

Thirty-five years after the fall of Saigon, the shedding of 'certain blood for uncertain reasons' (*IID*, 167) still remains, sadly, a topical subject. In spite of the renewed relevance of his writing to the contemporary global political scene, O'Brien is not very well known outside the United States; moreover, even in his own country, he is generally perceived – for reasons that are all too obvious – as a niche artist, the breadth of whose work, no matter how sharp in its insights and skilful in its execution, is confined within the realm of war literature, rather than being judged against the parameters of great literature *tout court*. This pigeon-holing, understandable in the light of O'Brien's compulsive return to the literal and figurative landscape of the Vietnamese conflict, and of his awareness of the challenges inherent in writing about unspeakable, traumatic events, fails to do justice to his achievements as a postmodern fabulator, an acute observer of the human condition and a sharp critic of American culture.

As my title indicates, this study is predicated on the conviction that Tim O'Brien has revitalized war literature, taking it beyond the contingencies of the experience of armed conflict to an exploration and an affirmation of the power of storytelling, through formal innovations, metanarrative reflections and a recurrent concern for pressing philosophical questions on matters such as individual agency, ethical responsibility and authenticity. In other words, while it would be close to impossible (and, if possible, then certainly counterproductive) not to acknowledge the centrality of the experience of the war in his writing, Vietnam is for O'Brien a productive starting point for the treatment of wider themes with a deep, universal resonance – the human need for love, the quest for meaning, the wrestling with ethical dilemmas, the coming to terms with one's failures – and for the development of thought-provoking formal experiments underpinned by a strong sense of one's moral accountability. O'Brien's narrative engagement with the war in Southeast Asia has also involved the development of a critical attitude towards those myths that inform America's perception of itself and, more generally, a number of ideological positions common in Western culture: the association between courage, heroism and masculinity, the celebration of the pioneering spirit in the frontier narrative, the unquestioned sense of superiority in the encounter with foreign civilizations, the fraught relationship between power and truth, or reality and imagination, and the ability and the right to articulate one's perception of things. These latter themes, in particular, prompt interesting considerations on the role and the responsibility of the storyteller, in what is undoubtedly an important corrective to postmodern writing practices, whose self-reflectiveness and linguistic and technical playfulness have often been perceived as a jettisoning of the ethical dimension. From this perspective, it cannot be emphasized enough how much O'Brien's rigorous ethical focus sets him apart from the narcissism, and the ostensible lack of political charge, of a more gratuitously playful postmodern aesthetics – from a 'high' postmodernism, that is, characterized by ironic appropriations, experimental excesses, depthlessness and a gusto for pastiche and virtuoso citationality.[3] O'Brien himself has resisted the label of 'postmodern writer', and taken a distance from what he sees as the 'gimmicky' and 'frivolous' nature of the fiction of this period[4] – although in this instance he too may be guilty of overlooking the serious, political potential of such literature. This study supports the validity of the claim that O'Brien partakes of a postmodern sensitivity, most clearly encapsulated in his deconstructive spirit, paired with a keen scrutiny of, and ultimately an investment in, the performative power of storytelling; and yet it is true that the question of 'how we know' takes centre stage in most of his narratives, thus aligning his work also to modernist, cognitive concerns.[5]

Taken to be an imaginative enterprise without any pretensions to mimetic accuracy, at least in a literal sense, storytelling for O'Brien is indeed in the first instance an epistemological tool with a role in the individual's quest for truth and signification. Naturally, such a quest becomes particularly urgent, and liable to generate controversy, in the case of war writing, where an objective perception of truth – should we be willing to posit its feasibility, in disagreement with postmodern (and modernist) theorizations – would have to come to life in spite of unarguably adverse conditions, given how wars are fought and won through propaganda, as well as on the battlefield. In Vietnam, the site of notoriously heated ideological clashes, both on the home front in the US and in the effort to win the 'hearts and minds' of the local population, the difficulty in reaching consensus over objective facts was further complicated, in the field, by the arduousness of deciding what was

---

3 Of course, claiming that postmodernism lacks altogether an ethical and/or political stance is, at the very least, an oversimplification, whose refutation would deserve a longer discussion than can be afforded in the present volume. For a persuasive problematization of the facile association between postmodernism and a fundamentally disengaged stance, see, for example, Linda Hutcheon's reminder of the wider political dimension of postmodern representation, which 'does work to turn its inevitable ideological grounding into a site of de-naturalizing critique'; *The Politics of Postmodernism* (New York: Routledge, 1989), p. 3.

4 Larry McCaffery, 'Interview with Tim O'Brien', *Chicago Review*, 33.2 (1982), pp. 129–49, p. 148.

5 On the basis of Brian McHale's definition of modernism and postmodernism as having, respectively, an epistemological/cognitive and ontological/post-cognitive dominant, Alex Vernon makes a compelling argument for considering Tim O'Brien as a modernist writer (cf. his *Soldiers Once and Still: Ernest Hemingway, James Salter and Tim O'Brien* [Iowa City: University of Iowa Press, 2004]). My own reading of O'Brien, instead, places greater emphasis on those qualities in his work that are more firmly on the postmodern side of the spectrum – although, in the end, given what I regard as the continuity between the two terms (and the fact that their use is meant to throw light on the work in question, rather than be an end in itself), an exact categorization of O'Brien's writing is something of a moot point.

real and what was the product of a besieged imagination, or of perception affected by the strains of combat and of an alien and hostile environment. More generally, the traumatic nature of the military experience and the extreme stress induced by a continuous proximity to death often produce a sense of estrangement and a radical reappraisal of the significance and the worth of human life, and of one's system of values. In this context, and quite apart from the epistemological scepticism characteristic of (post)modernism, the possibility of objectivity in Vietnam war writing recedes further and further into the distance. Against this background, and in line with a long-standing culture of suspicion towards the mimetic claims of formal realism, O'Brien chooses to emphasise the proximity between fact and fiction, and the mutual sphere of influence between imagination and reality; in doing so, he highlights how perceptions and impressions get channelled into stories, how we live life thinking of ourselves as the actors of these narrations, in a two-way process in which emotional veracity is, controversially perhaps, more important than factual accuracy.

O'Brien articulates these convictions most memorably and succinctly in setting up an opposition between two radically different concepts of truth. 'Happening-truth' and its antithesis 'story-truth' are central to O'Brien's poetics: the former makes a claim to literalness, factuality and objectivity in representation, while the latter rejects these qualities as unimportant, or even detrimental to the fundamental pursuit of the writer. According to O'Brien,

> [l]iterature should be looked at not for its literal truths but for its emotional quali-
> ties. What matters in literature, I think, are pretty simple things – whether it
> moves me or not, whether it feels true. The actual literal truth should be super-
> fluous. For example, here's a story: four guys go on a trail, a grenade sails out, one
> guy jumps on it, takes the blast, and saves his buddies. Is it true? Well, yeah, it may
> have happened, but it doesn't feel true, because it feels stereotypical, hackneyed;
> it feels like Hollywood. But here's another story: four guys go on a trail, a grenade
> sails out, one guy jumps on it, takes the blast, and dies; before he dies, though, one
> of the guys says, 'What the fuck you do that for?' and the dead guy says, 'The story
> of my life, man,' and starts to smile. He's dead. That didn't happen. Clearly, ever,
> and yet there is something about the absurdity of it and the horror of it – 'What
> the fuck you do that for?' – which seems truer to me than something which might
> literally have happened. A story's truth shouldn't be measured by happening but
> by an entirely different standard, a standard of emotion, feeling – 'Does it ring
> true?' as opposed to 'Is it true?'[6]

6 Martin Naparsteck, 'An Interview with Tim O'Brien', *Contemporary Literature*, 32.1 (1991), pp. 1–11, pp. 9–10. O'Brien mentions the same two stories about the four guys on a trail in 'How to Tell a True War Story' in *The Things They Carried*. The terms 'story-truth' and 'happening-truth' occur later on in the same narrative, in a vignette entitled

Consequently, O'Brien legitimizes and practises a certain narrative embellishment of factual reality in place of (the attempt at) a faithful account of things as they happened; in this way, he means to try to salvage, and then communicate, the exact intensity of the original impact of the narrated events on those who experienced them, either first-hand, or even only as powerful stories, i.e. as endeavours to wrench some narrative sense out of the inchoate, chaotic, subjective material that makes up our existence. In his doomed quest for precision, veracity and signification, O'Brien invests in the power of storytelling to invent – both in its etymological meaning 'to find out' and with its current connotations as 'to fabricate' – and make available to narrators and listeners/readers alike a partial and provisional 'story-truth'. 'Story-truth' is thus closely connected to the performative aspect of the narrative enterprise seen as an endless process of infinite repetitions and modulations of the same tales, in the hope of achieving an ever closer approximation to the elusive target of the 'true war story'. Not merely a function of storytelling as a perpetual work-in-progress, the performativity of O'Brien's narratives is also to be understood in terms derived from J. L. Austin's linguistic theory and his definition of performative speech acts: instead of being truth-evaluable, these utterances can either be felicitous or infelicitous. Similarly, rather than being measured against their veracity or falsity, O'Brien's stories are conceived and demand to be appreciated for their ability 'to make the stomach believe' (*TTC*, 75), for their narrative and affective success, as speech acts making real – if only momentarily, as an imponderable gut feeling, or a 'quick truth goose' (*TTC*, 34) – that which they are talking about.

O'Brien's investment in the affective strength of his stories is potentially controversial, particularly in the context of his recurrent military subject matter. The appropriateness, if not the legitimacy, of taking any liberties with factuality in writing about Vietnam has been raised even by readers sympathetic to O'Brien's practice. In an early interview with O'Brien, for example, Eric James Schroeder asks the inevitable question: 'Don't you see Vietnam in particular as a subject which shouldn't need embellishment?'[7] Of course, O'Brien disagrees, asserting once more his conviction that the 'lying' involved in fictional re-elaborations of certain experiences – such as the horror, or even the boredom, of war – eventually reveals a deeper truth. Besides, in the statement which had triggered Schroeder's original question, O'Brien had made an explicit connection between the author's right to exert his or her imaginative freedom and the very nature of fiction: 'The sense of embellishment, letting one's imagination heighten detail, is part of what

'Good Form'; interestingly, the two notions are not defined, but rather illustrated by the examples of two competing versions of the story about the enemy killed by the narrator.

7 Eric James Schroeder, 'Two Interviews: Talks with Tim O'Brien and Robert Stone', *Modern Fiction Studies*, 30.1 (1984), pp. 135–64, p. 141.

fiction-writing is about. It's not lying. It's trying to produce a story detail that will get at a felt experience.'[8] With this in mind, we need to recognize and appreciate that O'Brien's greatest achievement has been the harnessing of the postmodern sensitivity of his time towards the inquiry into matters of personal responsibility, without ever shirking the acknowledgement of the partiality of one's point of view, and of the cowardice or the iniquity of one's actions; he has done so relentlessly, even at the cost of alienating readers from his protagonists, as in his characterization of a self-righteous, self-pitying, desensitized 'Tim O'Brien' in 'How to Tell a True War Story'. Underpinned by a profound scepticism towards orthodoxies of any kind, O'Brien's oeuvre targets time-honoured US, and Western, myths, including the ideal connection between storytelling and self-improvement, particularly strong in the tradition of American autobiographical writing, so often geared towards charting the individual's spiritual growth and intellectual maturation. O'Brien openly demystifies the long-standing investment, particularly common in the century of psychoanalysis, in the narrative act as a vehicle of catharsis or consolation, or as a process of sense-making and (self-)instruction. Rather, he views storytelling as a means of inquiry which occasionally manages to capture an all too volatile truth, while forcing us to come to terms with our moral quandaries and obligations.

In exposing the hidden mechanisms of storytelling and in deliberately frustrating the readers' desire for a reliable source of information, however incomplete and approximate, O'Brien has been accused of indulging in postmodern, narcissistic gimmickry, in books – such as, most famously, *The Things They Carried* – where the narrator appears to be repeatedly pulling the rug from under his readers' feet with multiple, discordant accounts of the same event, while bedazzling his audience with the impossibility of separating fact from fiction, and autobiographical material from artistic licence and pure invention. Still, I would reiterate that these narrative strategies, practised with particular success in his most celebrated works, are intertwined with O'Brien's painful awareness of his inability to find catharsis in the act of storytelling. This poignant conviction, together with the reminder that we cannot delegate our individual responsibilities, is one of the few certainties that O'Brien is unstintingly determined to share with his readers. Thus, from the rubble of Western grand narratives, and American myths in particular, O'Brien propounds a small-scale, immanent notion of ethics, grounded on something akin to the storyteller's creativity: the human capacity for empathy, which extends from the ability to imagine what it would be like to be somebody else to the knack of envisioning – and subsequently embracing – an alternative future for oneself. Seen from this

---

8   Schroeder, 'Two Interviews', p. 140.

perspective, the failure to adopt an ethical position is often seen to begin with a 'failure of the imagination' (*GAC*, 296). This, too, is an important reminder that the stories we tell about ourselves, to ourselves and to other people, play a crucial role in mediating our relationship with reality and in fostering a more conscious and/or active engagement with it.

O'Brien's critical approach to distinctive American narratives and ideas is the main reason why the present volume, unlike other book-length studies of his work, is organized thematically, rather than chronologically. Both Steven Kaplan's pioneering *Understanding Tim O'Brien* (University of South Carolina Press, 1994) and Mark A. Heberle's *A Trauma Artist: Tim O'Brien and the Fiction of Vietnam* (University of Iowa Press, 2001) proceed chronologically, devoting one chapter to each individual book. Only Tobey C. Herzog has adopted, partially, a thematic approach in his *Tim O'Brien*, published in the Twayne's United States Authors Series in 1997. Herzog disrupts the sequential analysis of O'Brien's output by pairing up *Going After Cacciato* and *The Things They Carried* in a central chapter on the interplay between memory, reality and imagination. These three monographs chart the development of O'Brien's career up until the time of their respective publication: for this reason, Kaplan and Herzog conclude their studies with a reading of *In the Lake of the Woods* (1994), while Heberle is also able to include an analysis of *Tomcat in Love* (1998). To the best of my knowledge, the only author to have written a comprehensive account of Tim O'Brien's entire publishing career, from *If I Die in a Combat Zone* (1973) to *July, July* (2002), is Patrick A. Smith in *Tim O'Brien: A Critical Companion* (2005) in the 'Critical Companions to Popular Contemporary Writers' series of the Greenwood Press. Structured in the customary chronological sequence, with the analysis of each individual text supplemented by an alternative reading from a specific theoretical perspective, Smith's companion is aimed more towards a high-school audience than the academic community. Also different in scope from the present volume is the recent *Approaches to Teaching the Works of Tim O'Brien*, a collection of essays edited by Alex Vernon and Catherine Calloway, published by the Modern Language Association in December 2010. In adding my own voice to the rich scholarly debate on Tim O'Brien, I have been keen to take advantage of the possibilities opened up by my thematic approach.

Central to my attempt to go beyond Vietnam is also a focus on gender, stimulated by O'Brien's revision of traditional notions of masculinity and femininity; unsurprisingly, together with his metafictional experimentations, this is the other element of O'Brien's work to have generated much interest, and some critical controversy. For example, with its examination of the nature of courage, O'Brien's early writing has been widely interpreted as voicing the need for a feminization of this virtue, so as to temper the masculine (or macho) excesses that often imbue its characterization, particularly in a military context. Admirers of his work point this out as evidence of O'Brien's distance from the misogynist backlash that, according to cultural historians such as Susan Jeffords, swept through the United States in the aftermath of the Vietnam war; his detractors, on the other hand, argue that O'Brien's re-definition of courage, however well-meaning, ultimately does little more than perpetuate gender stereotypes, even as – or precisely as – it advocates the embrace of traditional feminine qualities. The narrative of the frontier – a major influence in American culture, and Vietnam war writing in particular – is another theme whose analysis demands a discussion of American masculinity. O'Brien's handling of this narrative and his creation of an alternative landscape of mythical (or rather, as we shall see, apocalyptic) resonance has also sparked much critical attention, often focused on exposing the misogyny still prevalent not merely in military culture and, by extension, in war narratives, but specifically in O'Brien's characterization of women and representation of the experience of trauma. Even the matter of the representation and interpretation of the reality of war, and of the communication dynamics at play in the articulation of potentially ineffable or otherwise problematic topics, has been approached by several scholars with a view to unpicking any gendered nuances in O'Brien's treatment of the subject. Particularly contentious is the allegation that O'Brien has a tendency to single out unsympathetic *female* interlocutors as the epitome of an uncomprehending, or even hostile, audience exposed to the plight of the war veteran. Thus, while each of my chapters focuses on a specific topic, they are also linked by a further, common thematic undercurrent, for they all address, with varied intensity and from different perspectives, the questions about gender definitions that are so often raised by – and in relation to – O'Brien's work, and war writing in general.

Chapter 1 provides an introductory context for the rest of the volume, outlining the postmodernity of the war in Vietnam, the influence of frontier narratives and of the Conradian trope of the journey into the heart of darkness on perceptions of the conflict, and the anti-heroic pattern of twentieth-century war writing. These issues are revisited in the main body of the monograph: beyond its thematic resonance as a study of the 'fascination of the abomination', the Conradian legacy illuminates O'Brien's scrutiny of the epistemological power of storytelling, and his embrace of a postmodern sensitivity. In turn, the relationship between the Vietnam war and the mood of postmodernity ties in with the analysis of the truth and morality of storytelling, while the impact of the frontier myth on expectations and representations of the conflict, and America's sense of itself in its aftermath, paves the way for the discussion of O'Brien's take on the American wilderness and of his topography of trauma. The identification of an ironic, anti-military tradition in war writing and of the fallout from the mythology of World War II lead directly to the analysis of O'Brien's re-definition of courage in Chapter 2, which thus focuses on the notion of authenticity – rather than the adherence to a masculine code of values – as the real theoretical framework for his critique of traditional views of heroism. This early chapter also illustrates O'Brien's awareness of the limitations of the *Bildungsroman* model, so common both in war and in anti-war writing, but rejected by most of his narratives. In this sense, O'Brien takes the lead from Stephen Crane's ironic treatment of the quest for military glory in *The Red Badge of Courage* (1895), but pushes the anti-heroic lesson one step further, disputing the need for experiential contact with the war in order to ascertain one's courage and moral integrity. Chapter 3 moves from the 'trilogy of courage' (*If I Die in a Combat Zone*, *Northern Lights* and *Going After Cacciato*) to an analysis of those novels set primarily in the United States: together, *Northern Lights*, *In the Lake of the Woods* and *The Nuclear Age* constitute a different pioneer country – identified for the most part with a daunting northern landscape, and its rigorous ethos – from the western frontier, from whose mythology O'Brien obviously wants to distance himself. The mapping of this alternative national landscape is complemented by an overview of O'Brien's exposure of the fallacy in the identification of Vietnam as a new 'Indian Country'. The disingenuousness of the projection of evil qualities on a (feminized) alien landscape is linked, in the following chapter, to a discussion of the charges of misogyny that have occasionally been levelled at O'Brien.

As already mentioned, the consideration of the extent to which and the ways in which O'Brien manages to eschew gender stereotypes and misogynist positions, while acknowledging their existence and their pervasive influence, particularly in the rhetoric of war, is a thread that runs through this entire study. It does so for obvious reasons, given the institutionalized sexism in much military culture, and given that the passionate critical debate on O'Brien's treatment of gender demands that the present discussion should also take a position on the issue. Chapter 4 is where O'Brien's writing choices are shown to be inextricably connected to the ineffable experience of trauma, and to an engagement with cultural perceptions/representations of gender. This is a crucial issue, deserving of the extensive analysis it receives, because it underpins the investigation of the core argument of this study: the nature of O'Brien's investment in the power of storytelling. While Chapters 2 and 3 deal primarily with thematic questions, in relation to O'Brien as a sharp critic of received orthodoxies, and an alternative mythographer in his own right, Chapter 4 instead begins the scrutiny of O'Brien's poetics and narrative techniques. For all that his writing theory and practice are tightly interwoven with the traumatic – and often 'politically incorrect', for lack of a better expression – nature of his subject matter, O'Brien consistently strives to soar above the strictures of war literature (in the narrow sense of literature about combat, and its aftermath), demystifying its commonplaces and developing its potential to 'magnify' universal quandaries.[9]

The first part of Chapter 4 shows how O'Brien rejects the association, common in the literature of the conflict, between Vietnam and the image of the *vagina dentata*; O'Brien's symbolic topography instead privileges the non-gendered trope of the *cloaca* – most famously visible in the image of the shit field, the prime locus of trauma in *The Things They Carried* – as a correlative of the horror of war. Having delved more specifically into the gender anxieties experienced by both the male and the female characters in O'Brien's narratives, the second part of this chapter moves into a preliminary analysis of the difficult communication dynamics at work between those with experience of the war, and those who have remained 'in the world' – a challenging rift that is indeed configured as corresponding, often but not inevitably so, to a binary gender divide. In fact, O'Brien always exposes the cultural conditioning behind stereotyped (self-)perceptions of men and women, highlighting in the process how the (masculine) investment in an ideal of (feminine) innocence is one of the results – to be perhaps sympathised with, but not condoned – of his characters' attempt to come to terms with trauma. The third section of Chapter 4 expands this line of investigation in order to consider O'Brien's concern with the universal longing for love, and the pain and frustration that accompany the traumatised subjects' difficulty in forming and maintaining healthy emotional relationships. These themes are the focus of *The Nuclear Age*, *Tomcat in Love* and *July, July*, O'Brien's three comic novels, which have been frequently ignored by academic readers and literary commentators.

O'Brien's caricatural excesses and penchant for the ridiculously and contemptuously comic, rather than for a less dark and scathing form of humour, partly explain why these fiercely argumentative texts – which well deserve to be defined as novels of ideas – have typically elicited a different response from the one reserved to O'Brien's other works: their protagonists' failure to be true to themselves is unmitigated in these cases by the appeal to sympathy inherent in the restrained narrative tone, and the nuanced characterization, to be found in O'Brien's more accomplished texts. Interestingly, however, for all its compositional limitations, it is the earliest of these comic novels, *The Nuclear Age*, that offers in Sarah Strouch the most developed

---

9 In a 1994 interview, O'Brien has indeed claimed that '[t]he environment of war is the environment of life, magnified'; Brian C. McNerney, 'Responsibly Inventing History: An Interview with Tim O'Brien', *War, Literature, and the Arts: An International Journal of the Humanities*, 6.2 (1994), pp. 1–26, p. 23.

female character in O'Brien's work. A strong, intriguing, rounded figure, and an anticipation of the transgressive Mary Anne Bell in 'Sweetheart of the Song Tra Bong', Sarah has the stature of the protagonist of a Greek tragedy, doomed as she is by a 'fatal flaw'. Nonetheless, she remains unwavering on her path towards authenticity, and has therefore a rightful claim to being the real heroine in the text, worthier of respect than her male counterpart. The final section of Chapter 4 turns to *The Things They Carried*, O'Brien's most celebrated work and the text where he most overtly outlines his poetics of reception. In his practice and in his metafictional theorizations in *Things*, O'Brien is critical *both* of masculine (rational, syntagmatic, metonymical) *and* of feminine (emotional, paradigmatic, metaphorical) declensions and responses to storytelling. By contrast, O'Brien argues for a non-gendered, visceral approach to his stories, which rely on ambiguities and ellipses in order to deal with the unspeakable issue of traumatisation.

After considering matters of narrative structure and technique in O'Brien's entire output, Chapter 5 opens with a section devoted to 'Sweetheart of the Song Tra Bong', one of the most arresting stories in *The Things They Carried*. In this short narrative, O'Brien acts on the idea that the war can only be understood 'as though it were a story' by engaging in a sustained and fruitful conversation with Joseph Conrad's *Heart of Darkness*, one of the most suggestive tales in the modern Western literary canon. The comparative close reading of the two texts highlights the evocative and sense-making power of 'Sweetheart of the Song Tra Bong' as a creative re-elaboration of the experience of Vietnam. O'Brien's encounter with Conrad's novella provides a critical and imaginative distance from factual constraints; this distance is crucial to the writer's attempt to convey and comprehend the true significance of the conflict. At the same time, the analysis of the differences between *Heart of Darkness* and 'Sweetheart of the Song Tra Bong' reveals a shift from a subtle modernist critique of patriarchal ideology to a postmodern deconstruction of the naturalness of gender roles, and from a modernist 'nihilistic' epistemological scepticism to the postmodern wilful recuperation of the notion of a truth (however local and provisional) to be yielded by the mythopoetic power of storytelling. To this end O'Brien reworks the Conradian sequence of embedded narratives that communicate and obscure – one might say 'envelop' – the truth about Kurtz (and Marlow) into a multivocal act of mythopoesis that marvels at, celebrates and engages each time anew with Mary Anne and her story. This case study begins to bring the volume to a close, for it provides an opportunity to offer some concluding remarks on the scope and the quality of O'Brien's output, while revisiting its main themes and the characteristics of its writing: O'Brien's literariness; his development of Conrad's modernist sensitivity into a postmodern one; his treatment of the Vietnamese environment, and of American preconceptions about it; his confrontation with the ideal middle landscape between wilderness and civilization, and the draw of this tension on the American imaginary; his representation of women and his view of gender relations; and, finally, his articulation of trauma, his poetics of reception and his investment in storytelling.

The second and third parts of Chapter 5 return to *The Things They Carried* in its entirety, in order to explore its articulation of the distinction between 'story-truth' and 'happening-truth', and the author's endorsement of the former over the latter as the only truth potentially available to the storyteller. In line with illustrious American predecessors, such as Nathaniel Hawthorne, whose theory of romance provides a luminous example, O'Brien's attitude towards the apprehension and the communication of truth is a celebration of the epistemological power of storytelling, and of fiction writing in particular. This optimistic engagement with an attempt at sense-making is accompanied by a less buoyant view of the potential for catharsis yielded by the whole process. Thus, O'Brien firmly rejects the moral authority typically associated with experience, in favour of a fragile, and always provisional, personal connection with the Other, to be sought after in the endless refashioning of stories and in the imaginative identification with the plight of fellow human beings – an imperfect foundation for our ethical commitments, and yet the only foundation available to us at all. Like the numerous thematic and formal concerns listed above, these lessons too are encapsulated in 'Sweetheart of the Song Tra Bong', whose intertextual and metafictional elements provide one of the most felicitous enactments of O'Brien's belief that stories should develop in more than one telling, and generate more stories, and continue to resonate with narrators and audiences long after their performance. At its best, O'Brien's writing certainly has the power to do all these things.

1

Vietnam and Beyond

'*There was a map of Vietnam on the wall of my apartment in Saigon and some nights, coming back late to the city, I'd lie out on my bed and look at it, too tired to do anything more than just get my boots off. That map was a marvel, especially now that it wasn't real anymore.*'[1] The opening lines of Michael Herr's *Dispatches* (1977) – among the most influential narratives of the war in Vietnam – suggest a fascination with the act of mapping, even in the knowledge of its historical contingency and fundamental inadequacy as an epistemological tool. While the mention of these limitations may be a counterintuitive place to start from, for a monograph intent on its own kind of charting, Herr's reference to the allure of the cartographer's work brings to mind a more famous recollection of the enthralling power of maps – Charlie Marlow's memory of the seductive power of the 'many blank spaces on the earth'[2] in Joseph Conrad's *Heart of Darkness* (1899), a canonical thematization of the ineffable enchantment that comes from the perception of alien lands as mysterious places waiting to be explored and deciphered, or conquered. Beckoning from the depths of Africa, on whose map – what used to be the biggest blank of all – it stands out as an 'immense snake uncoiled', the river Congo casts its spell on Marlow, and his audience: 'The snake had charmed me' (22). I am keen to start – as I will end, in much greater detail – with an allusion to Conrad's novella for a number of reasons. To begin with, given its thought-provoking treatment of the challenges inherent in the encounter – or rather, the clash – between different cultures, as well as in the articulation of such an experience and, more generally, in the investigation of the human potential for savagery, *Heart of Darkness* has played a considerable role in setting the place of the Vietnam war in our collective imagination and has had an enduring impact on American representations of the conflict, most notably, of course, through the mediation of Francis Ford Coppola's *Apocalypse Now* (1979). O'Brien himself has revisited the Conradian model

---

1 Michael Herr, *Dispatches* (London: Picador, 1978), p. 11.
2 Joseph Conrad, *Heart of Darkness* (London: Penguin, 1995), p. 22. Subsequent references are to this edition.

in 'Sweetheart of the Song Tra Bong', originally published as a short story in *Esquire* in July 1989 and subsequently incorporated into *The Things They Carried*. While the trope of the journey into the heart of darkness will be outlined later on in this chapter and analysed in depth near the end of this volume, for the time being the reference to Conrad's long shadow prompts a couple of quick, introductory points about O'Brien's work and Vietnam war literature in general.

One of the first considerations to strike O'Brien's readers – even when his intertextual connections are not as easily discernible as those in 'Sweetheart' – is that he is very much a writers' writer and a committed craftsman, conscious of his literary and cultural influences. He is a wordsmith with a clear interest in exploring the mechanisms of language, as well as in testing the technical and formal limits and the sense-making potential of his chosen medium, narrative writing. Those familiar with his working methods will also be aware that O'Brien, true to his belief that making sentences takes a lot of time and effort,[3] drafts and revises several versions of his material before he can be satisfied with the final result. Indeed, he has been known to make changes to his manuscripts at the very last minute: for example, *In the Lake of the Woods* contains significant revisions to the preview copy which had appeared only four months prior to the book's actual publication.[4] From the beginning of his career – in fact, particularly at the beginning of his career – O'Brien's intellectual and self-reflective drive has been most noticeable in his dialogue with other authors and other texts, and in his musings on the art of storytelling, from the overt philosophical and cultural references in *If I Die in a Combat Zone* to his all too heavy debt to Ernest Hemingway in *Northern Lights*, and the metanarrative scope of *Going After Cacciato*. Throughout his career, O'Brien has continued to adopt deliberately complex narrative structures, in order to avoid the mimetic fallacy that would have us see writing as a straightforward transcription or reproduction of reality. Indeed, with the exception of his first novel *Northern Lights*, O'Brien has always privileged the diegetic aspect of his texts – that is, the act of storytelling through which the events in the tale get processed and communicated to an audience – over what, as Gérard Genette shrewdly points out, is only ever the '*illusion of mimesis*' afforded by narrative writing (unless, of course, the narrative subject be language, or the act of writing itself).[5] Flagging up the existence and the

---

3   'Interview with Tim O'Brien', http://bigthink.com/timobrien, 15 April 2010 (accessed 10 July 2010).

4   Steven Kaplan, *Understanding Tim O'Brien* (Columbia, SC: University of South Carolina Press, 1994), p. 218, n. 4. O'Brien has also frequently published, as short stories in magazines, excerpts from longer works-in-progress.

5   Gérard Genette, *Narrative Discourse: An Essay in Method* [1972], trans. Jane E. Lewin (Ithaca, NY: Cornell University Press, 1980), p. 164. Other narratological terms that will be of use in my analysis of O'Brien's work are 'intradiegetic' and '*mise en abyme*'.

role of his narrators, emphasizing the context of the narrating situation, foregrounding all storytelling acts and exchanges, and generally never letting readers forget that they are accessing an inevitably mediated version of events, O'Brien constantly gives prominence to *diegesis* over *mimesis* in his works. The two terms should not be merely construed in the Platonic and Aristotelian opposition of 'narrative' vs. 'imitation', or 'reporting' vs. 're-presentation' (or even Wayne Booth's 'telling' vs. 'showing'[6]); besides being the mark of a preference for a particular kind of narrative delivery, O'Brien's embrace of the diegetic also signals the author's considerable investment in the power of storytelling to extract meaning from – or indeed inject meaning into – our (real or imaginative) perceptions of the world. Unprocessed by narrative filters, these perceptions would remain at the mere level of experience, which – no matter how objectively reliable (were such a thing ever possible) or first-hand or otherwise authoritative – O'Brien always finds relatively worthless and unenlightening. The relationship between story-telling and truth, together with other crucial issues such as the redefinition of courage, or the interplay between memory and imagination, is one of O'Brien's recurrent concerns. Throughout his career he has repeatedly engaged with the same key questions to be found at the heart of his early work, so that his overall output can be seen to form a coherent corpus, worth considering as a whole, for all the variations in the individual texts' success with the critics and the public, and in their respective technical accomplishments.

The reference to Conrad is also, much like the title of this study, a reminder that O'Brien writes about Vietnam always with the aim to go beyond literal thematic strictures and the other generic confines associated with the realm of combat narratives. As he has freely admitted in interviews, and has practised in all his work, O'Brien regards the 'framework of war' as a 'short cut' to apply immediate pressure on his characters and situations, and thus to allow him to deal with fundamental questions to do with 'the human heart'[7] – the latter an expression that significantly echoes Nathaniel Hawthorne's declaration of poetics, as we shall see in Chapter 5. With a slightly infelicitous turn of phrase – for, in his treatment of fighting, he in fact

'Intradiegetic' refers to the level of the narrative, rather than the extratextual world: for example, we have an intradiegetic Tim O'Brien, character and narrator in *The Things They Carried*, not to be confused with the real-life author of the same book. In literature, a '*mise en abyme*' is a story within a story. More generally, it indicates a mirroring between one element of a story and the narrative in its entirety, such as when a small episode foreshadows the main narrative arc or a wider theme in the text as a whole. It is in this latter sense that '*mise en abyme*' is typically used in this study.

6 Wayne C. Booth, *The Rhetoric of Fiction* (Chicago: University of Chicago Press, 1961).

7 Daniel Bourne, 'A Conversation with Tim O'Brien', *Artful Dodge*, 2 October 1991, http://www3.wooster.edu/ artfuldodge/interviews/obrien.htm (accessed 10 July 2010).

insists on the materiality of the horror of war, being very careful not to reduce it to a convenient figure of speech – O'Brien has talked about Vietnam as 'an essential or a life-given metaphor that, for [him], is inescapable'. As he goes on to explain: 'I've used it in the way Conrad writes about the sea [...] But Conrad is no more writing about the sea than I am writing about war.'[8] There is, of course, a danger in treating a specific experience – particularly one, such as the Vietnam war, so morally fraught and traumatic, and so liable to being conflated with a negative perception of an entire country – as a way to explore what it means to be human, itself a claim with more than a hint of problematic essentialism in its universalizing drive. For this reason, and for what would have to be regarded as a tendentious pro-Western/American bias, O'Brien has laid himself open to the same kind of postcolonial critique that has been brought against Conrad's use of Africa in *Heart of Darkness* (memorable, and still controversial, in this debate is Chinua Achebe's accusation that Conrad is 'a bloody racist' for his reduction of an entire continent and its inhabitants to 'the role of props for the break-up of one petty European mind'[9]). Other critics, on the other hand, have embraced O'Brien's attempt to transcend the contingencies of his subject matter, perhaps viewing it as a sign of the classic status that some of his narratives aspire to: given his choice of comparison, this was certainly the perspective adopted by Richard Freeman, whose glowing review for the *New York Times*, often reprinted on dust-jackets and back covers of later editions of the book, makes the bold claim that '[t]o call *Going After Cacciato* a novel about war is like calling *Moby Dick* a novel about whales'.[10]

While the politics of O'Brien's work will be discussed in the rest of the book, alongside the analysis of his thematic concerns, formal solutions and metanarrative reflections, this first chapter aims to provide a general introduction to the close reading of the primary texts. The following pages sketch the reasons for the common definition of Vietnam as a postmodern war, and the impact of this perception on the literature on the subject. The analysis then expands to consider the inscription of this view of the war within a specifically American cultural context: the myth of the frontier. The third section of this chapter develops my initial comments on the 'journey into the heart of darkness' as a paradigm in the perception of the war, and relates this trope to O'Brien's deconstruction of gender and racial stereotypes and to his mythopoetic sensitivity – both exemplary of a postmodern poetics, in spite of

8 Bourne, 'A Conversation with Tim O'Brien', n.p.
9 Chinua Achebe, 'An Image of Africa', *Research in African Literatures*, 9.1 (1978), pp. 1–15, p. 9.
10 Richard Freedman, 'A Separate Peace', *The New York Times*, 12 February 1978, http://www.nytimes.com/ books/98/09/20/specials/obrien-cacciato.html (accessed 21 July 2010).

O'Brien's firm disavowal of this label. The last section combines the very large and the very small, looking at the challenges inherent in writing about war *vis-à-vis* changed attitudes towards the notion of heroism, while also giving a brief overview of the specific literary and cultural models that O'Brien engages with, or has pointedly chosen to disregard.

A postmodern conflict

What do we talk about when we talk about Vietnam? And how do we – or how should we – talk about Vietnam? Herr's marvellous map of an unreal country seems to raise these, and similar, questions. While such queries necessarily elude final, comprehensive answers, a brief sketch of the possible meaning and the frame of reference for the use of 'Vietnam' as shorthand for the American conflict in the Southeast Asian peninsula, and for the soldiers' experience of the country of the same name, throws light on the historical and ideological context of the US military engagement and of its literary reinter-pretations. As a matter of fact, while this study will follow the convention of writing 'Vietnam' as one word (the common Westernized spelling of the indigenous *Việt Nam*), some critics, following Renny Christopher's example, have chosen to capitalize on the existence of alternative spellings in order to make a crucial distinction between the country and the conflict. Thus, in what is already a loaded definition of the two terms, we have '"Vietnam" – an ideological signifier for the futilely destructive American military, political, and economic intervention in Southeast Asia and its cultural and political ramifications within the United States and elsewhere; and "Viet Nam" – the nation that won the war and has a history and culture that transcends "Vietnam"'.[11] If it is relatively easy to draw a broad outline of the history of the country – the millenary Chinese rule (208 BC to AD 983), a long period of independence and the seventeenth-century division of one kingdom into two (the Trinh kingdom in the north and the Nguyen in the south), the slow progress of French colonization (from the arrival of the first missionaries in the seventeenth century to the gradual establishment of protectorates and colonies in the nineteenth century) until Ho Chi Minh's 1945 declaration of Vietnamese independence, which ironically opens with a reference to its American counterpart – things get much more complicated when it comes to attempting a chronicle of the Vietnam war, pinning down its exact duration, and indeed even the number of different, interlinked conflicts it entailed.

Several historians prefer to talk about 'Vietnam *wars*' in the plural, to

---

11 Mark A. Heberle, *A Trauma Artist: Tim O'Brien and the Fiction of Vietnam* (Iowa City: University of Iowa Press, 2001), p. xviii.

highlight how the American military engagement in Vietnam of 1965–73 (from the launch of operation 'Rolling Thunder' to the signing of a ceasefire agreement and the subsequent departure of the last American troops) 'was preceded by a failed French war of colonial reconquest, ran parallel with a southern Vietnamese civil war, and would be followed by a war of national reunification waged by North Vietnam and its southern supporters'.[12] Besides, as Marilyn B. Young points out, the 'Americans sent to Vietnam fought different wars depending on when they arrived and where (and whether) they were in combat'.[13] The official US presence in Vietnam had started with the arrival of the first American military advisors to train President Diem's South Vietnamese Army in 1956 – two such military advisors were to become the first American casualties in 1959 – and ended with the American Ambassador leaving Saigon after the fall of the city on 30 April 1975 in what marked a twenty-year interruption of diplomatic relations between the two countries. Yet the record of incontrovertible facts – arrivals and departures, movements of troops, place names, dates of significant operations, presidents and officers in command on both sides – tells only a small part of the story, and the least controversial one at that. The lack of certainties that surrounds the American perception of the conflict in Vietnam not merely on the matter of its opportunity and design – the issue of whether it was a war of aggression and an undue interference in another country's right to self-determination, or rather a necessary part of the fight against Communism – is perhaps best summarized by Mark Taylor, who opens his study of the Vietnam war in history, literature and film with the following, loaded question: 'What would victory have consisted of?'[14]

The American military involvement in Vietnam has often been described as the first postmodern war in history, for a number of well documented reasons.[15] The conflict's 'inconclusiveness', in the perceived lack of a clear

12 Kevin Ruane, *The Vietnam Wars* (Manchester and New York: Manchester University Press, 2000). For other references to the conflict in the plural, see also Marilyn B. Young, *The Vietnam Wars, 1945–1990* (New York: HarperCollins, 1991) and Justin Wintle, *The Viet Nam Wars* (London: Weidenfeld & Nicolson, 1991).

13 Young, *The Vietnam Wars, 1945–1990*, p. 172.

14 Mark Taylor, *The Vietnam War in History, Literature and Film* (Edinburgh: Edinburgh University Press, 2003), p. 1.

15 On the other hand, Alex Vernon makes a persuasive case for (re)contextualizing our understanding of Vietnam as a postmodern war, reminding us that 'many other wars – even most other wars – have been just as chaotic, fragmented and nightmarish for the participants'; *Soldiers Once and Still*, p. 10. He also points out that the classification of the Vietnam war as a postmodern phenomenon makes sense primarily – if not exclusively – from the perspective of the cultural or literary critic, and not necessarily from that of the soldiers or indeed in military terms. In other words, the postmodernity of Vietnam is in great part an inevitable product of the cultural/literary mood of its time, and its immediate aftermath: 'these veterans and *nonveteran* authors did not write in a postmodern way in response to the war, but in response to literary history. When other battlefields that were equally chaotic

final purpose, is certainly one of them, and was itself the result of a combination of concurrent causes. To begin with, the war seemed to lack clear objectives at a very fundamental level: fought according to the rules of guerrilla warfare, in a foreign country and on unfamiliar terrain, against both the People's Army of Vietnam (the regular North Vietnamese army) and the National Front for the Liberation of Southern Vietnam (most commonly referred to as the Viet Cong, who – recruited in the South – were therefore already in that part of the country whose independence from the North the US had pledged to defend), it appeared to the American soldiers as a conflict against an invisible enemy hiding amongst, and indeed often part of, the civilian population. Lacking the battle-lines of traditional military efforts, conducted as a war of attrition and intertwined with a civil war, Vietnam soon turned out to involve the American troops in a campaign to win the 'hearts and minds' of the very people they thought they had come to help.

In an interview with Tobey C. Herzog, talking about the rationale behind his war memoirs, Tim O'Brien explains that he wanted to write about 'the infantryman's experience through the eyes of a soldier who acknowledged the obvious: that we were killing civilians more than we were killing the enemy. The war was aimless in the most basic ways, that is, aimless in the sense of nothing to aim at, no enemy to shoot, no target to kill'.[16] The peculiar rules of engagement of a contained conflict with no definite front-line and an 'invisible' enemy also made it difficult to measure success on the battlefield: military progress thus ended up being gauged on the body-count of the respective casualties, a procedure which in turn encouraged the perverse syllogism that a dead Vietnamese must be a VC (not to mention the implicit legitimization of the mutilation of corpses to get a 'confirmed kill').[17] The American soldiers' limited tour of duty (a year for the Army, thirteen months for the Marines) together with the fact that they would join the war effort individually rather than as units dealt a further blow to the idea that the war in Vietnam had a final, collective purpose: although meant to guarantee that there were always experienced soldiers in combat units, this latter practice effectively turned individual soldiers into cogs in the military machine. Add to this the element of chance brought about by the draft lottery system, and

---

and fragmented did not produce chaotic and fragmented literature, the difference lies in literary history, not military history' (pp. 12–13). Of course, much like the distinction between 'Vietnam' and 'Viet Nam', theoretical disquisitions about the postmodernity of this conflict reflect the concerns (and the bias) of Western cultural critics, and not of the Vietnamese.

16 Tim O'Brien, quoted in Tobey C. Herzog, *Tim O'Brien* (New York: Twayne Publishers, 1997), p. 40.

17 For a discussion of the notions of the 'body count' and the 'confirmed kill' see, amongst others, Lloyd B. Lewis, *The Tainted War: Culture and Identity in Vietnam War Narratives* (Westport, CT: Greenwood Press, 1985), p. 101.

the increasingly vocal opposition to the war at home, and it is easy to see why the soldiers' disaffection would mount, even before they set foot on Vietnamese ground.

These practical issues, and their obvious repercussions on the troops' morale, can be regarded as a marker of the postmodernity of the conflict insofar as they partake of, and promote, a mood of uncertainty, scepticism and relativism, with their privileging of the communication and interpretation of information over other activities, and the prioritization of simulation over substance (see the already mentioned difficulty in ascertaining the difference between friends and enemies, or the notorious practices of the body count, and the kill ratio, to determine military progress). The depthlessness fostered by the fragmentation of knowledge and the proliferation of individual readings of the events is accompanied by other features of postmodernity, such as the negation of a strong teleological narrative implied by the vague strategic objectives of an endless war of attrition, and the flattening of temporality in the 'presentist' attitude pervading the conflict, perhaps best exemplified by each draftee's individual desire to survive his limited tour of duty, in the absence of the shared goal of a final collective victory.[18] Last but not least, Vietnam represents 'a new and virtually unimaginable quantum leap in technological alienation'[19] in modern warfare, both in the mechanization of the communication and processing of intelligence, and in its love affair with the potential for immediate, speedy, small-scale targeted operations afforded by the use of helicopters. The latter has become the most instantly recognizable symbol of the American presence in Vietnam, immortalized by Herr's image of the 'collective metachopper' in perpetual motion – 'saver-destroyer, provider-waster, right hand-left hand, nimble, fluent, canny and human; hot steel, grease, jungle-saturated canvas webbing, sweat cooling and warming up again, cassette rock and roll in one ear and door-gun fire in the other, fuel, heat, vitality and death, death itself, hardly an intruder'[20] – and by Coppola's memorable sequence in *Apocalypse Now* of the fleet of Hueys rising in flight and attacking a beach to the sound of Richard Wagner's 'Ride of the Valkyries'.

The iconic presence of these images also testifies to another peculiarity of this conflict: never before had a war been so intricately connected with the idea of spectacle, the two notions becoming blurred in their reciprocal interaction with the mass media. American soldiers went to Vietnam with a

---

18 See Chris Hables Gray, 'Postmodernism with a Vengeance: The Vietnam War', in *The Vietnam War and Postmodernity*, ed. Michael Bibby (Boston: University of Massachusetts, 2000), pp. 173–97, p. 175.

19 Fredric Jameson, 'Postmodernism, or the Cultural Logic of Late Capitalism', *New Left Review*, 146 (1984), pp. 53–92, p. 84.

20 Herr, *Dispatches*, pp. 15–16.

baggage of unrealistic expectations derived in part from their exposure to popular representations of previous wars. Hollywood accounts of World War II, in particular, gave rise to the widespread and obviously unprecedented phenomenon of the 'John Wayne Syndrome', with its reckless, unattainable model of heroism, accompanied by the dangerous feeling of being on a movie set rather than in a real combat zone. On the other hand, the everyday, immediate journalistic coverage of the war, and of the moral and political debate surrounding it, gave the event a mediatic quality with all the consequences of the case, not least a simultaneous closeness to and distance from the conflict and, eventually, a sense of information overload, which has most probably contributed to America's state of denial in the aftermath of its first military defeat.[21]

How else, then, can the inscription of Vietnam within the logic of late capitalism, so often associated with a privileging of efficiency and performance over truth, be said to have affected the representation and reception of the war? Even if at one point it had become something of a critical commonplace to assume that 'as a postmodern war, portrayals of the war in Vietnam demand a postmodern style to be meaningful, or indeed to be meaningless in order to reflect the meaninglessness of the war',[22] the postmodernity of the conflict has not necessarily been reflected in an analogous quality in its literary renditions.[23] In fact, a significant majority of books, as well as films, comics and other expressions of popular culture dealing with Vietnam, have no real artistic pretensions. On the narrative front, most accounts of the war can be categorized as combat novels focused on traditional and realistic descriptions of battle. At best, they read like adventure stories, making no great attempt to perform a deeper analysis of the psychology of war, or of the ethical and ideological assumptions underlying this particular conflict; at worst, they can be dismissed as '*trash literature*, with a significant proportion of texts whose combat setting is a mere pretext, as they zoom in onto episodes of sexual violence'.[24]

Nonetheless, from the reactionary and chauvinistic extreme of near-

---

21 On this issue, see Andrew Martin, *Receptions of War: Vietnam in American Culture* (Norman, OK, and London: University of Oklahoma Press, 1993), p. 76.

22 Taylor, *The Vietnam War in History, Literature and Film*, p. 24.

23 See, for example, Stefano Rosso, 'Narrativa statunitense e guerra del Vietnam: un canone in formazione' [US narrative and the Vietnam war: a canon in the making], *Acoma*, 4 (1995), pp. 73–85.

24 Stefano Rosso, 'La mascolinità problematica nella narrativa di guerra di Tim O'Brien' [Problematic masculinity in Tim O'Brien's war writing], in *Methodologies of Gender*, eds. Mario Corona and Giuseppe Lombardo (Rome: Herder, 1993), pp. 493–504, p. 493, my translation. Rosso grounds his argument on John Newman's *Vietnam War Literature: An Annotated Bibliography of Imaginative Works About Americans Fighting in Vietnam* (Metuchen, NJ: Scarecrow Press, 1988). See also Rosso, 'Narrativa statunitense e guerra del Vietnam: un canone in formazione'.

pornographic and/or pulp narratives through the documentary value of many fictional and non-fictional accounts of the conflict, Vietnam war literature has reached out to include some of the most innovative and creative works to have come out of the United States since the 1960s. Philip D. Beidler goes as far as to claim that 'such a body of writing has also suggested a major direction for the national literature towards an access of renewed creative energy [...], a possible way beyond what became known in the 1960s and early 1970s in the metafictionist argot as "the literature of exhaustion"'.[25] I would agree with Beidler that, generally speaking, Vietnam war literature – in its finest manifestations – has heeded John Barth's call for self-reflectivity, making a virtue out of the necessity to verbalize its inability to speak, and thus developing new thematic concerns and narrative strategies in order to handle its volatile material. This is certainly true of Tim O'Brien who, having discarded the notion that experiential memory and mimetic writing might respectively provide the foundation and the outlet for an authentic account of the war, also renounced the claims to authority of the first-hand participant in – and witness of – the events, and invested instead in the performative power of storytelling, i.e. in the power of narrative acts to process, mediate and organize our (imaginative, as well as real) experience of the world, and refashion it into a tentative sense-making activity.

Meaning is found, and at the same time created, in the interplay between the actual conflict (or rather, the individual subject's awareness of it), its collective cultural, symbolic significance and one's personal reinterpretation of the two combined. Devoid of any didactic or cathartic connotations, each individual, idiosyncratic act of storytelling is viewed as a speculative, and yet the only available, hermeneutical and expressive practice capable of offering an intermittent glimmer of 'truth' – a nugget of wisdom suddenly thrown into relief by what we might call, after Michael Herr, an inspired 'illumination round'. In the decades to follow the last official American departure from Saigon in 1975, this mythopoetic trajectory has come full circle, with the widespread acknowledgement – not only on O'Brien's part – that the stories we tell about Vietnam have been a catalyst for the representation and the analysis of the contradictions of American culture, and indeed of Western culture, at the end of the American century. More than that: Vietnam has been reimagined – and one cannot emphasize enough the wilful, constructed nature of this vision – as a 'perfect metaphor for our times', a symbol that 'both reflects and illuminates our larger predicament'.[26] O'Brien has exploited both veins in his writing, in which Vietnam figures always as an

---

25 Philip D. Beidler, *Re-Writing America: Vietnam Authors in their Generation* (Athens, GA: The University of Georgia Press, 1991), p. 2.
26 Ken Lopez quoted in 'Postscript' in Philip Caputo, *A Rumor of War* (London: Pimlico, 1999), p. 356.

urgent theme, deserving of obsessive attention both in its own right, *and* for its ability to flag up the tension between the individual subject and the often conflicting cultural discourses that make up his or her own sense of identity.

Old myths, new frontiers

The image most readily associated with World War I is the landscape of trenches and foxholes of the Western Front and its eerie, inorganic mockery of nature with barbed wire shrubbery and sandbag mounds. World War II moved the conflict to the skies, with the London Blitz, the bombing of Dresden and, most powerfully memorable of all in this catalogue of tragedies, the atomic mushrooms over Hiroshima and Nagasaki. The war in Vietnam is connected both with an underground, hellish dimension (the Viet Cong tunnels) and with mass destruction from the air (the American chemical downpour of napalm and Agent Orange across the land). The history of this conflict is that of a war waged against the enemy and his territory alike, the one perceived as the emanation of the other: hostile, impenetrable and undeniably alien. The iconography of the American intervention in Vietnam rests on the image of a triple-canopied jungle, with layers and layers of vegetation: enclosed and trapped in its unfamiliar majesty are camouflaged and scantily dressed GIs, often offering – particularly when transposed onto the big screen – a display of sun-tanned muscles which we are more used to seeing on Californian surfers and bathers than on the battlefield.[27] The tropical, luxuriant setting of the Southeast Asian peninsula is definitely one of the features to set this conflict apart from the paradigmatic examples of the two World Wars, which were fought mainly on European, hence familiarly Western, soil.[28]

The specific nature of the Vietnamese landscape had great material consequences on the military strategies, and indeed on the outcome, of the conflict, which the Viet Cong fought relying on their long experience of guerrilla warfare, forcing their opponent to develop anti-guerrilla techniques. The geography of Vietnam thus constitutes a first, natural barrier between the

27 Francis Ford Coppola foregrounds this conceit through the character of Lance Johnson, the surfing champion turned soldier, and especially through the larger-than-life and suggestively named figure of Bill Kilgore, a madcap Lieutenant Colonel (his is the infamous line 'I love the smell of napalm in the morning'). Kilgore, a surfing aficionado, insists that Johnson should give him a demonstration of his prowess, even as the bombs are falling on the beach where the soldiers have just landed.

28 The Korean War of 1950–53 is often referred to as the 'forgotten war'; it never quite captured people's imagination, and therefore does not figure as a paradigm for Vietnam. The unusual status of this conflict is also perhaps due to the fact that the American intervention in Korea was not preceded by an official declaration of war by the US Congress.

opposing armies, acting like a shield and a screen for VC operations, granting the natives a near total invisibility. Paradoxically, and somehow absurdly in the logic of war, American soldiers at times found it more difficult to reach the appointed destination, to cut their way through a thick, impenetrable vegetation, than to engage the enemy in battle. O'Brien himself testifies to this unnerving state of affairs in his memoir, where he recalls 'three silhouettes [...] tiptoeing out of the hamlet. They were twenty yards away, crouched over, their shoulders hunched forward. It was the first and only time I would ever see the living enemy, the men intent on killing me' (*IID*, 101–102). Added to the sheer physical fatigue of 'humping the Nam' were the constant apprehension of stepping onto a mine or being targets for an ambush, and the ensuing necessity to watch both the ground and the flourishing thickets for hidden dangers. This, in turn, led to the arduous and tiring choice to avoid easy trails and let oneself be swallowed by the untried jungle; all these elements caused American troops to perceive the Vietnamese environment as just as hostile as the people who lived in it. And, as if the snares fabricated by the Viet Cong were not enough, the American soldiers had to contend with the fear of the terrible traps harboured by the territory itself, seen as a breeding ground of unknown diseases and of poisonous, exotic insects and parasites. This perception gives an almost literal resonance to the view of Vietnam as the 'Garden of Evil', voiced by one of the characters in *The Things They Carried* as a possible explanation for the extraordinary behaviour of the American 'Adams' in a land where 'every sin's real fresh and original' (*TTC*, 76).

These material and psychological encumbrances ran counter to the American expectations of how the war would unfold; what is more, Vietnam failed to live up to its projected, metonymical representation of the wondrous Far East, an image burdened with well-established orientalist conceits – associations with sensual, captivating and mysterious revelations – perpetuated even by writers, such as Joseph Conrad, who are otherwise well aware of the spuriousness of a stark dichotomy between the Orient and the Occident.[29] While it may have been the site of ancient, enchanting and unchanging

29 See, for example, Marlow's first view of the East in 'Youth: A Narrative': 'And this is how I see the East. I have seen its secret places and have looked into its very soul; but now I see it always from a small boat, a high outline of mountains, blue and afar in the morning; like faint mist at noon; a jagged wall of purple at sunset. I have the feel of the oar in my hand, the vision of a scorching blue sea in my eyes. And I see a bay, a wide bay, smooth as glass and polished like ice, shimmering in the dark. A red light burns far off upon the gloom of the land, and the night is soft and warm. We drag at the oars with aching arms, and suddenly a puff of wind, a puff faint and tepid and laden with strange odours of blossoms, of aromatic wood, comes out of the still night – the first sigh of the East on my face. That I can never forget. It was impalpable and enslaving, like a charm, like a whispered promise of mysterious delight'; Joseph Conrad, 'Youth: A Narrative' in *Selected Short Stories*, ed. Keith Carabine (London: Wordsworth, 1997), pp. 69–94, p. 91.

civilizations, with a millenary culture of ascetic wisdom, as well as of fabled feminine submissiveness and hospitality, the Far East in Vietnam lent itself to being perceived (by subscribers to the myth of America as the 'redeemer nation'[30]) as home to a poor, rural population torn apart by years of civil war and therefore waiting, with arms wide open, for their Western saviour. The general orientalist preconceptions about Far East Asia, which go back centuries in Western culture to the time of Marco Polo's marvellous encounter with the court of Kublai Khan in the Kingdom of Cathay, were compounded by the distinctly American perception of this region as the natural extension of the US's own Pacific borders. Last but not least, the American vision, both of the Vietnamese country and people, and of the role that the soldiers would be called to fulfil in their expedition to this foreign land, was also coloured by the symbolic attributes of one of the founding myths of the United States: the great narrative of the frontier.

As is well known, the United States has built an important part of its national identity on its successful effort to conquer and tame the Far West: its self-perception as a progressive, enterprising and young-spirited country rests solidly on the assurance and persistence with which it has met the challenge of a wild and unexplored land. Such venture has required, in equal doses, reliance on the powers of civilization and a strong sense of adaptability and appreciation for the virtues of a more Spartan life, lived according to the rhythms of nature. The myth of the frontier thus rests on a complex tension between the values of civilization and those of the wilderness, as Frederick Jackson Turner and other cultural historians after him have pointed out. In this liminal place, later subsumed within the pioneering spirit of the entire country, the United States strikes the perfect balance of culture and nature, embodying the golden mean between over-civilized, decadent Europe, marred by the shame of its colonial politics and general spiritual decline, and the savagery of the Native Americans. Unsurprisingly, the myth of the frontier glosses over the American ignominies that accompanied the conquest of the Wild West, from the indentured and slave labour behind the construction of the railway system to the genocide of Native Americans. The frontier narrative unfolds as the story of the triumph of civilization: 'No society of any appreciable magnitude has ever chosen to reject westernization. [...] There is no reason why the Indians should not have shared in this almost universal trend if they so chose'.[31] Insofar as the United States has sought to distance itself from its European ancestors, whose moral corruption and religious intolerance first led the Pilgrim Fathers to cross the ocean, America has been

---

30 John Hellman, *American Myth and the Legacy of Vietnam* (New York: Columbia University Press, 1986), p. 6.
31 Alden T. Vaughan quoted in Richard Slotkin, *Gunfighter Nation: The Myth of the Frontier in Twentieth-Century America* (New York: HarperCollins, 1993), p. 493.

configured as a symbolic landscape where country, wilderness, nature and the unconscious carry positive connotations, set against the city, civilization, technology and the conscious.[32] However, the negative terms of these binary oppositions are all recuperated and redeemed within the mythical and the tangible geography of the frontier, where ingenuity, practicality, sophistication and material progress are highly valued, since they provide the measure of the pioneers' successful control over their environment. In this way, the frontier becomes the expression of an incorrupt form of civilization, making a claim for the innocence that Europe has irretrievably lost, while embracing the need for technological advancement in order to meet the challenge of the uncharted territory waiting to be mapped out and settled. This extraordinary reconciliation of opposites reflects the American 'self-image of limitless possibility, mastery over nature, democratic equality, self-reliant individualism, and special community mission'.[33]

Half a century after the closure of the original western frontier, at a time when the American pioneering spirit infused the new challenge of the space race, Vietnam was seized as an opportunity for the United States to relive one of the most thrilling and significant pages of its young history. On first glance, the American role in Vietnam appears to share several remarkable traits with the conquest of the west. The ingredients for another 'success' story are all there, beginning with the setting. As anticipated, East Asia can easily be imagined as the geographical and ideal continuation of the original frontier. Vietnam, in particular, was not only of course a place other than Europe, but a country plunged into its difficult predicament by European influences: there, the Americans had the chance to put to right what the French, with their crumbling colonial power, had not been able to resolve. All the same, though, and despite its very old civilization, Vietnam retained its exotic alterity, which was liable to be viewed as a form of weakness, even of savagery, by Western observers interested in asserting their moral superiority. Indeed, this is exactly the vision of Southeast Asia prevalent in America in the 1950s, due for the most part to the huge popularity of William Lederer and Eugene Burdick's *The Ugly American* (1958). Advertised as fiction based on fact, the book sold over four million copies – endorsed by J. F. Kennedy, it was given to each member of the Senate at the time of his Presidency – and in 1963 was made into a film starring Marlon Brando.[34] Set in the not-so-fictional country of Sarkhan, the text 'offered its readers an Indochina representing a frontier where Americans could return to the remembered virtues of their heritage and at the same time free themselves from the burden of their past'.[35]

32 Hellman, *American Myth and the Legacy of Vietnam*, p. 23.
33 Hellman, *American Myth and the Legacy of Vietnam*, p. 8.
34 See Taylor, *The Vietnam War in History, Literature and Film*, pp. 35ff.
35 Hellman, *American Myth and the Legacy of Vietnam*, p. 35.

The moral, utopian appeal of this vision informed the spirit, and the policies, of John Fitzgerald Kennedy's 'Camelot Years', whose faith in the possibility of universal progress was streaked with an awareness of distinctly American shortcomings, past and present crimes, and a consequent desire for national catharsis. For example, while the United States has never been – not officially, at least – a colonial power, a large part of its economy had depended on slavery, as well as on the exploitative system of indentured labour: thousands of Asian immigrants worked, and died, building the very railroads that would forever change the environment of the Great Plains and jeopardize the livelihood of the local Indian populations. Kennedy's New Frontier would make epic gestures of worldwide resonance, such as the space programme, with the climactic achievement of the 'giant leap for mankind' on the moon;[36] simultaneously, however, it would also seek symbolic redemption and material reparation of wrongs deeply entangled with the development of American history. Seen against the bloody legacy of the old, western frontier, Vietnam thus seemed to present a great opportunity for the United States to make amends to the 'dark man', albeit vicariously: the same country which had once crushed the Native Americans would now protect the Vietnamese and set them free. Slotkin remarks that Lederer and Burdick treat Asians in much the same way as Hollywood at the time treated Native Americans, while Hellman points out how *The Ugly American* reads like an act of imaginative atonement for the killing of the buffalo, when it is envisaged that the United States should introduce the cow to Sarkhan.

The violent aspect of the frontier myth introduces another series of conflicts to the list of paradigmatic military campaigns in American history: the extermination of Native Americans during the westward expansion of the country and, previous to that, the French-Indian wars fought by the British to secure control of their American colonies. Once again, the broad similarities between these early hostilities, easily coalesced in a seamless battle against savagery, and the much later experience in Southeast Asia, are striking: the difficulty in discriminating between 'good' and 'bad' Indians would be replicated with further complications in Vietnam, where the presence of enemies in the civilian population was a source of particular frustration and distress for the American soldiers, who had expected, especially in the early years of the war, to be hailed as benefactors and liberators of the country. In the original frontier narrative, the pioneers' encounter with the Native American populations had had very rewarding consequences for the newcomers who, exposed to the wisdom of the local cultures, were able to learn valuable lessons about survival in an unfamiliar

---

36 It seems no coincidence then that Tim O'Brien should choose to have David Todd, the soldier character from his latest novel *July, July*, get seriously injured in combat while Armstrong lands on the moon.

environment. Knowledge of the land and, perhaps more importantly, respect for the natural world were key traits in the development of the pioneer into what remains the most intriguing heroic figure in the mythology of the west: the 'White Indian', a character immortalized by James Fenimore Cooper in his *Leatherstocking Tales* (1823–41). Loosely based on the historical figure of Daniel Boone (1738–1820), Natty Bumppo (also referred to as Leather-stocking, Hawkeye and *La Longue Carabine*, or the scout, the deerslayer and the pioneer) embodies the ideal dweller of the middle landscape of the frontier, for he combines the innate moral and intellectual superiority of the white man with an intimate understanding of the Native American ethos of harmonious coexistence with the wilderness.[37] This archetypal western hero strikes a perfect balance between civilization and savagery, most significantly in his fighting skills: he is in command equally of Western technology and military strategies, and of Native American weapons and tactics. Bumppo's close relationship with his Indian mentors and allies undoubtedly makes him a mediator between the two different races and, to a great extent, a champion of the indigenous cultures; however, in time this kind of character is trans-formed into 'civilization's most effective instrument against savagery – a man who knows how to fight like an Indian, to turn their own methods against them'.[38] Incidentally, this early American mastery of non-conventional fighting techniques exposes one of the greatest ironies of the debacle in Vietnam, which is often blamed on the treacherousness and unpredictability of guerrilla warfare, when in fact this has been 'the most typical form of military operation during most of the army's history', from the first skirmishes against the Indians to the war of independence against the British colonial yoke.[39]

The figure of the 'White Indian', duly updated, was summoned to play a major role in the American taming of the Southeast Asian frontier in the guise of the Green Berets. These Special Forces had been instituted in the aftermath of World War II: trained as guerrilla experts, they were to provide assistance to the local armies in the event of a Soviet occupation of western

37 In the 1850 'Preface to the Leatherstocking Tales', Cooper makes explicit his intention to create in Natty Bumppo a composite figure, capturing the best of both worlds: 'removed from nearly all the temptations of civilized life, placed in the best associations of that which is deemed savage, and favorably disposed by nature to improve such advantages, it appeared to the writer that his hero was a fit subject to represent the better qualities of both conditions, without pushing either to extremes'; James Fenimore Cooper, *The Last of the Mohicans* (Oxford: Oxford World's Classics, 1990), p. 379. Subsequent references are to this edition.
38 Slotkin, *Gunfighter Nation*, p. 16.
39 Slotkin, *Gunfighter Nation*, p. 454. The opening sentence of *The Last of the Mohicans* could not make this any clearer: 'It was a feature peculiar to the colonial wars of North America, that the toils and dangers of the wilderness were to be encountered, before the adverse hosts could meet' (p. 15).

Europe. Employed in the Korean War, the Green Berets were amongst the first troops to be sent to Vietnam, by John Fitzgerald Kennedy, who in 1961 had sanctioned their right to wear their distinctive headgear (previously unauthorized by the US Army) in a deliberate move to set them up as a distinguished group with a special mission. Their prestigious status and their role of defenders of democracy and freedom, at the service of weaker, foreign lands, cast them as quasi-chivalric types, in tune with the spirit of Kennedy's presidency; the Special Forces' association with the President was such that they were soon dubbed 'Kennedy's Own'. Their popularity was boosted by Robert Moore's book *The Green Berets* (1965), later turned into a film by John Wayne, and by the song 'Ballad of the Green Berets', released in 1966. In Kennedy's vision, the Green Berets would excel as counterinsurgents in Vietnam because their skills as military tacticians would be matched by their ability to empathize with the plight of the local populations: like the western frontiersman of lore, the Green Beret would be soldier and diplomat, killer and peacemaker, interpreter between cultures, while ultimately proving the superiority of American civilization. President Johnson's escalation of the war effort in Vietnam inevitably relegated the Special Forces to a less prominent role, but it did not affect the mythical aura surrounding this outfit: on the contrary, this fall from favour can be seen to add to the mystique of the Green Berets as an elite minority, enmeshed in a complicated relationship with the institutions and, indeed, with any form of authority.

Ultimately, the Green Beret, like the western hero, is only restrained from succumbing to primitive and barbaric impulses by 'his own higher sense of natural law that is at one with his true civilized duty'.[40] This circular argument passes off as self-evident the righteousness of the Special Forces in their association with natural law rather than with the laws of men; dangerous as it undoubtedly is, the logic behind this statement is merely an extension of the idea that all American soldiers were fighting for a noble cause, being the bearers of the torch of enlightenment and progress. Needless to say, the reality of the war soon disclosed the delusive nature of this belief, and of the air-tight moral alibi proceeding from it: the Green Berets, for example, acquired a reputation for recklessness, often bordering on a crazy lust for violence and atrocity (and this is indeed how Slotkin's definition of the White Indian, quoted above, continues: 'In its most extreme development, the frontier hero takes the form of the "Indian-hater," whose suffering at savage hands has made him correspondingly savage, an avenger determined at all costs to "exterminate the brutes"'[41]). The American dream of redemption and rectitude turned sour as soon as the materiality of the conflict gave the lie

---

40 Hellman, *American Myth and the Legacy of Vietnam*, p. 64.
41 Slotkin, *Gunfighter Nation*, p. 16.

to the mythical expectations that had been projected onto Vietnam: the Eastern 'wilderness' would not lend itself to induce, nor to reflect, the Western display of good will and philanthropy, because these concepts were all clearly flawed cultural constructions and simplistic, spurious opposi-tions.[42] The encounter with an alien culture turned out to be as confusing for its failure to conform to preconceived ideas about what Vietnamese people, both friends and enemies, would be like and how they would respond to the American arrival, as for the genuine differences and mutual lack of trust between the foreign contingent and the local population. Thus, the experi-ence of Vietnam worked as a magnifying mirror reflecting the epistemolog-ical and moral arrogance underlying the self-appointed American neo-colonial mission and, by extension, the shallowness of its concept of civilization. In other words, faced with the defamiliarizing reality of an unmanageable war, compounded by a particularly frustrating relationship with the Vietnamese allies, the American soldiers embarked on a psycholog-ical journey of self-discovery which often left them with the painful aware-ness that the line between sanity and insanity, civilization and barbarity, justness and atrocity is difficult to discern and, therefore, easy to cross.

This psychological journey is a topic that O'Brien – like most other writers of the war – explores on several occasions in his work, most typically by exposing how perceptions of the landscape, be it the American or the Vietnamese wilderness, are coloured by the characters' prejudices, anxieties and projections, and often provide a building block for the creation of a trans-parent topography of trauma. Similarly, the 'fascination of the abomination' – often irresistible, if difficult to explain, let alone justify – is another frequent theme to crop up in the pages of war narratives. In O'Brien's writing, the lure of savagery takes a particularly poignant form in the account of episodes of gratuitous violence against the environment, shorthand for the primeval, unspeakable malice lurking behind the characters' need to release their pent-up feelings of helplessness or their blind desire for revenge. One such recurrent incident – highlighted with special vigour in *The Things They Carried*, but present also in *Going After Cacciato* and *In the Lake of the Woods* – is the killing of water buffalo, the animal most readily connected with the

42 This is reminiscent of Kurtz's movement in his report for the International Society for the Suppression of Savage Customs from a rhetoric with 'no practical hints' to the chilling 'Exterminate all the brutes!', which provides a paradigmatic example for twentieth-century dealings between different cultures: 'This was the unbounded power of eloquence – of words – of burning noble words. There were no practical hints to interrupt the magic current of phrases, unless a kind of note at the foot of the last page, scrawled evidently much later, in an unsteady hand, may be regarded as the exposition of a method. It was very simple, and at the end of that moving appeal to every altruistic sentiment it blazed at you, luminous and terrifying, like a flash of lightning in a serene sky: "Exterminate all the brutes!"'; Conrad, *Heart of Darkness*, pp. 83–84.

rural economy of Vietnam and, symbolically, with the ideal association between the Vietnamese and the Native Americans, and the mythology of the West. At other times, not-so-veiled references to the mindlessly destructive, even genocidal, potential of certain actions, and to the violence of the American fire-power against Vietnam, take a bathetic turn, as in the opening of *In the Lake of the Woods*, whose veteran protagonist burns the house plants with hot water – and, possibly, kills his own wife. A similarly ludicrous effect is achieved by the main character in *Northern Lights* who enters the scene 'ejaculating sweet chemicals that filled the great forest and his father's house' (*NL*, 16), engaged in a battle against mosquitoes conducted with copious amounts of insecticide in what must strike readers as an unsubtle but nevertheless disturbing echo of the napalm-bombing of the jungle.

The use of bathetic images or a bathetic register is one of the recurrent strategies adopted by O'Brien in his critique of the frontier myth, and indeed of other conventional (masculine) narratives. Courage, physical prowess, the demands of patriarchy, patriotism are all variously undercut by O'Brien's recourse to a form of comedy which, suffused with embarrassing or mock-heroic undertones, invites ridicule and contempt, rather than cheerful, good-humoured and light-hearted laughter. The frontier myth, whether applied to America's perception of itself or to the projection of this narrative onto the Vietnamese landscape, is further deconstructed by O'Brien's exposure of the culturally determined nature of these operations. By contrast, as we shall see, O'Brien envisages an alternative symbolic geography in order to try to capture the traumatisation of his protagonists, as well as to sketch a poetics of reception that would transcend gender differences and bridge the gap between those who have remained 'in the world' and those who have travelled 'in country', where the country in question is not just Vietnam, or the war, or any war, but rather the murky, unmappable territory of the human predicament.

Retelling the journey into the heart of darkness

The epigraph to Mark Baker's *Nam: The Vietnam War in the Words of the Men and Women Who Fought There* (1981) reads: 'You want to hear a gen-u-ine war story? I only understand Vietnam as though it were a story. It's not like it happened to me.' It is no surprise that a collection of oral testimonies, otherwise introduced as an earnest attempt to 'bring us closer to the truth than we have come so far',[43] should be prefaced by an immediate disclaimer

---

43 Mark Baker, *Nam: The Vietnam War in the Words of the Men and Women Who Fought There* [1981] (London: Abacus, 1982), p. xv.

of the notion of factual truth and an affirmation of the need for literary licence if one is to begin to make some sense out of the experience of war. Meaning can only be accessible to the narrator-witness if he dissociates himself from his immediate knowledge of Vietnam: paradoxically, the genuineness of a personal account can only be attained through a creative, fictional re-elaboration of the storyteller's first-hand experience of the conflict. The inexplicable nature of Vietnam, in its dual identification with an alien land and with a harrowing military enterprise, goes perhaps some way towards casting light on its unmanageable yet compelling status as a subject for storytelling, or indeed for linguistic definition. 'In country', 'Indian country', 'the boonies', 'Fantasyland', 'Disneyland', 'the Nam': the soldiers' slang finds inspiration in a crescendo of binary oppositions, in which the contrast between civilization and wilderness is superseded by the dichotomy between the real and the surreal (or even the non-real). Larger than life, given gravity and substance by the presence of the definite article, 'the Nam' is variously renamed as a savage, inimical land, a sort of parallel, self-contained universe where the rules of reality do not apply: 'Vietnam was written off as a place too incomprehensible to exist. People did not go home. They "went back to the world"'.[44] Beyond the reach of language, Vietnam becomes an experience which ultimately transcends its materiality to become 'a state of mind',[45] a byword for a psychological condition, as well as for the most private and unfathomable recess of human nature.

The metaphor of the physical journey as an exploration of the meandering of one's consciousness, probably as old as storytelling itself, is thus an accurate reflection of the soldiers' metamorphosis in response to their experience of war in an unfamiliar country, whose cultural makeup and natural environment were often perceived as both hostile and impenetrable. The radical alterity of Vietnam compounds the displacement of the romantic expectations – the dreams of heroism and courage – that traditionally underlie the military ethos: as Herzog sums up, 'the realities and ironies of combat forever destroy [the soldiers'] naïveté and lead them to crucial insights about human nature and war. Some soldiers submit to this spiritual and psychological journey; others resist as they hold on to civilization's trappings, saving illusions, or surface details' (4). Soldiers are therefore subject to a double threat of alienation, from their physical surroundings and from the system of values that seemingly validates their actions. The US confrontation with Vietnam can thus be seen to involve a geographical and an existential journey which, in its turn, triggers a critique of Western ideology.

44 Philip D. Beidler, *American Literature and the Experience of Vietnam* (Athens, GA: The University of Georgia Press, 1982), p. 6.
45 Oliver Stone, quoted in Tobey C. Herzog, *Vietnam War Stories: Innocence Lost* (London and New York: Routledge, 1992), p. 1. Subsequent references are to this edition.

The complexity of a similar scenario is masterfully captured in Conrad's *Heart of Darkness*, whose account of Marlow's progress upriver in the Congo and Kurtz's surrender to the 'fascination of the abomination' is an apt, established precursor for the challenges, and the charm, of the experience of guerrilla warfare in Vietnam. In fact, while the opposition between light and darkness, in reference to the realms of epistemology and morality alike, pervades the fictional and critical discourse on war at large, in the case of Vietnam narratives the metaphor of the journey into the heart of darkness has become the most recurrent and resonant literary transcription of the soldiers' experience of combat and, ultimately, of human nature.[46] This is of course an image rich not only in symbolic implications, but also in intertextual allusions, rooted as it is in Conrad's eponymous novella, first published in 1899.[47] Besides, the centrality and suggestiveness of this metaphor are widely acknowledged beyond the confines of academia by popular culture, following the cult status of Francis Ford Coppola's *Apocalypse Now* (1979), the text responsible for relocating Marlow's journey from the Congo to the Vietnamese jungle.

Eleven years after the release of Coppola's bold cinematic take on *Heart of Darkness*, Conrad's narrative exploration of the cruelty that inhabits 'the dark places of the earth'[48] is revisited once more within the gruesome context of the Vietnam war in 'Sweetheart of the Song Tra Bong', one of the chapters in Tim O'Brien's *The Things They Carried*.[49] The fundamental analogy between O'Brien's story and *Heart of Darkness* has been noted before on several occasions but, to my knowledge, nowhere has it been explored in depth, as I shall do in the final chapter of this study.[50] In their respective

---

46 The first direct allusion to a connection between the experience of Vietnam and 'some heavy heart-of-darkness trip' appears in Michael Herr's *Dispatches* (p. 15). Following Herr's cue, Tobey C. Herzog identifies in the 'Heavy Heart-of-Darkness Trip' one of the five thematic contexts in his overview of Vietnam war literature: the other four are the ironic spirit, the John Wayne syndrome, the confrontation with the past and the relationship between the uniqueness [postmodernity] of the Vietnam war and the narratives it has produced.

47 'The Heart of Darkness' was first published in three monthly instalments between February and April 1899 in *Blackwood's Magazine*. It was later revised for publication in book form and included, with 'The End of the Tether', in *Youth: A Narrative; and Two Other Stories* (Blackwood, 1902). This forms the basis for all subsequent editions of *Heart of Darkness*.

48 Psalms 74:20, quoted in *Heart of Darkness*, p. 18, henceforward referred to in the text as *HD*.

49 For ease of reference, throughout this study I will refer to *The Things They Carried* as to a novel, although the text is probably best described as a collection of interrelated short stories, or as a short-story cycle. On this issue, see Chapter 5.

50 For example, '"Sweetheart of the Song Tra Bong" is O'Brien's *Heart of Darkness*, Americanized, Vietnamized, and surrealized (and possibly encouraged by Francis Ford Coppola's film version of Conrad, *Apocalypse Now*...)'; Heberle, *A Trauma Artist*, p. 184; and 'In "Sweetheart of the Song Tra Bong" [...] O'Brien tells a strange and unlikely tale,

investigations of the alienating effect of the Western colonial enterprise and the (neo-colonial) American war in Vietnam, both Conrad and O'Brien find themselves scrutinizing the lure of power and of transgression, as well as their interrelationship. However, in line with O'Brien's vocal critique of the masculine bias – and machismo – embedded in the military mentality, 'Sweetheart' plays a provocative variation, through its *female* protagonist, on the typical theoretical and literary approach to the phenomenon of American soldiers 'going native' during the conflict. The crumbling of moral certainties and cultural (and gender!) differences in O'Brien's acknowledgement that even 'civilized' Americans (and, more shockingly, an American sweetheart) feel the pull of barbarity and of the unknown Vietnamese natural environment – most immediately expressed in an exhilarated response to the violence and the chaos of war – unfolds in neat parallelism with the anti-colonial thesis of the Conradian model.

In *Heart of Darkness* the strain on the individual's ability to adapt and survive the mysteriousness of Africa is accompanied by a general cultural critique, exposing the weakness of Western rationalizations of the colonial enterprise, what we might call with Conrad the 'redeeming idea'.[51] And yet, the common preoccupation with the evils of imperialism and violence, particularly – it ought to be said – on their very perpetrators rather than their victims, is only the superficial thematic analogy between *Heart of Darkness* and 'Sweetheart'. Eventually, both texts delve deeper into general considerations about the frailty of human nature, while raising interesting questions about identity and gender relations. What is more, Conrad's novella and its later creative rewriting share a distinct self-reflective concern, and deliberately foreground the indefiniteness and lack of closure of the narrative act, even as they clearly also invest the process with an urgent necessity and the potential to lead to (fleeting) revelations. *Heart of Darkness* famously opens on the Thames, on a cruising yawl. Waiting for the tide to turn, the men on board the *Nellie* are soon to become the addressees of a story which does not promise to yield easy satisfaction, told as it is by Charlie Marlow, a seaman

vaguely reminiscent of both the story and the plot of *Heart of Darkness*'; Stefano Rosso, *Musi gialli e Berretti Verdi: Narrazioni USA sulla Guerra del Vietnam* [*Yellow Faces and Green Berets: US Narratives about the Vietnam War*] (Bergamo: Bergamo University Press, 2003), pp. 198–99, my translation. Herzog also makes a quick reference to the '"heart-of-darkness" experience' narrated in 'Sweetheart' (*Tim O'Brien*, p. 110), while Lorrie Smith argues that the short story 'can be read as a gendered and perhaps parodic version of *Heart of Darkness* and its derivative retelling *Apocalypse Now* – those explorations of the imperialist male psyche gone off the deep end'; '"The Things Men Do": The Gendered Subtext in Tim O'Brien's Esquire Stories', *Critique*, 36.1 (1994), pp. 16–39, p. 32.

51 Cf. 'The conquest of the earth, which mostly means the taking it away from those who have a different complexion or slightly flatter noses than ourselves, is not a pretty thing when you look into it too much. What redeems it is the idea only' (*HD*, 20).

known for his evocative tales, and significantly introduced to the readers in 'the pose of a Buddha preaching in European clothes and without a lotus-flower' (*HD*, 20). When Marlow finally breaks a long silence, with the casual recollection of his one stint as a fresh-water sailor, the narrator of the frame immediately comments: 'we knew we were fated, before the ebb began to run, to hear one of Marlow's inconclusive experiences' (*HD*, 21).

With a similar intent to draw attention both to the compelling nature, and to the impenetrability, of some tales, 'Sweetheart of the Song Tra Bong' begins: 'Vietnam was full of strange stories, some improbable, some well beyond that, but the stories that will last forever are those that swirl back and forth across the border between trivia and bedlam, the mad and the mundane. This one keeps returning to me' (*TTC*, 87). The obvious protracted, tantalizing resonance of this story for 'Tim O'Brien', the (partly autobiographical) narrator of *The Things They Carried* (and, of course, of the tale about to begin), replicates the attitude of Rat Kiley, the intradiegetic narrator of Mary Anne's story in 'Sweetheart', whose grip on his material is much less firm than Marlow's, at least in terms of the authoritativeness of his status as an eye-witness and a participant to the events that make up his account. This and further, subtle adjustments to the narrative structure, and to the way in which the scope of the storytelling act is configured, provide a clear illustration of the shift in emphasis from cognitive to post-cognitive questions that characterizes the passage from a modernist to a postmodern sensibility.[52] In fact, set against Conrad's inspiring example, O'Brien's departure from the (derivative) modernism of an early work like *Northern Lights* becomes particularly evident. Like Brian McHale, I see modernism and postmodernism in a relation of mutual definition and continuity, as evidenced by the essential agreement between Conrad's and O'Brien's practice on a number of crucial points such as, for example, the correspondence between narrative form and content and the problematization of the notion of truth. On the other hand, as we shall see, it is the question of the nature and final accessibility of signification that tantalizes the most, and sets apart from each other, the two authors: while *Heart of Darkness* diffuses any hope in the success of the epistemological quest, 'Sweetheart' – and indeed O'Brien's entire oevure – enacts the belief that truth can be painstakingly summoned and *momentarily* glimpsed through the performativity of the narrative act.

---

52 Brian McHale's theory of the change in dominant underpins my periodization of the two primary texts under scrutiny: if we choose to read *Heart of Darkness* as a modernist text on the strength of its fundamental epistemological uncertainty and lack of closure, we must acknowledge the postmodernity of 'Sweetheart' as it bypasses the cognitive impasse of its predecessor with an act of faith in the performative power of storytelling (foregrounding ontological questions in the process).

War writing and the death of heroism

Tim O'Brien's assessment of his participation in the conflict in Vietnam can be summed up in the epigrammatic pronouncement that closes 'On the Rainy River' in *The Things They Carried*: 'I was a coward. I went to the war' (*TTC*, 55). Punchy, paradoxical and memorable, O'Brien's reversal of the customary connection between bravery and military life feeds into the sceptical attitude towards the notion of heroism that pervades most twentieth-century war literature. Cynical rather than tragic in tone, critical rather than celebratory in mood, this counter-tradition to the epic ethos is a direct consequence of the advances in modern military technology and the ensuing disappearance of face-to-face combat. When killing the enemy becomes as easy as pulling a trigger or as impersonal as dropping a bomb on an indistinct swarm of people, the possibility for classical heroism, rooted in the prowess of the single warrior measuring himself against an equally valiant adversary, is effectively vanished. It was during the Great War that the reality of modern combat first became evident on a scale so large as to initiate an epochal change in the perception of individual valour and personal sacrifice. It is hard to disagree with Paul Fussell's thesis that World War I is essentially responsible for the ironic and anti-heroic stance which characterises the twentieth-century sensibility and which inevitably marks the great war literature of the past one hundred years. While it is customary to cite the poetry of Wilfred Owen and Siegfried Sassoon, or the narratives of Ernest Hemingway, or Erich Maria Remarque's *All Quiet on the Western Front* (1929) as the earliest, exemplary literary critiques of the perverse mechanism of twentieth-century warfare, the frenzied organization of the military forces and the effective scope for heroic behaviour in battle had already been explored, from a disenchanted perspective, in Stephen Crane's *The Red Badge of Courage* (1895) at the end of the nineteenth century.[53] Set during the American Civil War, Crane's short novel displays an impressionistic attention to detail and offers a distinctly unorthodox rendition of the plot development, from innocence to self-awareness, to be expected of a narrative charting the initiation of the young soldier into combat.

By definition, the inexperienced recruit comes out of the battle – whether victorious or defeated, whether alive or dead – having faced his fears and responsibilities; in other words, having become a man. First-hand knowledge of war makes soldiers grow up and turns them into veterans, i.e. into *old* men

---

53 In pointing to Crane as an interesting term of comparison for O'Brien's work, even if his influence remains unacknowledged by O'Brien himself, I am indebted to Tobey C. Herzog, who uses *The Red Badge of Courage* as the literary context for the analysis of *If I Die in a Combat Zone* and *Going After Cacciato* in Chapter 4 ('Consideration') of his *Vietnam War Stories*.

('veteran' deriving from Latin, *vetus* = 'old'). Crane's narrative, by contrast, provides at best an ambivalent picture, if not an outright ironic dismissal, of this *Bildungsroman* model: the development of its protagonist, Henry Fleming, proceeds in fits and starts, and it ultimately leads nowhere, since the young soldier's final demonstration of courage is little more than an involuntary reflex.[54] Crane thus anticipates and sets the standard for twentieth-century representations of war in a number of ways that will later be revisited by O'Brien, particularly in his first book, *If I Die in a Combat Zone*. He describes the battleground in short and vivid vignettes, while dwelling on the disturbing anticipation and the actual chaos of combat through his protagonist's skewed and muddled perspective. He also emphasises the role of the soldier as an anonymous cog in the machine (Fleming is most often referred to simply as 'the youth' and it is not until near the end of the narrative that we are told his full name) and focuses relentlessly on the motivations behind his decision to join the fighting. Such rigorous psychological scrutiny is in itself evidence of the demise of the epic notion of heroism: in demystifying the grandeur of battle and probing into the hidden facets of valorous behaviour, Crane unmasks the absence of the *gratuitous* hankering for excellence that is the mark of the true hero.

Heroic excellence works according to tautological rules, in tune with the self-evident logic of mythical thinking; it is an ideal for which the hero himself is the final measure: 'Achilles, the prototypical hero, does not serve a cause (or, if he does, then he serves it badly) and fights for no purpose that could be situated in time and space. He is a hero because he pursues a model of heroic perfection which he has interiorized'.[55] The hero is already the embodiment of an ideal perfection; the cause of his contingent acts of courage is immaterial, the proof of his excellence is always redundant. By contrast, Fleming's desire to prove his manhood in the pursuit of military glory is a puerile obsession that both fuels and is fuelled by the unconfessable fear of the (male) fate worse than death: cowardice. Crane's protagonist *does* have something to prove but, in an ironic analogy with the status of the classical hero, he ends up concentrating on his personal trial even to the detriment of the success of the communal military enterprise. In enlisting into battle because of a *private* worry over his adequacy to the *culturally* sanctioned ideal of male daring, Fleming clearly departs from the self-sufficiency of the epic hero: the glorious autonomy of the ancient model becomes instead a small,

---

54 This achievement counterbalances, and ironically throws into relief, Henry's previous cowardly retreat, a mad scramble during which the young soldier had been injured. The ignominy of Henry's behaviour is compounded by his failure, after the first battle, to disclose the truth about his wound, the deceitful 'red badge of courage' of the title which is, in reality, a red badge of shame.

55 Tzvetan Todorov, *Facing the Extreme: Moral Life in the Concentration Camps*, trans. Arthur Denner and Abigail Pollack (London: Phoenix, 2000), p. 47.

personal matter about living up to conventional expectations and gaining – or retaining – a certain status within society. Fleming's doomed quest for gallantry is neither gratuitous, nor redundant, and – in its solipsism – it antic-ipates the divergence between individual and national goals that informs the various 'separate peaces' embraced by the anti-heroes of twentieth-century war literature (most notably, Frederic Henry's in *A Farewell to Arms* and Yossarian's in *Catch-22*). O'Brien does not fit into this tradition: a separate peace is impossible for him to achieve, or rather, it would bring no solace to the soldier who knows that he has betrayed himself by acquiescing in the draft call. He should *never* have left for the war in the first place.

Of course, from a different perspective, characters like Henry Fleming are the upshot of the rise of modern individualism, when the cult of the epic hero as the perceived ideal embodiment of communal values, and the hero's disin-terested display of glory, is replaced by the private pursuit of happiness as the main goal in life. That the United States subscribes to this value is clear, as witnessed by its prominent mention in the Constitution, as well as by the entire mythology of the American Dream which ratifies the self-conscious American championing of the right to personal success and self-improve-ment. Crane's description of Fleming's naive disappointment at the demise of the old warrior spirit reveals, through a clever transition from focalization to third-person narrative, that the current stakes are much more partisan than ever before and a natural extension, in war-time, of the practical ideal of the pursuit of happiness: 'Greeklike struggles would be no more. Men were better, or more timid. Secular and religious education had effaced the throat-grappling instinct, or else firm finance held in check the passions. He had grown to regard himself merely as a part of a vast blue demonstration. His province was to look out, as far as he could, for his personal comfort.'[56] Civilization may have smoothed over the primeval brutality of mankind but, significantly, the humanizing triad is not complete until the influence of rationalism and piety are joined by a solid economic pragmatism. It seems that already before the battle, and in direct contradiction to his investment in the ennobling experience of combat, Fleming begins to have an inkling of the hard-nosed reality of war and reviews his priorities accordingly, in what looks like an uncanny anticipation of the logic of personal survival, which devel-oped in Vietnam as a response to the experience of the war as a timed event with the introduction of the policy of the year-long tour of duty. Fleming's fledgling susceptibility to change as a result of the introspection prompted by the mere idea of his future engagement in combat suggests a potential for development (or self-expression) that precedes the young soldier's participa-

56 Stephen Crane, *The Red Badge of Courage and Other Stories*, ed. Pascal Covici, Jr. (London: Penguin, 1991), p. 50. The same passage, with slight variations, appears also on page 46. Subsequent references are to this edition.

tion to the war. This is an idea that O'Brien will exploit fully in *If I Die in a Combat Zone*, whose protagonist's greatest struggle, and most humiliating defeat, takes place before he has even set foot on Vietnamese soil. Nevertheless, for all these subtle correspondences, given his suspect allegiance to the belief that war is, after all, the way to a 'quiet manhood' (211), Henry Fleming does not figure in O'Brien's list of examples of heroic behaviour in *If I Die in a Combat Zone*, which turns Crane's literary model on its head at the same time as it follows in its footsteps as a sustained meditation on the nature of courage. Fleming thinks of himself as a potential hero, and must learn that he is a coward. The O'Brien protagonist of *If I Die*, who does not believe in Fleming's notion of heroism, thinks of himself as intellectually superior to his fellow soldiers, but he too must learn that he is really no different from the mass. If anything, his intellectual superiority makes him a hypocrite, and more of a brute than the other soldiers, who lack his self-awareness.

The ancient Greek model of heroism, still looming large, for all its cracks, over the American recruits to Vietnam – 'We come to Fort Lewis afraid to admit we are not Achilles, that we are not brave, that we are not heroes' (*IID*, 45) – is not the only martial ideal that O'Brien needs to renegotiate. For the soldiers fighting in Vietnam, the most recent and authoritative incarnation of the perfect warrior was John Wayne, who had built since the late 1920s a larger-than-life cinematic persona in the cognate genres of the western and the World War II epic drama. For the young people of O'Brien's generation, John Wayne represented the quintessential American hero, endowed with extraordinary courage and, above all, with an innate righteousness: 'In the movies in which John Wayne portrays the war hero, the aggression unleashed as overt violence is legitimated by the end it is designed to serve. Wayne performs in the heroic mode to defeat Fascism – Evil Incarnate – in those WWII epics. The absolute wickedness of the enemy sanctifies massive bloodletting. (In the marginally cited genres – cops/robbers and cowboys/Indians – equally definitive forces of evil are annihilated: lawlessness and savagery)'.[57] The figure of John Wayne, however, is noticeable for its near-absence in O'Brien's writing. This omission is easily explained, especially in *If I Die*, by the fact that O'Brien was a very reluctant fighter, definitely 'not soldier material' and deeply troubled by a war that would draw 'certain blood for uncertain reasons' (*IID*, 31, 167). Unlike Ron Kovic and Philip Caputo, whose *Born on the Fourth of July* (1976) and *A Rumor of War* (1977) form with *If I Die* an early, canonical corpus of memoirs from the Vietnam war, O'Brien was one of the unlucky winners of the draft lottery. The dilemma at the core of O'Brien's inquiry on courage – should I take part in a war that I believe to

---

57 Lewis, *The Tainted War*, p. 29. For a seminal analysis of the John Wayne myth, see also Richard Slotkin's *Gunfighter Nation*.

be morally wrong? – completely bypasses Kovic and Caputo, who both joined the military in order to fight in Vietnam and thus prove their courage; needless to say, both writers mention the myth of John Wayne as one of the inspirations behind their enlistment.

Having said that, it is certainly true that World War II was the 'paradigm war'[58] for the Vietnam generation of soldiers: as the conflict of their fathers, it was an almost tangible point of reference, an event whose legacy had played a manifest role in their young lives. O'Brien is quick to acknowledge the long shadow cast by the aftermath of this momentous victory on the American psyche:

> I grew out of one war and into another. My father came from leaden ships of sea, from the Pacific theatre; my mother wore the uniform of the WAVES. I was the wrinkled, swollen, bloody offspring of the great campaign against the tyrants of the 1940s, one explosion in the Baby Boom, one of the millions of new human beings come to replace those who had just died. My bawling came with the first throaty note of a new army in spawning. I was bred with the haste and dispatch and careless muscle-flexing of a rejuvenated, splendidly triumphant nation giving bridle to its own good fortune and success. I was fed by the spoils of 1945 victory. I learned to read and write on the prairies of southern Minnesota, in towns peering like corpses' eyeballs from out the corn. (*IID*, 21)[59]

This passage opens the second chapter, with the significant heading 'Pro Patria', of O'Brien's war memoir. It provides an immediate contextual counterpoint to the beginning of the narrative, a sketch entitled 'Days'. A description *in medias res* of a typical episode of life on the battlefield, 'Days' captures the mundane, distressing monotony of the war, which for the most part unfolds in an unbroken blend of tedium and fear. The flattened temporality of guerrilla warfare – '"Snipers yesterday, snipers today. What's the difference?"' (11) – is followed in 'Pro Patria' by the wide historical perspective on the soldiers' cultural background, which is given a distinct mythical dimension: the parental figures are transfigured into fabulous images (witness the epic ring of the 'leaden ships of sea' or the identification of the mother with the corps of the WAVES). At the same time, O'Brien casts himself as the archetypal 'Baby Boomer', an expression whose explosive connotations are deliberately detonated here. While father and mother shed their individuality to be endowed with an iconic and heroic quality, the movement from a unique to a collective identity enveloping the sons unfolds in a completely opposite direction, towards anonymity and undifferentiation.

58 Lewis, *The Tainted War*, p. 154.
59 The mythical resonance of this passage is noticed also by (amongst others) John Hellman, *American Myth and the Legacy of Vietnam*, p. 105.

Entering the scene in a clearly traumatic fashion ('wrinkled, swollen, bloody'), the Baby Boomers are described as spare parts, clones, the expendable results of intensive rearing or reproduction by spawning. In this dystopian vision, even the prairie, the fertile landscape of the frontier narrative, is distorted into a surreal and macabre apparition. If the previous generation ascend, as a group, to a heroic status, the sons' loss of individuality is unmatched by any gain or positive connotation, and speaks of the young soldiers' anxiety about what seems to be configured – again, in mythical terms, but this time with a clear ironic intent, for the myth turns out to be a nightmare – as the inexorable, cyclical progress of history in whose context Vietnam will be the fall which must succeed one of the country's greatest military triumphs.

O'Brien's rejection of the popular mythology of World War II, glamorized by Hollywood and invested with a further, more private allure by its emotional connections with parental figures, explains at least in part why, especially in his early writing, he looks at literary models who deal with the horrors of the Great War.[60] As its suggestive epithet constantly reminds us, this conflict has the dubious privilege of being the first modern confrontation on a global scale. Another major difference between the two world wars, in so far as their cultural representations are concerned, is to do with the media which codified and fixed them in the popular imagination. The events of World War II proved to be perfect raw material for the big screen, as evidenced by John Wayne's charismatic grip on his audience; conversely, the literature of the same conflict, which includes American classics such as Norman Mailer's *The Naked and the Dead* (1948), Joseph Heller's *Catch-22* (1961), Kurt Vonnegut's *Slaughterhouse-Five* (1969) and Thomas Pynchon's *Gravity's Rainbow* (1973), appeared much later, often decades after the end of the conflict, and took longer to acquire canonical status. In the end, before and during the American engagement in Vietnam, the influence of these now celebrated war narratives was in no way comparable to the popular reach of blockbusters like John Wayne's *Sands of Iwo Jima* (1949; directed by Allan Dwan) or even the less gung-ho but mythically titled *From Here to Eternity* (1953; starring Montgomery Clift, Burt Lancaster and Frank Sinatra, directed by Fred Zinnemann, from a script based on the eponymous 1952 novel by James Jones) and *To Hell and Back* (1955; starring Audie Murphy and directed by Jesse Hibbs).

World War I by comparison generated a more considerable impact on the

---

60 The Horatian motto 'Dulce et decorum est pro patria mori', scathingly revisited by Wilfred Owen as an 'old lie', is embedded, in a jumbled-up order, in the title of three chapters of *If I Die. Northern Lights* is virtually a rewriting of Hemingway's *The Sun Also Rises*, while *Going After Cacciato* opens with an epigraph from Siegfried Sassoon, 'Soldiers are dreamers'.

international literary scene; it may even be said to have given rise to a new genre, with the brutal, surreal indictment of the reality of combat in the poetry of Wilfred Owen and Siegfried Sassoon, whose impassioned critique of the rhetoric of war is acknowledged by O'Brien's early writing. In fact, British war poetry – the category hardly needs the 'first world' qualifier, since it is so readily associated with the image of the trenches on the Western front – represents a seminal example of 'literature of protest', with the soldier-artist exposing time-honoured conventions and common (mis)representations of the truth for the cultural, ideological constructions that they really are.[61] The revolutionary impact of the Great War and its literature on (for lack of a better term) the Western world is rightly identified as one of the key reasons for its persistence in the twentieth-century imaginary. More specifically, cultural historians see an obvious analogy between the effect of the First World War on Europe (particularly on the British Empire) and the terrible blow that Vietnam dealt to the US's perception of itself. The image is that of a rude awakening, a fall from grace, the end of a golden era, as Freeman Dyson already argued in 1979: 'The Vietnam War produced in American life the same fundamental change of mood that the First World War produced in Europe. The young Americans of today are closer in spirit to the Europeans than to the Americans of thirty years ago. The age of innocence is now over for all of us'.[62] Besides prompting the moral controversy about the role of the US on the global scene and challenging its identity as the redeemer nation, the war in Vietnam, *pace* Richard Nixon and General Westmoreland, still remains the only substantial blot on the American military record.[63] Again, even leaving aside any ethical issue, this defeat is so much more humiliating when one considers the disproportion in wealth and technological resources between the two countries.

Last but not least, World War II turned out to be an inadequate precursor to the experience of Vietnam because the latter proved to be a more awkward

---

61 Of course, the literature of protest substitutes its own constructions for the old ones: for example, it is virtually predicated on the (self-)perception of the soldier as a victim or even a martyr. O'Brien seems aware of this danger, which is why he is so concerned with exploring the notions of authenticity and personal responsibility.

62 Quoted in Herzog, *Vietnam War Stories*, p. 69.

63 In *No More Vietnams* (1987), Richard Nixon wrote, 'On January 27, 1973 almost twenty years after the French had lost the first Vietnam War, we had won the second Vietnam War. We signed the peace agreement that ended the war in a way that won the peace. We had redeemed our pledge to keep South Vietnam free'; quoted in Susan Jeffords, *The Remasculinization of America: Gender and the Vietnam War* (Bloomington and Indianapolis: Indiana University Press, 1989), p. 2. General Westmoreland also famously stated his belief in the American victory, even if with a telling proviso: 'Militarily, you must remember that we succeeded in Vietnam. We won every engagement we were involved in out there'; quoted in Kermit D. Johnson, *Realism and Hope in a Nuclear Age* (Louisville, KY: John Knox Press, 1988), p. 28.

moral quagmire than anybody could have ever imagined. Vietnam lacked the self-evident moral certainties of 'the great campaign against the tyrants of the 1940s' and stirred an unprecedented and occasionally violent opposition on the home front: only John Wayne could produce and star in a film clearly in support of the war while the conflict was about to escalate amid growing perplexity.[64] The Great War did not possess that unshakeable kernel of righteousness, and the necessity of the continuing massacre was audibly called into question, most famously by Sassoon, who in July 1917 expressed his strong objections to the war in 'A Soldier's Declaration': 'I believe that this war, upon which I entered as a war of defence and liberation, has now become a war of aggression and conquest. [...] I have seen and endured the suffering of the troops, and I can no longer be a party to prolong these sufferings for ends which I believe to be unjust and evil.'[65] Interestingly, Sassoon's own sense of duty and loyalty towards his soldiers is what convinced him to suspend his protest and rejoin the war: the bond, in this case between an officer and his troops, and more generally between fellow-soldiers, becomes the supreme commitment, particularly when allegiance to one's state and to the cause of the conflict begins to wane. This consideration brings me to two more points to be made about the wide cultural context of O'Brien's position as a war writer – both revolving around the ideological battles being fought on the home front, and both fuelled by the feeling of ingratitude and hostility perceived by the veterans back in the US: the sense that the soldiers had been betrayed by their fathers, and their experience of a direct, American threat to their masculinity. In both cases, O'Brien's writing departs from these widespread responses to the war and their literary articulations.

Acquiring particular resonance in the comparison between Wolrd War I and Vietnam, the first of the above-mentioned issues flags up the hiatus between the pull of the individual's sense of obligation towards his or her ancestors and the inevitable tension and discrepancies in the conduct and values of different age groups: in other words, what Milton Bates calls the 'generation war'.[66] Of course, the generation gap is a constant of human

64 The film in question is *The Green Berets*, released in July 1968. It performed well with the public, who probably got what they expected, i.e. a movie in the John Wayne tradition. Even so, it was generally perceived to be little more than propaganda and, to this day, it continues to be derided not only for its simplistic, clear-cut politics and ridiculous patriotism, but also for its blatant factual inaccuracies. Notorious amongst these mistakes is the film's ending on an improbable sunset on the east-facing South China Sea. For a discussion of *The Green Berets*, see Taylor, *The Vietnam War in History, Literature and Film*, pp. 48ff.

65 Siegfried Sassoon published 'A Soldier's Declaration' as an open letter to *The Times* on 31 July 1917. The declaration is reproduced in his 1930 *Memoirs of an Infantry Officer* (London: Faber & Faber, 2000), pp. 224–25.

66 See Chapter 5 of Milton J. Bates, *The Wars We Took to Vietnam: Cultural Conflict and Storytelling* (Berkeley and Los Angeles: University of California Press, 1996).

existence, but both the Great War and the Vietnam war contributed very significantly to the intensification of the cultural clash and the shift in the prevailing mood that often accompany the passage from one generation to another. Memories of the class of 1914 are inevitably slipping away, while the tag 'Vietnam generation' retains common currency; both denote an epochal change in sensitivity, the irrevocable onset of a new age and the dismissal of old beliefs. There is, however, a fundamental difference between those whom the young soldiers of the two conflicts held to be responsible for the perpetuation of the wrong ideals: in Vietnam things got very personal. The rude awakening to the unprecedented scale of destruction caused by modern armed conflict during the First World War was of truly historic significance, because at the beginning of the twentieth century war itself was an event barely within human memory in Europe and the US: 'No man in the prime of life knew what war was like. All imagined that it would be an affair of great marches and great battles, quickly decided'.[67] Both in World War I and in Vietnam those who had not yet reached their prime would bear the brunt of the inaccuracy of these expectations. War is always fought by the young; unsurprisingly, their disillusionment with military life is often mingled with resentment towards what looks like the undeserved and/or misused authority of the older generations, of their institutions, of their values.

In Vietnam, this ideological clash took place in a private dimension, as well as in the public arena. Memories of a relatively recent war, and a just and noble war at that, prevented the recurrence of the peculiar military amnesia that had preceded the First World War, but were the cause of even more terrible misconceptions. To the Baby Boomers deployed in Vietnam, the memories had come charged with emotional connections, since it was the soldiers' own fathers who could guarantee, first-hand, their authenticity and, by implication, the validity of the principles they stood for: 'Fathers taught sons the nature of war using their own experiences in WWII as a model. By levying on the notions of manhood and duty [...], the fathers presented war as a blessed event. Had the Vietnam War proved itself amenable to the world view of the fathers, those notions would have survived intact to be re-transmitted by the sons to future initiates'. Besides raising critical questions of the nation's system of beliefs, the rupture of this seamless continuity damaged the most basic form of social cohesion, breaking the relationship of trust within the family: 'Vietnam made a whole generation of fathers look like liars and betrayers, and a whole generation of sons victims of their own initiation'.[68] If the reality of trench warfare shattered myths of gallantry and brilliant military action that were truly time-honoured, the Vietnam war

---

67 A. J. P. Taylor, quoted in Paul Fussell, *The Great War and Modern Memory* (Oxford: Oxford University Press, 2000), p. 21.
68 Lewis, *The Tainted War*, pp. 49–50.

pitched the young soldiers against their own fathers, the veterans of a conflict in which glorious purposefulness and the possibility of heroism seemed indeed to have resurfaced.

I would argue, however, that the much more personal nature of the American soldiers' feeling of betrayal in Vietnam is the product not merely of the contingent circumstances of the war, but also of the mythical and actual legacy of the peculiar history of the United States. The bond of duty between one generation and the next is loaded by the Puritan vision of America as the 'City upon a Hill' or, in its secular manifestation, the land of freedom and possibilities.[69] Whether in a sacred or a lay version, a tradition of *individualistic* utopianism underpins the foundation of America and becomes the unwritten covenant that binds all its citizens, as private human beings, to the fulfilment and the defence of its principles. The autonomy and the rebellious spirit of the pioneer bear witness to the strength of American individualism even within the context of a collective, 'civilizing' mission. By contrast, the British Empire's call for allegiance to God, King and Country rests on a much longer shared history and remains devoid, in spite of any religious reference, of the messianic sense of purpose that informs the foundation of the United States. Finally, the very status of America as a country of immigrants, to be built on individual volition, heightens the sense of mutual responsibility, as well as the attrition, between fathers and sons, particularly when the parental figure is perceived to be a link with the corrupt European past. The deposition of the (European) Father is, after all, a constant of the early American novelistic tradition.[70] While father figures loom large in many of O'Brien's narratives, where they often assume larger-than-life proportions (most notably in the case of the patriarch in *Northern Lights*), they are for the most part supportive of their children and nowhere are they held directly responsible for the fate of their sons in relation to Vietnam. Undoubtedly critical of the cultural coordinates that he has been given, O'Brien remains concerned in his entire output with exposing the kernel of personal responsibility that his protagonists must acknowledge in facing their experience of the war or indeed of any other event in their lives.

The disparaging exposure of the dubious motives behind the conflict and the perception of the soldiers as victims rather than as agents of destruction have another interesting aftermath in the American troops' perception of their ordeal: the idea that they had been callously forced to engage in what was at best a senseless enterprise underpins the portrayal and (self-)percep-

---

69 The Puritan legacy for Vietnam is mentioned in almost every literary study of the literature of the war (see, for example, Herzog's *Innocence Lost*), but Philip Melling makes it the main object of study in his *Vietnam in American Literature* (Boston: G. K. Hall, 1990).

70 See Leslie Fiedler, *Love and Death in the American Novel* (Champaign, IL, and London: Dalkey Archive Press, 2003), p. 79.

tion of the Vietnam veterans as 'emblems of an unjustly discriminated masculinity',[71] a near-ubiquitous notion in the re-evaluation of the war and the reapportioning of blame that took place in the 1980s. In her seminal book *The Remasculinization of America*, Susan Jeffords argues that the US's involvement in Vietnam, and its unprecedented military defeat, triggered a distinctly conservative and misogynist backlash, which found expression in an extreme re-evaluation of male bonding as the prime form of human relationship. Ironically, to all intent and purposes, this line of reasoning ends up running counter to the American patriotic spirit, since it claims that soldierly camaraderie is to be privileged not only over familial and romantic ties, but also over the social pact between each individual and the larger national community. In other words, allegiance to one's brotherhood finally supersedes allegiance to the flag. Jeffords focuses on the cultural revisionism spawned by the proliferation of personal, fictional and historico-political accounts of the war from the late 1970s onwards; her research shows how these representations and appraisals of the conflict turn Vietnam into a spectacle of masculine prowess and mutual loyalty, while inviting the fetishization of the male body. They are also instrumental to the redemption of the image of the soldier, who is cast in the role of victim of an ineffective and feminised government and of an unsympathetic mother-country. The American troops are thus seen to be threatened with emasculation by their own superiors, by the political apparatus and by the people at home, perceived respectively as incautious strategists, useless negotiators and passive, if not hostile, observers. Given these premises, it would follow that, had hot-blooded male Americans been allowed to unleash their righteous and muscular power without constraints, the war would have been won and the natural order of things would have been restored. In this imaginary scenario, the (feminine) doves are no match for the (masculine) hawks.

The general scapegoating and denigration of femininity is completed by the projection of feminine qualities onto the invisible, unfathomable enemy and onto the Vietnamese landscape, often effectively configured as a *vagina dentata* or as another castrating, feminine monstrosity. While O'Brien's gender politics are occasionally problematic, and at times even deliberately shocking, they never fail to draw the readers' attention to pressing questions and unresolved contradictions, as well as to the inadequacy of the traditional military identification between courage and masculinity. This latter point is analysed obsessively throughout O'Brien's work, from the expansive philosophical meditations of his early autobiographical narrative, to the concise and peremptory tone of the epigrammatic sequence of paradoxical pronouncements about the nature of war contained in 'How to Tell a True

71 Jeffords, *The Remasculinization of America*, p. 116.

War Story'. After the chiasmic reiteration, in slightly different terms, of the simultaneous feelings of exhilaration and revulsion prompted by the experience of combat – 'War is nasty; war is fun. War is thrilling; war is drudgery' – O'Brien's final quip shakes up the old equation between military enterprises and male rites of passage, with a deadpan reminder of what is ultimately at stake for the soldier: 'War makes you a man; war makes you dead' (*TTC*, 77). Such a cynical, disenchanted take on the impact of war on the individual's growth is clearly intertwined with a radical re-evaluation of traditional notions of courage and gallantry. The following chapter will explore O'Brien's re-definition of these terms, particularly in the early phases of his writing career.

2

The Courage of Authenticity

Courage is an indispensable quality in Western definitions of masculinity. Whether embodied by the mythical heroes of ancient and medieval epics, or by the self-made pioneers of modernity, whether nostalgically yearned for by the lost generations of the twentieth century or celebrated, tongue-in-cheek, by the anti-heroes of postmodernity, courage remains at the heart of what it means to be a man. The word has long been a synonym of 'virtue', whose etymology (from Latin, *vir* = 'man') betrays a masculine bias in the definition of excellence – hence, one might argue, of heroism at large. Inevitably, war literature is one of the privileged textual arenas in which the association between bravery and masculinity is articulated and pondered over; the existence of a manly code of honour and the meaning and possibility of male heroism are inextricably linked with our understanding of conflict and armed warfare. Particularly, but not exclusively, within a mythical, sacred ethos,[1] war has been seen as the ultimate rite of passage, an event that separates the men from the boys, an opportunity to test oneself and prove one's valour, either in victorious survival or in the extreme sacrifice of one's life. The pervasiveness of this idea, even in the disillusioned context of the post-Vietnam era, is such that we find the celebratory sanctioning of masculinity through combat voiced by the least plausible advocates of its truth: those American men and potential draftees who, for a number of disparate reasons, did not actually fight the war. In 'Apocalypse Continued', a 1985 article for the *New York Times Magazine*, the psychotherapist Edward Tick summarises the plight of his fellow Vietnam veterans *manqués*: '[we] suffer because we chose not to perform a primary and expected rite of passage. We were never inducted, not merely into the Army, but into manhood. […] I have had some of the usual rites – marriage, educational and professional

---

1 I use the terms 'mythical' and 'sacred' in Mircea Eliade's sense of the words, as outlined in *The Myth of the Eternal Return* (1949), where they characterize the investment in ritual gestures as purveyors of meaning for their participation in the primordial temporality of the eternal present. According to Eliade, this attitude is typical of, but not exclusive to, pre-modern, traditional, 'primitive' cultures; *The Myth of the Eternal Return or, Cosmos and History*, trans. Willard R. Trask (Princeton: Princeton University Press, 1974).

recognition. But no matter how many passages or accomplishments I garner, I never quite feel complete'.[2]

What is striking in testimonies such as Tick's is not so much the regret for not having been through the archetypal masculine formative experience, within the scenario that allegedly fosters the most meaningful and authentic male bonding, but rather the resolute conviction that these experiential gaps rule out the possibility of ever feeling whole – a possibility, one surmises, that would have been available to these men had they marched on to war. Tick's lament for a never-to-be-achieved ideal wholeness is endorsed by Michael Herr's confession, near the end of *Dispatches* (1977), of the insoluble dilemma facing those participants and witnesses to the war who finally manage to wean themselves off its influence. The necessity of finding a way out of Vietnam, physically and mentally, lest one should become addicted to it – or, as Herr's popular wisdom would have it, lest one should become 'one of those poor bastards who had to have a war on all the time' – is counterbalanced by the bittersweet fate awaiting the veteran: 'We got out and became like everyone else who has been through a war: changed, enlarged and (some things are expensive to say) incomplete.'[3] In the most severe instances, the feeling of loss, Herr argues, engenders sensations similar to the phantom-limb pains suffered by amputees: the survivor-witness of combat cannot but mourn the disappearance of a part of him that used to be alive. Vietnam is thus remembered as a time tending towards the ideal of a blissful, eternal presence, as conveyed by Herr's image of an idyllic infancy: 'A few extreme cases felt that the experience there had been a glorious one, while most of us felt that it had been merely wonderful. I think that Vietnam was what we had instead of happy childhoods' (195). This final, often quoted, pronouncement is an epigrammatic version of Tick's analytical stance on the war, an event perceived as a defining adventure and a vehicle for male camaraderie and fulfilment.[4]

Herr's provocative reference to 'happy childhoods' also introduces the idea of war as a locus of experiential immediacy and of authenticity, whose participants are offered the rare chance to be fully and truly themselves.[5] In

2 Quoted in Bates, *The Wars We Took to Vietnam*, p. 147.
3 Herr, *Dispatches*, p. 195.
4 Here and in the previous quotations about the 'poor bastards who had to have a war on all the time', Herr is referring specifically to correspondents, like himself, who had turned into 'war junkies' and relinquished the professional objectivity of the reporter to become deeply embroiled in what they were supposed to observe (as he explains in another memorable line: 'I went to cover the war and the war covered me' (24)). Still, as Tick's pained recognition of the experiential bond provided by the war, and indeed Herr's blurring of the notion of participants and observers, both testify, these comments can easily be interpreted to apply to the plight of the military veterans of Vietnam.
5 I talk of 'authenticity' in existentialist terms, as a radical quest for and expression of one's individuality, and as such caught up in an endless attempt to transcend the established,

this chapter, I will argue that authenticity provides the conceptual context of O'Brien's analysis of courage and masculinity – although, I should hasten to add, O'Brien rejects in no uncertain terms the notion of war as a male rite of passage and Herr's deliberately shocking comparison between the conflict in Vietnam and an edenic state of being when one's true self is naturally encouraged to come through. This theoretical framework also accounts for O'Brien's departure from the traditional storytelling modalities of war writing. Authenticity is a state of existence: something one *is*, rather than becomes or performs. It is a private quality, and it does not have an immediate impact on, nor is it directly influenced by, the social sphere. This helps to explain why O'Brien's narratives typically eschew the *Bildungsroman* formula or, when they adopt it, as in the case of *Going After Cacciato*, they do so only to provide very small-scale revelations. O'Brien's analysis of the meaning and the cost of bravery is thus underpinned by a rigorous philosophical quest, and it is the focus of his first three books, which have therefore been described as forming a 'tripartite "myth of courage"'.[6]

As anticipated in the previous chapter, the autobiographical *If I Die in A Combat Zone* departs from the narrative pattern of other personal accounts of Vietnam, such as Caputo's and Kovic's, because O'Brien does not conform to the type of the recruit who is enlightened about the evil of war by his involvement with it. Unlike his fellow veteran-memoirists, O'Brien did not believe in the rightness of the war in the first place and, unlike them, he cannot ascribe to his writing any cathartic or didactic value. O'Brien's assessment of his integrity does not need the support of experiential elements acquired in the field, because what is really under scrutiny is not the nature of war but the intimate drama of a character who chooses to go to Vietnam against his conscience. The debt of *If I Die* to the rich modern literary tradition of war writing as protest and demystification of an old-fashioned heroic

communal sense of morality. This latter set of values finds its most powerful and suggestive articulation in mythical storytelling, as argued, for example, by the cultural historian Mircea Eliade and – after him – by literary critics such as Northrop Frye and Frank Kermode. The slippery notion of 'authenticity' is perhaps best explained in contrast to qualities such as 'honesty' and 'sincerity', which in turn 'can be defined as a congruence between one's inclinations and the prevailing ethos, or as a congruence between one's behaviour and one's innermost essence. Authenticity, however, is not in keeping with such a definition. Not only does it deny any rigid a priori essence, but it also rejects any intrinsic value in compliance with a given set of standards. It regards any such compliance as a flight from one's responsibility for freely forming one's selfhood. Authenticity defines itself in lacking any definition. It is a pathos of incessant change, as opposed to a passive subordination to one particular ethic'; Jacob Golomb, *In Search of Authenticity: From Kierkegaard to Camus* (London and New York: Routledge, 1995), p. 3.

6 Heberle, *A Trauma Artist*, p. 72. Heberle borrows the idea of the 'myth of courage' from Milton J. Bates, 'Tim O'Brien's Myth of Courage', *Modern Fiction Studies*, 33.2 (1987), pp. 263–79.

code is similarly not straightforward, as a further, brief comparison between this text and *The Red Badge of Courage* (1895) will illustrate. Heberle distinguishes between '[t]he two conventional purposes of combat narratives – denouncing war or validating its formative effect on personal identity' (53), but in modern war writing the former is usually a sub-species of the latter, given how the lesson of technological warfare is more often than not about the immense destructive power that man can exercise over his fellow human beings. Whether they be two separate issues or deeply interconnected, protest and personal maturation are beyond the scope of O'Brien's memoir, because 'either scenario would be dishonest to [the writer's] own experience' (54).

The inadequacy or hypocrisy of the *Bildungsroman* model is further exemplified by *Northern Lights*, a text which clearly foregrounds questions about gender identity alongside its analysis of bravery. The gender politics in O'Brien's work are arguably more problematic than his take on courage – or rather, his reflections on courage appear to become problematic when they overlap with gender issues. Still, in the trilogy of courage O'Brien clearly distances himself from the gung-ho mentality and the machismo endorsed by the military, and by the misogynist streak and the male revanchism that Susan Jeffords and James William Gibson have traced in American culture in the post-Vietnam years.[7] *Northern Lights* has generally been read as an expansion of the invitation to the feminine 'wise endurance' propounded by *If I Die*, as a story revolving around the education of the male protagonist, who must learn to move from the rejection of the paternal misogynist model to the embrace of his wife's femininity. This interpretation, however, does not do justice to O'Brien's more complex approach to gender relations and definitions – an approach that goes beyond the mere inversion of the binary opposition between masculinity and femininity. The same is true of *Cacciato*, the one novel whose protagonist undergoes a process of maturation as a result of the war, ostensibly because of the positive example of feminine role models. Even in this case, however, the protagonist's real growth is only tangentially related to questions of gender; the soldier's maturation does not consist of the ability to temper one's essential maleness with feminine touches, but rather resides in the acknowledgement of one's personal responsibility in the face of societal pressures. Thus does the trilogy come full circle: for O'Brien, courage is a matter of authenticity.

---

7 James William Gibson is the author of *Warrior Dreams: Violence and Manhood in Post-Vietnam America* (New York: Hill and Wang, 1994), an analysis of the burgeoning of paramilitary culture in the US in the 1990s. Gibson's study can thus be said to be a development of one of the strands of Susan Jeffords's *The Remasculinization of America*.

The battle before the battle

Published in 1973, the first of his eight book-length narratives to date, *If I Die in a Combat Zone* remains one of the most interesting and most frequently analysed of O'Brien's works. The reason for its popularity goes well beyond its significance as an early documentary account of the war. In spite of O'Brien's protestations that it is a 'faithful representation of Vietnam',[8] the book has sparked endless discussions of its unusual structure and approach to its autobiographical material. The history of reception of *If I Die* is marked by uncertainty about whether it belongs to the realm of fiction or of fact. Its early critics have referred to O'Brien's memoirs in several different ways, picking up on the episodic nature of the narrative ('snapshots' and 'sketches'), or highlighting its opaque cautionary tone ('parable'), or simply hedging their bets because of the obvious literariness of an account that remains clearly based on its author's life ('semi-fictionalized story'). 'Ironically, even the paperback publisher was confused about the appropriate category by placing the letters "FIC" (fiction) on the spine of the 1979 Laurel Edition and "NF" (nonfiction) on the 1987 edition'.[9] O'Brien was indeed amongst the first writer-witnesses of the war to produce a memoir which artfully employs fictional strategies, and thus provides an alternative, but no less authentic, perspective on the conflict from the accounts of the media. The text's departure from a strict chronological pattern is the most obvious sign of its formal adherence to a fictional rather than a conventionally autobiographical structure; this straddling of fiction and history is a feature that *If I Die* shares with Norman Mailer's and Truman Capote's New Journalism, and with the most popular example of the genre to come out of Vietnam, Michael Herr's *Dispatches*.

However, while Herr's idiosyncratic story unfolds as a movie, complete with its own popular music soundtrack and psychedelic montage, *If I Die* is a distinctly *literary* book, beginning with its learned epigraph from Dante's *Divine Comedy*, quoted in Italian in the text.[10] The reference to free will, God's greatest gift to man, sets up the tone of philosophical inquiry that underscores the narration and introduces the main concern of the text: the drama of conscience faced by the draftee convinced of the iniquity of the war. The literariness of the memoir, a trait that in the weakest parts of the narra-

---

8   Travis Elborough, 'Relying on Memory and Imagination: Travis Elborough Talks to Tim O'Brien', in *IID*, pp. 2–9, p. 9.
9   Herzog, *Tim O'Brien*, p. 41.
10 The epigraph reads: '[L]o maggior don che Dio per sua larghezza / fesse creando ... / ... fu de la volontà la libertate, *The Divine Comedy Par.* V, 19 ff.'. The quotation can be translated as 'the greatest gift that God, in his generosity, / offered in his creation / was freedom of will'.

tive verges on a bookish excess, should therefore not be merely ascribed to the anxiety of influence and lack of self-confidence of a first-time writer still searching for his own voice. In fact, O'Brien deliberately cultivates the image of himself as 'College Joe' (*IID*, 33), the atypically mature and educated draftee, definitely 'not soldier material' (*IID*, 31), who tries to reason his way out of the moral stand-off caused by his two contrasting allegiances: to his country and to his personal beliefs. That the dilemma is primarily a philosophical one is also made clear by the sustained intertextual references to the Platonic dialogues in which Socrates's reflections on the nature of courage, together with a radical pursuit of virtue, provide a luminous, and extremely demanding, model of behaviour for the young O'Brien. Like *The Red Badge of Courage*, *If I Die* is a war story whose priority is the investigation of the nature of bravery and of personal *integrity* (a matter of individual *wholeness*, which manifests itself in the seamless adherence to one's own ethical code), rather than the factual account of combat. Famously, Crane had no direct experience of war when he wrote his novel, while O'Brien – who was instead in the position to write a chronicle of his year 'in country' – devotes a significant part of his narrative to the agonizing choice between going to Vietnam or deserting and leaving America behind. The deliberation is protracted from Basic Training to Advanced Infantry Training at Fort Lewis, from the receipt of the draft letter to the moment when O'Brien alights at Cam Ranh Bay, and beyond. The real battle, in other words, is what goes on in the soldier's mind. In a sense, the narrative in *If I Die* begins where the story of Henry Fleming had ended: while Fleming's self-delusions are shaken by his confrontation with combat, so that his questionable growth finally amounts to a more refined ability to examine himself and his surroundings, O'Brien does not seem to need the encounter with the war, and with military life in general, in order to face his private demons.

From the start, O'Brien is already an insightful and uncompromising observer and self-critic, no more inclined to expose the contradictions of the people and institutions involved in the war than he is to denounce his own failings. While Fleming scrutinizes his fellow soldiers in the hope of discerning traces of the self-doubt and fears that plague him in the wake of the battle, O'Brien focuses his gaze inwardly, in a rigorous self-analysis, which is the first mark of his independence and individuality; where Fleming seeks confirmation of the normality of his feelings, O'Brien holds on to his intimate, non-compliant attitude to the homologizing machismo of the army training. His description of Fort Lewis revolves around the opposition between his unique self and the indistinct, unthinking crowd, the 'horde of boors', 'jungle of robots', pack of 'savages' (*IID*, 40, 41) constituted by his fellow recruits, who have become, without realizing it, prisoners of the Army, animals in a 'cattle pen' or in a 'hopeless zoo' (*IID*, 52). The mixed metaphor of the '*jungle* of robots' is particularly telling in view of the conditions in which the war was fought and of the fact that the attributes traditionally associated with this term are the idea of wilderness and unruliness, in direct contrast to the qualities normally attached to the nature of the military organisation. Another significant reversal of the usual combination of semantic fields and referents is the use of 'savages' to denote the American army rather than the enemy.[11] O'Brien is very harsh in the judgement of his fellow recruits:

> I hated the trainees even more than the captors. I learned to march, but I learned alone. I gaped at the neat package of stupidity and arrogance at Fort Lewis. I was superior. I made no apologies for believing it. Without sympathy or compassion, I instructed my intellect and eyes: ignore the horde. I kept vigil against intrusion into my private life. I maintained a distance suitable to the black and white distinction between me and the unconscious, genuflecting herd. (*IID*, 41)

This is a deliberately unsympathetic self-construction: the character's vehement superciliousness is bound to push readers away even as they are alerted to the unthinking nature, and the particular brand of arrogance, of his fellow trainees and of the army machine. Such a high sense of oneself, so early in the narrative, is a natural prelude for a fall: like Henry Fleming, O'Brien seems ripe for a change, but the protagonist's transformation does not occur as a result of his experience of the battleground. If anything, both the army training and his employment as an infantryman strengthen O'Brien's, and the readers', contempt for the brutality and the pointlessness of war. What needs purging is the all too swift association, in the character's mind, between his intellectual self-awareness and his moral fibre, because the one does not immediately translate into the other, as he naively seems to imply. On the contrary, given that he did not refuse to leave for the war, O'Brien's ability to see through the strategies used by the army to indoctrinate the soldiers, paired with his misgivings about the appropriateness of the military efforts in Vietnam, mire his credibility as the reliable moral centre of the narrative. What the character must learn, he can learn through a piercing, honest examination of his failure to say no to the draft call, which is tantamount to an admission of moral weakness completely unrelated to the experience of fighting. In other words, O'Brien's acknowledgement of the hypocrisy that lurks even behind his censorious attitude to the army could have – and indeed should have – accompanied his military career right from the start: the character's self-doubts and recriminations do not concern his likely behaviour under fire, but the failure of nerve that has landed him in this position in the first place.

11 See also sections in Chapter 1 ('Old myths, new frontiers') and Chapter 3 ('Indian Country') for a further discussion of these themes.

O'Brien's musings and self-analysis for the most part, therefore, precede his actual engagement in combat, drawing on literary and philosophical models, and effectively pre-empting the need for experiential evidence in the definition and test of courage. This challenge to the necessity of experience is an even more extreme rejection of the *Bildungsroman* pattern which had already been given an ironic treatment by Stephen Crane. Needless to say, having renounced the authority of witness, O'Brien also discards any didactic claim for his narrative: 'Can the foot soldier teach anything important about war, merely for having been there? I think not. He can tell war stories' (*IID*, 32).[12] Triggered by a missed opportunity for self-assertion and moral growth, *If I Die* cannot unfold as a progressive narrative of personal development, nor can it be a retrospective warning, to future generations, about the evils of war: O'Brien's protest is aimed primarily at himself, and at his incapacity to be true to his convictions.

A sober realism and the ability to do the right thing, even when that involves the risk of social censure or the certainty of a solitary destiny, is what distinguishes O'Brien's heroes: 'Nick Adams, Alan Ladd of *Shane*, Captain Vere, Humphrey Bogart as the proprietor of Café d'Américain, Frederic Henry. Especially Frederic Henry' (*IID*, 142). This list of role models zeroes in on the type of the American loner, a man 'removed from other men, able to climb over and gaze down at other men' (*IID*, 142). Solitude is the condition that allows him a clearer vision of his world than most, and therefore, paradoxically, a stronger sense of responsibility for his actions. Hemingway's Frederic Henry is singled out both for his lack of conceit and for the poignant decision at the heart of his 'separate peace': far from being a desperate gesture of cowardice, desertion in his case signals the acceptance of his most urgent responsibility as a human being, as a companion to Catherine Berkeley and a father to their unborn child. Of course, within the context of a reflection on courage, the reference to the protagonist of *A Farewell to Arms* (1929) brings to mind his blunt condemnation of the abstract ideals of heroism and the emotive jargon of military propaganda:

> I was always embarrassed by the words sacred, glorious, and sacrifice and the expression in vain. [...] There were many words that you could not stand to hear and finally only the names of places had dignity. Certain numbers were the same way and certain dates and these with the names of places were all you could say and have them mean anything. Abstract words such as glory, honor, courage, or hallow were obscene beside the concrete names of villages, the numbers of roads, the names of rivers, the numbers of regiments and the dates.[13]

12 For a discussion of the wider implications of this statement, see Chapter 5.
13 Ernest Hemingway, *A Farewell to Arms* (London: Arrow Books, 1994), p. 165.

Scepticism towards a self-aggrandizing perception of courage, the aware-ness of one's limits, is another common trait of these *fictional* inspirations, whose example finds an unassuming, real counterpart in Captain Johansen, the 'living hero' who taught O'Brien that 'human beings sometimes embody valour and that they do not always dissolve at the end of a book or movie reel' (*IID*, 144). O'Brien's sincere admiration for Johansen is still inscribed within the constant comparison between the fictional and the real.[14] Later on, O'Brien would continue to blend factual and fictive suggestions in the character of Major Callicles, named after Socrates' antagonist in Plato's *Gorgias*, who represents in *If I Die* the false courage of the reckless and point-less expedition.[15] In the same vein of deliberate confusion between history and myth, O'Brien's early, polemic list of real heroes includes 'Kennedy, Audie Murphy, Sergeant York and T. E. Lawrence' (*IID*, 53), people invested with a legendary aura that makes them quasi-fictional creations.[16] In Captain Johansen, instead, for once life appears to approximate the ideal. The excitement for this small revelation is tempered by O'Brien's knowledge that Johansen would not share such a flattering opinion of his courage. The corol-lary of the Socratic motto is the hopelessness of ever seeing oneself as a hero: 'That's the problem. Knowing yourself, you can't make it real for yourself' (*IID*, 146).

It is finally another Socratic idea that links all of O'Brien's heroes: courage as 'wise endurance', a concept developed in Plato's *Laches*, where Socrates contends that 'men without courage are men without temperance, justice, or wisdom, just as without wisdom men are not truly courageous' (*IID*, 140). Courage seems to reside in the awareness of danger and, more importantly, of one's limitations; it is in the continuous attempt to approximate the ideal

14 Captain Johansen was a member of Amundsen's expedition to Antarctica in 1910–12. He criticized Amundsen's disastrous false start in the race with Scott for the South Pole, and openly questioned his poor leadership and selfish quest for personal glory, which had led him to put the lives of his men at risk. Amundsen later dismissed Johansen from his party and refused to acknowledge his crucial contribution – Johansen had saved the life of a less experienced fellow explorer – to the expedition. In 1913 Johansen committed suicide. Like O'Brien's eponymous captain, Johansen is an unacknowledged hero.

15 In *Gorgias*, Callicles attacks Socrates and indeed philosophy in general. He is an advocate of natural justice, i.e. supremacy of the strong over the weak.

16 President Kennedy needs no introduction: of his role in the Vietnam War and of the Arthurian spirit of his Camelot Years, we have already spoken in Chapter 1. Audie Murphy was the most decorated American soldier of World War II, and went on to star in the autobiographical *To Hell and Back* (1955), as well as in a number of westerns and war movies; he played the youth (i.e. Henry Fleming) in the cinematic version of *The Red Badge of Courage* (1951). Alvin York, an erstwhile conscientious objector, was the most decorated American soldier of World War I; Gary Cooper played him in the biographical 1941 film *Sergeant York*, which was the highest-grossing production of the year. T. E. Lawrence, an officer of the British Army, rose to fame for his role in the Arab Revolt (1916–18) and was immortalised as Lawrence of Arabia by David Lean's epic 1962 film.

balance between the four parts of virtue that make up the Platonic vision of true excellence. It is not recklessness, or gamesmanship. It is not what most people immediately conjure up as the image of the hero: the instinctive warrior waging a one-man spectacular attack against the enemy, unconcerned for his life, spurred on by the strength of his passion. The memory of one such assault provides a clear exemplification of O'Brien's point: 'Arizona bulled out across a flat piece of land, just like the captain, and I only remember his long limp body in the grass. It's the charge, the light brigade with only one man, that is the first thing to think about when thinking about courage. People who do it are remembered as brave, win or lose. They are heroes forever. It *seems* like courage, the charge' (*IID*, 135, my italics). O'Brien juxtaposes to this deceptive example of bravery the low-key, composed model provided by Johansen. What makes the captain's action heroic, and earns him the recognition of 'the steady, blood-headed intensity of Sir Lancelot', while Arizona's feat is quickly reduced to the image of a lifeless shape in the grass, is not the success of the enterprise, but the frame of mind that preceded it. Johansen is moved by a burning desire to be brave, but also by a constant uncertainty about what this longing implies and what courage really means. Arizona, instead, is obviously part of the unthinking herd, 'bulling' through the field, in a blundering private charge which O'Brien associates with the terrible immolation of the five hundred of Tennyson's ballad. In this vignette, O'Brien dismantles traditional representations of heroism, from Tennyson's ode to sacrifice, to Henry Fleming's pathetic (self-)deception – 'Soldiering is not a red badge of courage' (*IID*, 141) – and even, at a first glance, Hemingway's famous definition of courage as 'grace under pressure' (*IID*, 146).

On closer inspection, however, it is plain that O'Brien is challenging the literal, *mis*interpretation of Hemingway's motto, arguing that grace and poise are too easily affected. In fact, the distinction between courage and its affectation is one that Hemingway himself makes very clear in *The Sun Also Rises* (1926), a text that O'Brien knows very well. One of the climactic moments of *The Sun Also Rises* revolves around the bull-fighting in Pamplona, a ritual with quasi-religious force for Jake Barnes, the narrator-protagonist of the novel, a man still trying to come to terms with the aftermath of the Great War and with the consequences of the wound that has emasculated him. The war has left Jake unable to establish a mutually fulfilling relationship with the woman he loves, Brett Astley, herself a troubled, directionless character. An emancipated figure, Brett then embarks on a number of doomed, destructive affairs; the idealistic Robert Cohn and the self-possessed Pedro Romero, who both subscribe, albeit in different ways, to a traditional view of gender roles, are amongst her lovers. Unsurprisingly, Brett cannot commit to either of them. Jake, on his part, like Hemingway, is obsessed with finding a model of masculinity unscathed by the uncertainties and self-consciousness of modernity. In Jake's eyes, it is Pedro Romero, the young bull-fighter, who embodies this rapidly disappearing ideal of manhood against the showmanship of his older, histrionic predecessors.

> Romero never made any contortions, always it was straight and pure and natural in line. The others twisted themselves like corkscrews, their elbows raised, and leaned against the flanks of the bulls after their horns had passed, to give a faked look of danger. Afterward, all that was faked turned bad and gave an unpleasant feeling. Romero's bullfighting gave real emotion, because he kept the absolute purity of line in his movements and always quietly and calmly let the horns pass him close each time. He did not have to emphasize their closeness. [...] since the death of Joselito all the bullfighters had been developing a technique that simulated this appearance of danger in order to give a fake emotional feeling, while the bullfighter was really safe. Romero had the old thing, the holding of his purity of line through the maximum of exposure, while he dominated the bull by making him realize he was unattainable, while he prepared him for the killing.[17]

Romero combines the old Achillean model of heroism – collected, self-sufficient, an end unto itself – with the modern attribute of authenticity, of truthfulness to one's unique self, a human quality that, as already adumbrated, developed with the rise of individualism and began to wane with its twentieth-century crisis, as Hemingway's protagonists testify. Romero is clearly an exception, part of a rare class of men whose existence is still possible in the mythical dimension of the fiesta, in a country as yet untouched by the malaise of modern life, the latter epitomized in the novel by Paris and the 'lost generation' of Jake and his friends. With his lack of self-consciousness and his refusal to pander to the taste of his audience, Romero embodies an authenticity that remains an unattainable ideal in Jake's, and our, disillusioned world. At the end of the century, (O'Brien's) heroes can no longer be unselfconscious, but they still strive for integrity, the sense of wholeness attained when one's essence expresses itself freely, fluidly and seamlessly. Arizona's gesture clearly runs counter to this quest for authenticity: his is the mechanical action of a kid who has grown up watching too many war movies and who ends up fighting (and dying) in the attempt to be the replica of a replica, hankering for a simulacrum, nurturing his very own 'John Wayne wetdream' (24), to borrow Michael Herr's colourful expression. By definition, the search for authenticity often ends up clashing with the individual's integration within a community. Lionel Trilling distinguishes between this

---

17 Ernest Hemingway, *Fiesta: The Sun Also Rises* (London: Arrow Books, 2004), pp. 145–46. Subsequent references are to this edition.

deep, and highly personal, quality, and the more superficial dictates of sincerity (or honesty): this latter attribute is achieved through a coincidence between the self's hidden motives and the established morality of the day. The sincere/honest individual is thus a social construct, defined by his or her adherence to externally sanctioned values and by the correspondence between his or her inner self and its outward manifestations (in demeanour, actions, utterances, etc.). Paradoxically, neither parameter recognizes the sincerity of the self by looking exclusively at the very self under scrutiny: in the first instance, the individual is measured against something over and above himself or herself, while the second perspective implies a split in the self, which is therefore perceived as made of two parts which might or might not be in accordance. Authenticity instead is a rigorous extolling of one's deepest essence, shed of all societal bindings and influences until the very notion of selfhood becomes untenable. The authentic individual is therefore seamless, whole and self-contained and, at the same time, indefinable and ever-changing: these are the conditions for one's disenfranchisement from any standard.

The wider scenario of the contrast between the subject's authenticity and the mandates of the state is once again illustrated in *If I Die* by Socrates, who was sentenced to death for the alleged anti-democratic nature of his teachings. As O'Brien reminds us, Socrates – who had served Athens as a young soldier – refused both to recant his doctrine and to escape from the city under whose laws he had been happy to live all his life: 'he reminded himself that he had had seventy years in which he could have left the country, if he were not satisfied or felt the agreements he'd made with it were unfair. He had not chosen Sparta or Crete. And, I reminded myself, I had not thought that much about Canada until that summer' (*IID*, 28). All wrapped up in the momentousness of his dilemma, the narrator is completely oblivious to the bathetic shift from Socrates and Sparta to himself and Canada, nor does he dwell on the fundamental difference between his predicament and that of the ancient philosopher. In accepting his inevitable death, Socrates does not go back either on his personal beliefs or on the laws of his country; by comparison the draftee would have had a similar, yet infinitely easier option, in the choice to face prison. And yet, somehow, this prospect is *never* envisaged in any of O'Brien's narratives. This scenario seems to be literally unthinkable. Why?

We have come here to the heart of the matter, to the real reason why O'Brien cannot find the strength to act in accordance with his individual moral principles: going to prison would mean incurring the kind of social censure that one's anonymity in Canada or Sweden might not invite (although guilt is inescapable in either case). What O'Brien does not want to lose is ultimately what Captain Vere – significantly the only hero whose wisdom is questioned in *If I Die* – also could not afford to jeopardize: social order. O'Brien's parallelism with Melville's Captain Vere is particularly poignant since both figures are cast as readers, observers and thinkers, as well as, in due course, *judges* of the stories in which they are involved. O'Brien is the recruit who has 'read too many books' (*IID*, 63), as the battalion chaplain scathingly replies to the soldier's lucid explanation of his qualms about the war.

The obvious quality of *If I Die* as 'an educated and literate man's response to war' has led Maria Bonn to remark that O'Brien's 'attitude toward the written text initially seems uncomplicated. The good guys read books and the bad guys don't.'[18] Captain Vere, on his part, is equally atypical as the learned commander of the *Bellipotent*, 'with a marked leaning toward everything intellectual',[19] as well as being 'the most undemonstrative of men', 'intrepid to the verge of temerity, though never injudiciously so' (338). Both characters in the end are engaged in a verdict that must deliberate between innocence of intentions and innocence of deeds, and consequently in the choice between alternative linguistic systems to apprehend the world. O'Brien characterizes his final resolution to join the war as a slow abdication of will, the passive surrender to a default setting:

> All the personal history, all the midnight conversations and books and beliefs and learning, were crumpled by abstention, extinguished by forfeiture, for lack of oxygen, by a sort of sleepwalking default. It was no decision, no chain of ideas or reasons, that steered me into the war. It was an intellectual and physical stand-off, and I did not have the energy to see it to an end. I did not want to be a soldier, not even an observer to war. But neither did I want to upset a peculiar balance between the order I knew, the people I knew, and my own private world. It was not that I valued that order. But I feared its opposite, inevitable chaos, censure, embarrassment, the end of everything that had happened in my life, the end of it all. (*IID*, 31–32)

The certainty of 'inevitable chaos' is the counterpart of O'Brien's reliance on what he sees as a motivated, transparent reality, a world organized according to familiar, decipherable categories, in a language that is clearly intelligible.

Paradoxically, the preservation of this order requires the execution of what to him are unmotivated, arbitrary actions – drawing 'certain blood for uncertain reasons' (*IID*, 167) – as well as the participation in a conflict in which a constative, referential use of language – one, for example, that would provide

18 Maria S. Bonn, 'Can Stories Save Us? Tim O'Brien and the Efficacy of the Text', *Critique*, 36.1 (1994), pp. 2–15, p. 3.
19 Herman Melville, 'Billy Budd, Sailor' in *Billy Budd, Sailor and Other Stories*, ed. Harold Beaver (London: Penguin, 1985), pp. 317–409, p. 340. Subsequent references are to this edition.

a clear definition of the enemy – has been replaced by an arbitrary or disingenuously twisted use of words, as in the infamous, unwritten rule about how to identify the opponent: if it is dead and Vietnamese, then it is a VC. In the first linguistic model, the relationship between words and actions is predetermined and fixed, however conventionally; in the second, instead, actions precede and give a morally perverse meaning to words. The gap between intentions and deeds, inner and outer expression of the individual's consciousness, crops up again in O'Brien's final pronouncement on what constitutes a man's virtue: 'I believe [...] that a man is most a man when he tries to recognize and understand what is good – when he tries to ask in a reasonable way about things: is it good? And I believe finally that a man cannot be fully a man until, deciding that something is right, his actions make real the suspect bravery of the mind' (*IID*, 57).

This is the same crux at the heart of Captain Vere's dilemma in *Billy Budd*, where intentions and actions never coincide, with tragic results. Melville's novella, published posthumously in 1924, tells the story of its eponymous protagonist, an innocent young sailor much loved by his fellow crew on board the *Bellipotent*, with the exception of the Master-at-Arms John Claggart, who falsely accuses him of mutinous designs. Incapable, because of a speech impediment, of an immediate verbal response to Claggart's charges, Billy instinctively strikes his opponent and inadvertently causes his death. Thus, Billy's innocence and status as a '*motivated* sign',[20] i.e. a figure whose purity and transparency of purpose is reflected in a good-looking frame, is contradicted by his involuntary, violent reaction to Claggart's slanderous accusation. Conversely, prompted by an unmotivated hatred of the 'Handsome Sailor', Claggart's defamatory charge against Billy turns out to be true, insofar as the young man does end up committing a crime: Claggart's pronouncement of guilt becomes indeed a self-fulfilling prophecy, however incapable of capturing Billy's essence. Captain Vere, who is aware both of Billy's de facto crime and of his intrinsic innocence, must fall back – for the sake of order – on social conventions, which at the time of the Mutiny Act and under conditions of warfare demand that Claggart's killing be followed by the harshest possible punishment.

As in O'Brien's quandary, Vere's preservation of order comes at the cost of the disconnection between his inner desire (to save Billy) and his social responsibility (to sentence him to death). Vere's case, however, differs from O'Brien's in the real limitations on the Captain's ability to exercise his individual agency. As members of the King's Navy, Vere and his crew have abdicated – to a large extent – the right to make independent decisions.

20 Barbara Johnson, 'Melville's Fist: The Execution of *Billy Budd*', *Studies in Romanticism*, 18.4 (1979), pp. 567–99, p. 573.

Moreover, Vere's analysis of their situation outlines the consequences of what O'Brien's own response to the draft call will imply: 'in receiving our commissions we in the most important regards ceased to be natural free agents. When war is declared are we the commissioned fighters previously consulted? We fight at command. If our judgments approve the war, that is but coincidence.'[21] Billy's sentence, like any other martial duty, is already out of the Captain's hands before the trial begins; Vere's position of responsibility within a network of social laws, sanctioned by his title, dictates his verdict, which he must necessarily reach so as to avoid the disturbance that Billy's crime might create on the *Bellipotent*. In a way, Vere's action – the fulfilment of a duty which comports a touching demonstration of self-denial – can be interpreted as the sacrifice of an exemplary individual (the Christ-like Billy) and of an exemplary judge (the father-like Vere, who must suppress his paternal feelings for the Handsome Sailor) for the benefit of the many (the crew). O'Brien's decision instead is inscribed within a much less pressing social context, under circumstances that allow a greater degree of personal freedom, and lacks the justification of having been made in view of the common good. O'Brien's inability to follow the dictates of his own conscience, to opt out of the social pact with his fellow-countrymen in response to a greater moral imperative, is an act of self-indulgence rather than self-denial.

The writer stages this crisis in a nautical drama of his own in the chapter in *The Things They Carried* entitled 'On the Rainy River', the account that most vividly describes the draftee's concrete opportunity to turn his back on a war he had never believed in, and probes into the reasons for the protagonist's failure of willpower. The early reference to Dante's *Comedy* and to 'de la volontà la libertate' ('freedom of will') in *If I Die* has a faint echo in the structure and the theme of this story, which charts Tim O'Brien's (unsuccessful) journey of enlightenment during the summer before his enlistment. Unable to cope with the pressure of his impending conscription, the young character leaves home – and the gory job at a meatpacking plant that would have seen him to graduate school – and finds temporary refuge in a lodge on the mountains, along the river that marks the border between Minnesota and Canada. The impromptu trip towards the borderline between conscription and freedom has an equally suggestive point of departure and destination: from the river of blood of the pigs' carcasses (reminiscent perhaps of the Phlegethon, to whose boiling, bloody waters the violent are confined in the seventh circle of Hell), O'Brien ascends to the majestic wilderness surrounding the Tip Top Lodge, presided over by Elroy Berdhal, a seemingly omniscient, unobtrusive yet deeply sympathetic landlord.

21 Melville, 'Billy Budd, Sailor', p. 387.

Under the silent scrutiny of this godlike figure, O'Brien ponders his situation.[22] The final crisis occurs when the old man takes him fishing, pushing the boat into Canadian waters, as if to present Tim with the reality of this option and the urgency of either embracing it or dismissing it for good. The momentous nature of the decision triggers off a kaleidoscopic parade of characters from O'Brien's private life and from his American cultural and historical inheritance, a phantasmagoria of images from his past and his future, a series of ghosts all waving at him 'from the far [Minnesota] shoreline' (*TTC*, 53). Faced with the opportunity to jump ship and desert, the protagonist-narrator of this tale is held back by a spurious loyalty towards his country: O'Brien's sense of responsibility and belonging to the American community is brutally exposed as amounting to no more than a fear of embarrassment. (Vere's) respect for public duty is demeaned to a petty, narcissistic dread of private derision:

> All those eyes on me – the town, the whole universe – and I couldn't risk the embarrassment. [...] [I]n my head I could hear people screaming at me. Traitor! they yelled. Turncoat! Pussy! I felt myself blush. I couldn't tolerate it. I couldn't endure the mockery, or the disgrace, or the patriotic ridicule. Even in my imagination, the shore just twenty yards away, I couldn't make myself brave. It had nothing to do with morality. Embarrassment, that's all it was. And right then I submitted. I would go to the war – I would kill and maybe die – because I was embarrassed not to. (*TTC*, 54)[23]

The story closes with a quick, almost cinematic fast-forward, a condensation of the events to come, while O'Brien is driving back home. The narration suddenly speeds up towards its anticlimactic finale: 'I passed through towns with familiar names, through the pine forests and down to the prairie, and then to Vietnam, where I was a soldier, and then home again. I survived but it's not a happy ending. I was a coward. I went to the war' (*TTC*, 55).

So far, the analysis of O'Brien's view of courage has led us to consider two

---

22 'Elroy Berdahl remained quiet. [...] His eyes were flat and impassive. He didn't speak. He was simply there, like the river and the late-summer sun. And yet by his presence, his mute watchfulness, he made it real. He was the true audience. He was a witness, like God, or like the gods, who look on in silence as we live our lives, as we make our choices or fail to make them' (*TTC*, 54).

23 Cf. also the title chapter from *The Things They Carried*, where O'Brien exposes the universal nature of these feelings: 'They carried the soldier's greatest fear, which was the fear of blushing. Men killed, and died, because they were embarrassed not to. It was what had brought them to the war in the first place, nothing positive, no dreams of glory and honor, just to avoid the blush of dishonor. They died so as not to die of embarrassment. [...] It was not courage, exactly; the object was not valor. Rather, they were too frightened to be cowards' (*TTC*, 17–18).

interdependent manifestations of this quality: a spiritual kind, related to the idea of integrity and the ability to stand by one's own moral principles, and a more physical kind, something akin to military prowess and lack of fear in the face of material dangers. As we have seen, unlike Frederic Henry (and Bogart, Shane, Nick Adams, as well as Vere himself, who believes, after all, that what he is doing is right and is convinced, with good reason, that even Billy appreciates the justice of his verdict), O'Brien portrays a factual and fictional picture of himself as a character who fails to live up to his convictions; he betrays them not for a greater good, but in a hypocritical acquiescence in a social order which he knows to be flawed. O'Brien's plight can be summed up as the sacrifice of authenticity for what Lionel Trilling calls 'sincerity' and what we might more familiarly refer to as honesty; in his respect for cultural conventions and expectations, O'Brien discards truthfulness to his self for the adherence to society's standards. O'Brien's struggle for this kind of courage precedes the battle; the breach of integrity that comes with the acceptance of the departure for Vietnam in itself effectively prevents the achievement of real bravery. The knowledge of this original, and crucial, failing, however, does not prevent the soldier O'Brien from reflecting upon the different kind of resources that he is called to draw upon when courage implies most immediately the ability to cope with fear of the enemy and fear of death. This martial aspect of courage, rather than its earlier, contemplative counterpart, is more readily associated with a masculine ideal. It is to O'Brien's view of masculinity (and femininity) in the context of the definition of courage that this study will now turn.

In Hemingway's footsteps

If one were to summarize the conclusion reached by *If I Die in a Combat Zone* as a philosophical meditation on the nature of courage, one could do worse than draw on O'Brien's Platonic formula of 'wise endurance'. This definition of bravery has certainly catalysed the critics' attention (see, for example, Bates's 1987 essay 'Tim O'Brien's Myth of Courage'). It has often been described – and indeed even praised, for its open-minded, liberal, non-chauvinistic spirit – as a 'feminization of virtue', a powerful subversion of 'militarized male fortitude'.[24] Of course, the perception of 'wise endurance' as an androgynous virtue depends on gender stereotypes – the equation of masculinity with physical strength and a resolute moral fibre, against the gentler qualities of passive contemplation and restraint, traditionally seen as attributes of the 'fair sex'. It is not surprising that the presence of a qualifier

24 Heberle, *A Trauma Artist*, p. xx.

for the term 'endurance' should have prompted a lively critical discussion, given how telegraphic O'Brien's style can be, especially in certain sections of *If I Die*, where adjectives and adverbs are often 'noticeably missing'.[25] Besides, it is true that within the context of O'Brien's memoir, the appeal to the four parts of virtue provides a deliberate, if understated, theoretical contrast to the military practice, from Major Callicles's irresponsible, showy, inane machismo, to the callous incompetence and desire for glory of the higher ranks of the Army (see, for example, the unnamed colonel in the chapter entitled 'July'). Such a minimalist style and the reliance on showing, rather than telling, the reality of the war are traits inherited from Ernest Hemingway, the most evident literary influence on O'Brien's early attempts to come to an understanding of the notions of heroism and masculinity, and of their mutual relationship.

Hemingway's legacy is, as one might expect, never felt more strongly in O'Brien's oeuvre than in his first novel: *Northern Lights*. Critics are nearly unanimous in acknowledging that, while showing promise, this book has serious limitations, given the way that it occasionally verges on an unwitting parody of Hemingway.[26] O'Brien himself is the harshest judge of his initial full-length foray into fiction; with typical honesty, he provides what has now become the ultimate evaluation of *Northern Lights*: 'That's a terrible book. I'm embarrassed by it; it's hard to talk about it. It's the first novel I ever tried to write, and unfortunately it was published.'[27] For all its faults, however, *Northern Lights* remains an interesting read for the critic, and offers a valuable insight into O'Brien's approach to significant themes of (American) war literature: the paternal role model, the test of manliness in the wilderness, and the polarization of masculine and feminine qualities. The following analysis will show how this text, much like the earlier memoir, does not quite follow the *Bildungsroman* pattern that scholars have often identified in it; this corrective to the received critical opinion will demonstrate that the perspective on gender in O'Brien's first novel is more nuanced than has generally been recognized.

Northern Lights tells the story of Paul Perry, a disaffected husband and federal agent for the Department of Agriculture, and his immediate circle of friends and family, in the Arrowhead country in Minnesota. The other protagonists are Harvey, Paul's younger brother, who has just returned from his tour of duty in Vietnam; Grace, Paul's caring and docile wife, and Addie,

---

25 Kaplan, *Understanding Tim O'Brien*, p. 50.
26 See, for example, 'the book's major defect is its unmistakeable origins in Hemingway's *The Sun Also Rises*' (Herzog, *Tim O'Brien*, p. 65). Herzog then goes on to quote Roger Sale's review of the book: 'Is it possible to read *The Sun Also Rises* too often?' (p. 65). There is a clear implication that, in O'Brien's case, the answer would appear to be yes.
27 Naparsteck, 'An Interview with Tim O'Brien', p. 2.

reminiscent of Brett in *The Sun Also Rises*, a young, independent, sensual woman, who appears to feel a reciprocated attraction for the unavailable Paul, and who later gets involved with Harvey instead. The most memorable character in this novel, in spite of the fact that he has been long dead, is Paul's father, Pehr Lindstrom Peri, an imposing patriarchal figure, who continues to exert influence on his two sons even in his absence. A severe Lutheran minister and a messenger of apocalyptic visions (like William Cowling in *The Nuclear Age*, he is obsessed with making preparations for what he thinks is an impending nuclear holocaust), he clearly embodies an unwise male endurance: he preaches hardiness and stoicism, and feels an undisguised hostility towards femininity, to the point of excluding women from his life, as his own father (Pehr Peri) had done before him.

Paul and Harvey thus belong to an exclusively male lineage; their mother is barely mentioned, having died in giving birth to Harvey (*NL*, 82). We are never told her name. Similarly, nothing is known of Pehr Lindstrom Peri's own mother, other than a surname so common amongst the Scandinavian immigrants in that part of the country as to make her identification impossible; nevertheless her son erases even that trace of her existence, dropping his middle name (his maternal legacy) and Americanizing Peri into Perry. An authoritarian and crushing *pater familias*, Pehr Perry thus appears to be an emanation of the intimidating northern territories: configured as a cold, male domain, the latter are a different kind of pioneer country from the mythical frontier of the West. The only trait that these two landscapes seem to have in common is the fact that both have witnessed the Native Americans being driven away and supplanted by European settlers. The Arrowhead region attracted waves of German, Scandinavian and Finnish people, already accustomed to an unwelcoming climate and wild natural environment. Of an austere, Lutheran, northern stock, reserved, hard-working and frugal, these northern pioneers are also characterized by resilience, patience and stamina. These are the virtues that Pehr Perry has tried to instil in his sons: his teachings still shape the two brothers' lives, even when – as in Paul's case – they cannot and will not put them into practice.

While Harvey does try, and often manages, to approximate his father's ideal of manliness, Paul is the black sheep, the son who fails, or refuses, to live up to paternal expectations. Harvey instead appears to be at ease with the woods, and willingly indulges his father's only fear, building, single-handedly, a nuclear shelter for the family. His return from Vietnam, where he suffers an injury that leaves him blind in one eye, marks the end of only the latest of his adventures – although the dismal reception that he receives from his family and from the wider community dispels any illusion, on the reader's if not on Harvey's part, that we are witnessing the homecoming of a war hero. The lukewarm response to Harvey's return is unrelated to his military conduct, but is part of a general mood of disillusionment and indifference towards great national events felt by the inhabitants of an isolated, shrinking and neglected region; the ideal of military heroism does not seem relevant to the people of Sawmill Landing who, for all their hardiness and respect for patriotic duty, can do little against the decline, in population and importance, of their community. From this disaffected perspective, courage in battle is devoid of any particular glamour, and is reduced to one of the many possible manifestations of male identity. Paul's exclusion from his brother's military experience is therefore not the only reason why his sense of self and feelings of worth are wavering.

Direct engagement with war aside, Paul Perry is like Jake Barnes in *The Sun Also Rises*: they are both emasculated characters, hurt and simultaneously redeemed by their psychological and physical scars. Jake's genital wound is a sign of lost male potency and wholeness; it is also, paradoxically, what keeps him from crossing over into the opposite side of the male spectrum, Robert Cohn's 'genteel, sentimental, and implicitly feminine masculinity'.[28] Similarly, Paul's incompetence in male pursuits and lack of interest in abiding by his father's rules saves him from his brother's destiny, which, as the book progresses, turns out to be no more than a superficial adherence to antiquated and unrealistic modes of male behaviour. Harvey's dreams of adventure are hollow, good only in so far as they provide a theoretical affirmation of masculinity, never to be translated into action; besides, as he reveals in a pathetic confession to Paul, his male swagger is dictated by fear rather than by a sincere belief in the paternal values (*NL*, 254ff.). By the end of the narrative, it is clear that Harvey's nickname, 'the bull', must be read ironically: it represents, like Arizona's doomed charge, an unthinking macho posturing or even, as a slang abbreviation, the gross inaccuracies and vain exaggerations underpinning Harvey's perception of himself.

With this bathetic reversal, gone are the mythical intertextual connotations of this symbol: Harvey's bull is not Hemingway's sacrificial victim, whose death endorses the bull-fighter's courage and masculinity; and gone, also, is the overt reference to the mythical 'bull of Karelia', the epitome of 'stoic endurance and unflinching acceptance of the end' of the Finnish epic poem *Kalevala*.[29] Incidentally, it is worth emphasizing how these two mythical incarnations of the bull, already *per se* a symbol of masculinity, are charged with completely different connotations: Jake Barnes yearns for participation, however surrogate, in the life-affirming Mediterranean *tauromachia*, a tradition that is culturally alien to him, whereas Paul must shed the much more gloomily fatalistic northern inheritance, an 'indigenous' legacy since it has

28 Greg Forter, 'Melancholy Modernism: Gender and the Politics of Mourning in *The Sun Also Rises*', *The Hemingway Review*, 21.1 (2001), pp. 22–37, p. 26.
29 Bates, 'Tim O'Brien's Myth of Courage', p. 264.

reached him through his ancestors. The bull of Karelia is therefore an apocalyptic figure, in keeping with the general, intercultural mythical framework of the novel, whose epigraph is provided by a passage from Revelation:

> and, lo, there was a great earthquake; and the sun became black as sackcloth of hair, and the moon became as blood. And the stars of heaven fell unto the earth even as a fig tree casteth her untimely figs, when she is shaken of a mighty wind. And the heaven departed as a scroll when it is rolled together; and every mountain and islands were moved out of their places [...] For the day of his wrath is come. And who shall be able to stand? (Revelation 6: 12–17)

Posing a rhetorical question about our ability to withstand the wrath of God at the end of time, this passage offers an immediate clue about the imposing and unforgiving presence of the father figure in the narrative. *The Sun Also Rises* instead opens with a quotation from Ecclesiastes about the continuity of generations, set in contrast to the vanity of individual human existence.[30]

The diametrically opposite mythical framework of the two novels explains in part the perceived gap between Hemingway's nostalgic disillusionment, with Jake's betrayal of his *afición* and the perpetual impasse of his impossible relationship with Brett, and O'Brien's seemingly more optimistic conclusion. This is perhaps one of the reasons why *Northern Lights* has been mistakenly read as a *Bildungsroman*, describing Paul's progress from the misogynist darkness of his father's and his culture's apocalyptic credo to a more balanced, positive view of the world, capable of embracing the feminine principle, embodied by the suggestively named Grace. This misreading is further encouraged by the figurative scope of names and imagery in the narrative, which is at times obvious to the point of clumsiness, and which consistently draws attention to the characters' gendered attributes and to their ability to open up to some kind of enlightenment. Harvey's inability to do so, for example, is neatly symbolized by his Vietnam war wound to the eye; by contrast, Paul's congenital lack of vision appears to be less irreversible: he bears its mark in his second name, Milton, the blind poet of *Paradise Lost*, and in his short-sightedness. Besides, should we have missed the further implications of his (first) name, the novel provides us with a further hint at a crucial point in the story: while he is lost in the snow, Paul

---

30 'One generation passeth away, and another generation cometh; but the earth abideth forever. The sun also ariseth, and the sun goeth down, and hasteth to the place where he arose. The wind goeth toward the south, and turneth about unto the north; it whirleth about continually, and the wind returneth again according to his circuits. All the rivers run into the sea; yet the sea is not full; unto the place from whence the rivers come, thither they return again' (Eccl. 1:4–7).

prays, thinking of Damascus Lutheran, a clear reference to the conversion of Saul (*NL*, 174).

Following these clues, critics such as Kaplan and Bates have meticulously traced Paul's gradual and discontinuous progress: the loss of his glasses during the disastrous adventure in the woods with his brother has been read as Paul's adoption of Harvey's blind recklessness. By the same token, Paul is also perceived to mature when, having realized that such recklessness is not a true virtue, he almost ritually shaves off his beard and buys a new pair of spectacles. This interpretative line is all too easy to follow, since Paul's entire predicament can be summed up with imagery pertaining to the field of a pathological vision: he sees too much, or too little, either way with a hint of morbidity (Addie calls him 'Peeping Paul', remarking on the voyeuristic, passive trait in his personality). Paul is always scrutinizing his own behaviour and finding it inadequate, with a self-consciousness that is both crippling and wholesome. His faulty vision and the awareness of his limitations, equally experienced as a threat to masculinity, function exactly like Jake's wound: it is precisely the (real and metaphorical) wound, or the knowledge thereof, that prevents Paul and Jake from falling into the sentimental/mock-heroic/nostalgic trap that Harvey and Cohn fall into. Whether Paul ultimately finds a convincing way forward, an alternative to Harvey's naive fantasies, is another matter altogether – and this is where my reading of the novel differs from the standard interpretation.

At the beginning of the narrative, Paul is clearly about to face a crisis, the long-term result of traumas rooted deeply in the past and in his relationship with his father. Paul cannot leave this ghost behind, scarred as he is from the memory of his many failures in the paternal eyes. His near-drowning in Pliney's Pond during a swimming lesson, his dropping out of Divinity School while trying to follow in his father's professional footsteps, and his refusal to accede to his father's dying wish and help Harvey build the nuclear shelter all mark Paul as unworthy of the paternal physical, intellectual and spiritual inheritance. For these reasons, Paul feels less of a man than Harvey, whose return from Vietnam catalyses once again the elder brother's sense of inadequacy. His relationships with women are also very unsatisfactory. Paul's marriage – to a woman despised by his father for her motherliness – has grown stale; he cannot or will not make love to Grace, who, on her part, seems happy to comfort and fuss over him: her caresses can be occasionally sexual, as it would appear in the monologue that ends the first section, entitled 'Elements' (although the passage could be almost read as a parodic, mundane reversal of Molly Bloom's free-flowing stream of consciousness), but are more usually maternal and not at all erotically charged. Grace's role seems to be confined to soothing a husband-child, with relaxing rubs and babyish terms of endearment. The other woman in Paul's life is Addie, the opposite of Grace in both appearance and attitude: wild, adolescent-like, lively and sensual, vaguely exotic (she claims to be from New Guinea, but is also associated with the Native Americans), she teases Paul and dreams up adventurous fantasies of escape with him. Paul, however, does not know how to respond to her half-playful advances.

Paul's passivity is further emphasized by his infantilization, as Grace mollycoddles and pities him as her 'poor boy' several times in the narrative. Even his job, in which he feels trapped, is described by Harvey as 'sucking the Federal Titty' (*NL*, 30). Harvey's return from the war aggravates the crisis, forcing Paul to face up to his perceived inadequacy from yet another perspective. Harvey seems to be able to do everything that Paul cannot do: besides being a fighter, an adventurer, and his father's legitimate moral heir, he is also capable of conquering Addie (who calls him 'the pirate'), while treating Grace with the respect she deserves. Yet Harvey also unwittingly precipitates his own and Paul's reversal of fortune, when he suggests a holiday to Grand Marais, so that the two men can take part in a skiing competition and the women enjoy the festivities. The highlight of the trip is to be the brothers' skiing expedition back home, a real adventure and the archetypal test of manhood in the exploration of the wilderness. Before Paul and Harvey set off on their homeward journey, however, the holiday has already degenerated into a series of disappointments, with Paul's continuing inability to relate to Grace, Addie's defection from Harvey to a young, promising skier (O'Brien's counterpart to Hemingway's Romero) and Harvey's pitiful and hung-over athletic performance (he falls during the race, while Paul does not even take part in it). The final adventure therefore does not begin under the most promising circumstances and soon turns into a complete disaster, when Harvey fails to navigate accurately and a furious storm gets the two brothers even more hopelessly lost. It is at this point that Paul must take over, tending to his sick brother, foraging for food, and looking for help. Paul undoubtedly does all of these things, but his success as a real man is always underscored by the unheroic nature of his accomplishments: his skills as a hunter are confined to battering a torpid woodchuck to death (*NL*, 278ff.), and his success in finding assistance is foolhardy and fortuitous, as a couple of decidedly unimpressed local men point out in no uncertain terms (*NL*, 312ff.).[31] During the storm, Harvey confesses his admiration for Paul's ability to stand up to their father, but not even this startling admission alerts Paul to the vacuity of his reclaimed masculinity; on the contrary, for a while, he cultivates the ruggedness he thinks he has gained in the forest.

Critics have interpreted Paul's eventual rejection of the superficial

---

31 For a further analysis of the woodchuck episode, see the section 'Indian Country' in Chapter 3.

trappings of a manly mask, and his renewed efforts to become closer to Grace, as evidence of his maturation into a human being who can finally recognize the need for a balanced blend of masculine and feminine elements in his personality and in his life. Much has been made of Paul's changed attitude towards Grace, who, by the end of the novel, seems to take on the role of muse and mentor to her husband. Following her gentle lead, Paul makes plans to sell his father's house and relocate to her native state, Iowa, which is significantly related to the idea of a tame and fertile agricultural landscape, as opposed to the hostile territory of northern Minnesota. In another noteworthy episode, during a walk in the woods, Grace teaches Paul how to see and appreciate the feminine, gentle side of the wilderness and, by implication, how to love her for the first time. In a scene with clear baptismal undertones, Paul wades into the waters of Pliney's Pond, teeming with life and associated with Grace throughout the narrative; he comes out of this amniotic fluid a new man, with a restored vision (after his immersion, Paul manages to see the northern lights that he had failed to notice before) and a regenerated vigour. Again, the imagery could not be clearer: the narrative had started with Paul 'ejaculating' poison to kill mosquitoes (a self-evident bathetic counterpart to the American war effort in Vietnam) and ends with him finally making love to and presumably impregnating Grace.

It is difficult not to be taken in by the neat symmetry of this structure, and by the blatancy of the other textual clues that suggest the emotional progress of the main character. However, Paul's transformation from self-loathing child into wise man is not entirely convincing, nor does it offer a strong model of identity, grounded in the solid reconciliation of positive male and female qualities. Like Anthony Beavis, the protagonist of Aldous Huxley's *Eyeless in Gaza* (1936), another text revolving around the imagery of impaired vision and the necessity, for the main character, to learn how to love, Paul Perry comes under the sphere of influence of several different people and each time, one may argue, he is easily swayed by their presence. In virtually all his major choices, Paul *re*acts to the prompts of his friends and family, be they deliberate or inadvertent, constructive or provoking. His marriage to Grace is a case in point, a decision which seems to make itself, partly as a rejection of (posthumous) paternal authority, partly as a calm acquiescence in an act that seems to require no conscious volition: 'After all the years with his father, after pursuing the old man's winter tracks, ice fishing and hunting and fiery sermons, after all that Grace had come with her whispers and understanding, and marrying her after graduation had been as easy and natural as falling asleep in a warm bath. By then the old man was dead' (*NL*, 24). After the collapse of Harvey's plans of adventure and of Addie's dreams of escape (she leaves Sawmill Landing, not for the exotic Badlands but for life in metropolitan Minneapolis), Grace's wish for domesticity becomes the next available fantasy and as good an aspiration as any.

In fact, the illusoriness of Paul's progress is underscored by the cyclical structure of the novel, which is inscribed within the mythical passage from 'Black Sun' to 'Blood Moon', in two symmetrical sequences made up of 'Heat Storm', 'Elements' and 'Shelter' and separated by the climactic 'Blizzard'. Particularly if compared to *The Sun Also Rises*, the novel's ending appears unconvincing and inconclusive; by the same token, Paul's tempering of his northern roots sounds at best half-hearted, at worst disingenuous *vis-à-vis* Jake's renewed nostalgic disavowal of the pre-modern ideal of masculinity. The final scenes of the two novels share remarkable similarities and equally striking differences. In *The Sun Also Rises*, Jake and Brett mutually acknowledge the impossibility of their dream in a memorable exchange: "'Oh Jake," Brett said, "we could have had such a damned good time together." [...] "Yes," I said. "Isn't it pretty to think so?"' (216). These modernist characters are the broken, cynical heirs of Romanticism, with its yearning for an unreachable wholeness: Jake's final line states his subscription to this impossible desire even in the knowledge that – should fulfilment be available – it would not yield its promise. Jake continues to wish for old-fashioned, pre-modern idols (the myths of heroism, masculinity, romantic love, authenticity) even as he knows that they are illusions. *Northern Lights* instead ends with a near-caricature of this passage, with Harvey's preposterous dreams of adventurous camaraderie and Paul's characteristic refusal to commit: "'What do you think?" Harvey said. "We'll have us a fine time, won't we?" [...] Perry shut his eyes. "Doesn't it sound great?" Harvey kept saying. "Doesn't it?"' (*NL*, 363).

Paul's silence is ambivalent: it provides a neat contrast to the ridiculousness of Harvey's excitement, but it also fails to rein him in. O'Brien pointedly excludes Grace from this final sketch, except in a passing and revealing mention. Harvey asks: "'...You really going to Iowa?" "Grace seems to like the idea. We'll see what happens"', says Paul (*NL*, 361). While *The Sun Also Rises* ends with a kind of negative epiphany, *Northern Lights* ends with no epiphany at all. Paul's final utterance in the novel is 'maybe' (*NL*, 362), and his whole attitude betrays the proposed settling down with Grace in Iowa as a very low-key happy ending. One must also wonder how much the relocation is prompted by the fact that Paul loses his job half-way through the novel: again, Paul seems to go along with whatever life throws at him, rather than make responsible and independent decisions. The truth is that Grace's alternative to Pehr Perry's uncompromising credo, and to Harvey's delusional dreams, is itself flawed and fragile: at no point in the novel does Grace convincingly live up to the redeeming connotations of her name. She is certainly not damaged like Brett, whose psychological scars make her a kindred spirit to Jake, in her unavailability; she embodies a diminutive standard of cosy domesticity, rather than a powerful, instinctive, healing, mother-earth figure.[32] Interestingly, her femininity, just like the waters of the pond with which she is associated, is characterized in ambivalent terms: her 'womanly, wifely, motherly sympathy', which 'ooze[s] like ripe mud' both attracts and repels Paul, comforting him but also threatening to smother or sully him (*NL*, 24). Likewise, the pond's waters are not merely swarming with life. They are also stagnant and vaguely putrescent. They smell simultaneously of burgeoning life and slow decay; they are both amniotic fluid and a *cloaca*, where Paul can discharge his black bile like diarrhoea (*NL*, 351).

In this first novel, the characters who seem to conform most closely to monolithic stereotypes, the austere, law-giving patriarch (Pehr Perry) and the sympathetic, nurturing mother (Grace), are revealed to be monstrous or deeply flawed in their nature. Harvey and Addie, who represent slightly more nuanced specimens of masculinity and femininity, also expose the limitations of their gendered identity, but in a more pathetic way, once it is clear that their aspirations are nothing more than shallow posturing. Given the lack of viable options and positive role models, it is not surprising to see Paul hovering unconvinced on the brink of a spurious change in the parodic and nihilistic ending of the novel. As a meditation on courage and integrity, *Northern Lights* strikes me as a much darker narrative than *If I Die*, which at least posited, at the end of the chapter on 'Wise Endurance', a modicum of value in the *conscious* attempt to change, to try harder, to improve. 'Wise courage' is not a quality that one possesses once and for all, but rather something one must strive for, incessantly and deliberately. It is a work in progress. And, finally, the attempt is all: 'You promise, almost moving your lips, to do better next time; that by itself is a kind of courage' (*IID*, 147).

Dreams and responsibility

The discussion of bravery and of its relation to ideas of masculinity and femininity in O'Brien's writing would not be complete without an analysis of his third book-length publication, *Going After Cacciato*. The novel can be seen as the final part of the trilogy of courage, although the themes broached here will continue to crop up in O'Brien's later works. *Going After Cacciato* begins with an immediate reference to 'the ultimate war story', an episode that – like the memory of all the other casualties of the Third Squad, First Platoon, Alpha Company – haunts the entire narrative: Billy Boy Watkins's

---

32 It has been remarked that 'Grace is the antithesis of Pehr Peri, and one would be tempted to call her an earth-mother except that she is usually associated with a stagnant body of water called Pliney's Pond'; Bates, 'Tim O'Brien's Myth of Courage', p. 265.

death. The primacy of this death over the other fatalities mentioned in the novel is perhaps due to the singular cause of this soldier's demise: Watkins is a casualty of fright, an inexperienced soldier literally scared to death, killed by fear rather than by physical wounds. In spite of the fact that this story seems to endorse an 'either/or' reading of O'Brien's pithy decree about the effects of war, denying the full force of its paradoxical meaning – war will make a man out of you, if it does not kill you first, Billy *Boy* Watkins's parable appears to say – the novel in its entirety clearly takes its distance from a macho view of courage.

To an extent, O'Brien's first Vietnam war novel is a more clearly fictional re-elaboration of the same fundamental predicament outlined by the protagonist of *If I Die*, a character whose involvement in Vietnam is the result of vague and questionable reasons (fear of embarrassment and social censure), or even no reason at all (a paralysis of the will or inertia). The reluctant soldier's feeling of disorientation and confusion, of complete and utter estrangement from the world of the war, is unmitigated, in *Cacciato*, by the account of the protagonist's military training and soul-searching prior to his arrival in country. Paul Berlin, the main character in the novel, is an average American kid with no intellectual pretensions, devoid of the sense of superiority and the (ultimately naive) self-awareness of the College Joe figure carefully portrayed by O'Brien in his memoir. This difference provokes a slight shift in the immediate scope and tone of the analysis of the notion of bravery. In *If I Die*, O'Brien is represented as a character who belongs to an intellectual elite: the fact that he is better educated than most American draftees, that he is articulate and thoughtful and clearly destined for further 'superior' pursuits, makes his deployment as a foot soldier – what in earlier wars might have been called 'cannon fodder' – a scandalous option, according, of course, to the first person narrator's partisan line of reasoning. It is on the strength of this conviction that O'Brien takes a chance, turning down the opportunity offered during basic training to enlist in the Army for three years, the only guaranteed way of escaping infantry duty. As he recalls, with more than a hint of self-contempt gained in hindsight: 'I had gambled, thinking they would use me for more than a pair of legs, certain that someone would see the value of my ass behind a typewriter or a Xerox machine' (*IID*, 56).[33] O'Brien's self-portrait is deliberately painted in such a way as to

---

33 This idea is reiterated more vehemently in 'On the Rainy River' in *The Things They Carried*: 'I was too *good* for this war. Too smart, too compassionate, too everything. It couldn't happen. I was above it. I had the world dicked – Phi Beta Kappa and summa cum laude and president of the student body and a full-ride scholarship for grad studies at Harvard. A mistake, maybe – a foul-up in the paperwork. I was no soldier' (*TTC*, 40–41). In *Cacciato*, instead, Berlin is shown to be aware of the encouraging odds of landing a relatively safe assignment in Vietnam; the laws of probability are the only reason why he entertains the hope of being spared combat duty: 'The ratio of support to combat personnel

highlight the intellectual pride and moral smugness of the narrator-character, to the point of making his representation less than sympathetic at times, and unquestionably risible in the unspoken claim to immunity to the draft call. At the same time, however, from a dramatic perspective, O'Brien's lofty opinion of himself heightens the poignancy of his collapse: the higher you stand, the greater the fall. For a character of strong principles, sound mind and keen sense of justice, the inability to act on one's convictions is an unforgivable ignominy, configured as a defeat, a surrender and a slow suffocation of one's true self (cf. the extinguishment 'by forfeiture, for lack of oxygen, by a sort of sleepwalking default', quoted above).

Paul Berlin, on the other hand, lacks the initial self-righteousness and the developed aptitude for self-analysis displayed by O'Brien in *If I Die*; without the framework of an individual conscience struggling to come to terms with an act of self-betrayal, the scrutiny of one's acquiescence in the Vietnam war becomes more open-ended. What might have been lost in immediacy, with the move from first- to third-person narration, is gained in the more 'everyman' quality of Berlin, whose own inertia and confusion are perhaps ultimately easier to relate to than O'Brien's philosophical reflections and unflinching moral judgements. While it is clear from the start that there is no hope for redemption for the protagonist of *If I Die*, *Going After Cacciato* unfolds instead as a journey whereby the possibility of development and change can be still entertained for the duration of the narrative, even if it is finally denied in the end. Berlin's is a strange, phantasmagorical flight: a journey of the mind and of the conscience, perhaps, but a real journey nonetheless. The presence of a protagonist like Berlin – inexperienced, but not simple, politically and philosophically green, but not oblivious to the larger implications of his participation in the war – allows O'Brien to move the focus from the failures of nerve and judgement of the individual to the objective moral and epistemological difficulties involved in making the right decision about Vietnam.

Through Berlin, O'Brien declares the impossibility of pinning down the exact causes and consequences of the war, or to fathom the benefits (however dubious) of the American intervention when they are measured up against the global political scenario. He then proceeds to pose more and more radical epistemological and ethical quandaries: can the truth be disentangled from the lies of propaganda and the deceptions of bad faith? Is it possible to identify – let alone adopt – a single, universally valid, moral stance? In a novel which propounds the cognitive value of imagination, these reflections are aptly framed within Berlin's hypothetical conversation with a little Vietnamese girl, years from the end of the war:

> was twelve to one. Paul Berlin counted it as bad luck, a statistically improbable outcome, to be assigned to the 5th Battalion, 46th Infantry, 198th Infantry Brigade' (*GAC*, 46).

[...] he would explain to her why he had let himself go to war. Not because of strong convictions, but because he didn't know. He didn't know who was right, or what was right; he didn't know if it was a war of self-determination or self-destruction, outright aggression or national liberation; he didn't know which speeches to believe, which books, which politicians; he didn't know if nations would topple like dominoes or stand separate like trees; he didn't know who really started the war, or why, or when, or with what motives; he didn't know if it mattered; he saw sense in both sides of the debate, but he did not know where truth lay; he didn't know if communist tyranny would prove worse in the long run than the tyrannies of Ky or Thieu or Khanh – he simply didn't know. And who did? Who really did? Oh, he had read the newspapers and magazines. He wasn't stupid. He wasn't uninformed. He just didn't know if the war was right or wrong or somewhere in the murky middle. And who did? Who really *knew*? So he went to war for reasons beyond knowledge. (*GAC*, 249–50)[34]

What is articulated here is a more essential stalemate of the reason than the one experienced by the protagonist of *If I Die*, who declared himself in possession of a firm opinion about the iniquity of the Vietnam war.

In a chapter with a significant title and strategically placed near the conclusion, *Cacciato* instead takes us through the intricate debate about the necessity of the war: 'The Things They Didn't Know' is the penultimate section in the strand of the narrative made up of sketches and recollections from Berlin's first six months in country, as well as some general musings about the war.[35] It is only at this point, having established the contingent difficulty in ascertaining the truth about the war – and having cast legitimate doubt, by implication and through the cumulative structure of his main argument, on the possibility of knowing anything at all – that O'Brien reverts to a familiar theme and prevents us (and indeed his protagonist himself) from looking at the epistemological and moral confusion about Vietnam as a justification for Berlin's behaviour. Berlin's 'reasons beyond knowledge', when further articulated, echo the confession at the core of *If I Die*, and O'Brien's

34 The Vietnamese girl is the male protagonist's projected idealization of innocence, as well as a character that epitomizes – again, in Berlin's mind – a complete separateness from the war. Such male investment in young female figures is recurrent in O'Brien's work, as I shall discuss further in Chapter 4.

35 The novel also comprises a series of chapters recording Berlin's thoughts during a six-hour night-shift on the observation post, and, of course, the account of the squad's fantastic pursuit of Cacciato on the way to Paris. As critics have often remarked, the trajectory of the pursuit sub-plot is surprisingly straightforward, both spatially (in a manner of speaking, of course) and chronologically (see Slabey or Vannatta, for example). The more thematically realistic sketches about the war, instead, are presented in a jumbled order, while the ten 'Observation Post' chapters, which can be said to partake of the setting of both other strands (reality and Berlin's mind), follow each other in the right temporal sequence. For a further discussion of the three narrative strands in *Cacciato*, see also Chapter 5.

own feelings about his participation to the war; the above-mentioned passage continues with an implicit allusion to the noble ideas upon which the American nation, and democracy in general, is founded, with a reminder of the social pact that underpins its political system. This sequence of observations ends with a refrain familiar to O'Brien's readers from his memoir – the somewhat humiliating disclosure of the real reason behind Berlin's answer to the draft call, his desire not to bring shame upon himself:

> [So he went to war for reasons beyond knowledge.] Because he believed in law, and law told him to go. Because it was a democracy, after all, and LBJ and the others had rightful claim to their offices. He went to the war because it was expected. Because not to go was to risk censure, and to bring embarrassment on his father and his town. Because, not knowing, he saw no reason to distrust those with more experience. Because he loved his country and, more than that, he trusted it. Yes, he did. Oh, he would rather have fought with his father in France, knowing certain things certainly, but he couldn't choose his war. Nobody could. (*GAC*, 250)

Insofar as this revelation is concerned, *Cacciato* can be said to end where *If I Die* had begun, that is from the acknowledgement that the fear of social censure is stronger than the fear of violence and death. Even after the completion of his Advanced Infantry Training, for the protagonist of *If I Die* the option of desertion remains an all too feasible, tantalizing possibility. The reader is made party to the agonizing confrontation with this dilemma, as O'Brien starts making serious plans to flee to Sweden, a safer destination for the American deserter than Canada, where most draft-dodgers escaped to. Having worked out the logistical arrangements – bus from Seattle to Vancouver, flight to Dublin, followed by a boat ride to the Swedish shores – O'Brien must admit to himself that 'it was truly possible. [...] There was no doubt that it could be done' (*IID*, 60). The plans come to nothing, however, and O'Brien never makes it past Seattle, where he goes through a delirious, sleepless night in which physical illness and moral paralysis of the will are conflated: 'I was a coward. I was sick' (*IID*, 73). The main drama charted by *If I Die* is about this malaise, and the issue of O'Brien's courage, and defiance of social expectations, is resolved once and for all before he gets to Vietnam.

Paul Berlin's own exploration of the possibility of desertion, and the related deliberation about the real meaning of courage, takes the shape of a book-length, fantastic journey in pursuit of Cacciato, a fellow-soldier from Alpha Company who one day decides to leave the war and sets off on his way to Paris. Interestingly, if O'Brien's fear in the face of his two unpalatable options – leaving his old life behind to seek asylum in Sweden, losing his reputation into the bargain, or joining the war and losing his self-respect, and possibly his life, instead – finds a physical manifestation in recurrent bouts of vomiting during his fateful weekend in Seattle, Berlin's dread of the war is immediately configured in terms of corporeal symptoms which, in their turn, substantially affect the character's manner of envisaging, and presumably responding to, his moral quandary. Berlin has an excess of fear 'biles', which provokes, amongst other disorders, 'paralysis of the mental processes that separate what is truly happening from what only might have happened; float-ingness; removal; a releasing feeling in the belly; a sense of drifting; a lightness of head' (*GAC*, 35). Chapter 2, the first 'Observation Post' section, contains an unequivocal hint about what might have triggered Berlin's whole imaginary journey to Paris, which does otherwise take its cue from Cacciato's actual flight from the war: 'This Cacciato business – it's the work of the biles. They're flooding your whole system, going to the head and fucking up reality, frying in all the goofy, weird stuff' (*GAC*, 35), Doc Peret, the squad's medic, says to Berlin. As readers are told at the very beginning of the novel, and of the squad's pursuit of their comrade, when the narrative is still in the realm of actual facts, Berlin suffers an attack of the biles after the explosion of a booby-trap set up by Cacciato. In the grip of panic, Berlin loses control of his bowels and, as it turns out much later, in a not altogether unpredictable denouement at the end of the novel, he loses consciousness too.

The flight to Paris, however, is not simply the product of an unconscious vision from which Berlin wakes up in the final chapter of the novel (appro-priately entitled 'Going After Cacciato', just like the opening chapter, when the fainting fit takes place); throughout the parallel narratives of the guard-duty at the observation post and of the adventures on the road to Paris, Berlin often tries to imagine, or is encouraged to imagine, a happy ending for this crazy venture. Thus, the pursuit of Cacciato is simultaneously represented as a creation of Berlin's subconscious and a reverie for Berlin to indulge in at night-time, an activity so enjoyable that he is willing to prolong his shift at the observation post for the sake of working out the odds of Cacciato's success and/or dreaming up a positive conclusion for the latter's adventures – and, at an imaginary level, his own and the squad's. Whether a subconscious vision or a wilful fantasy, the journey to Paris is a way for Berlin to explore the real nature of courage and measure his own aptitude for bravery. The option of desertion, which O'Brien had already identified in *If I Die* as the only true courageous alternative for any draftee opposed to the war, is deliberated through the (more or less conscious) power of the individual's imagination – and this is where the novel explores in more depth an issue only intimated in the memoir and later revisited in *The Things They Carried*: the connection between the inability to do the right thing and a 'failure of the imagination' (*GAC*, 296).

Whether in a bile-induced hallucination or in a controlled reverie, the squad's flight to Paris is never fully entertained by Berlin as a straightforward act of desertion; rather, in spite of Harold Murphy's early refusal to follow the search party beyond the Vietnamese border, and of further subsequent reminders of the soldiers' precarious status outside the war zone (see, for example, the execution of a young Iranian boy accused of having gone AWOL in the chapter entitled 'Atrocities on the Road to Paris'), the journey to Paris is constantly justified by the need to apprehend Cacciato, even when the appeal of ulterior motives is so strong as to overshadow, more and more frequently, the original goal of the soldiers' expedition. After all, the flight to the French capital can be seen as the fulfilment of fantasies of escape from the horror and the chaos of combat in the pursuit of romantic love, or in the accomplishment of a collective mission with a definite aim, or in the pleasure of a challenging, exotic trip towards a fascinating destination. In this sense, the possibility of desertion is always investigated in a doubly mediated form, not merely through the buffer of imagination, but also as an experiment prompted by Cacciato's own fanciful decision to set off on the 8,600-mile-long march to *La Ville-Lumière*. Interestingly, both the squad's expedition and Cacciato's journey are primarily configured as movements *towards* an objective, rather than flights *away* from the status quo – although, of course, in the end the two options really amount to the same thing.

On its part, the final destination of the soldiers' journey summons up a host of suggestive images: in the first instance, within the immediate context of the Vietnam war, Paris is where the inconclusive peace talks between the US and North Vietnam had been taking place since 1968 in an attempt to find a diplomatic alternative to the military conflict. Of course, Paris is also the city where the independence of the United States from Great Britain was first internationally recognized in 1783. The memory of the American shedding of the colonial yoke in Paris makes an ironic historical counterpart to the fate of Vietnam which, divided in the colony of Cochinchina, and the two protectorates of Amman and Tonkin, would fall prey to France's own imperialistic drives and become part of French Indochina in 1887. Paris also embodies a number of more general contradictions, as the city of the Enlightenment *and* of Terror; a symbol of sophistication and a den of debauchery; the most romantic place in the world, but also an aggressively sensual and sexual place, particularly in the Puritan American imaginary (see Lieutenant Corson's immediate response to the disclosure of Cacciato's destination: 'So Cacciato's gone off to gay Paree – bare ass and Frogs everywhere, the Follies Brassiere', *GAC*, 12). Last but not least, in this series of connotations, is the fact that Paris is located at the end of a long march *westward*, thus bringing to mind the mythology of the frontier.

Guiding his squad to this loaded destination is the pre-eminently uncomplicated Cacciato who, by virtue of his innocence, acts as perfect foil for Berlin's exploration of his own desire for escape, while also providing, with his eccentricity, a very convincing starting point for the whole mad enterprise. Introduced, on the second page of the novel, in the matching words of two of his comrades ('Dumb as a bullet, Stink said. Dumb as a month-old oyster fart, said Harold Murphy', 10), Cacciato is repeatedly described as almost pathologically simple and with strangely unmemorable features:

> 'It's the Mongol influence,' Doc Peret had once said. 'I mean, hey, just take a close look at him. See how the eyes slant? Pigeon toes, domed head? My theory is the guy missed Mongolian idiocy by the breath of a genetic hair. Could've gone either way.' And maybe Doc was right. There was something curiously unfinished about Cacciato. Open faced and naïve and plump, Cacciato lacked the fine detail, the refinements and final touches, that maturity ordinarily marks on a boy of seventeen years. The result was blurred and uncolored and bland. You could look at him then look away and not remember what you'd seen. All this, Stink said, added up to a case of gross stupidity. The way he whistled on guard, the funny little trick he had of saving mouthwash by spitting it back into the bottle, fishing for walleyes up in lake country. It was all part of a strange, boyish simplicity that the men tolerated the way they might tolerate a frisky pup. (*GAC*, 15)

On closer look, however, the negative associations of Cacciato's simplicity can be replaced by much more even-handed and flattering explanations; the fuzziness of his features, for example, makes Cacciato into something of a blank slate – an ideal character on which to pin one's deepest desires – and creates a sense of mystery about him, while constantly reminding the reader that this soldier, like most of his comrades, is still little more than a boy. Cacciato displays the physical traits of a baby (the soft flesh, the big eyes, the pale skin tone) and the mannerisms of a child without a care in the world (the constant smiling, whistling and chewing gum), so that his dumbness is better described as playful, nutty and even immature 'tomfoolery' than as incapacitating idiocy (after all, the squad are completely outsmarted by Cacciato's smoke-grenade, the 'booby's booby trap', *GAC*, 27). What is more, Cacciato is recognized by general consensus to have distinguished himself not merely for his ability to cope with the toughest aspects of life as a grunt, but also for some memorable acts of bravery, so that the hypothesis that fear is the reason behind his decision to quit the war is decidedly ruled out of the question (*GAC*, 22). Seen in this light, then, his crazy enterprise looks like an impulsive, audacious escapade of the kind that would appeal to a boy who lives in the moment and who would therefore take no notice of such trifles as practical considerations and military rules.

This utter disregard for the realm of rationality and common sense ties in very well with Cacciato's association with the moon (its shape is recalled in the roundness of his face), hence with the (traditionally feminine) faculties of intuition and imagination. To this dyad, I would add the quality of purity or innocence, which is also one of the constitutive traits of Artemis/Diana, the virginal goddess of the moon, and of the hunt, in ancient Greek and Roman mythology. Cacciato's lunar connotations are further emphasized by the reference to the 'caccia' ('hunt' in Italian) contained in his name, which translates into 'the hunted' or even possibly 'the shunned'. The latter, looser interpretation is perhaps a hint to Cacciato's separateness from the group – a distance which acquires particular significance when we remember that Cacciato is the only squad member who refuses to be actively implicated in the fragging of Sidney Martin, the young lieutenant executed by his men for putting their lives at risk (and for causing the deaths of Frenchie Tucker and Bernie Lynn) with his rigorous insistence on Standard Operating Procedures when dealing with VC tunnels. All in all, with his quirks and ingenuousness, Cacciato makes an unlikely hero, and certainly a very unlikely male role model, devoid as he is of any conspicuously manly traits. In fact, in the course of their search, his comrades dismiss the suggestion that the fugitive might be found looking for 'booze an' bimbos' like any 'red-blooded Joe', while one of the squad members goes as far as to doubt that 'the guy knows women from french fries' (*GAC*, 116–17).

O'Brien's use of the metaphor of the hunt – an image already present in other Vietnam war narratives, such as Norman Mailer's *Why Are We in Vietnam?* (1967) and Michael Cimino's *The Deer Hunter* (1978) – also strikes me as an ironic quotation of 'the prototypical American figure, the isolated hunter in the wilderness'.[36] It is true that, in relation to Berlin, Cacciato gradually changes from his original role as quarry to the active function of guide and source of inspiration, but he remains a very unorthodox scout figure. Elusive, unpredictable, bizarre, even comic, Cacciato is an odd kind of pathfinder: his skills, the nature of his adventures and the tone of their representation could not be more different from the solemn earnestness of the frontier myth. On the other hand, Cacciato does partake of some of the traditional qualities of the pioneer: his singleness of purpose is perhaps fuelled more by a simple-minded doggedness than by manly hardiness but, on the plus side, Cacciato is definitely endowed with the sense of ease with himself

36 Robert M. Slabey, '*Going After Cacciato*: Tim O'Brien "Separate Peace"', in *America Rediscovered: Critical Essays on Literature and Film on the Vietnam War*, eds. Owen W. Gilman, Jr and Lorrie Smith (New York and London: Garland Publishing Inc., 1990), pp. 205–24, p. 208. In his article, Slabey reminds us of the widespread critical proposition that 'warfare, as treated in American fiction, is an avatar of the frontier spirit, with the soldier replacing his progenitors, the cowboy and the frontiersman [...]. With the widespread use of imagery from the hunt and Indian warfare Vietnam becomes an extension of the American Westward movement' (p. 208).

and the infinite adaptability to his surroundings typical of the scout (from this perspective, his ostensible lack of interest in women can be assimilated to the celibacy and self-sufficiency of the White Indian). More than that, Cacciato is always and seamlessly himself; his simplicity and indeterminacy are finally marks of an authentic individual, whole and self-contained, and therefore always potentially at loggerheads with the rules of common sense and common morality. If authenticity is the key to true courage, then Berlin could not have found a better trailblazer for his journey of self-discovery and for his inquiry into the right course of action necessary in order to maintain one's integrity and prove one's valour in Vietnam.

Alongside Cacciato, Berlin finds another spiritual guide and role model in Sarkin Aung Wan, a young refugee from Cholon who joins the squad on the Vietnamese border with Laos, to which she had been travelling with her two elderly aunts – their final destination, in the girl's own words, 'The Far West' (*GAC*, 60). Seemingly fragile and in need of protection, but in fact full of energy, physically tough and strong-willed, Sarkin is also – or perhaps I should say unsurprisingly: she is, after all, a figment of Berlin's imagination – fetching and exotic. She soon becomes an active member of the expedition to Paris, in spite of some initial reservations on the part of old Lieutenant Corson (Sidney Martin's replacement). In line with his nostalgia for the certainties of conventional combat with proper rules of engagement and clear demarcations between friends and enemies, Corson maintains that war is no place for civilians – least of all, the implication seems to be, when they are women.[37] Undaunted by the Lieutenant's scepticism, Sarkin is immediately charmed by the prospect of reaching Paris, where she would love to visit the famous monuments, stroll along the Seine, admire the shops and perhaps even put down roots, establishing a beauty parlour and setting up home. As she tells Berlin, there is a possibility that they might fall in love in Paris. In her vision, Sarkin combines the thrill of a holiday and the magic of romance with the peaceful appeal of domesticity, thus painting an idyllic picture that – the reader surmises – would naturally come to mind, enticingly, to Berlin

---

37 Lieutenant Corson wistfully reminisces about his engagement in an earlier Southeast Asian conflict: 'In Korea, by God, the people liked us. Know what I mean? They *liked* us. Respect, that's what it was. And it was a decent war. Regular battle lines, no backstabbing crap. You won some, you lost some, but what the heck, it was a war' (147). The implication is that Vietnam is not even a war, let alone a decent war. While O'Brien gives voice through the old-fashioned lifer to the familiar argument about the particular challenges of the American intervention in Vietnam, he later on maintains, through Doc Peret (another sympathetic character), that all military conflicts are the same: 'The point is that war is war no matter how it's perceived. War has its own reality. War kills and maims and rips up the land and makes orphans and widows. Any war. So when I say that there is nothing new to tell about Nam, I'm saying it was just a war like every war' (*GAC*, 190). In voicing this latter view, O'Brien takes an atypical stance in the literary and cinematic canon that has developed around the war in Vietnam.

as the best possible development of the daydream triggered by Cacciato's flight to Paris. Throughout the course of the narrative, Sarkin continues to spur Berlin on his imaginary journey, acting both as an essential part of his wildest fantasies and as the key character to prompt and/or resolve crucial incidents in the plot, such as the squad's escape from the VC tunnels or Berlin's honest reflection on the reasons for his inability to follow completely in Cacciato's footsteps, both in reality and in the realm of fiction.

O'Brien's early descriptions of Sarkin Aung Wan manage to strike a perfect balance between exotic, seductive, even primitive connotations and more familiar, innocent and unthreatening traits: 'A girl, not a woman: maybe twelve, maybe twenty-one. Her hair and eyes were black. She wore an *ao dai* and sandals and gold hoops through her ears. Hanging from a chain about her neck was a chrome cross' (*GAC*, 60); 'smooth skin, dignity, eyes that were shy and bold, coarse black hair. She was young, though. Much too young. She smelled of soap and joss sticks' (*GAC*, 62). Dark and beautiful, demure and confident, Sarkin wears her contradictions on her body: the fresh scent of soap and the more pungent fragrance of incense, the cross on her chest complementing her local attire and sparkling earrings. If she is a cliché – which to an extent, of course, she is, particularly in her first intimate moment with Berlin, as she 'purr[s] from somewhere below his knees' while clipping his toenails (*GAC*, 113) – we should not mistake the conventional imagery as a failure on O'Brien's part to create a complex, three-dimensional female character. Rather, this is the logical consequence of the fact that Sarkin is a product of the mind of an inexperienced, timid young soldier, who is quite the opposite of a ladies' man; a consummate day-dreamer and procrastinator, always wavering about his options, something of a drifter, plagued by an 'inability to decide' (*GAC*, 217), Berlin is no material for a lead romantic role, in a war narrative or otherwise.

Readers are given the measure of his personality in a couple of vignettes about his life as a young man back home: the school counsellor's disbelief ('Don't you know there's a war on?', *GAC*, 217) when Berlin quits college only four credits short of graduation and in the full knowledge that this act might speed up his draft call, or the clumsy courtship of a high-school sweetheart ('In high school, Louise Wiertsma had almost been his girlfriend. He'd taken her to the movies, and afterwards they had talked meaningfully about this and that, and afterward he had pretended to kiss her', *GAC*, 175). The late, sensitive disclosure of these details prevents them from being used to dismiss Berlin with a few easy labels (the college drop-out, the loser); rather, they put the finishing touches to a poignant, rather than pathetic, picture. Bearing all this in mind, it comes as no surprise that Berlin should latch on to common orientalist imagery (e.g. the submissive Asian girl) and create out of this raw material – which, admittedly, is problematic for some of the gender and ethnic stereotypes that it perpetuates – a perfectly idealized figure within the strict boundaries of what her architect dares to imagine. The relationship between Sarkin and Berlin quickly develops into a romantic liaison, framed by the Parisian promise of fulfilment, but it remains plausibly chaste – plausibly, that is, when we think that this is the dream of the same boy who could not bring himself to kiss his date back in the States.

Tailor-made to fit her creator's emotional needs and desires, Sarkin is also a positive, vibrant and engaging figure *tout court*. When she first enters the scene – two bawling aunts in tow, mourning the loss of one of their water buffalo at the hands of Berlin's squad – she appears to be offering, as a vulnerable refugee, an orphan and a victim of American violence, a feminine, domestic, civilian counterpoint to the soldiers' plight. Soon enough, however, through the passion of her vision, evidence of her resourcefulness, and the discreet, early disappearance of her elderly relatives, she turns her escape from the conflict into a life-affirming mission towards a brighter future. At the beginning of the marvellous journey towards Paris, it is Sarkin who encourages Berlin not to give up his dream, which at this stage has developed beyond the initial aspiration to follow Cacciato – i.e. a thinly disguised wish to leave a controversial war – into a more complex desire that includes the fulfilment of a romantic fantasy with a beautiful, caring and spirited young woman. Sarkin's vision of playing house in Paris is Berlin's own fantasy in both senses of the word: Berlin is merely projecting onto Sarkin, a figment of his imagination, a desire which he strongly cherishes himself and which he cannot freely express without her mediation, because it is incompatible with his duty as a soldier – and with traditional gender roles. Like Cacciato before her, Sarkin functions as a foil for Berlin's own inadmissible desires: the hunt for the deserter masks Berlin's longing to take a moral, if not physical, distance from the war. Similarly, imagining the wish for domesticity as Sarkin's own daydream is Berlin's way of letting himself entertain the same fantasy vicariously, and therefore not as a full-blown betrayal of manly virtues and of the military ideal of male bonding.

Significantly, Berlin will not be able – even in the realm of fantasy – to overcome his reservations about the legitimacy of this romantic dream: when getting a flat in Paris with Sarkin becomes a real option – in the fantastic subplot, of course – he feels guilty about walking out on his comrades. Having overcome these misgivings, Berlin cannot make the final leap of imagination into the much longed-for scene of domestic bliss: the police catch up with the squad, who therefore must relocate all together into the flat recently rented by the couple; what was meant to be a love-nest becomes a military headquarters from which to resume the collective search for Cacciato with renewed earnestness. In the initial stages of the adventure, by contrast, Sarkin's confidence in the power of Berlin's imagination had not been disappointed; one of the most surreal episodes of the journey occurs at the moment when the soldiers and the three Vietnamese refugees appear doomed to go their separate ways, in accordance with Lieutenant Corson's orders. This particular plot development is prevented at the last minute by a truly extraordinary invention, as the earth opens under the travellers' feet and the entire party falls, Alice-in-Wonderland-like, down a hole on the road to Paris. The squad find themselves in a tunnel complex presided over by Li Van Hgoc, a prematurely aged Viet Cong major, whose promising future has been thwarted by the draft call. After Li Van Hgoc's bizarre attempt to seize control of his enemies – which amounts to nothing more than a feeble declaration of intent since, as Corson sums up, the major is '[o]utmanned, outgunned, and outtechnologized' (*GAC*, 95) – the American soldiers are made to realize a new meaning of the expressions 'prisoner of war': Li Van Hgoc has spent ten years in his underground maze, with 'tunnels leading to more tunnels, passages emptying in passages, deadends and byways and twists and turns, darkness everywhere' (*GAC*, 98). There is no exit. They are all trapped. *Xa*, the land, is their common enemy. As if the metaphor were not clear enough already, Sarkin and Li Van Hgoc go on to explain that the ancient ideogram does represent the land, but also 'community, and soil, and home. [...] *Xa*, it has many implications. But at heart it means that a man's spirit is in the land, where his ancestors rest and where the rice grows' (*GAC*, 87).

Americans and Vietnamese alike are prisoners of a conflict whose resolution is not clearly in sight, for all the military superiority of the American armed forces; furthermore, while the indigenous connection with the land is self-evident, for the American soldiers *Xa* cannot but signify the bond of duty to one's country, what it stands for and what it requires of its loyal citizens. Faithful to her role as a migrant, dispossessed and in search of a new home, and as the voice of possibility and imagination, Sarkin embraces a paradoxical logic perfectly suited to the squad's present circumstances ('"The way in," she repeated, "is the way out. To flee *Xa* one must join it. To go home one must become a refugee"', *GAC*, 99) and guides them out of the hole, through a subterranean environment marked by the stench of death, by sewage and by sludge. This part of the soldiers' expedition to Paris is thus configured as a re-birth, the journey that follows (for those lucky enough to make it) the catabasis, i.e. the (often cathartic) descent into the underworld, itself a place of decay, waste and dirt. The reference to the labyrinth also suggests a perilous, difficult passage, where one is likely to get lost or to encounter monsters, where both one's sanity and one's life are seriously under threat. Sarkin – a novel Ariadne or, as intimated by Slabey, a novel Beatrice – leads the soldiers out of their labyrinthine *selva oscura* to the conclusion of this part of the journey, in Mandalay, a location no doubt much more mundane than Dante's Paradise, but still possessed of a legendary ring in the Western world, with its promise of the love of a languid 'Burma girl' and memories of the golden days of the British Empire.[38]

The soldiers' progress continues in a series of curious adventures and encounters from Mandalay through India, Iran, Turkey and then across Europe to Paris where, in the last chapter completely devoted to the fantastic sub-plot ('The End of the Road to Paris'), Sarkin and Berlin hold their own personal peace talks in a climactic showdown during which imagination must be finally translated into reality or abandoned for good. Confronted with Sarkin's peremptory plea for him to start living his marvellous dream, Berlin is forced to admit that, even at an imaginary level, he cannot overcome the moral and emotional obligations that keep him tied to the war. Berlin's address concludes with a much quoted sequence of three sentences which sum up the 'failure of the imagination' at the heart of this book. The final paragraph of Berlin's confession deserves to be reported in full, for its eloquent exposition of the pressure that society exerts on the individual (a point subtly emphasised in the shift from the first person singular to the first person plural in this passage) or, in the terms of my analysis of bravery, of the conflict between sincerity/honesty and authenticity:

> Perhaps now you can see why I stress the importance of viewing obligations as a relationship between people, not between one person and some impersonal idea or principle. An idea, when violated, cannot make reprisals. A principle cannot refuse to shake my hand. Only people can do that. And it is this social power, the threat of social consequences, that stops me from making a full and complete break. Peace of mind is not a simple matter of pursuing one's own pleasure; rather, it is inextricably linked to the attitudes of other human beings, to what they want, to what they expect. The real issue is to find felicity within limits. Within the context of our obligations to other people. We all want peace. We all want dignity and domestic tranquillity. But we want these to be honorable and lasting. We want a peace that endures. We want a peace we can live with. We want a peace we can be proud of. Even in imagination we must obey the logic of what we started. Even in imagination we must be true to our obligations, for, even in imagination, obligation cannot be outrun. Imagination, like reality, has its limits. (*GAC*, 302–303)

The announcement of the limits of imagination, almost like a performative

---

38 The image of the Burma girl (or 'broad', in the American vernacular) wishing her British soldier back to Mandalay, 'where the old flotilla lay' and 'where there ain't no Ten Commandments' (but rather, the sound of 'crazy [temple] bells calling' to lazy days in a luxuriant landscape, the wind blowing amidst the palm trees, while the flying fish play in the sea) originally comes from Rudyard Kipling's poem 'Mandalay'. The first and last stanzas of this poem were edited and put to music by Oley Speaks in 1907 as 'On the Road to Mandalay', a song popularized in America by Frank Sinatra in the late 1950s.

speech act, brings the negotiations to a halt: Berlin and Sarkin leave the room from separate exits, and the girl effectively disappears from the novel. We later find out that she is heading all the way back to Vietnam with Lieutenant Corson, the character who, in the aftermath of Berlin's attack of the biles and Cacciato's successful flight across the Vietnamese border with Laos, concludes the novel with a declaration of hope against all the odds, a tentative suggestion ('Maybe so', *GAC*, 317) that Cacciato might make it. The lieutenant's cautious optimism explains why Berlin has imagined him as Sarkin's companion on her return journey to Vietnam; in the realm of reality, Corson is the one character who, with Berlin, seems to believe in and wish for the possibility of Cacciato's enterprise succeeding. Corson is the good, caring lieutenant, as opposed to Sidney Martin, a bad leader for his insistence on military discipline and regulations. On this subject, it is worth pointing out that O'Brien never depicts Martin as an outright villain, fully deserving his violent death: while Corson is undoubtedly a much more sympathetic character, loved by his men (and by Sarkin, who treats him like an ailing father), Martin is also portrayed as a perfectly decent, intelligent and percep-tive man. His murder remains perhaps the most traumatic and heinous incident in the novel, so terrible that it is the only truly unspeakable death in the narrative. The circumstances of the other American casualties are all accounted for, even if not in the right chronological order, but rather deliv-ered in a mixture of prolepsis and analepsis; by contrast, we never see Oscar Johnson throwing the grenade that, having been touched by all the other squad members, kills the lieutenant. Rather than playing down the magni-tude of the event being glossed over, this remarkable ellipsis draws the readers' attention to issues of collective, and individual, responsibility.

Berlin's confession of his inability to stand up to social pressure is only a fraction of what the young soldier discovers in the exploration of his own soul under Sarkin's tutelage. During the war, the encounter with 'a little girl with gold hoops in her ears and ugly scabs on her brow' (*GAC*, 248), in need of medical attention, had prompted Berlin to wonder whether she, and her fellow villagers, could sense his compassion for them, his desire for mutual kindness and collective happiness, his horror of violence, and his fear. Dabbing iodine on the girl's sores, Berlin had embarked on a silent, heartfelt explanation, aimed at the entire village, of the extent and the nature of his personal involvement in the conflict, a desperate attempt to absolve himself from any sense of guilt:

> His intentions were benign. He was no tyrant, no pig, no Yankee killer. He was innocent. Yes, he was. He was innocent. [...] [He would have told them h]ow it made him angry and sad when ... a million things, when women were frisked with free hands, when old men were made to drop their pants to be searched, when, in

a ville called Thin Mau, Oscar and Rudy Chassler shot down ten dogs for the sport of it. Sad and stupid. Crazy. Mean-spirited and self-defeating and wrong. Wrong! He would have told them this, the kids especially. But not me, he would have told them. The others, maybe, but not me. Guilty perhaps of hanging on, of letting myself be dragged along, of falling victim to gravity and obligation and events, but not – not! – guilty of wrong intentions. (*GAC*, 249)

In a similar bid to establish his distance from the war, during his first day of combat, Berlin – like a toned-down version of the Tim O'Brien from *If I Die* – had worked out his own strategy of resistance against assimilation into the military pack: going through the moves of the comradely trooper, he would look, smell, learn how to clean and how to use his weapon like the other soldiers, and perhaps even laugh at their macabre jokes, pretending to find them funny, without letting on. Acting his role in the most superficial manner, he would thus preserve his integrity and individuality. 'The trick was not to take it personally. Stay aloof. Follow the herd but don't join it' (*GAC*, 204; notice the recurrence of the word 'herd' from *If I Die*). At the end of the novel, however, and particularly after his confrontation with Sarkin – who, as the reader will have noticed by now, is really a composite figure, modelled partly on Louise Wiertsma, partly on the 'little girl with gold hoops in her ears' – Berlin realises that his earlier excuses and rationalizations do not exonerate him from his individual share of culpability as a soldier, albeit a reluctant one. Before launching into the final part of the harangue in which he declares his failure of imagination, Berlin in fact acknowledges in no uncertain terms that the fear of social censure, even as it explains his inability to oppose the war, does not provide him with a moral justification for his behaviour (*GAC*, 301ff.). By the same token, the distinction between tagging along and being guilty of the wrong intentions is a specious one: this realization, which provided the premise of *If I Die*, is the greatest lesson that Berlin learns from his journey.

In conclusion to the analysis of *Cacciato* and of the more general argument on the nature of courage, a few observations about the gender politics of this novel are perhaps in order, particularly in view of the fact that academic discussion of O'Brien's take on the notion of bravery has tended to focus on his marked rejection of a masculine, heroic conception of this ideal in preference of the androgynous virtue identified in *If I Die* as 'wise endurance'. My own insistence on authenticity as the key to understanding O'Brien's definition of courage aims to complement previous studies of this subject, but also to moderate the emphasis placed on the endless debate about the opposition between masculinity and femininity which – quite justifiably, of course – pervades the study of war literature, and has inevitably become the privileged perspective from which to approach an author like O'Brien, especially in his attempt to define a quality so traditionally intertwined with manliness. As shown by this reading of *Cacciato*, the creation of a feminine figure like Sarkin is due more to the need for psychological faithfulness to the character of Paul Berlin than to O'Brien's desire to attach a gender to courage, imagination or hope. (Needless to say, these notions are all gendered enough in our culture.) It is true that Berlin's other guides – Cacciato, and even Corson – are somewhat feminized, and not always in the most flattering terms. The former is branded as an idiot, the latter is a sick man: the language of pathology is used in reference to both figures. It is also true that when Sarkin encourages Berlin to embrace his dream in spite of (what she sees as) a misguided loyalty towards his comrades (a camaraderie that he must have succumbed to in the face of his early resistance to the lure of the 'herd'), she might be construed as a female threat to the male bond – a bond that Cacciato did not have to break because it was never there for him in the first place.

On the whole, however, it seems to me that any dubious connotations ascribed to feminine or feminized characters are more than counterbalanced by the novel's attempt to provide an honest representation of the complexity of the bond between the soldiers, not to mention its unmistakable critique of the ridiculous machismo that pervades the entire hierarchical structure of the army. For example, the sketch about Berlin's interview with the battalion promotion board, in the realistic strand of the novel, exposes the obscenity and inanity of the 'tough-guy' military posturing in the committee's grotesque, bullying repartee with the soldier (*GAC*, 251ff.). On the other side of the spectrum of gender stereotypes, the parade of wacky characters in *Cacciato* does include a girl from California, a 'revolutionary', or rather the parody of a hippie, from whom the squad hitch a ride near Zagreb. Without having given the soldiers time to explain the purpose of their flight to Paris, the girl over-zealously proclaims her affinity with their rebelliousness, emphasizing their common rejection of rules, their contempt for institutions, and their desire to separate themselves from evil. Exasperated by the girl's off-hand, if well-meaning, comments about the similarity of their plight, Oscar puts the rifle against her ear and gets her to pull over. Knowing Oscar's quick temper and having witnessed his mounting irritation, the reader is not too surprised by what follows: the van is hijacked, the girl is dumped on the road. Not so the girl, who mistakes Oscar's brutal recourse to his weapon as the preliminary to another kind of violence, and quickly interjects, smiling: 'Look, rape isn't necessary. I mean, hey, I really dig sex. Really. We can rig up a curtain or something' (*GAC*, 261). With these words, this vapid figure confirms the tritest misogynistic ideas that the military – who, it ought to be pointed out, in the promotion board vignette, were self-proclaimed 'swingin' dicks' (*GAC*, 253) – entertain about women: they are stupid, they cannot understand the war, they are sluts. Besides being the character who, more than anybody else in the novel, seems to represent the unbridgeable divide between those who have fought the war and those who have not (and women, by definition, traditionally epitomize the latter category), the girl from California embodies another misogynistic cliché with her sexual behaviour.

The girl from California certainly is a mono-dimensional character who could be (mis?)construed as a misogynistic caricature. However, one wonders, should this be read as an expression of misogyny on O'Brien's part, rather than a representation of the prejudices held by his characters or even, by extension, of the misogyny present in our culture? The answer, I think, is no, although I appreciate that the Californian girl's unwillingness to listen and inability to understand seem to prefigure similar failings ascribed to other women in O'Brien's best known book, *The Things They Carried*, whose war stories fall on the deaf ears of sisters who do not write back and elderly ladies of humane convictions who do not get the point. We shall return to this issue in Chapter 4, but for the time being, one thing is for sure: particularly through his early work and his recurrent meditations on the nature of courage, O'Brien clearly takes his distance from what Susan Jeffords has called the 'remasculinization of America' in the aftermath of Vietnam. At the most basic level, the guiding presence of Sarkin Aung Wan makes sure that the journey to Paris, i.e. the real test of courage in the novel, is not 'that men without women trip' that perpetuates the myth of male bonding as the one good thing to come out of extreme situations like combat.

More to the point, *Cacciato* tries to supersede the scrutiny of gendered role models that had informed *If I Die* and *Northern Lights* and continues O'Brien's relentless probing into the issue of personal responsibility not merely for one's actions, but also for one's failures to act. The novel acknowledges the pressures of social conditioning and military training – Berlin, after all, is a more malleable recruit than the protagonist of *If I Die* – but at no point does it suggest that he, or any other soldier for that matter, is a guileless victim of the system or that society is to blame for the ferocity (or even the indifference or cowardice) of its people. On the contrary, in *Cacciato* Berlin shows that keeping away from a gung-ho mentality must be accompanied by a frank acknowledgement of one's individual responsibility and failings. This is perhaps why, after his trilogy of courage, O'Brien has been able to move on to the exploration of a character like William Cowling – the anti-hero of *The Nuclear Age* – who, however flawed (and O'Brien's protagonists are always troubled and flawed), appears to have the guts to stick to his beliefs at the cost of unpopularity and social censure.

3
Remapping the National Landscape

Throughout his career, O'Brien has alternated between narratives primarily set in Vietnam and narratives primarily set in the United States, with *If I Die*, *Going After Cacciato* and *The Things They Carried* being followed respectively by *Northern Lights*, *The Nuclear Age* and *In the Lake of the Woods*. This alternation has only ceased with O'Brien's two most recent novels, *Tomcat in Love* and *July, July*, which are both very dark, often grotesque comedies, like *The Nuclear Age* before them. Unlike *The Nuclear Age*, and unlike O'Brien's other American novels, though, these two later texts do not immediately engage with the symbolic resonance of the American wilderness, but rather concentrate on the psychological journey of their protagonists, whose lives unfold for the most part against a metropolitan or suburban background. Regardless of their actual environment, however, O'Brien's characters share one fundamental trait: from the autobiographical narrator of *If I Die* to the variegated, dysfunctional cast of the 'Class of '69' in *July, July*, they all experience the loss of their physical and/or moral coordinates. It is true that, whether set primarily on home ground or 'in country', O'Brien's narratives all return imaginatively to Vietnam: even in *The Nuclear Age*, the only novel not to include amongst its protagonists a veteran from the war, the main character's life is significantly shaped by his decision not to answer the draft call. And yet, as already adumbrated at the beginning of this study, in a way Vietnam can be read as a landscape of the mind, a metaphor for the mysterious, and often treacherous, psychological terrain that we must navigate in our progress through life, constantly facing, as we all do, intellectual, emotional and moral quandaries, whether consciously or otherwise.

In the pursuit of his role as a postmodern mythographer, O'Brien has also made clever use of the symbolic potential of the American settings in his novels; they provide an interesting counterpart to – and, some may argue, a much needed equivalent of – an analogous figurative take on the alien Vietnamese territory. O'Brien is certainly not the first American writer to exploit the mythical connotations of the geography of his land. As a matter of fact, the trope of a dangerous natural location as the place of sinister encounters, as the repository of one's innermost – and often wicked – drives is deeply ingrained in American culture, most notably through the 'Puritan image of the wilderness as the land of the terrible unconscious in which the dark dreams of men impress themselves on reality with tragic consequences'.[1] O'Brien appears to have taken up this imaginative legacy in his recurrent descriptions and allusions to the impenetrable forests of northern Minnesota or to the hostile expanses of the Wild West, with its savage inhabitants. In particular, his overt references to the American conquest of the original Indian country are part of a deliberate revision of the myth of the frontier, a narrative that is evoked on several occasions in his work, from a critical perspective. O'Brien in fact deflates, or otherwise complicates, any symbolic reading of the American landscape; his use of established tropes exposes the dark underbelly of these conventional images and leads to their mockery and critique. The following pages will therefore provide an analysis of the literal and mythical geography of O'Brien's oeuvre, concentrating on those novels which capitalize on the austere connotations of the northern frontier, itself set against the national epic of the conquest of the West. Neither landscape, as we shall see, repays the contemporary 'pioneer' with a sense of security and belonging. Undoubtedly Vietnam is the geographical location of the most visible traumas in O'Brien's narrative universe: still, like all good war literature (and I am using the term in its widest possible sense here), O'Brien's writing deals with deeper, radical questions, with insecurities and ordeals that are part of ordinary human experience. With their ever increasing focus on American society and culture, O'Brien's stories imply, in no uncertain terms, that it is just as easy to get lost in the apparent safety of familiar surroundings as in the unknown territory of Vietnam.

The American wilderness

The American Mid-West provides the general background to O'Brien's fiction: even when it is not the immediate setting of the narrative, this region figures as the place of origin and the general cultural reference for the great majority of O'Brien's protagonists. The narrator of *If I Die* describes himself as a Baby-Boomer from 'the prairies of southern Minnesota' (*IID*, 21); O'Brien was born in Austin, Minnesota and brought up in Worthington, on Lake Okabena, a small town boasting the self-appointed title of 'Turkey Capital of the World' (*IID*, 23). This same location reappears, appropriately, as home to (the fictional) Tim O'Brien in *The Things They Carried*, while its buoyant pride and provincial mentality are recreated in Owago, the 'Rock

---

1 Richard Slotkin, *Regeneration Through Violence: The Mythology of the American Frontier 1600–1860* (Norman, OK: University of Oklahoma Press, 2000), p. 475.

Cornish Hen Capital of the World' (*TL*, 53), birthplace of Professor Thomas H. Chippering, as well as setting for the original trauma that triggers his entire, convoluted narration in *Tomcat in Love*. With the partial exception of *July, July*, whose Darton Hall College appears to be located in the metropolitan space of the Twin Cities, all the other narratives written by O'Brien are primarily set against smaller communities, caught between naive or, at worst, parochial instincts on one hand, and a strong ethical drive and a belief – or a desire to believe – in fundamental human decency on the other. This is the picture typically associated with small-town America, particularly in the Mid-West, a part of the country often defined for what it is *not*, rather than for what it is, according to facile stereotypes: neither cosmopolitan and vibrant like the East Coast, the financial, political and intellectual hub of the nation, nor genteel and decadent like the South, nor even free-spirited and wild like the West.

Alongside a sizeable slice of suburban American life, O'Brien's Mid-West also provides – in two memorable representations of its native wilderness – an altogether harsher physical and moral panorama of isolation and asperity, hard work and integrity. *Northern Lights* and *In the Lake of the Woods*, the two novels that immediately allude to their geographical location in their titles, are both set in northern Minnesota, whose inhabitants suitably reflect, in their disposition, the impervious and secluded nature of the landscape. The locals are portrayed as subscribing to a culture of endurance and reserve, and as coupling their strong sense of morality with a mistrust of authority and a keen spirit of independence. This is a different kind of pioneer country from the canonical frontier, whose westward development is identified with ideas of movement, expansion and progress, and whose individualism is associated with lawlessness on one hand, and a positive entrepreneurial flair on the other. O'Brien's description of the Swedish settlement in the Arrowhead region represents instead a dour, unglamorous reality:

> Perry learned about the hardships. Hardship was something the old man stressed. He learned that the Swedes broke ploughs on base rock, got robbed on prices, seeded soil meant for spruce and not corn, wore silent hard faces. He learned that they left Sweden in famine and, in perfect irony, came to Minnesota just in time for more of the same: locusts and drought, fierce winter and boulders; they left bad soil for worse soil, rock for rock, pine for pine. In some miserable genetic cycle, they did not leave at all and they did not arrive. (*NL*, 76)

This is the earliest sustained description of the northern environment in O'Brien's entire oeuvre: introduced by a comprehensive chronological history of the land – from the Ice Age, through the arrival of a sequence of Indian tribes and, later, of successive waves of European immigrants – the passage works by repetitions and accretions, the faint echo of biblical cadences highlighted by the image of the 'locusts and drought'. In spite of its detailed genealogy, this unruly terrain – not barren, but impossible to domesticate – is connected with a certain timelessness: the wilderness remains intact and, even more alien to the concept of the frontier, the immigrants' journey is characterized by stasis, disappointment and resignation. Thus, Perry's lesson gives the lie to the narrative of progress of the American Dream and of the conquest of a territory ready to be tamed, while supporting instead the idea that '[a]t the time of its founding, Minnesota was a fanciful invention used to draw immigrants to the state with the enticement of all the land they wanted in a "bracing and invigorating climate"'.[2]

At no point in either novel, nor indeed in any of his books, does O'Brien endorse a mythical vision of this setting as the backdrop for a national epic of heroism and for smaller narratives of individual spiritual growth and self-realization. If O'Brien's treatment of the northern landscape were to be related to a strand of American culture, it would not be connected to the pioneer's faith in the unstoppable march of progress, but perhaps to the Puritan suspicion of the wilderness as the locus of dangerous encounters with one's inner demons. The forests and lakes of Minnesota are coloured by the characters' moods: rather than a way into positive epiphanies, they reflect the onlookers' doubts and anxieties, and add to the atmosphere of narrative inconclusiveness. As we have seen in the previous chapter, in *Northern Lights* the ability to commune with nature – be it the masculine challenge of the cross-country skiing expedition or the feminine enjoyment of the luxuriant undergrowth – appears to be set up as an opportunity for redemption; an opportunity, however, that ultimately proves to be illusory. Short of being a route to self-assertion, the Hemingwayesque encounter with the wilderness is deflated into a pathetic misadventure, while the appreciation of the less imposing elements of the landscape (the pond and the brushwood, both teeming with life) fails to lead to any meaningful realizations.

O'Brien sketches a diminutive, comic version of Paul Perry's near-fatal trial in the forest with the account of a disastrous father–son activity at Indian Guides in *Going After Cacciato*. Early on in the narrative, in the middle of a chapter recording new recruit Paul Berlin's first impressions of the American military organization in Vietnam, there is a brief, yet conspicuous, passage describing how as a child, 'with his father, he had gone to Wisconsin to camp and be pals forever. Big Bear and Little Bear' (*GAC*, 47). Paul, whose very name recalls the protagonist of *Northern Lights*, has his own small-scale initiation rite in the wilderness: this time the cultural significance of the

---

2   Joseph A. Amato and Anthony Amato, 'Minnesota, Real and Imagined: A View from the Countryside', *Daedalus*, 129.3 (2000), pp. 55–56.

experience is highlighted by its inscription within the practice of the Indian Guides, an organization clearly reminiscent of Baden-Powell's Boy Scouts, as well as drawing on the mythology of the frontier. The congregation of these father-and-son pairings around the campfire is a wishful-thinking enactment and celebration of the ideal American social system, based on democratic arrangements and a shared sense of belonging, as well as on the belief in the individual's ability to survive and prosper under the spiritually rejuvenating influence of nature. Unfortunately, even a controlled, child-friendly replica of the Native American experience of the wild – 'Yellow and green headbands, orange feathers. Powwows at the campfires' (*GAC*, 47) – proves to be too much for Little Bear: on the third day, he gets lost during a scouting exercise, unable to follow his father's tracks, and is finally found 'bawling in the big Wisconsin woods' (*GAC*, 47). Paul's misadventure leaves him with a feeling of sickness that will only go away when, having decamped early, father and son make their way back home, and the conversation moves to baseball and other 'white man talk' (*GAC*, 47).

The bathetic ring of this episode, compared to Paul Perry's (already unheroic) encounter with the wilderness, is emphasized by the contrast between the two fathers: unlike Pehr Perry, 'Big Bear' is a benign figure, an accommodating and affectionate parent. Paul Berlin does not harbour any resentment, nor has he suffered from any long-term emotional damage as a result of his early failure to live up to ancestral standards and commune with his well-meaning father. In fact, Berlin appears to have internalized the paternal lesson after all, in plain denial of his previous inability to put it successfully into practice. The debacle at Indian Guides thus works as an ironic gloss to a previous passage in the narrative when, at the end of the first chapter of the novel, in a moment of relative peacefulness, 'as if a mask had been peeled off, the rain ended and the sky cleared and Paul Berlin woke to see stars' (*GAC*, 31). This seems to be no mundane awakening, but rather the possible harbinger of a revelation: nature itself lets up and Berlin is immediately drawn to look at the sky, in what reads like a typical soldierly idyll. The stars provide a reassuring image and the comfort of well-known names and patterns and, most importantly, the promise of reliable coordinates:

> They were in their familiar places. It wasn't so cold. He lay on his back and counted the stars and named those that he knew, named the constellations and the valleys of the moon. He'd learned the names from his father. Guideposts, his father had once said along the Des Moines River, *or maybe in Wisconsin*. Anyway – guideposts, he'd said, so that no matter where in the world you are, anywhere, you know the spot, you can trace it, place it by latitude and longitude. (*GAC*, 31, my italics)

The recollection of Wisconsin is quickly dismissed, and with it Berlin chooses to ignore the previous inefficacy of his own sense of direction and of his father's role as a guide.

In the comparative reading of these two episodes from *Cacciato*, the legacy of the paternal interpretative grid is devalued and, by extension, the validity of a whole set of cultural coordinates is placed under scrutiny: does America really know where she is and where she is heading to? The answer must be no, as it is further testified by Berlin's irredeemable confusion upon his arrival in Vietnam: 'He was lost. He had never heard of I Corps, or the Americal, or Chu Lai. He did not know what a Combat Center was' (*GAC*, 43). The description of Berlin's hopeless disorientation – past and present, for the Indian Guides episode follows it shortly – is ironically contained in a chapter entitled 'How They Were Organized', which also records how, on the third night after his arrival in country, Berlin writes to his father and asks him to 'look up Chu Lai in a world atlas' (*GAC*, 45). Thus, the campsite vignette works as a *mise en abyme* of Berlin's experience of the war, faced by the young soldier with the same misguided reliance on a paternal guidance that is once again doomed to be pitifully inadequate to offer a secure sense of direction. Having exposed the fragility of the American sense of purpose, and having questioned the reliability of traditional epistemological systems and certainties, *Going After Cacciato* can then proceed to explore a different way of coming to terms with reality and with its moral quandaries through a sustained praise of our imaginative resources, one of O'Brien's most typical and powerful themes. The naivety of Berlin's attempt to get his geographical bearings is later subsumed within his immense creative effort to envisage a way out of the war in his imaginary flight to Paris, a westward journey towards a resonant, yet ambivalent, destination, as already discussed in Chapter 2.

The incomprehensibility of the wilderness, and the denial of any cathartic function in the encounter with it, is at the centre of *In the Lake of the Woods*, which, more than any other narrative by O'Brien, exploits the connotations of the seclusion and impenetrability of its setting. The Northwest Angle is an extreme, and eccentric, manifestation of the awesome landscape of northern Minnesota: from the main body of the country, it 'juts like a thumb into the smooth Canadian underbelly at the 49th parallel. A geographical orphan, stranded by a mapmaker's error, the Angle represents the northernmost point in the lower 48 states, a remote spit of woods and water surrounded on three sides by Canada' (*LW*, 289). A cartographer's oversight, a parentless oddity, an alien body puncturing the otherwise regular border between Canada and the United States, the Angle projects images of alterity, menace and aloneness. Within it, the Lake of the Woods 'gazes back on itself like a great liquid eye. Nothing adds or subtracts. Everything is present, everything is missing' (*LW*, 290). Sometimes people get lost here, and disappear forever. 'Thickly timbered, almost entirely uninhabited, the Angle tends towards infinity. Growth becomes rot, which becomes growth again, and repetition itself is in the nature of the angle' (*LW*, 290). The tension towards infinity described in this passage, for all that it may sound like a Transcendentalist borrowing, conveys a different message from the sublime communion with the wilderness famously envisaged by Emerson.[3] Here, nature's gaze is narcissistic, the landscape is complete and self-sufficient, caught up in an endless loop, indifferent – if not hostile – to man. O'Brien's scenario is absolutely secular: its temporality is not the 'perpetual youth', the time of eternity of Emerson's epiphany, but a vertiginous deferral of meaning, the flickering of presence, an inescapable cycle of repetition without solution; in short, it expresses an undisguised incredulity about the possibility of attaining closure and signification, which is the underlying theme of the whole novel.

The nature of the Angle/(narrative) angle is intimated at the very beginning of the story, and indeed signalled as the reason why John and Kathy Wade seek refuge in the woods: the two protagonists are trying to escape the limelight in the aftermath of the scandal that has destroyed John's reputation and political career. About twenty-six years after the event, John's involvement with the My Lai massacre has finally (and not implausibly) come to light during his electoral campaign for the US Senate. The secret that John had guarded even from his wife resurfaces to wreak a double revenge, devastating both his public and private life: defeated by the landslide victory of his political opponent, John must also face the strain that this shocking revelation has placed upon his marriage with Kathy. From this perspective, it is easy to see the lure of Lake of the Woods, its isolation, its 'secret channels and portages and bays and tangled forests and islands without names. Everywhere, for many thousand square miles, the wilderness was all one thing, *like a great curving mirror*, infinitely blue and beautiful, always the same. Which

---

3 Cf. these familiar words from 'Nature': 'In the woods, is perpetual youth. Within these plantations of God, a decorum and sanctity reign, a perennial festival is dressed, and the guest sees not how he should tire of them in a thousand years. In the woods, we return to reason and faith. There I feel that nothing can befall me in life, – no disgrace, no calamity, (leaving me my eyes,) which nature cannot repair. Standing on the bare ground, – my head bathed by the blithe air, and uplifted into infinite space, – all mean egotism vanishes. I become a transparent eyeball; I am nothing; I see all; the currents of the Universal Being circulate through me; I am part or particle of God. The name of the nearest friend sounds then foreign and accidental: to be brothers, to be acquaintances, – master or servant, is then a trifle and a disturbance. I am the lover of uncontained and immortal beauty. In the wilderness, I find something more dear and connate than in streets or villages. In the tranquil landscape, and especially in the distant line of the horizon, man beholds somewhat as beautiful as his own nature'; Ralph Waldo Emerson, *Essays and Poems by Ralph Waldo Emerson*, ed. Peter Norberg (New York: Barnes and Noble, 2004), p. 12.

was what they had come for. They needed the solitude. They needed the repetition, the dense hypnotic drone of woods and water' (*LW*, 1, my italics). The image of nature as a blank slate, or as a series of anonymous hiding places, the refuge sought after as the catalyst for a new start in life, acts in fact as a magnifying mirror, giving back a merciless reflection of the protagonists' shortcomings, and is as elusive and meandering as their most mysterious motives.

At the heart of the novel, lost in the labyrinth of waterways and vegetation, lies the pivotal incident in the main narrative: Kathy's disappearance, which is eventually followed by her husband's one-way journey northward into Lake of the Woods. The novel is interspersed with eight chapters, all entitled 'Hypothesis', offering a variety of equally inconclusive speculations about what might really have happened to Kathy: was it an accident, a suicide or murder? Did she suddenly decide to run away from her husband or had they planned the escape, and final reunion, together from the start? The uncertainty surrounding Kathy's disappearance inevitably translates onto the role played by John in the event: is he an ignorant victim of circumstances, an abandoned husband or an accomplice? Is he guilty of manslaughter, or perhaps even murder? Besides the tentative series of hypotheses, *In the Lake of the Woods* contains three more distinct groups of chapters: the ones somewhat misleadingly entitled 'Evidence' are made up of testimonies from the inquests on Kathy's disappearance and on the My Lai massacre, as well as references to other fictional and historical texts; hovering between the speculative character of hypothesis and the claim to objectivity of evidence, there is a group of meditative, almost essayistic chapters on 'The Nature of' concepts as diverse as loss, marriage and war; finally, the remaining chapters provide the one chronological, 'factual' narrative sequence in the novel, charting the Wades' story from their arrival in Lake of the Woods, through John's memories of the night when Kathy vanished, to the subsequent investigation and John's final departure for the wilderness.[4]

In the Lake of the Woods revisits – expanding its symbolic connotations – another narrative strategy already found, on a small scale, in the previous novel: while in *Going After Cacciato* the memory of the Wisconsin forest works as a *mise en abyme* of Berlin's helplessness and confusion during the war, the intricate depths of the northern setting of *In the Lake of the Woods* parallel, and envelop, the hidden layers of events preceding the time of the main narrative: the tragedy of My Lai, but also silent domestic dramas, such as John's troubled relationship with his father, and the latter's suicide, as well

4   As I show in Chapter 5, this categorization builds upon the tripartite division of *Going After Cacciato*, whose narrative structure comprises a series of realistic war sketches, Berlin's introspective meditations while on duty at the observation post and the account of the squad's fantastic journey to Paris in pursuit of Cacciato.

as Kathy's secret life of little rebellions against her husband's suffocating love and her unspoken discontent with her lot as a trophy wife. The wilderness that finally takes Kathy and John in becomes the objective correlative of the wilderness within the two characters, and ultimately within human nature itself: it is not just the secret of John's counterfeited Army records and compromising presence in My Lai to be replaced by the mystery of his venture into the northern woods. Kathy's vanishing act – whether voluntary or otherwise – is slowly revealed to be the last in a series of brief disappearances and escapes, possibly her most successful attempt to elude her husband's possessive surveillance, and undoubtedly the climactic event in her history of reticence and silences. Like a 'great curving mirror', the natural world reflects in its impenetrability the web of ellipses, gaps and subterfuges that characterize the Wades' public profile and, significantly, also their self-awareness and mutual relationship. At the beginning of the novel, for example, John and Kathy appear to be in denial about the repercussions of John's electoral defeat, desperately trying to imagine, in a futile game of make-believe, a happy future together: 'At night they would spread their blankets on the porch and lie watching the fog move toward them from across the lake. [...] They pretended things were not so bad. The election had been lost, but they tried to believe it was not the absolute and crushing thing it truly was' (*LW*, 1–2). From the start, numbed by the emotional weariness that has been creeping on them like the approaching haze, the couple seem unable to bridge the distance between them.

Readers are later made to realize that this void is rooted deep in John's secretive and manipulative nature and in Kathy's own enigmatic past and reservations about her husband's behaviour. As the narrative progresses, the entire spectrum of human relationships, from the familial and marital to the social and political, is shown to be constantly subject to misreadings and hesitations, deceptions and prejudices, prey to epistemological limitations and ethical shortcomings. Indeed even the characters' own perceptions of themselves prove to be unreliable: John and Kathy deceive themselves and each other when they fail to admit their unhappiness; John deceives himself when he tries to atone for My Lai by serving a second term in Vietnam; Kathy deceives herself when she sacrifices her unborn baby and plays along with the role of the candidate's wife in spite of her loathing for the political game. The dimension of history, accompanied by an emphasis on the social aspect of human existence, is much more evident in this text than in any other novel written by O'Brien, given the narrative engagement with what is perhaps the most notorious episode of the Vietnam war and the creation of two protagonists whose lives unfold – and unravel – in the public eye.

The heightened focus on the social sphere finds expression in O'Brien's portrayal, in broad strokes, of the dichotomy between the metropolitan and the 'rural', i.e. the city and the backwoods, an opposition that is much clearer and starker here than in *Northern Lights*. The two worlds are perfectly epitomized by the careerist, unscrupulous Tony Carbo, Wade's spin-doctor, and by the earnest, uncompromising local deputy sheriff, Vinnie Pearson. Carbo's reaction to John's secret about his presence in My Lai is dictated for the most part by purely pragmatic considerations: he can understand John's desire to keep quiet about it – 'who the hell wouldn't?' (*LW*, 199) – and is even prepared to believe that John's political ambitions might have been a genuine attempt to atone for his role within the war. However, his analysis of John's decision to hide the truth ultimately boils down to matter-of-fact, cynical comments: in a run for the US Senate '[t]he *shit* had to come out: a principle of politics' (*LW*, 200).[5] Similarly, when asked to speculate about the events in Lake of the Woods, Carbo, who inclines towards the hypothesis that the double disappearance might have been planned from the start, draws his conclusions without being at all judgemental: 'reputation shot, no more career, bills up the gazoo. Christ, I'd run for it too' (*LW*, 299). In marked contrast, Vinnie Pearson, a former Marine who tellingly remarks that he '[d]idn't kill no babies' (*LW*, 128), is very outspoken in his contempt for John Wade: in the eyes of this fellow Vietnam veteran, Wade's connection with My Lai is seen as an irredeemable mark of criminality. Throughout the narrative, Pearson is the most relentless advocate of Wade's guilt in relation to Kathy's disappearance: from 'The guy offed her' (*LW*, 12) through 'The fucker did something ugly' (*LW*, 30) to 'Something was wrong with the guy. No shit, I could almost smell it' (*LW*, 148), Pearson's lapidary and violent accusations continue to convey his adamant, unproven conviction of Wade's culpability.

The middle ground between Carbo's detached and amoral stance and Pearson's personal and judgemental attitude is represented by Ruth and Claude Rasmussen, the owners of the lakeside cottage rented by the Wades. The couple are typical Minnesotans of Scandinavian stock, with all the connotations characteristic of their background already outlined at the beginning of this section: a no-nonsense, rough (yet generous) sense of hospitality, paired with an instinctive reserve and an impatience with the niceties and hypocrisies of so-called civilized society. An 'old-time party contributor', Claude is barely acquainted with the Wades; yet, after the disaster of the primary, his offer of 'the cottage and clean air and two weeks without newspapers' had reached John as 'the only phone call that mattered', and had been accepted as it should have been, at face value, the gesture of a 'tough old bird'

---

5 The choice of expletive is not remarkable *per se*, given that recourse to scatological language is very common in references to unfortunate or difficult circumstances: even so, as we shall see in the next chapter, O'Brien seems to be particularly keen to exploit this connection, to the point that he develops and outlines an entire emotional landscape around the image of the war as a scatological horror.

devoid of ulterior motives (*LW*, 88). The relationship between the two continues along these lines: a man of few words, Claude teases John by referring to him as 'Senator', and by dwelling without any qualms on the scale of his defeat. At the same time, however, Claude cultivates a deliberate ambiguity in the expression of his political faith, and ultimately of his solidarity with John:

> '…Say what you mean, mean what you say. One thing I don't care for, it's pussy-foot politics.'
>
> There was silence while the old man refilled his glass.
>
> 'Anyhow,' he said, 'can't say I voted for you.'
>
> Wade shrugged. 'Not many can.'
>
> 'Nothing personal.'
>
> 'No. It never is.'
>
> Claude gave him a sidelong glance, amused. 'Other hand, I'm not saying I *didn't*. Maybe so, maybe not. What surprised me – the thing I don't get – you never once asked for help. Money-wise, I mean. You could've asked.'
>
> 'And then what?'
>
> 'Hard to say. People claim I'm a sucker for lost causes.' (*LW*, 93)

Claude's evasiveness continues to leave ample room for readers to infer his disapproval of John's mistakes – a disapproval that, presumably, extends to John's conduct in Vietnam.

Nonetheless, his censure appears to be tempered by an unwillingness to pass judgement and by the awareness that John is already a ruined man. Rather than genuine sympathy, Claude displays a reluctance to add to John's misery, as if in obeisance to an old-fashioned ethos of sportsmanship, dictating that you should not kick a man who is already lying on the ground. There is a sense of equanimity and fair play about Claude's attitude to John, particularly in relation to his role in the mystery of Kathy's disappearance; the old man joins in the debate about the extent of Wade's present (and past) guilt to point out the need to keep an open mind, and to argue for the necessity to give Wade, if not the pardon implicit in the offer of a second chance in public life, at least the benefit of the doubt even in the face of past errors: 'That's what I keep telling people. Guy yells wolf, he gets stuck with the mistake, can't say a goddamn thing to change anybody's mind' (*LW*, 249). Claude's peroration is both a concession to the possibility of atonement and an indictment of the hasty conclusions often reached by a public opinion only too keen on reaching some kind of closure. Having initially refused to let John go on his own in search of his wife, Claude eventually provides him with a boat and a chart book, and encourages him, in a brief note, to set off for Canada and 'evaporate':

'Whether you're nuts or not, I don't know,' Claude had scrawled, 'but I can honestly say that I don't blame you for nothing. Understand me? Not for *nothing*. The choices funnel down and you go where the funnel goes. No matter what, you were in for a lynching. People make assumptions and pretty soon the assumptions turn into fact and there's not a damn thing you can do about it. Anyhow, I've got this theory. I figured what happened was real-real simple. Your wife got herself lost. The end. Period. Nothing else. That's all anybody knows and the rest is bullshit. Am I right?' (*LW*, 282)

In the end, just like the taciturn Elroy Berdhal in 'On the Rainy River', Claude becomes an accessory to the protagonist's rendezvous with his conscience: he sends John away to battle with his own demons – possibly to commit suicide by losing himself in Lake of the Woods – rather than acquiesce in a less than perfect, summary justice that, in the absence of a clear conclusion, would still condemn him to social censure and ruin.

In a narrative one quarter made up of hypotheses, and where everybody has a theory, Claude's 'speculation' amounts to little more than a reminder of the facts. Significantly, this is also the position advanced early on by the narrator – an anonymous veteran who started his tour of duty one year after Wade's arrival in Vietnam – who invites those requiring solutions to 'look beyond these pages. Or read a different book', for 'evidence is not truth. It is only evident' (*LW*, 30, n. 21) – or, in other words, only available to consideration and susceptible to different interpretations. As I have already suggested, this epistemological relativism is reflected by the unspoken role played by the natural environment in this story; rather than representing the permanence and reliability of nature, even the cycle of the seasons highlights the precariousness and subjectivity of perception and exposes a nihilistic logic whereby different elements and impressions cancel each other out, instead of creating a fuller and clearer picture: 'It is by the nature of the angle, sun to earth, that the seasons are made, and that the waters of the lake change color by the seasons, blue going to gray and then to white and then back again to blue. The water receives color. The water returns it. The angle shapes reality. [...] The mathematics are always null; water swallows sky, which swallows earth' (*LW*, 291).

This passage is reminiscent of a previous, overt intervention on the narrator's part, an attempt to communicate his sense of what might have triggered the My Lai massacre: 'It was the sunlight. [...] The unknown, the unknowable. The blank faces. The overwhelming otherness. [...] Twenty-five years ago, as a terrified young PFC, I too could taste the sunlight. I could smell the sin. I could feel the butchery sizzling like grease just under my eyeballs' (*LW*, 203, n. 88). While the characterization of the enemy as an unfathomable, invisible, even malign entity conforms to orientalist constructions of the Other as ultimately provoking and deserving its oppression, the insistence of the entire text on how reality is always shaped by the angle of perception – by a trick of the light, one might say – and the shift to the first person in this passage give the lie to any apportioning of blame to the victims of the massacre and fails to exonerate people like Wade, or the narrator himself, even as they acknowledge the complexity of the plight of the American soldiers. It is clear that one of O'Brien's aims in writing this novel is to prevent My Lai from slipping away from our collective memory;[6] yet, in its investigation of the burden of responsibility and the legacy of guilt for the atrocities committed in Vietnam, the narrative ultimately focuses on the predicament of the individual and, interestingly, refuses to damn its main character completely.

The exposure of John's role in the massacre is accompanied by several intimations that his second tour of duty, and indeed his political career, may have been motivated, in part at least, by a desire to redeem himself, crucially *in his very own eyes*, given his initial success in covering up the exact record of his time in Vietnam (the plausibility of this hypothesis is indeed heightened by the endorsement it receives by Tony Carbo, whose calculating character makes him otherwise always ready to believe the worst of people). Conversely, Wade's role in his wife's disappearance is kept deliberately and painstakingly obscure. Steven Kaplan observes that the final draft contains a last-minute change to the text of the advance preview copy of the book, aimed at toning down the implication that John might have been literally responsible for Kathy's vanishing.[7] John Wade is certainly not a likeable character, and his motives and actions remain less than pure and unselfish, but neither the narrator, nor – one suspects – the author, is willing to cast the first stone. The alternative is not a psychological justification, or a rationalization of the events, but rather a confrontation with 'the mystery of evil' that touches us all. Wade's story is an opportunity for the narrator to face up to his own Vietnamese ghosts: 'I have my own PFC Weatherby. My own old man with a hoe' (*LW*, 301; n. 127). This confession, with its reference to the two men killed by Wade in My Lai, is an unequivocal admission of guilt, presumably voiced as an indirect plea for forgiveness, both for the teller and, by implication, for the main character of this tale.[8]

O'Brien himself suggests that his protagonist's and his narrator's negotiation of their guilt works as a vicarious admission and processing of *his own*

6 See, on this matter, Herzog, *Tim O'Brien*, pp. 152ff.
7 Kaplan, *Understanding Tim O'Brien*, p. 218, n. 4.
8 The 'old man with the hoe' is vaguely reminiscent of 'the man at the well', protagonist of the eponymous vignette in *If I Die*: the kind, 'blind old farmer' is struck in the face by a carton of milk thrown, for no reason, by a 'blustery and stupid' American soldier (*IID*, 104–105).

implication with the war: 'the My Lai thing, in its grotesque, monstrous, obscene evil, seems a fitting corollary. It seems to fit the sense of evil that I live with day by day and the guilt I feel day by day'.[9] Significantly, for a story whose main plot is triggered by the disastrous public disclosure of Wade's personal disgrace, and for a novel so engaged with the realm of history and of collective memory, *In the Lake of the Woods* can be read as a quest for catharsis dictated by a very private need, both on the narrator's and on O'Brien's part. Even John Wade is left wandering alone, lost, uttering rambling monologues into the airwaves and later to the wilderness, once the radio has been dropped overboard and the twin Johnsons have been fired up to swing the boat further north into the lake (*LW*, 288). While we cannot completely exclude the possibility that this might be the final act in a finely tuned, premeditated performance, the narrative ends with a series of questions that invite us to think otherwise.

Whatever the truth about his crimes, the image of John's grief as he heads north seems to suggest that it is our own individual conscience and our awareness of the consequences of our actions that is the harshest judge, the one that we all must inescapably face – a point that reiterates O'Brien's emphasis on personal responsibility and on the rigorous moral standards that the authentic self is unable to ignore. Written after *The Things They Carried*, in which O'Brien explores and ultimately denies the possibility of achieving individual catharsis through storytelling, *In the Lake of the Woods* begins with the protagonist's undeniable complicity in an infamous war crime, and draws immediate attention to the impact of the revelation of one's guilt in the communal sphere, where private narratives enter a truly public domain. As the novel progresses, however, the focus shifts again to the intimate dimension of the quest for self-forgiveness, atonement and individual redemption. After all, legal justice can be manipulated or evaded with relative ease, as testified by Wade's lies and particularly by his final escape, sanctioned by Claude, the character who provides through his initial reserve the moral centre of the book and who explicitly questions the soundness of public assumptions. The fact that the core of the text is a concern with *individual* moral struggles is confirmed by the presence of a narrator whose declared investment in Wade's story and whose idiosyncratic compilation of the 'Evidence' chapters make his mediation of the story fraught with personal issues.

Previous readings of *In the Lake of the Woods* (cf. Kaplan, Herzog and Heberle) have focused on the experimentalism and the metafictional aspect of the text, which undoubtedly highlights the constructed nature and the partiality of official history and its status as one of the many possible,

9   Quoted in Herzog, *Tim O'Brien*, p. 153.

competing versions of an event. In fact, I would not hesitate to use Linda Hutcheon's term 'historiographic metafiction'[10] to define this text, which continuously blurs the boundary between factual account and imaginative fabrication, with its fictional rendition of the events in My Lai, alongside accurate quotations from historical sources of varied evidential value, such as the records of Lieutenant Calley's court-martial or Robert Caro's political biography of Lyndon Johnson or Richard Nixon's political memoir *Six Crises* (1962). The courageous revisitation of My Lai in *In the Lake of the Woods* has won this narrative the American Historians' Cooper Prize for best historical novel; yet, in spite of the text's reflections on the production of history, and of its concern with the past and its secrets (foregrounded by the complex temporality of the tale, and its frequent prolepses), the main axis of the narrative remains spatial rather than chronological: *In the Lake of the Woods* reads more like a travelogue, the story of an exploratory mission, than like a chronicle of the rise and fall of a flawed character. The chronology is as labyrinthine as the physical and moral geography of the landscape and of the characters, but of course the main topos of the narrative is the Wades' *journey* of reconciliation or their decision – mutual or otherwise – to go their different ways, or even John's slow descent into murder and madness. The first two alternatives imply a voyage of self-discovery as well as the need to get to know one's life-partner once again: what used to be familiar territory must be newly mapped out in the aftermath of the revelations triggered by John's exposure, which include Kathy's confession of her resentment for the constant prioritization of John's political career over any other plan. The third option is a story of perdition and annihilation.

Whatever the scenario, the most recurrent motif in the novel is the sense of getting lost or disappearing, the feeling of disorientation and the lack of a secure grip on reality. In fact, the relationship between John and Kathy revolves around the two characters grounding and simultaneously losing themselves in each other. This is particularly true of how John thinks about Kathy, as exemplified by the following passage, which foreshadows the final, already quoted, description of the nature of the angle with its circular sequence of engulfments ending in a null mathematical operation:

> He said he was lost without her. He said she was his sun and stars. He compared their love to a pair of snakes he'd seen along a trail near Pinkville, each snake eating the other's tail, a bizarre circle of appetites that brought their heads closer and closer until one of the men in Alpha Company used a machete to end it. 'That's how our love feels,' John wrote, 'like we are swallowing each other up, except in a *good* way […] Just like those weirdo snakes – one plus one equals zero!' (*LW*, 61)

10 Linda Hutcheon, *A Poetics of Postmodernism: History, Theory, Fiction* (New York and London: Routledge, 1988).

The image of John's voracious desire to gobble up his wife recurs in more graphic detail later on: 'Such eyes, he'd think. He'd want to suck them from their sockets. He'd want to feel their weight on his tongue, taste the whites, roll them around like lemon drops' (*LW*, 72). This fantasy of physical incorporation is combined with John's equal and opposite wish to become part of Kathy in a sort of *regressus ad uterum*: 'There were times when John Wade wanted to open up Kathy's belly and crawl inside and stay there forever. He wanted to swim through her blood and climb up and down her spine and drink from her ovaries and press his gums against the firm muscle of her heart' (*LW*, 71; notice how the mention of 'gums' rather than 'teeth' contributes to John's infantilization. This kind of regression is a recurrent trope in O'Brien's writing).

Although Kathy's feelings for John do not seem to match the eerie intensity conveyed by these images – possibly because the narrative focuses for the most part on John and gives less space to the articulation of Kathy's psychology – there is a clear intimation that she may have experienced the desire to lose herself in John (*LW*, 187). This hypothesis is given a certain authoritativeness by the fact that it is advanced by Pat, Kathy's cynical sister, who is bemused at the very thought that anybody might wish for such self-abandonment and such dependence on somebody else. Admittedly, the description of the amorous passion with reference to space is not at all unusual: one need only mention its representation as *ek-stasis*, i.e. the displacement and loss of the self, or the expression 'to fall in love', a dead metaphor whose literal aspect is emphasized by John in his final monologue.[11] Having said that, in *In the Lake of the Woods* even themes that we would perhaps expect to unfold along a temporal axis, such as the Wades' hopes and dreams for the future, are configured in spatial terms: the restoration of happiness, for example, is envisioned by the couple as 'a physical place on earth, a secret country, perhaps, or an exotic foreign capital with bizarre customs and a difficult new language' (*LW*, 3). The arduousness of the Wades' journey towards this and other destinations is compounded by the meaning of their name, with its connotations of impeded movement and slow progress.

The image of a strenuous and encumbered advancement towards an impossible goal is also used by the narrator to describe his long, stubborn pursuit of the truth about John (and, by extension, about his own heart as well as 'the human spirit' in general); ultimately, the gathering of information and

---

11 John's linguistic analysis draws attention to the relinquishment of individual agency implied by certain expressions: 'Do we choose sleep? Hell no and bullshit – we *fall*. We give ourselves over to possibility, to whim and fancy, to the bed, the pillow, the tiny white tablet. And these choose for us. Gravity has a hand. Bear in mind trapdoors. We fall in love, yes? Tumble, in fact. Is it *choice?* Enough said' (*LW*, 287).

the writing of this very novel, together with the reasons – contingent or universal – behind similar enterprises are all seen as a frustrated, yet irresistible, epistemological quest:

> [...] for all the travel and interviews and musty libraries, [John Wade's] soul remains for me an absolute and impenetrable unknown, a nametag drifting willy-nilly on oceans of hapless facts. [...] What drives me on, I realize, is a craving to force entry into another heart, to trick the tumblers of natural law, to perform miracles of knowing. It's human nature. We are fascinated, all of us, by the implacable otherness of others. And we wish to penetrate by hypothesis, by day-dream, by scientific investigation those leaden walls that encase the human spirit, that define it and guard it and hold it forever inaccessible. (*LW*, 103, n. 36)

This metafictional notation – which extends the spatial metaphor from the level of the story to the experience of the narrator and to the process of story-telling itself – is typical of the paradoxical postmodern coexistence of the awareness of the impossibility to achieve and communicate secure knowl-edge, and of a narcissistic, undaunted faith in the suggestive power of fiction. While a deeper analysis of O'Brien's view of storytelling will have to wait until Chapters 4 and 5, it is difficult to ignore the recurrent association in the above-mentioned passage between the acquisition of knowledge and an act of violent invasion (the 'impenetrable unknown' to be conquered, 'a craving to force entry', a 'wish to penetrate') with possible sexual undertones. It is possible to read the obsessive, brutal desire to apprehend information and gain full intellectual mastery over it as a (critical? tongue-in-cheek?) exagger-ation of the project of the Enlightenment, whose narrative of human progress has nonetheless often sidelined alternative world-views, and even legitimized the oppression of marginal cultures. O'Brien's choice of words is uncomfort-able – necessitating perhaps the buffering provided by the fictional narrator – but it is illustrative of a particular epistemological problem, rather than of O'Brien's personal solution to it, as we shall see particularly in the analysis of his representation of the ultimate unknowable and unrepresentable, the dead enemy, in 'The Man I Killed' in Chapter 5.

Indian Country

The representation of man's problematic relationship with the wilderness and nature, and the projection of one's moods onto the landscape, are common enough literary themes, not only in the American context. The American cultural makeup is unarguably much more informed by geograph-ical – as opposed to historical – discourses than its various European counterparts; nonetheless, the dichotomy between nature and culture, in its multiple incarnations (the country vs. the city, wilderness vs. civilization, etc.), is a recurrent feature of post-Romantic Western thought, even as it finds a unique American expression in the myth of the conquest of the Wild West. The most distinctly American legacy of the narrative of the frontier in Vietnam war literature is the perception of the foreign land as an enemy – and, more specifically, of Vietnam as 'Indian Country' – paired with the lingering presence of feelings of national guilt inherited from the violent subjugation and destruction of native American cultures. The final part of our discussion of the impact of the frontier myth on O'Brien's writing deals with the noticeable cross-references, in the narratives that we have analysed so far, between the military experience of Vietnam and the genocide of the Native Americans, a tragic part of US history uneasily subsumed within the comedic plot of the national epic of westward expansion and civilized progress.

Unsurprisingly, *In the Lake of the Woods* adopts the conceit of the landscape as a reflecting mirror, or a blank canvas coloured in by one's expectations, prejudices and state of mind, in relation both to the forests of Minnesota and to the unfamiliar and disquieting reality of Vietnam. Against the drudgery and the horror of the war, Wade's skills as a magician – the result of a youthful hobby that had earned him his father's scepticism and mockery – are transfigured into truly extraordinary qualities, transforming Wade from loner and outsider to 'Sorcerer', the oracle and lucky charm of Charlie Company, or the 'company witch doctor' (*LW*, 38), as he boasts in a letter to an unimpressed Kathy. With his new identity as Sorcerer, the once shy and solitary Wade finds himself 'in his element', in a country which, in its turn, has been reinvented as a land of dark incantations and hidden evil. Vietnam

was a place with secret trapdoors and tunnels and underground chambers populated by various spooks and goblins, a place where magic was everyone's hobby and where elaborate props were always on hand – exploding boxes and secret chemicals and numerous devices of levitation – you could *fly* here, you could make *other* people fly – a place where the air itself was both reality and illusion, where anything might instantly become anything else. It was a place where decency mixed instantly with savagery, where you could wave your wand and make teeth into toothpaste, civilization into garbage – where you could intone a few syllables over the radio and then sit back to enjoy the spectacle – pure mystery, pure miracle – a place where every object and every thought and every hour seemed to glow with all the unspeakable secrets of human history. The jungles stood dark and unyielding. The corpses gaped. The war itself was a mystery. Nobody knew what it was about, or why they were there, or who started it, or who was winning, or how it might end. Secrets were everywhere – booby traps in the hedgerows, bouncing betties under the red clay soil. (*LW*, 72–73)

The language of magic is used here to provide euphemisms for violent acts of war and to articulate the perceived alterity of the enemy: Vietnam, like an illusionist's stage, or an otherworldly realm, is a place with carefully guarded secrets, a location where the rules of nature and common sense are continuously suspended, where one would do well not to believe one's eyes, a laboratory of endless, dangerous transformations. And yet the genealogy of Wade's passion for illusionism as an escape from reality, and the swiftness of his metamorphosis from taunted loser to acclaimed, charmed performer, are strong reminders of the artificiality, partiality and arbitrariness of the entire account.

It is clear that the representation of Vietnam as a cross between a malign fantasy-land and a deranged magician's workshop is the product of the same narrative that has cast Wade in the role of witch doctor, possessed with genuine magic talents; in other words, Sorcerer and the wondrous quality of Vietnam are closely intertwined cultural constructs: they shape each other and need each other in order to preserve their respective illusions. Treachery and violence are not objectified and projected onto Vietnam, as the country's evil emanations; rather, they are shown to be already present in Wade/Sorcerer's nature and already circulating in the soldiers' frame of mind, in their attempt to verbalize and exorcize – even through patently irrational narratives – the inexplicable and terrifying experience of war. If the Vietnamese setting and the war coalesce, as the irrationality of both is proclaimed, their indiscriminate conflation is exposed precisely for what it is: a crude rhetorical operation, one that banks very adroitly on the derogatory and sinister connotations of a particular kind of magic – the magic that purports to connect the human with the spirit world – in non-Western culture. Herzog points out that in *In the Lake of the Woods* the references to the illusionist's craft reveal, at a metafictional level, enlightening similarities with the storyteller's bag of tricks and relationship with his or her audience, a parallel that O'Brien had developed in more depth in a 1991 essay entitled 'The Magic Show', published in *Writers on Writing*.[12]

By contrast, at the diegetic level – the level of the characters', rather than the author's, opinions – the view of Vietnam as a place of 'spooks and goblins' and a land locked into a perverted version of the eternal present of primitive societies ('a place where every object and every thought and every hour seemed to glow with all the unspeakable secrets of human history'), together with Sorcerer's self-congratulatory acceptance of the role as 'company witch

12 Herzog, *Tim O'Brien*, p. 166.

doctor', contain disturbing undertones and cultivate the more ominous, and ideologically loaded, aspect of the semantic slipperiness of the word 'magic'. The above-mentioned passage and Sorcerer's subtle metamorphosis from prestidigitator to medicine man conflate the idea of illusionism as a spectacular performance and the notion of witchcraft, or shamanism, as the expression of an archaic belief in the possibility of communing with the sacred, a possibility that in Wade's view of reality – and indeed our own – is regarded contemptuously as tantamount to superstition:

> In Vietnam, where superstition governed, there was the fundamental need to believe – believing just to believe – and over time the men came to trust in Sorcerer's powers. Jokes, at first. Little bits of lingo. 'Listen up,' somebody would say, 'tonight we're invisible,' and somebody else would say, 'That's affirmative, Sorcerer's got this magic dust, gonna sprinkle us good, gonna make us into spooks.' It was a game they played – tongue-in-cheek, but also hopeful. At night, before heading out on ambush, the men would go through the ritual of lining up to touch Sorcerer's helmet, filing by as if at Communion, the faces dark and young and solemn. They'd ask his advice on matters of fortune; they'd tell each other stories about his incredible good luck, how he never got a scratch, not once, not even that time back in January when the mortar round dropped right next to his foxhole. Amazing, they'd say. Man's plugged into the spirit world.
>
> John Wade encouraged the mystique. It was useful, he discovered, to cultivate a reserved demeanor, to stay silent for long stretches of time. When pressed, he put on a quick display of his powers, doing a trick or two, using the everyday objects all around him.
>
> Much could be done, for example, with his jackknife and a corpse. Other times he'd do some fortune-telling, offering prophecies of things to come. 'Wicked vibes,' he'd say, 'wicked day ahead,' and then he'd gaze out across the paddies. He couldn't go wrong. Wickedness was everywhere.
>
> 'I'm the company witch doctor,' he wrote Kathy. 'These guys listen to me. They actually *believe* in this shit.' (*LW*, 37–38)

Wade himself disparages the belief system adopted collectively and only half-jokingly by his company, even as he appropriates and encourages it for his own personal ends. Interestingly, the admission that the soldiers' trust rests on 'shit' is delivered only after Wade has redefined his powers: from magic tricks, to more macabre transformations in the maiming of enemy corpses, to end significantly with bogus prophecies, a 'gift' subtly – perhaps even unconsciously – associated with Native American practices and with the belief in the 'spirit world'. The latter expression is indeed most frequently used in the novel by Richard Thinbill, a Chippewa soldier, who resorts to this image in order to capture the dreadful aftermath of the massacre. Incidentally, Wade's racist slip is so much more telling when we consider that Thinbill is his closest friend in the company: the fact that Wade is prepared to speak up in Thinbill's defence against Lieutenant Calley, in a tense discussion in which the argument about the legitimacy of the American killings is momentarily deflected onto the deliberation of Thinbill's ethnic origin, highlights the deep-rooted nature of the prejudice behind Wade's mocking reference to his own role as the company's witch doctor.

Thinbill is the first soldier to make a public show of taking his distance from the Lieutenant's inexcusable justification of the incidents in My Lai: his silent censure provokes in his superior an aggressive rebuttal, which relies not only on the deliberate falsification of the actual events, but also on a flippantly abusive dismissal of Thinbill's cultural heritage with the obvious intent of belittling the man and discrediting his opinions.

> Gooks were gooks, he [Calley] said. They [the American soldiers] had been told to waste the place, and wasted it was, and who on God's scorched green earth could possibly give a shit? [...] Thinbill glared at the lieutenant and got up and moved away.
>
> Calley glanced over at Sorcerer. 'What's Apache's problem? Not some weenie roast.'
>
> 'Chippewa,' Sorcerer said. 'Thinbill is.'
>
> 'Is he now?'
>
> 'Yes, sir.'
>
> [...] 'Not up on my tribes, I reckon, but you can still tell him it was a slick operation. Lock an' load and do our chores.'
>
> 'Yes, sir,' Sorcerer said.
>
> 'Search and waste.'
>
> 'Except there weren't any weapons to speak of. No incoming. Women and babies.'
>
> Calley brushed a fly off his sleeve. 'Now which babies are these?'
>
> 'The ones... You know.' (*LW*, 209)

After this exchange, Wade's tentative allegiance with Thinbill is promptly suppressed by Calley's official narrative of the massacre, a conspiracy of silence that rests on the denial of the truth of one's senses: there are no babies, or butchered women, or any other atrocities to be seen, just as there are no flies to be heard 'buzzing murder' over the bloated corpses, who certainly do not look as though they belong to innocent civilians.

Against the scandalous perversion of one's physical perceptions demanded by Calley – and subscribed to, more or less willingly, under the pressure of his command, by the entire company – there are a couple of alternative recollections of the scene. At a first glance, Wade apprehends the location of the massacre as an oxymoronic 'living deadness' (*LW*, 214), the corpses still appearing to wriggle with what is in fact the movement of millions of flies; 'An illusion, Sorcerer knew' (*LW*, 214). And, as already mentioned, Thinbill does resort on several occasions to the image of the 'spirit world' in order to describe the spectral aftermath of My Lai: the stench, the flies, the horror of the ditch full of civilian corpses and, even more unearthly, the strange shapes and silhouettes that animate the twilight in the mountains, still visible to the west even from the company's new camp by the coast.[13] However, while Thinbill obsessively recalls and utters the ghastliness of the scene, both in its material brutality and in its more ethereal, haunting dimension (the ditch and the flies glowing in the dark, the curious shadows against the violet twilight), soon enough Wade turns to playing 'mind-cleansing tricks' (*LW*, 217) in the attempt to forget what he has witnessed and taken part in. Thinbill's apprehension of the massacre, in spite of the mystical undertone of its articulation, represents a true vision of the appalling barbarity of the war, in direct contrast with Wade's disingenuous self-delusions.

O'Brien thus reverses the implicit and derogatory connotation of the Native American connection with magic and the unearthly, for it is only in relation to Wade and the other soldiers that magic becomes trickery, illusion and self-delusion and that the 'spirit world' is shorthand for superstition. Thinbill's own references to the 'spirit world' – like, to a certain extent, the narrator's gloss about the 'mystery of evil' in footnote 88 – are instead a pressing reminder of the indescribable violence committed against the Vietnamese and of the unmanageable, eerie images that will forever follow its perpetrators and witnesses alike. In support of this hypothesis, Thinbill's insistent recollection of the buzzing flies can be read as an allusion to Beelzebub, the 'Lord of the Flies' or 'Lord of the Dung' of the Old Testament.[14] More than everybody else, Thinbill is thus aware of the potential for evil ominously lurking in the human heart. A similar reversal of clichés takes place in relation to the identification of the land itself with evil, an idea that extends as a matter of course to the local people, who are seen as ghoulish emanations of their country. This conceit provides the opening for 'The

---

13 See, for example, p. 203 and p. 209. Thinbill's first remark is glossed in a footnote by the narrator, who appropriates the term 'spirit world' with reference to the alterity of the Vietnamese enemy, perceived as invisible, alien, unknowable by the American soldiers (*LW*, 203, n. 88; see above).

14 This suggestion is backed up by 'The Nature of the Beast', the title of Chapter 13, which contains the first sustained description of the My Lai massacre. The 'Beast' is another name popularly associated with the devil, and Beelzebub in particular, in no small part through the influence of William Golding's 1954 novel *Lord of the Flies*. For a reading of the intertextual allusion to *Lord of the Flies* in *In the Lake of the Woods*, see David J. Piwinski, 'My Lai, Flies, Beelzebub in Tim O'Brien's *In the Lake of the Woods*', *War, Literature and the Arts*, 12.2 (2000), pp. 196–202.

Nature of the Beast', the chapter on the My Lai massacre: in the brief but effective build-up to the events of 16 March 1968, we read about Lieutenant Calley referring to the Vietnamese as 'gookish fucking ghosts', a remark echoed by a soldier, in the dark, doing 'witch imitations' (*LW*, 104). In the eyes of the Americans, Vietnam is clearly a 'spook country. The geography of evil: tunnels and bamboo thickets and mud huts and graves' (*LW*, 105). Once again, Calley is the most vehement advocate of this idea, as he urges his soldiers to 'Kill Nam', while firing his weapon against the earth, the grass and a palm tree (*LW*, 105) – a deranged attack on the land that heralds the indiscriminate carnage soon to explode in the following paragraph.

As in a palimpsest, the description of the violence that engulfs the entire village of My Lai, destroying the huts and the vegetation, killing domestic and wild animals alike, and not even stopping to spare old people and children, contains several, unmistakable references to previous atrocities in the original Indian country. This time, however, it is the 'cowboys' who have become savages: Wade himself sees a 'pretty girl with her pants down' and her hair gone, and 'a GI with a woman's black ponytail flowing from his helmet' (*LW*, 108). Significantly, the extent of Thinbill's participation in the massacre amounts to the killing of some water buffalo, 'a grotesquely benign revision of analogous episodes in O'Brien's previous works'[15] but also, surely, an allusion to the long-gone livelihood of the American Indians.[16] With images like these, it is impossible not to pursue the connection between this war and the genocide of the Native Americans, and not to rethink the simplistic Manichaean distinction between good and evil that underpinned the systematic destruction of entire indigenous cultures – an odious distinction that is echoed in the brutality of Calley's reprisal, in the name of civilization and rationality, against the perceived subterranean malice of the Vietnamese. The troubling identification of the American intervention in Vietnam as a re-enactment of previous episodes of US history is a major theme in O'Brien's collation, in the penultimate 'Evidence' chapter, of excerpts from various historical records of the American military past. In the aftermath of the 1775 battles of Lexington and Concord, an anonymous

---

15 Heberle, *A Trauma Artist*, p. 236.
16 In the analogous episode in *Going After Cacciato*, as already hinted at in Chapters 1 and 2 above, the killing of the water buffalo is also clearly associated with the mythology of the Wild West: Stink Harris drops on one knee in order to shoot Sarkin's aunts' buffalo, thus adopting a recognizable western pose (*GAC*, 57), and his self-congratulatory comment on his hit – 'Fastest hands in the West' (*GAC*, 58) – reprises a stock cliché of westerns. The fact that the whole novel is pervaded by allusions to the western lore, as pointed out by Slabey, marks the strength of the influence of this foundation myth on Berlin, who is responsible for colouring the account of the imaginative chase after Cacciato with such vivid hues, while in reality the killing of a water buffalo by the American soldiers is reported in a laconic and matter-of-fact way (*GAC*, 105).

British infantryman recalls how the American troops fighting for independence from their European rulers were an irregular army, invisible and savage enemies, 'as bad as the Indians for scalping and cutting the dead men's ears and noses off' (*LW*, 262). The analogy between the American predicament in the War of Independence and the Vietnamese resistance against colonial power and neocolonial interference is completed by the accounts of a couple of British officers bearing witness to their soldiers' shameful retaliation against the civilian population for their losses at Lexington and Concord.

With the War of Independence and Vietnam as apt bookends, the mid-nineteenth-century campaigns against the Native Americans constitute the chronological and emblematic core of O'Brien's swift, but carefully edited, outline of America's history of total warfare and gratuitous (even in a military context) violence. O'Brien's selection of episodes from the Indian Wars focuses on a couple of seminal events and iconic historical figures, such as the infamous Sand Creek massacre of a Cheyenne village in 1864, captured in a particularly gruesome quotation,[17] and General William Tecumseh Sherman, whose most significant legacy as a military strategist is indeed the successful implementation of the concept of total warfare, as testified by his ruthless 'scorched earth' policy during the American Civil War, and by his positive endorsement of the decimation of the buffalo population as a way of fighting the Plains Indians. In *In the Lake of the Woods*, Sherman makes a brief appearance as the influential advocate for the retaliatory annihilation of the Native Americans: 'We must act with vindictive earnestness against the Sioux, even to their extermination, men, women, and children' (*LW*, 260) runs his telegram to General Grant, prompted by the news of Fetterman's massacre in December 1866.[18] This notorious excerpt finds its way onto the pages of O'Brien's book via Evan Connell's account of Custer's Last Stand, for Custer himself had recorded Sherman's telegram in his own autobiography, *My Life on the Plains* (1874). Thus, with a few chosen, wide-sweeping allusions, O'Brien sketches the violent past of his nation, zeroing in on the uncomfortable parallelism with the Vietnamese conflict offered by the American role as foreign – and often reckless and overconfident – invaders of the original Indian country.

17 'No prisoners were being taken, and no one was allowed to escape if escape could be prevented. A child of about three years, perfectly naked, was toddling along over the trail where the Indians had fled. A soldier saw it, fired at about seventy-five yards distance, and missed it. Another dismounted and said: "Let me try the little ——; I can hit him." He missed, too, but a third dismounted, with a similar remark, and at his shot the child fell [...] The Indians lost three hundred, all killed, of whom about half were warriors and the remainder women and children' (*LW*, 260–61, n. 97).

18 Fetterman and his seventy-nine men were lured by decoys over Lodge Trail Ridge where they were surrounded by Sioux and killed. After Custer's Last Stand, this is probably the most disastrous defeat of the American army at the hands of the Plains Indians.

The very mention of Custer, while it recuperates a common topos in the discursive representation of the war, must also be read as a deliberate reference to one of the most cryptic and evocative traumas of American history, an event whose heroic resonance contributed to the founding of the myth of the Wild West, and to its spectacularization of violence and war, as well as to the crystallization of the glorious image of the forces of gallantry and civilization committing the ultimate sacrifice in their fight against savagery and mayhem.[19] While the emotional legacy of Custer's problematic heroic model is more conspicuous in *The Nuclear Age*, the controversial figure of this 'national totem', 'a dashing cavalier embedded like a fossil in American folklore' makes an interesting term of comparison for the protagonist of *In the Lake of the Woods*.[20] Like Custer, John Wade is a calculating self-styled hero and a very ambitious man, indefatigable in promoting his own cult of personality, betrayed in the end by his own sense of invincibility. At the narratorial level, on the other hand, the fascination of Custer's and Wade's stories rests on their mystery, 'which both frustrates and fascinates' (*LW*, 269, n. 117).[21]

Of course, in spite of the narrator's obsession with his protagonist as a cipher, even in the fictional world of the novel, 'Senator' Wade remains at best a pathetic figure, a man who can only aspire to mythical fame, a risk-taker whose debacle deservedly achieves immediate and inglorious notoriety. Sorcerer is a larger-than-life character only in his own mind, which he has painstakingly purged of its most shameful recollections. Under the intense psychological strain of the events in My Lai, he fails to stand up to the collective madness of Calley's troops, even as he resists the lure of unchecked violence committed in the name of a spurious desire for revenge. His two killings during the massacre betray an impulsiveness that can only be partly explained by an instinctive drive for self-preservation. While this urge convincingly accounts for Wade's murder of an old Vietnamese man with a hoe, tragically mistaken for an enemy armed with a rifle, the assassination of

19 In Vietnam the US soldiers' identification with the doomed Seventh Cavalry at the Little Bighorn was 'epidemic', as argued by Bates, *The Wars We Took to Vietnam*, p. 9.

20 Evan S. Connell, *Son of the Morning Star: General Custer and the Battle of the Little Bighorn* (London: Picador, 1985), pp. 107, 105. Subsequent references are to this edition.

21 Custer remains a controversial myth – '[e]ven now, after a hundred years, his name alone will start an argument' (Connell, *Son of the Morning Star*, p. 106) – for the simple reason that the facts around the battle of Little Bighorn are still uncertain. Connell also points out, quoting Paul Hutton, that with the revision of the conquest of the frontier, Custer's image has been 'gradually altered into a symbol of the arrogance and brutality displayed in the white exploitation. [...] The only constant factor in this reversed legend is a remarkable disregard for historical fact' (p. 107). It is interesting to notice how both O'Brien and Connell are caught up in a game of Chinese whispers: O'Brien gives us Custer via Connell's mediation. Connell in his turn sums up the rise and fall of the General's image quoting Hutton. This, in itself, is symptomatic of the proliferation of tales that surround this painful chapter in American history.

a fellow American soldier reads more like an execution than as an act of self-defence, and is certainly not quite the automatic reflex that Wade would have himself believe. The details of this episode of 'friendly fire' are particularly illuminating: Wade is found at the bottom of an irrigation ditch, caught up in slime and surrounded by Vietnamese corpses, by PFC Weatherby, one of the most violent and callous of the American soldiers, the very man responsible, more than any other, for turning the agricultural landscape into an open-air mass grave. Weatherby, whose name recalls an American gun manufacturer famous for its production of rifles and high-powered magnum cartridges, had been 'killing whatever he could kill. [...] The almost-dead did twitching things until [he] had occasion to reload and make them fully dead' (*LW*, 109). In the face of such an impassioned and crazed lust for blood, Wade's own brutal reaction as Weatherby looks in on him is a plausible mistake, made by a traumatized soldier, surrounded by dead men and desperate not to take any chances with his own survival. Nonetheless, the moment of Weatherby's killing is represented *twice* in the narrative, with a curt, definite emphasis on the contrast between the soldier's comradely acknowledgement of Wade and the latter's unflinching gesture: '"Hey, Sorcerer," Weatherby said. The guy started to smile, but Sorcerer shot him anyway' (*LW*, 112); and again, '"Hey, Sorcerer," Weatherby said. He started to smile, but Sorcerer shot him' (*LW*, 220). According to Piwinski, and for all that his interpretation of the passage is more open-ended than mine, this is the episode that marks Wade's complicity in the collective iniquity perpetrated by the American soldiers in My Lai: 'Whether this act was, to quote from Wade's thoughts at the start of the massacre, "madness" (hysterical reflex?) or "sin" (intentional evil?) is one of the many ambiguities of this novel; nevertheless, Wade clearly has been infected by the murderous evil that he will continue to associate with the flies at My Lai.'[22]

The idea of evil spreading by contamination is certainly suggestive, given the way in which Wade (*nomen omen?*) is mired in the blood and excrement – the very stuff of Beelzebub – oozing out of the innocent victims piled up in the irrigation ditch. And yet, surely, Wade's gesture, even if intentional, or *particularly if intentional*, must be interpreted as an act of retribution on behalf of the corpses crowding the muddy ditch after a pointless massacre, rather than as a conscious display of unfettered malice. Even so, Wade lacks the moral stamina to pursue a lawful and systematic campaign for justice: were he to be assigned a place in Dante's Inferno, instead of being consigned to the Phlegethon (the boiling river of blood where the violent receive their punishment), he would be fully immersed in the muddy water of the Styx, as befits those guilty of the sin of *akedia*, who, unable to care, cannot bring

22 Piwinski, 'My Lai, Flies, Beelzebub', p. 200.

themselves to take action and carry out what they know to be the right thing
to do. In this sense, the irrigation ditch is a resonant central feature in the
haunting landscape of My Lai: Styx-like, it mirrors the geography of the
Fifth Circle of Hell, where the wrathful fight one another, and the slothful,
engulfed in mud, are left eternally speechless and gasping for breath. The
killing spree, sanctioned by Calley's mocking misreading of the Old Testament ('Eyeballs for eyeballs [...]. One of your famous Bible regulations', *LW*,
104), is an act of wrongful ire against the Vietnamese civilians. Not actively
involved in this particular crime, his two murders notwithstanding, Wade
slides – literally and metaphorically – to the bottom of the ditch, where he
cannot move and cannot breathe, seized as he is by an unstoppable fit of the
giggles. "'I guess that's the right attitude. Laugh it off. Fuck the spirit
world'" (*LW*, 220), Thinbill reluctantly concedes in the closing words of
'The Nature of the Spirit', which, focusing on the immediate aftermath of
My Lai, is the companion piece of the much earlier 'The Nature of the Beast'.
With this laconic pronouncement, Thinbill seals off the failure of his tentative suggestion to Wade that they should team up and report the massacre to
the authorities. On his part, only from the ditch, as a 'dead' man, can Wade
commit a fraught and ambiguous moral act in the execution of Weatherby.

As we shall see in the next chapter, this scenario is typical of O'Brien's
topography of trauma, where underground traps and/or shelters repeatedly
provide the background for characters' confrontation with sudden horrors
and painful epiphanies. Of course, *In the Lake of the Woods* maps out the
harrowing geography of the war in another, more literal sense, with its courageous depiction of My Lai as the latest in a series of barbaric incidents
involving the American military forces. Left with no doubts about the
irredeemable cruelty of characters such as Calley and Weatherby, the reader
is nonetheless encouraged to ponder over the nature of evil and the causes of
violence: fear, ignorance, blind hatred, desire for revenge, lust for blood,
survival instincts, spiritual inertia and moral cowardice all play a part in the
slaughter and its aftermath. As Wade's personal body-count suggests,
however, Vietnam and its people have got very little to do with this madness.

Northern Lights, the other novel whose narrative and imaginative centre
lies in the protagonist's gruelling engagement with the American landscape,
also contains allusions to a connection between American Indians and the
Vietnam war. Admittedly, this association of ideas is much more veiled than
its counterpart, presented as 'Evidence', in *Lake*. As in *Lake*, though, the
pervasiveness of this image as a constant, prejudiced reminder of the
supposed inferiority of alien cultures is exposed as a naive (when not
malicious) self-deception. Milton Bates identifies the subtle details that,
paired with the presence of the veteran Harvey, make *Northern Lights* a
Vietnam war novel: Paul thinks of killing rats in the town dump as an

ambush; the unpredictable Addie, nicknamed 'Geronimo' by the old mayor, has black eyes interchangeably described as Indian or Asian; the narrative makes frequent references to the history of conflict between native populations and white settlers in the Arrowhead region, a tradition of hostility embraced even by Paul and Harvey in their youthful pranks. The clearest connection between Vietnam and the Indian country – and the most derogatory image of the Vietnamese, alongside their implicit identification with vermin – is provided by the implication that 'Pliney's Pond, septic with sewage and Indian feces, is the closest thing to a rice paddy in Sawmill Landing'.[23]

The insistence on America's uneasy past – references to the Arrowhead provide the symbolic framework of the novel – puts into perspective the indiscriminate coalescing and belittling of foreign cultures, but O'Brien's critique of these attitudes does not stop at their faithful representation against the wider background of the prehistory of the land. In fact, the disturbing connection of the Vietnamese with pests and the image of the pond are both presented in a bathetic light in scenes which ultimately ridicule the American claim to cultural and military superiority, as well as the notion of heroic masculinity. For a start, Paul lacks the nerve to rise to Harvey's tasteless challenge of killing a rat – not a bad thing, one might argue, given the gratuitous cruelty of the entire affair – when the two brothers, accompanied by Grace and Addie, resort to the popular local pastime of shining headlights into the trash in order to liven up their evening. The motif of the hunt is revisited later on in the narrative, when Paul faces a much more critical challenge, whose gravity, however, is undermined by its dismal, risible outcome. Lost in the woods, with Harvey knocked out by a fever, Paul leaves the shelter to search for food, only to kill what looks like a grotesque reincarnation of the target that he had previously missed: a woodchuck with 'eyes glittering in a way Perry had never seen before, except for the junkyard rat' (*NL*, 279). Paul's success is seriously undercut by the way in which the entire episode is recounted: he imagines himself setting off on a hunting expedition of epic proportions, when he will finally get to prove his mettle. Armed with his brother's knife and buoyed by a new-found feeling of bravery, Paul hopes to track down a deer, but ends up bashing a small rodent to death with a 'thick bough nearly twice his own height' (*NL*, 278). Harvey's open and jovial mockery of Paul's trophy voices the readers' feelings towards a very unheroic killing, one of the many factors to make the brothers' adventurous survival in the woods a dubious test of manliness.

Similarly, Paul's conquest of his revulsion for the stinking waters of Pliney's Pond hardly suggests mastery or even reconciliation with what this

23 Bates, 'Tim O'Brien's Myth of Courage', p. 269.

place represents, characterized as it is as a sort of primordial broth, teeming both with life and with decay ('Mosquito eggs, crayfish, larvae, slime and Junebugs, frogs and newt and snakes and toads and lizards, Indian shit and rot…', *NL*, 72). In the previous chapter we have already seen how the musty pond provides an apt setting for Paul's unconvincing rebirth as a man, firm and courageous in his convictions (and in shaking off the long shadow of his father's education) but also accepting and responsive to a feminine – and therefore ultimately more balanced – outlook on the world. If Paul's rebirth as a well-adjusted man is illusory, his surfacing from the pond as a martial figure is even more ludicrous: to the twenty-first-century reader, the image looks like an *ante litteram* comic reversal of the iconography of the hyper-masculine Vietnam veteran epitomized by John Rambo, emerging from the mud as an ironic male Venus, or rather a fully-formed Mars, muscles glinting in the tropical rain, deadly look in his eyes, ready for the kill. By the same token, the disturbing dual function of Pliney's Pond as a locus of procreation and elimination – its waters part amniotic fluid, part Indian sewage – must be read as a projection of Paul's fears, and a realistic representation of the psychology of this character, rather than as a reflection of misogynist and racist tendencies on O'Brien's part. The problematic allusions to the Vietnamese and to the Native Americans that find their way into the novel – primarily through Paul's perspective – are ultimately derided, just as the limitations of Paul's early foibles and of his later pretensions to renewal are clearly exposed, in spite of the fact that the narrative remains sympathetic to the plight of its protagonist. In the end, Paul's predicament is not at all uncommon. It is the staple of modern, and modernist, literature: a human being looking for his or her place in the large scheme of things and, in doing so, coming to terms with his or her own – and other people's – frailty.

A review of the references to the history of the American Indians in O'Brien's work would not be complete without a mention of the crucial resonance of the massacre of the Little Bighorn in the plot of *The Nuclear Age*, whose initial setting in Fort Derry, Montana, makes sure that the image of this tragedy underpins the entire narrative. The story of the battle is etched in the memory of the novel's protagonist, William Cowling, from a very early age, given his father's role as the doomed General in the commemoration of Custer's Last Stand that takes place in the town each year. Enjoying the typical fare of summer pageants – ice-cream, candyfloss, root beer and other fun-fair treats – the citizens of Fort Derry unite in their annual remembrance of their local celebrity, while William's father gets to die a hero's death, basking in the limelight until the very last scene (his is the final exit), his dignity, as Custer's, unharmed in spite of defeat. Cowling-as-Custer is not simply a figure from the nation's past facing 'the inescapable scripting of history' (*NA*, 11); the yearly re-enactment of the slaughter is reminiscent of a cathartic ritual, with the sacrifice of an innocent victim – often, as in the fertility rites studied by James George Frazer, the very god of vegetation or the sacred king – performed periodically in order to guarantee the community's renewal.

The representation of the Last Stand aims for symbolic resonance, rather than historical accuracy, as witnessed by the poetic licence taken in relation to well-documented details about Custer's demise. The General is shown riding a white stallion and brandishing a silver sword, conjuring up the image of the knight in shining armour, with a princely deportment and pure intentions; the sacrificial nature of Custer's death is emphasized when the indisputable hero of the performance is turned into a martyr and subjected to the most demeaning affront, as Crazy Horse (another convenient dramatic embellishment, since the great Indian warrior's whereabouts and his exact role in the battle remain unknown) 'gallop[s] away with [Cowling's] yellow wig' (*NA*, 11). In actual fact, Custer's horse, Vic, was a Kentucky sorrel, i.e. chestnut in colour, and – according to what is most likely to be only a legendary account of the story and yet remains the most popular version of the events – the General was not scalped, nor mutilated in any way, a sure sign of respect for the great white chief on his enemies' part. The creative liberties in the dramatization of the Last Stand are small but significant, for they elevate a controversially heroic historical figure to a mythical status with near-sacred implications: the spotless champion, whose death assumes particularly violent and humiliating connotations, becomes effectively a scapegoat. He dies so that the community may live, a momentous image in a novel whose protagonist-narrator is consumed by a fear of nuclear annihilation and obsessed by a desire for survival. In line with the symbolic magnitude of the event, William faces his father's ordeal with a mixture of terror and fascination: 'I worshipped that man. I wanted to warn him, rescue him, but I also wanted slaughter' (*NA*, 10–11).

Interestingly, William's feelings for his father, undoubtedly one of the most positive paternal figures in O'Brien's canon, are described at this stage as a case of hero-worship, with the provincial real estate agent transfigured into an idol worthy of adoration. This throws into relief Mr Cowling's status as 'a decent man', 'an ideal father', 'a regular guy' (*NA*, 28–29). He is a good parent, but all too human and ordinary, completely at a loss in connecting with his son's apocalyptic nightmares in a way that would immediately make sense to William, i.e. at an imaginative level, by maintaining, for example, William's illusion of safety in his make-shift shelter under the ping-pong table. Mr Cowling's failure of sympathy and imagination results in a reversal of roles in his relationship with William, as the son sees through his father's well-meaning ruses to divert him from his obsessive fears. The promise of a chemistry set and the challenge of a late-night game of ping-pong cause a mixture of embarrassment and anger in William, who eventually chooses to spare his father's feelings and humour his transparent, ineffective attempts to drive the nuclear terror away. This entire set-up is the exact opposite of the paternal dynamics outlined in *Northern Lights*: Cowling, unlike Pehr Perry, is not a hated, overbearing patriarch, a self-righteous authority who, having set the law, is always ready to pass judgement. On the contrary, if Pehr Perry is the gloomy prophet of the apocalypse, Cowling is the apocalypse denier. In this respect, he truly has one thing in common with General Custer – and this is where the meaning of the novel's reference to the Little Bighorn becomes most immediately evident.

As Steven Kaplan points out, the tragedy that triggered the final escalation of the hostilities between the US and the Native Americans is representative of a worrying pattern in American history: the country's reluctance to bow out in a timely fashion in the face of potential disaster, the negative legacy perhaps of the all-American virtue of self-reliance and of the belief in the nation's Manifest Destiny and invincibility.[24] Like the father coming 'from leaden ships of sea' in *If I Die*, or Big Bear imparting his wisdom to Little Bear at Indian Guides in *Cacciato*, Mr Cowling embodies the good, wholesome American man – principled, law-abiding, patriotic, his legacy more subtle but just as heavy as the crippling denigration poured on their children by the negative paternal figures portrayed in *Northern Lights* and *In the Lake of the Woods*. Whether supportive or critical towards their sons, the fathers in O'Brien's writing – who, as already intimated in Chapter 1, are never held directly responsible for their children's participation in the war – provide in shorthand a key to the development of their sons' lives. A sense of belonging, a connection to the national past, the obligations tied in with the entitlement to the American way of life, but also feelings of inadequacy, and the earliest and most hurtful betrayals constitute the cultural and emotional baggage that fathers pass on to their sons in O'Brien's novels. America, it seems, is a father-country, for good and for bad. Significantly, the male lineage is short-circuited on the two occasions when the narrator-protagonists become fathers themselves, in *The Nuclear Age* and *The Things They Carried*: here, the two narrators are on the receiving end of an intense questioning from their little girls, who act as projections of the main characters' frustrated desire for meaning and love, and signs of their post-traumatic inability to establish successful adult relationships.

Before moving on to the exploration of O'Brien's topography of trauma, it is worth making a final observation about the mythical geography of the United States in *The Nuclear Age* (and in O'Brien's work in general). In the

---

24 'Custer's refusal to retreat at the Little Bighorn suggests America's refusal to cry "uncle" in Vietnam and the inability of the inhabitants of the nuclear age to say they have had enough'; Kaplan, *Understanding Tim O'Brien*, p. 150.

early pages of the novel, just after the description of Custer Days, William reports his father's assessment of Fort Derry:

> 'Culture's that way,' my dad would say, pointing east, 'and if you want it, civiliza-
> tion's somewhere over that last ridgeline, more or less,' then he'd hook a thumb
> westward, as if hitchhiking. Isolated. Fifty-eight miles from Yellowstone, eighty
> miles from Helena, twenty miles from the nearest major highway. (*NA*, 11)

Thus, in no uncertain terms, O'Brien's darkest novel makes a familiar point: as the characters find themselves stranded, or indeed brought up since birth, in a no-man's-land, the relativity of the concepts of culture and civilization is once again brought to the foreground. This idea was already present in O'Brien's first book; the precariousness of civilization is brilliantly and poignantly captured in *If I Die* in the description of the soldiers' fear of getting lost while walking at night through Vietnam:

> The man to the front and the man to the rear were the only holds on security and
> sanity. We followed the man in front like a blind man after his dog, like Dante
> following Vergil through the Inferno, and we prayed that the man had not lost his
> way, that he hadn't lost contact with the man to his front. [...] The man to the
> front is civilization. He is the United States of America and every friend you have
> ever known; he is Erik and blonde girls and a mother and father. He is your life,
> and he is your altar and God combined. And, for the man stumbling behind you,
> you alone are his torch. (*IID*, 83)[25]

In Vietnam, civilization is nothing more than the man at the front, the symbol of all that is good and noble and familiar. And yet, as it transpires from O'Brien's later works, the fragility of this link with our cultural and existential certainties accompanies us wherever we are. In O'Brien's narrative universe, the American frontier is less the place to test and consolidate a strong sense of identity than a space of insecurity and self-questioning, where substances and appearances blend, while characters are left on their own to work out the moral implications of their interpretation of reality and of their actions. By the same token, whether at home, or in Vietnam, the threatening landscape of the 'Indian Country' is exposed as the projection of deep-rooted, subjective fears, a place haunted by imported ghosts. In the end, civilization, rationality and culture are always somewhere else, even in America.

25 Erik is the like-minded trainee whom the protagonist of *If I Die* makes friends with at Fort
Lewis. The two are united by a common belief that the American intervention in Vietnam
is without just reason. Unlike O'Brien, who gambles on the belief that he is too good to
become a grunt, Erik chooses at the beginning of basic training to enlist for three years, thus
securing his escape from infantry duty.

4

Trauma, Gender and the Poetics of Uncertainty

Michael Herr's *Dispatches* opens with a marvel: an old map of Vietnam. Stretching between the 26th and the 9th parallel, the country unfolds like a long, thin 'S', swelling up in the Red River delta in the North and the Mekong River delta in the South, the 'two rice bowls at the opposite ends of a carrying pole'.[1] Interestingly, Herr offers a description of the map, but not of what it represents; the poster on the wall – the work of French cartographers – has clearly seen better days. Worn out by the heat and the humidity of the local climate, and made obsolete by the passage of time, it has ceased to provide correct geopolitical coordinates. The anachronism of the old colonial names for the protectorates and territories of French Indochina is part of the incantation of this vision: names such as Tonkin, Annam and Cochin China must have had by the late sixties a mythical, exotic ring, especially when juxtaposed, as on Herr's map, with fabulous places such as the kingdom of Siam. Yet, with the exclusion of the misguided help of this old-fashioned nomenclature, readers are left to their own devices in order to picture the serpentine drawing that appears to have bewitched the narrator. Like Herr's outdated map, this 'blank' image of Vietnam gains in evocative power in proportion to its lack of referential accuracy: map and country, signifier and signified are so much more fascinating as they are respectively inadequate mimetic tool and mysterious object of contemplation, empty signs holding the promise of a host of interpretative possibilities.[2]

Although part of a self-conscious, cynical and often self-deprecating narrative, Herr's partial mapping perpetuates orientalist prejudices about the Far East: for Herr in 1967, reading the shifting image of Vietnam, constantly reshaped by the escalating war 'was like trying to read the faces of the Vietnamese, and that was like reading the wind'.[3] Herr's statement immedi-

1 Larry H. Addington, *America's War in Vietnam: A Short Narrative History* (Bloomington and Indianapolis: Indiana University Press, 2000), p. 1.
2 This brings to mind the enigmatic 'immense snake uncoiled' that opens *Heart of Darkness* where, beckoning from the depths of Africa, the river Congo casts its spell on Marlow and his audience: 'The snake had charmed me' (p. 22). On this issue, see also the opening sections of Chapter 1, above, and Chapter 5, below.
3 Herr, *Dispatches*, p. 11.

ately questions the very possibility of mimetic representation and mutual understanding between different cultures, but it also lends itself to the charge of having stylized and romanticized – or worse, reduced to the status of brute, natural force – the object of one's observations. If not quite the 'blank space of delightful mystery' reminiscent of Marlow's boyish fantasy of exploration in *Heart of Darkness* (22), Herr's Vietnam, much like its people, is virtually invisible, not merely concealed by the old colonial boundaries, but effectively erased by the ongoing military conflict: 'We also knew that for years now there had been no country here but the war' (11). The opening image of *Dispatches* flags up a number of problematic issues that inform critical reflections on the Vietnam war, as well as textual representations of the Vietnamese landscape: while the realization of the impossibility of total and accurate mapping ties in with the modernist and postmodern reaction to the mimetic illusions of formal realism, and can be seen as part of the twentieth-century disenfranchisement from grand narratives, in tune with a poststructuralist take on language, Herr's orientalist perception of the Vietnamese and his coalescence of the conflict with the land it ravaged are emblematic of recurrent issues specific to the ways in which the Vietnam war has been narrativized in the United States.[4] We have already seen that O'Brien explores and deconstructs the *a priori* of mythical reductions and/or aggrandizements of his own country: his allusions to the symbolic geography of the United States – the harshness of the northern wilderness, the bloody violence of the Far West – are evidence of his critical attitude towards the foundational national narrative of the frontier, while his descriptions of the American landscape are closely intertwined with the psychological mapping of his characters, in the awareness of the human tendency to project (collective or individual) emotions onto the environment.

In a similar deconstructive spirit, O'Brien's representation of Vietnam is successful, for the most part, in eschewing and/or exposing the racist and misogynist stereotypes of much literature on the war. Together with the revision of traditional American locations, O'Brien's attempt to capture the soldiers' ambivalence towards the Vietnamese territory and its inhabitants is

---

4 In fairness, in *Dispatches* Herr does not claim an impartiality and completeness of vision. If anything, he does the opposite, with his focus on the American experience of the war, which explains (without justifying it) the flattening of Vietnam onto Western preconceptions and stereotypes: the ethnic and political diversity within Vietnam and the opacity of the overall picture of this 'alien' culture are as much a matter of Western perception and representation as the products of the history and geography of the place. After all, the paradox of the 'screening' nature of language itself, let alone cultural differences (cf. the ambivalence of the screen as a canvas on which images can be projected, but also as a partition that obscures things from view) is already present in Herr's title, the call to an obvious attempt at communication, always already doomed to misfire and do away with ('dispatch') final meaning.

subsumed within a vast figurative landscape – made up of holes and ditches, orifices and wounds – that recurs throughout his writing. O'Brien's penchant for this imagery has often been at the centre of heated critical discussions, because it can be read too easily as yet another gendered, misogynist construction, as in the case of the obscene shit field that claims the life of one of the soldiers in *The Things They Carried*. The charting of O'Brien's symbolic topography of trauma, as well as of his portrayal of the relationships between male and female characters, offers a fruitful entry point in outlining his non-gendered politics of reception, and in dealing with the question of the (im)possibility of representing the unspeakable and understanding the incomprehensible. I shall argue that it is in the light of this impasse in communication – thematized so obsessively in *Things* – that the holes in O'Brien's narratives find their most meaningful explanation.

A matter of holes and ditches

The feminization of the land is a common trope in Western narratives of exploration and conquest of faraway or even hostile territories, whose posses-sion is often configured as a game of (more or less forceful) seduction.[5] The American intervention in Vietnam is no exception, as several critics (Susan Jeffords perhaps most famously) have pointed out. In the chapter on gender conflicts in *The Wars We Took to Vietnam* (1996), Milton Bates quickly reminds us of the persistent sexualization of combat in various well-known, and all-but naive, narratives about the war: from Philip Caputo's literary memoir *A Rumor of War* (1977), in which the rush felt in leading a surprise attack is described as akin to 'the ache of orgasm',[6] to Michael Herr's ever-quoted *Dispatches*, in which the mood of dread and exhilaration during a firefight is compared to the experience of undressing a girl for the first time (112). As Bates remarks, this imagery is completely in line with more author-itative and public discourses about the war, such as the American 'eroticized foreign policy [of the time]. President Johnson notoriously compared escala-tion of the war to the seduction of a woman: it had to be sufficiently gradual that China would not slap him in the face'.[7] When it comes to the represen-tation of the soldiers' relationship with the Vietnamese territory, particularly in mass-market productions, such as cinematic franchises like *Rambo* or *Missing in Action* or the pulp combat novels which constitute the vast majority

---

5   Richard Slotkin and Annette Kolodny have traced this sexual motif in the utilitarian and imaginative literature of the frontier, showing how male settlers tended to regard the landscape as female. On this issue, see Bates, *The Wars We Took to Vietnam*, p. 46.

6   Caputo, *A Rumor of War*, p. 268.

7   From *Pentagon Papers*, vol. 3, quoted in Bates, *The Wars We Took to Vietnam*, p. 143.

of the narrative production on the war,[8] the feminization and sexualization of the land, and of the enemy, assume much more sinister and violent undertones.[9]

As already mentioned, the Southeast Asian peninsula, conceived in the American imaginary prior to the war as a fertile, luxuriant and exotic continuation of the western frontier, disappointed the expectation that the GIs would be welcomed as liberators of a troubled, developing country trying to assert its independence from evil and unwanted foreign influences – a scenario which in itself suggests a stereotypical gender opposition, with Vietnam playing damsel in distress to Uncle Sam's 'cavalry'. In fact, anybody envisaging the American intervention in Vietnam in terms of a rescue mission, not to mention an act of seduction, would have to come to terms with the lie of the old colonial cliché that sees the (often virginal) foreign land as being there for the taking, passive and scantily defended, if not positively ready to be plucked. The truth is that, if one were to continue with the sexual metaphor (and the hyper-masculine army mentality would certainly encourage us to do so), the Vietnamese territory could not be taken by conventional military means, i.e. a slow advance across regular battle-lines, a steady conquest of previously forbidden positions. Rape, rather than seduction, appears to provide a better figurative equivalent to the often indiscriminate fire-bombing of the jungle, the systematic deforestation of the land and the destruction of entire villages carried out by the American armed forces in response to the enemy combat strategy. In the context of guerrilla warfare, with the triple-canopied, thick vegetation constantly in the way of the foot soldiers' advance, while providing a perfect hiding place for the native adversary, the soil itself harbours all sorts of dangers: trails concealing

---

8   As Stefano Rosso has repeatedly pointed out, Vietnam war writing (particularly in the sub-genre of the combat novel) is characterized by a predominance of 'stylistically coarse, monologic, ideologically naive, if not outright reactionary' texts (*Musi gialli e Berretti verdi*, p. 34, my translation). There is an entire current of 'trash literature' in which the Vietnamese setting is only a pretext, an appropriate enough background for near-pornographic stories revolving around a mixture of sex and violence. Titles such as *No Virgins in Cham Ky*, *Vietcong Rape Raiders*, *Abused Vietnamese Virgins* – mentioned in Rosso, 'La mascolinità problematica nella narrativa di guerra di Tim O'Brien', p. 493 – sadly speak for themselves.

9   Some of these accounts are so exaggerated and grotesque that they would be comic, if they were not also unbelievably disturbing. Just to give a relatively tame example, *Welcome to Vietnam, Macho Man: Reflections of a Khe San Vet* (1987), Ernest Spencer's fictionalized memoir, whose title immediately betrays a gung-ho mentality, contains a section on 'Lady 881 South', the hill manned by the author's platoon: 'A mountaintop bastion ringed like a lady's neck with fine strands of diamonds – barbed wire wet from the morning mist reflecting the sun like sparking jewels. [...] Charlie did not give her up easily. And now I hold her for us. And we don't just hold her, we flaunt her. We cut down all the trees around the top and clear the brush for better vision and fields of fire. And do we ever wire the bitch' (New York: Bantam, 1991), p. 68.

underground traps (holes filled with spikes, on which the enemy would become impaled), mines and, of course, the extensive system of VC tunnels. The impenetrability of the land would therefore be construed as hostility, rather than coyness; similarly, the idea of the unfamiliar, mysterious quality of the territory would give way to an impression of treacherousness, creating the image of a monstrous femininity, intent on destroying the soldier. In short, the Vietnamese landscape has often come to be represented, in American narratives of the war, as a *vagina dentata*, a symbol that finds its realistic (!) correspondent in the widespread rumour amongst American GIs that Vietnamese women would hide razor-blades or glass in their vaginas and entice soldiers to have sex with them, so as to emasculate them or bleed them to death.[10]

The shocking awareness that danger lurks in unsuspected places thus ensures that GIs have, at best, an ambivalent relationship with their environment, and especially with the ground they tread on; the perception of Vietnam as a conflict whose unprecedented violence will strike out of the blue, even in the absence of the actual enemy, unpredictably triggered by as simple an act as walking, is presented as a source of constant anxiety for the infantrymen:

> We *were* making history: the first American soldiers to fight an enemy whose principal weapons were the mine and the booby trap. That kind of warfare has its peculiar terrors. It turns an infantryman's world upside down. The foot soldier has a special feeling for the ground. He walks on it, fights on it, sleeps and eats on it; the ground shelters him under fire; he digs his home in it. But mines and booby traps transform that friendly, familiar earth into a thing of menace, a thing to be feared as much as machine guns or mortar shells. The infantryman knows that any moment the ground he is walking on can erupt and kill him; kill him if he's lucky. If he's unlucky, he will be turned into a blind, deaf, *emasculated*, legless shell. It was not warfare. It was murder.[11]

While acknowledging the foot soldier's 'special feeling for the ground', and the role of weaponry in the metamorphosis of the land from an almost sentient being ('friendly, familiar') to a dangerous, impersonal entity ('a thing of menace, a thing to be feared'), Caputo's explanatory passage does highlight the terrible power of the Vietnamese earth to annihilate the humanity – and, more significantly, the manhood – of its victims. O'Brien too records the often ambivalent feelings experienced by the American soldiers in the relationship with their foreign surroundings, but he does so without objecti-

10 See Bates, *The Wars We Took to Vietnam*, p. 143.
11 Caputo, *A Rumor of War*, p. 288, my italics.

fying Vietnam or reducing it to a giant, monolithic, symbolic landscape, founded on the misogynist imagery of the gaping vaginal opening, and of a preying and deathly female sexuality. Particularly in his early books, O'Brien, like Caputo, reminds his readers of the particular bond between the grunt and the land, a provider of safety, comfort and strength, as well as a source of anxiety and a place of unexpected dangers.[12]

If I Die in a Combat Zone, for example, ends with the vignette of the protagonist's flight back home, a sketch in which the manufactured sterility and perfection of the environment on board the aircraft – presided over by 'blonde, blue-eyed, long-legged, medium-to-huge-breasted' stewardesses, America's thank-you for its loyal veterans – conveys an impression of distance and unfamiliarity, poignantly contrasted to the foot soldier's feelings for the receding ground:

> It's earth you want to say good-bye to. The soldiers never knew you. You never knew the Vietnamese people. But the earth, you could turn a spadeful of it, see its dryness and the tint of red, and dig out enough to lie in the hole at night, and that much of Vietnam you would know. Certain whole pieces of the land you would know, something like a farmer knows his own earth and his neighbour's. You know where the bad, dangerous parts are, and the sandy and safe places by the sea. You know where the mines are and will be for a century, until the earth swallows and disarms them. Whole patches of land. Around My Khe and My Lai. Like a friend's face. (*IID*, 201–202)

What begins like a contained declaration of intimacy, defined by immediate proximity with a diminutive, hospitable portion of the soil and set against a profound ignorance of fellow human beings (whether allies or foes), gradually becomes a more expansive commemoration of the Vietnamese earth: imagined as a source of livelihood, recognized, for the present, as a sometimes dangerous place, the land is also seen, within a larger time-frame, as a self-healing and protective entity, to be finally identified with specific locations, called by name and perceived as a friend. (The mention of My Lai seems particularly significant in this context.) One of the final passages of O'Brien's memoir, this nuanced and unapologetically subjective image of the Vietnamese landscape eschews any symbolic reductions with its repeated focus on the very small and on unheroic comparisons: the soldier's familiarity with the soil is akin to the farmer's; the land looks like a friend's *face*. This latter detail reveals a deliberate care to personify Vietnam in such a way as to confer on it a genderless humanity. It ought to be noted too how O'Brien here

---

12 By the mid- to late 1970s, several novels and memoirs about the war had been published to critical acclaim and success with the public: O'Brien's early writing is thus underpinned by a stronger documentary desire than his later works.

reverses the respective emphasis placed on the two paradoxical elements that inform the GIs' (experiential and imaginary) perception of the territory: it is the memory of his close physical contact, sublimated into an emotive affinity, with the ground that will remain the veteran's most abiding memory of his encounter with the Vietnamese.

O'Brien's meditation on the earth in *If I Die* is repeated, with striking similarities, in 'How the Land Was', a relatively short chapter from *Going After Cacciato*, where the image of the hunter at home in his favourite forest is briefly – and unsurprisingly, given the theme and the mythical context of the novel – associated with the more appropriate, local figure of the farmer, well acquainted with his acreage. In this expanded description of the land, the farming reference is developed as Berlin muses about the rural economy of Vietnam, whose people are connected to the land in a more essential way than the inhabitants of industrialized countries. The paddies, of course, are the most distinctive feature of the cultivated soil. They give the land a depth that Berlin has never known before; to Berlin's mind, the contrast with the smoothness and wholesomeness of the corn crops in the American Plains is not unpleasant: 'there was nothing loathsome about the smell of the paddies. The smell was alive: bacteria, fungus and algae, compounds that made and sustained life. It was not a pretty smell, but it was no more evil or rank than the smell of sweat' (*GAC*, 239). The reminder of the Vietnamese reliance on the land in time of peace, voiced by the most average and sympathetic protagonist-soldier in O'Brien's oeuvre, demystifies the representation of the enemy country as a malignant feminine entity that is common to much literature about the war. This particular description of the paddies, incidentally, is also vaguely reminiscent of Pliney's Pond in *Northern Lights*; this latter location, however, differs from the Vietnamese landscape in one crucial aspect: its clear symbolic role in the economy of O'Brien's first novel finds no counterpart in the geography of the war in the realistic strand of *Cacciato*. Berlin's attitude towards various Vietnamese environments is grounded in his experience of combat and not in a misogynist personification of the land which, even in the imaginary journey towards Paris, is never reduced to a hostile feminine place. Thus *Xa*, referred to as a neuter noun, is described as a maze full of sewage and mud, bringing to mind the anatomy of the organs of elimination, rather than of the female reproductive system.

On the observation post, Berlin is comforted by the presence of the sea: the water protects his back and offers the impression of remoteness from the war and 'a feeling of connection to distant lands [...] to Samoa, maybe, or to some hidden isle in the South Pacific, or to Hawaii, or maybe all the way home' (*GAC*, 52–53). Berlin experiences a similar sense of security sitting with his back to the Song Tra Bong, 'deep in his hole, glad to have water behind him' (*GAC*, 109). In the dark, the river, like the sea, is connected in Berlin's mind to memories of home, of his father's ability to distinguish the sounds of the streaming current from those made by the moving grass and the trees out in the countryside. These relations of contiguity – the sea connecting Asia to the American West Coast or the Song Tra Bong standing in for a more familiar river (see Berlin's fond recollection of the Des Moines River on p. 53) – are by no means the only reason why Berlin feels so safe in proximity to water that he rules it out from the catalogue of places where he can imagine finding his own death: 'In the thick forest, maybe, or on the slope of a mountain, or in one of the paddies. But not beside a river' (*GAC*, 109). Berlin's conviction is less idiosyncratic and fanciful than it appears at first glance, for his assessment of the dangerousness of the Vietnamese geography is based on facts, and not on the symbolic resonance of any particular location. Piecing together the jumbled account of the casualties of Third Squad, First Platoon, Alpha Company reveals that Berlin is afraid of those places where his comrades have been killed: Billy Boy is the first victim, with his memorable and grotesque death by fear, unable to cope with the shock of having lost a foot in stepping onto a mine (*GAC*, 208–10); Frenchie Tucker and then Bernie Lynn are killed in a tunnel (*GAC*, 69–73); Rudy Chassler is also killed by a mine, in an accident which breaks a long lull of uneventful days, shortly after the platoon have waded through a river (*GAC*, 110); Ready Mix dies on a charge towards the mountains (*GAC*, 199), in World's Greatest Lake Country, an area filled by the American bombs with craters; Lieutenant Martin is fragged – a death never actually described in the book, but planned, and presumably executed, in Lake Country; Buff dies by a ditch (*GAC*, 263) and Pederson in a paddy, gunned down by friendly fire (*GAC*, 128-30).

The list of fatalities is accompanied by a less immediately obvious catalogue, a taxonomy of holes in the shape of gashes, wounds and hollows. In the realistic strand of the narrative, the holes are signs of explosions, tears in the flesh and in the land, harbingers or traces of death: from the bullet holes in the hull of the Chinook, whose gunners mistakenly shoot Pederson in response to the enemy fire, to the bowl-shaped craters, lifeless lakes full of rainwater, which have taken the place of the luxurious forest on the scorched earth (*GAC*, 223). These images of indiscriminate, and often disproportionate, violence are perhaps best epitomized by the expression 'fire in the hole', which indicates an explosive deliberately detonated in a suspected enemy hideaway (not necessarily before the place has been searched), bringing to mind, of course, the quarrel about Standard Operating Procedures, the killing of Frenchie Tucker and Bernie Lynn in the tunnel, and the subsequent collective execution of Sidney Martin. In the novel, however, O'Brien uses the same expression as a title for the chapter about the aftermath of Pederson's death, when the surviving soldiers – drenched in paddy slime and caked in soft and greasy muck, like the dead man – call for white phosphorous in retaliation for the attack that has indirectly caused the demise of their comrade: even as the rounds keep hitting the ground, Third Squad line up and shoot into the burning village until it is reduced to a hole (*GAC*, 81).

In *Cacciato*, the recurrent association of holes with death is completely factual, devoid of intimations of monstrous femininity; rather, if anything, it is connected with images of muck and messiness (again, this would seem to allude to the excretive system instead of the female genitalia), as well as, possibly, with indirect references to an unspoken guilt, given the nature of the particular traumas present in the story: Pederson's manslaughter, the annihilation of the village, the plot against the lieutenant, the soldiers' reluctance to compose Buff's disfigured body, and more generally the relief experienced with each casualty, since somebody else's death is irrationally perceived to make one's own survival more likely. While there is no denying that holes provide a recurrent central – and inevitably very suggestive – element in many of O'Brien's novels, the proliferation of such images can often be easily explained by the topography of the battle ground. After all, the same was true of the paradigm modern conflict, as Siegfried Sassoon pointed out: 'When all is said and done, the war was mainly a matter of holes and ditches'.[13] This matter-of-fact summation of the Great War reads like a cautionary statement for the critic too keen to unearth the deep meaning of O'Brien's own dugouts and ditches: traps and shelters, hence often charged with diametrically opposite connotations, the holes in the Vietnamese landscape are reminiscent of the trenches, which were simultaneously places of safety and of hazardous confusion. The latter feeling, which is perhaps less immediately associated with the idea of trench warfare, where in the first instance it is no-man's-land – and not the dugout – that is synonymous with mortal danger, is clearly expressed by Fussell in his mapping of World War I: 'To be in the trenches was to experience an unreal, unforgettable enclosure and constraint, as well as a sense of being unoriented and lost. One saw two things only: the walls of an unlocalized, undifferentiated earth and the sky above. [...] It was the sight of the sky, almost alone, that had the power to persuade a man that he was not already lost in a common grave' (51). The disturbing idea of finding safety in an open grave is also intimated by the image of Berlin asleep in his foxhole, his mind entertaining both reassuring and oppressive visions: 'At night he slept in the holes, his back against the cold earth, dreaming of basketball and moles and tombs of moist air' (*GAC*, 107).

The underground dimension – obscure, clammy and claustrophobic – is a natural *memento mori* for Berlin and his fellow soldiers, even as it provides

13 Quoted in Fussell, *The Great War and Modern Memory*, p. 41.

shelter and an opportunity to muse on one's condition and to try to perceive reality from a different angle: at an imaginative level, this is what Berlin and the others experience in Li Van Hgoc's tunnel, where it is made clear that their feelings of confusion and entrapment are also the lot of their 'unfathomable' enemy. Besides, the labyrinthine underground, as anticipated in Chapter 2, is associated with decay in the form of sludge and excrement, not an unexpected idea when one thinks of how easily expendable human life is – and how horribly mangled and reduced to nothing bodies can be – in modern mass warfare. Like other Vietnam war writers, O'Brien reminds us that one of the many euphemisms adopted by the soldiers to talk about death exploits this very association of ideas between mortality, expendability and lowliness, while also carrying connotations of injudicious use and dissipation of resources: people are not 'killed'; they are 'wasted'.[14] Interestingly, a similar term is quoted by Fussell in his gloss to Sassoon's bathetic remark about the Great War: Fussell reminds us that, if it is true that the war was mainly a matter of holes and ditches, it is also true that 'in these holes and ditches extending for ninety miles, continually, even at the quietest times, some 7000 British men and officers were killed and wounded daily, just as a matter of course. "Wastage," the Staff called it' (41). Even if it were unconnected with ideas of precarious safety and impending death within the context of war, the underground would naturally summon the image of a miserable and debased existence: in trench and guerrilla warfare, for the most part, the soldier's lot is at best a grotesque and unheroic assimilation into the land, which for the unlucky ones becomes a tragically final condition.

This impression of abjection is further intensified in the epigraph of *The Nuclear Age* which aptly sets the scene for the apocalyptic theme of the novel and foreshadows the uncompromising, doom-like tone of the first-person narrative of its protagonist, William Cowling – even as the apocryphal origin of the biblical quotation is perhaps a first intimation to the reader that Cowling is a minor and eccentric sort of prophet. The epigraph indeed opens with a description of destruction on a global scale: 'And the dead shall be thrown like dung' (Second Book of Esdras, 16:23), a scriptural passage which makes explicit the scatological connotations of death in its reference to the deceased as the lowest form of excreta, while the few survivors remain 'hidden in the thick woods or in holes in the rocks' (16:29). O'Brien's suggestive symbolic topography is exploited to the full in his first foray into the realm of (black) comedy, a generic subscription immediately announced, as I have just mentioned, in the ironic gap between the portentous prophecy of the epigraph and the switch to an odd first-person narrator, a prophet-with-a-poster denouncing the dangers of the nuclear age. The journey

14 See, for example, *GAC*, 15 or *TTC*, 231. See also Caputo, *A Rumor of War*, p. 220.

underground, culminating in the most precarious of ascents, is thus the central trope of a comedic narrative whose dominant image of the hole – in the guise of a 'home-made' nuclear shelter – provides the catalyst for the strand of the plot set in the present time, as well as the obvious location for the nightmarish denouement of the story.

The novel itself begins as William Cowling digs the first spadefuls of earth in his garden, in the middle of the night, in order to build this refuge: his action is the impromptu, compelling actualization of a life-long obsession with safety, triggered in its turn by a pathological fear of a nuclear war. O'Brien's faithful readers will immediately notice how this motif is an expansion, in much darker tones, of a detail in the plot of *Northern Lights*, where Pehr Perry nurtured similar apprehensions about the end of the world being near. What these two post-Vietnam novels really share, though, is the rather unsubtle quality of their symbolism, which, while imputable to inexperience in the earlier text, is deliberately cultivated in *The Nuclear Age* for its caricatural effects. The shelter in *Northern Lights* epitomised Pehr Perry's gloomy, merciless religious beliefs as well as his despotic grip on his children. In *The Nuclear Age* too O'Brien explores the sinister side of a fanatical quest for security, emphasizing the clash in the contradictory notions associated with Cowling's several underground retreats: his hideaways provide safety and the illusion of safety (as a child, he finds comfort under his ping-pong table, modified to 'withstand' nuclear radiations with its coating of lead pencils) or a different kind of threat (a draft dodger, he gets embroiled with a violent terrorist group, undergoing a strenuous paramilitary training conducted by two Vietnam war veterans). The hole represents a desire for survival, but also a withdrawal from life; it is a sign of sanity, as a logical precaution in the face of one's fears, and the proof of lunacy, given the obsessiveness of Cowling's plan. Engineered to protect his nearest and dearest, the shelter alienates Cowling from his wife and daughter, becoming by the end of the novel a prison and a potential family grave. The land itself bestows on Cowling immense riches, but also a legacy of guilt when he discovers and decides to exploit a vein of uranium ore, a compromising source of wealth because inextricably linked in his mind with 'the Bomb', under whose terrifying shadow he has lived all his life.

Fear of nuclear annihilation is the dominant emotion in Cowling's existence, but *The Nuclear Age* is interesting primarily for the way in which it weaves this topic into the figurative geography of the narrative and into the protagonist's relationship with his women and their attitude to reality and to language. Already as a young boy, William understands his predicament as a no-win situation: one can either be an eccentric loner, a 'screwball' devoted to unpopular fixations – 'like that ex-buddy of mine, a chemistry set bozo, testing nails for their iron content' (*NA*, 29) – or one can be a 'regular guy'

(*NA*, 29), like Cowling's father, a well-adjusted human being, decent, accepted and sane, but also perhaps lacking in the single-mindedness necessary to identify and forestall danger. For love of his concerned parents, William tries to keep his eccentric tendencies under wraps, going through the motions of a regular adolescence and developing something of a double life, for he feels for the trappings of high school – a microcosm of society at large – the same hostility and the same sense of superiority felt by the Tim O'Brien of *If I Die* towards the macho military ethos: 'I was above it all. A little arrogant, a little belligerent. I despised the whole corrupt high-school system: the phys-ed teachers, the jocks, the endless pranks and gossip, the teasing, the tight little self-serving cliques' (*NA*, 35). As in the case of the O'Brien of *If I Die* and *Things*, the protagonist's pondering over his options in the face of conscription is later configured as a solitary, paralysing, excruciating process, an impossible dilemma that gets resolved only by default: 'I did not want to die, and my father understood that. It wasn't cowardice, exactly, and he understood that, too, and it wasn't courage. It wasn't politics. Not even the war itself, not the coffins or justice or a citizen's obligation to his state. It was gravity. Something physical, that force that keeps pressing toward the end' (*NA*, 140). Thus, the novel resorts to the familiar image of the stand-off, the 'sleepwalking' (*NA*, 119), the succumbing to the laws of physics and, while ostensibly framing the protagonist's dilemma within a different moral context from the one surrounding the definition of courage, in fact it reiterates, if only by negation, the thesis put forth by O'Brien in *If I Die* and 'On the Rainy River': William can dodge the draft call because he is already a social pariah, and because he has nothing to lose and everything to gain by taking a stand that consolidates his relationship with Sarah Strouch, the burgeoning political activist with whom he has fallen in love. The novel skirts over the issue of courage and cowardice, but effectively rephrases that dichotomy in terms of sanity and madness, notions which – besides their socially sanctioned meaning – are seen by William to stand for the individual's logical adherence to his beliefs: it is in this sense that O'Brien can claim that William is the only hero that he has written.[15] (Still, as I argue in Chapter 4, the presence of Sarah Strouch plays a decisive role in strengthening William's resolve and securing the success of his disappearance underground.) In fact, even William's brave choice must eventually reckon with the lure of (re)integration within society, and, in the long run, it succumbs to the unbearable burden of embarrassment and the pressure to conform, just as the same pressure brings about the 'cowardly' decision to go to war on the part of the protagonist-narrator in *If I Die* and *Things*.

Incapable of seeing himself as anything other than an 'oddball', and

15 Naparsteck, 'An Interview with Tim O'Brien', p. 5.

retaining his (by now half-hearted) rejection of a regular 'above-ground' existence, William nonetheless tries to adapt to the other readily available lifestyle: the quiet, settled family man, rooted in the land. Having initially made the choice that O'Brien could not summon the courage to make, Cowling at last confesses that he has had enough of his self-imposed exile: 'It sounds trite but I longed for America. Out on the fringe, alone, there wasn't a day when I didn't feel a sense of embarrassment nudging up on shame. Unhinged and without franchise, prone to the odd daydreams, I had trouble sleeping' (*NA*, 210). A cooling period of solitary home life in a cottage near Fort Derry and discreet visits to his family are followed, five years later in 1976, by the official request for pardon as a draft-dodger and by the enrolment as a graduate student in geology in 1977. As William readily admits, the latter experience provides an apt (and legal) counterpart to his previous 'subterranean' work as a courier for the terrorist organization that Sarah had got him involved with: 'for the next two years I went underground in a completely different way' (*NA*, 262). Already as a child and, later on, as a university student, William had found in geology a refuge from the volatility of global circumstances: '*Terra firma*, I'd think. Back to the elements. A hard thing to explain, but for me geology represented a model for how the world could be, and should be. Rock – the word itself was solid. Calm and stable, crystal locked to crystal, there was a hard, enduring dignity in even the most modest piece of granite. Rocks lasted. Rocks could be trusted' (*NA*, 68). This time the return to geology is a means of achieving material security and social respectability, besides intellectual comfort: through the exploitation of a vein of uranium ore in the Sweetheart Mountains, William becomes a millionaire and can thus successfully pursue Bobbi, a woman he had rather whimsically fallen for ten years before. The financial and emotional stability promised by this turn of events, however, do not mark the end of the protagonist's private anxieties; in fact, they are accompanied by a resurgence of William's obsessive fears of a nuclear holocaust, now further exacerbated by his sense of guilt at having made his position in life through the sale of the basic component of atomic bombs. With the retrospective account of these plot developments, the novel finally catches up with the narrative present, which sees William busy digging a nuclear shelter in the garden of the house he shares with his wife, Bobbi, and their daughter Melinda. In the final chapter of the novel, William's psychological meltdown threatens to lead to tragedy, when he drugs and transports Bobbi and Melinda into the makeshift shelter, and sets out to blow the entire thing up. This is the culmination of a hallucinatory frenzy, in which the hole/shelter teases William with the lures of annihilation, such as the promise of wholeness, lack of separation, the disappearance of contradictions, absolute correspondence:

Light the fuse! What's to lose? Like a time capsule, except we dispense with time. It's absolute! Nothing dies, everything rhymes. Every syllable. The cat's meow and the dog's yip-yip – a perfect rhyme. Never rhymes with always, rich rhymes with poor, madness rhymes with gladness and sadness and badness ... I could go on forever. I do, in fact. (NA, 299, italics in original)

This realm of perfect rhymes presided over by the rule of similarity, where everything is like everything else, is a world of pure metaphor; as I shall discuss in more detail in the final section of this chapter, O'Brien is deeply sceptical of the totalizing power of metaphorical language, while recognizing – as in the conclusion of *The Nuclear Age* – its strong allure as the privileged medium for all-encompassing explanations and consolatory grand narratives. William is finally rescued from this deadly appeal by the incursion of the sheer materiality of existence, when twelve-year-old Melinda stands up to him, demanding that he should abandon any thoughts of death and any fears for the future in order to concentrate on the present moment. As elsewhere in O'Brien's work, the hole in *The Nuclear Age* represents a locus for trauma: it is physically the location where traumatic events occur and it is a symbol for the traumatization of certain characters. In his novels, O'Brien unearths these holes without filling them up. They remain the sites of irreconcilable paradoxes and unspeakable experiences.

Another such hole is the one at the centre of O'Brien's most famous – and most written about – work: the shit field which engulfs and kills Kiowa, one of the main characters in *The Things They Carried*. More than the death of Curt Lemon or of the one enemy soldier killed by the narrator, two other harrowing events to be told several times in the course of the novel, Kiowa's drowning in the overflowing village latrine along the banks of the Song Tra Bong is the pivotal trauma in *Things*. The centrality of this episode to the economy of the entire narrative derives from the overwhelming horror of the events: Kiowa's slow sinking is witnessed at close quarters by one of his fellow soldiers who, overpowered by an insurmountable physical revulsion, abandons his rescue attempt. The image of Kiowa being sucked into the shit field is made even less susceptible to a faithful representation by O'Brien's deliberate reluctance to provide an unambiguous and trustworthy version of the story. The episode is revisited in three sequential chapters offering different versions of Kiowa's death: 'Speaking of Courage', 'Notes' and 'In the Field'. 'Speaking of Courage' follows Norman Bowker in his endless driving around the lake in his home town. A veteran alone with his own thoughts and memories on the Fourth of July, Bowker is obsessively musing over how to talk about his failure to save Kiowa and thus win a Silver Star for bravery. This poignant experience recalls another dramatic event, and its similarly guilt-ridden aftermath, from the pages of *Going After Cacciato* where, in Chapter 12, one of the 'Observation Post' sections, Paul Berlin also thinks about 'the time he almost won the Silver Star for Valor' (*GAC*, 82), crawling into a tunnel to retrieve the body of Frenchie Tucker. Instead, on that occasion, it had been Bernie Lynn who had gone into the tunnel, and died for his act of valour.[16]

'Notes', a brief metanarrative sketch, reveals how an earlier draft of 'Speaking of Courage' had been written for *Going After Cacciato*, but would not fit within the temporal flow of that novel because of its clear setting in the aftermath of the war. In 'Notes', O'Brien proceeds to reflect on the other reason for the initial failure of the previous piece: the original version of 'Speaking of Courage' had avoided any reference to the shit field. Retrospectively, this omission appears to O'Brien to have deprived his narrative of the 'natural counterpoint' for the lake around which Bowker would drive endless circuits, trapped in his inability to articulate his grief and lay the past to rest: 'A metaphoric unity was broken. What the piece needed, and did not have, was the terrible killing power of that shit field' (*TTC*, 158). The lake, on its part, works as a mirror image of the shit field. 'Fed by neither springs nor streams, the lake was often filthy and algaed, relying on fickle prairie rains for replenishment' (*TTC*, 140). It also has a killing power of its own: Max Arnold, a friend of Bowker's and a believer in the necessity of the idea of God as 'a final cause in the whole structure of causation' (*TTC*, 140), had drowned in it. (This death foreshadows the search for causation later undertaken by the soldiers in their attempt to allocate the blame for Kiowa's drowning.) Together with an explanation of the genesis of 'Speaking of Courage', 'Notes' also gives the rationale for its own inclusion in *Things*: Norman Bowker's 'simple need to talk' provides the 'emotional core' (*TTC*, 157) of this short narrative and therefore – the reader is left to surmise – a crucial topic for a text so concerned with 'how to tell a true war story'. The most interesting piece of information delivered by 'Notes', though, comes with its conclusion, which casts doubts on the identification of Norman Bowker as the soldier who failed to rescue Kiowa. Having confessed his reluctance to think about Kiowa's death and about his own burden of complicity in this tragedy, O'Brien ends this short piece with an important, and ambiguous, explanation: 'In the interests of truth, however, I want to make it clear that Norman Bowker is in no way responsible for what happened to Kiowa. Norman did not experience a failure of nerve that night. He did not freeze up or lose the

---

16 A full account of this episode is given in Chapter 14, 'Upon Almost Winning the Silver Star'. Quite apart from this self-reflective intertextual connection, 'Speaking of Courage' has a marked thematic affinity with Ernest Hemingway's 'Soldier's Home' from *In Our Time* (1925). For an excellent comparative reading of these three texts, see Michael Kaufmann, 'The Solace of Bad Form: Tim O'Brien's Postmodernist Revisions of Vietnam in "Speaking of Courage"', *Critique*, 46.4 (2005), pp. 333–43.

Silver Star for valor. *That part of the story is my own'* (*TTC*, 159, my italics).
While Bowker is fully exonerated from Kiowa's death, O'Brien's role in the
actual unfolding of the tragedy and its eventual retelling remains muddled,
suspended as it is between the two possible interpretations: the final sentence
can be read as a declaration of creative licence, claimed as a storyteller's right
elsewhere in the novel, and/or an admission of guilt (notice how this state of
affairs is clearly reminiscent of the narrator's predicament in *In the Lake of
the Woods*).

The third and final story in the series, 'In the Field', continues to cast an
aura of uncertainty around the mechanics of Kiowa's death. It does so by
going back to the morning after the event, with the platoon's search for the
corpse, the individual soldiers' apportioning of blame, and their deliberation
over Lieutenant Jimmy Cross's responsibility for their comrade's grotesque
demise. The aftermath of the tragedy unfolds in a double search, for Kiowa's
body and for a recognizable principle of causation; these would seem to
provide respectively the beginning and the ending (and a sense of closure) to
the story of this particular casualty. The collective quest in its turn is paral-
leled by two more private efforts, both marked by the need to leave things
unsaid: the lieutenant's tentative phrasing of a letter of condolence to Kiowa's
family and a young soldier's frantic search in the muck for the photograph of
his girlfriend. Out of decency, the lieutenant omits the shit field from his
letter, and focuses on the fine qualities of the deceased. The nameless soldier
hides a more troubling secret. His reconstruction of the chain of events that
has led to Kiowa's death revolves around the lost photograph of the girl: the
soldier is convinced that the mortar attack of the previous evening had been
triggered by his reckless decision to switch on a flashlight so as to illuminate
the portrait of the girl and have Kiowa admire it. Needless to say, the line of
thought behind the interpretation of this horrible sequence follows the
twisted logic of guilt, for Kiowa's nameless best friend and self-confessed
culprit is none other than the distraught soldier defeated by the shit field in
his rescue attempt. The suggestion, first intimated in 'Notes', that O'Brien
might be this close friend is supported by the characterization of his relationship with Kiowa throughout the narrative, and particularly in 'Field Trip',
the account of O'Brien's post-war return to Vietnam in the company of his
ten-year-old daughter Kathleen. The journey is a sort of pilgrimage to the
scene of Kiowa's drowning, where the narrator wades into the murky water
and lays his friend's moccasins in the marshland – a private ritual performed
in the uncomprehending presence of the little girl and under the silent gaze
of an old Vietnamese farmer.

Set twenty years after the war, and clearly focused on the enduring, painful
impact on the narrator of Kiowa's death, 'Field Trip' emphasizes once more
the centrality of this tragic episode, and of the shit field, as a sort of *mise en*

abyme of the experience of war. In 'Notes', O'Brien had already highlighted the need to mention the field as a counterpart to Bowker's lake: together, the two locations constitute an essential 'metaphorical unit' which, if broken, would irredeemably impair the success of the story (i.e. the strength of its grip on the reader and its ability to convey an approximate truth about Bowker's experience). It is important to notice at this point that it is only in their mutual, contrapuntal relationship as signs in a self-contained system of signification that O'Brien endorses the metaphorical association of ideas that reverberate from the pairing of lake and shit field. Taken individually, and analysed for their respective ability to gesture to an actual referent, the two signs work in strikingly different ways, placed as they are on opposite ends of the continuum between metaphorical and metonymical language. The reason why the lake fails to work by itself is because it relies primarily on its metaphorical connotations (its silent, reflecting, deep, circular nature an apt mirror to Bowker's state of mind) in order to have an emotional impact on the reader. The shit field, by contrast, marks a powerful, uncompromising, *metonymical* adherence to utter abjection in the image of 'death by waste', the best possible approximation to the otherwise unspeakable nature of the traumatic experience of war. According to David Jarraway's incisive reading of the use of scatological imagery in the text, in this way, 'Tim O'Brien eradicates all possibility for responsive uplift in *The Things They Carried* by reducing even the metaphorical import of waste. As a measure of atrocious acts and imbecile events, waste's claim on all concerned, accordingly, is seen to be absolutely *literal*. At this zero-degree level of rectitude, then, war becomes the equivalent of human waste – "a goddamn *shit* field" […] – in which an entire platoon must immerse itself in order to register most completely the nauseous vacuity and repulsive futility of their lives at war'.[17]

In an acute psychoanalytic reading of the topography of trauma in *Things*, Brian Jarvis digs deeper into the symbolic import of the image of the shit field to reveal how this place conjures up the memory of a greater trauma than the loss of a particular individual, however close to the narrator. Not only is Kiowa the name of an entire Indian tribe, but the mode of the soldier's slow disappearance into the muck until only one knee is protruding 'might be read as a "crypt effect" in which the last major armed conflict between the Native Americans and the US Army [the Wounded Knee massacre of 1890] surfaces'.[18] Similarly, the second major traumatic casualty in Alpha Company, the death of Curt Lemon, blown to pieces by a booby trap and left

17 David R. Jarraway, '"Excremental Assault" in Tim O'Brien: Trauma and Recovery in Vietnam War Literature', *Modern Fiction Studies*, 44.3 (1998), pp. 695–711, p. 696.
18 Brian Jarvis, 'Skating on a Shit Field: Tim O'Brien and the Topography of Trauma', in *American Fiction of the 1990s: Reflections of History and Culture*, ed. Jay Prosser (London New York: Routledge, 2008), pp. 134–47, p. 140.

hanging in a tree, might be read as an allusion to the other main strand of racial violence in US history: the murder of African Americans (Curt's face appears 'suddenly brown and shining' in the 'fatal whiteness' of the explosion, *TTC*, 69, 79). Jarvis's insightful observations uncover the traces of previous national tragedies behind the smaller-scale losses compulsively, but always inadequately, recounted in *Things*. At the same time, the solid psychoanalytic underpinning of Jarvis's analysis takes us back to the recurring debate about the presence of a monstrous femininity at the core of O'Brien's perception of Vietnam, a hypothesis that appears particularly compelling in the interpretation of Bowker's unsuccessful attempt to *deliver* Kiowa from the shit field. As Jarvis maintains, '[t]he psychogeography of this scene suggests antipodal birth traumas in the *anus mundi*: one "newborn" survives to be haunted by meconium aspiration (when a baby swallows its own feces during labor), but the other undergoes a rectal absorption which recalls Freud's "cloaca theory" (a misconception amongst some children that women have only one pelvic orifice and birth occurs through the anus)' (136). Beyond its monitory allusion to the Native American genocide (a haunting crime doomed to resurface as a repressed memory in Indian Country), the shit field would therefore reveal O'Brien's perpetuation of a problematic – if not outright misogynist – image of femininity.

Such a mapping of O'Brien's topography of trauma, however, strikes me as both a little ungenerous and as too keen to ascribe to this particular text what Jarvis himself recognizes as the 'generalized gender anxieties apparent within the libidinal economy of war' (137). After all, quite apart from the context of the hyper-masculine army training, the identification of the land with Mother Earth is such a conventional, widespread idea that it is all too easy to see 'the maternal imago haunt[ing] a landscape of fecund jungle, intrauterine tunnels and invaginating fox holes, swamps, rivers and a shit field'.[19] O'Brien cannot completely avoid this troublesome connection, which was effectively inescapable in the military culture at the time of the Vietnam war and most likely remains so even now, given the pervasiveness of the Mother Earth figure in our culture, so conveniently available to brand the enemy territory with the mark of a feminine aberration. Having said that, in 'In the Field', the final piece to revisit this crucial location, two decades after the end of the war, O'Brien makes it clear that beyond the projections of traumatized soldiers, crushed under an unbearable weight of terror and guilt, there lies an ordinary little field, decidedly not the monstrous place that he has remembered all along, since Kiowa's death.

There were birds and butterflies, the soft rustlings of rural-anywhere. Below, in

19 Jarvis, 'Skating on a Shit Field', p. 135.

the earth, the relics of our presence were no doubt still there, the canteens and bandoliers and mess kits. This little field, I thought, has swallowed so much. [...] Still, it was hard to find any real emotion. It simply wasn't there. After that long night in the rain, I'd seemed to grow cold inside, all the illusions gone, all the old ambitions and hopes for myself sucked away into the mud. Over the years, that coldness had never entirely disappeared. There were times in my life when I couldn't feel much, nor sadness or pity or passion, and somehow I blamed this place for what I had become, and I blamed it for taking away the person I had once been. For twenty years this field had embodied all the waste that was Vietnam, all the vulgarity and horror. Now, it was just what it was. Flat and dreary and unremarkable. (*TTC*, 185–86)

Suggestive as the idea of the entrapping womb might be, both in this passage and in the description of Kiowa's death, it ultimately lurks behind the image of the cloaca (the repository of muck and of the undigested traces of the soldiers' passage) and of the voracious mouth, sucking and swallowing (this latter image makes a logical counterpart to the cloaca, at the other end of the digestive tract).[20] In spelling out the figurative import of the field, O'Brien insists on its quite literal representation of the indescribable *waste* and the irredeemable horror of the war; besides, in its association with the image of the *anus mundi*, O'Brien's shit field is bound to summon the memory of Auschwitz, the place of utter abjection and unspeakable traumas in relation to which that very expression has been infamously used.

Scatological imagery, itself all too common in the soldier's crude vernacular, and references to the grotesque body are a frequent presence in O'Brien's writing, where they mark the protagonists' deepest responses – their gut reactions, so to speak – to sheer panic and awesome realizations: see, for example, O'Brien's bouts of vomiting in *If I Die*, Paul Perry discharging his black bile in the waters of Pliney's Pond in *Northern Lights*, or Paul Berlin and William Cowling soiling themselves under the stress of combat in *Going After Cacciato* and *The Nuclear Age* respectively. Thus, for a writer who has otherwise already made extensive use of such graphic imagery to try to capture his characters' encounter with essential feelings of fear, shame, terror and guilt, the shit field, in its lurid materiality, must have seemed like the obvious locus of trauma – an apt correlative and a concrete, metonymical summation for the experience of war, and of the physical annihilation and the moral squalor that come with it. After his hermeneutical *tour de force*, even Jarvis has his own misgivings about the dangers of abandoning oneself to the metaphorical appeal of O'Brien's topography of trauma: 'how sure can one's

20 As Mikhail Bakhtin points out, swallowing is a 'most ancient symbol of death and destruction'; *Rabelais and his World* [1965], trans. Hélène Iswolsky (Bloomington: Indiana University Press, 1984), p. 325.

footing be in a shit field? Perhaps my own scatter-bombing, or even muck-spreading, has ignored the possibility that sometimes a shit field is just a shit field? By dumping so much on this site, do we risk flushing away the phenomenological materiality, the shittiness and fundamental thingness of things?' (146). Indeed, in my opinion, we do.

As part of the literal and figurative setting of O'Brien's novels, holes and underground (and underwater) passages are ambivalent places at best: the possibility of rebirth or redemption adumbrated by the characters' reaction to these locations is always configured as fragile and temporary, and it is often fraught with guilt. Paul Perry's 'epiphanic' immersion into the primordial broth of Pliney's Pond – a pseudo-baptismal ablution clearly linked to ideas of reinvigoration and spiritual growth – is followed only by the most tentative and precarious drive for change, in tune with the general bathetic tone of the denouements in *Northern Lights*. In *Going After Cacciato*, Berlin's imaginary flight from Li Van Hgoc's tunnel marks the beginning of his journey of development and his alliance with Sarkin Aung Wan, but the soldier's attempt to take his distance from the war is ultimately doomed to failure. In *The Nuclear Age* Cowling's emergence from the nuclear shelter is a last-minute response to his daughter's life-wish; given the protagonist's history, however, the reprieve from his nightmares is bound *not* to be a lifelong affair. Even more dubious as a wilful act of reparation is Wade's execution of PFC Weatherby from the depth of the corpse-strewn irrigation ditch in *In the Lake of the Woods*, while the shit field in *The Things They Carried* completely rules out the possibility of salvaging any dignity and of drawing any redemptive lessons from the war. It would be impossible to deny the irresistible appeal of a symbolic reading of these environments: such (hard to avoid) figurative readings often open up perfectly legitimate and fruitful hermeneutical avenues. Even so, as this brief overview reminds us, the most persuasive – and evident – interpretation of these recurrent locations in O'Brien's oeuvre often hinges, rather simply, on the recognition of their presence as places of indeterminacy and confusion, where the gaps in our understanding, and accounts, of things are mercilessly exposed.

Speaking of (damaged) men and women

The success or failure in the portrayal of female characters is one of the most contentious issues in the reception of O'Brien's work, even in the case of those novels which have otherwise found wide acclaim, both with academics and reviewers, and with the general public. The charge most typically made against O'Brien's representation of women is that his female characters are flat and undernourished creations, instrumental figures devoid of a life of their own, only necessary to the illustration of an idea, or to the development of the plot and of the male protagonists. There is an element of truth in these accusations but, at the risk of stating the obvious, I would argue that O'Brien's occasional failure to create convincing and sympathetic female characters, whose existence is not subordinated to the fleshing out of the male protagonists' predicament, is an inevitable result of the choice to filter his narratives through a perspective that is clearly masculine, and clearly perturbed and uncomfortable with itself: a masculinity that feels permanently ill at ease and under threat. This masculine anxiety is flaunted, inviting an all too easy Freudian response, even by the protagonist of *If I Die in a Combat Zone*, the narrator-witness who otherwise denounces the misogynist bias of the Army in censorious terms.

In his first book-length narrative, O'Brien makes an immediate, implicit allusion to the institutionalized misogyny of the Army, for the marching song that gives the memoir its title contains numerous offensive references to women: for example, the first verse, cited by O'Brien, goes 'If I die in a combat zone / Box me up and ship me home. / An' if I die on the Russian front, / Bury me with a Russian cunt' (*IID*, 50). In the testosterone-fuelled context of Fort Lewis, O'Brien and Erik – quiet, reflective, educated young men – are doomed to the role of outsiders: branded as the 'college pussies' (*IID*, 53) by the company drill sergeant Blyton, they become the object of scorn even on the part of the military authority. His passive resistance to the culture of machismo fostered by the Army takes its psychological toll on the young O'Brien. In Vietnam, during a night ambush, he recalls a dream that he had had as a fourteen-year-old, 'the only dream I ever remembered in detail' (*IID*, 93) – a dream which 'surely cries out for psychoanalytic interpretation', as T. J. Lustig argues in his lucid analysis of this episode.[21]

> I was in prison. The prison was a hole in the mountain. During the days, swarthy-faced moustached captors worked us like slaves in coal mines. At night they locked us behind rocks, every prisoner utterly alone. They had whips and guns, and they used them on us at pleasure. The mountain dungeon was musty. Suddenly we were free, escaping, scrambling out of the cave. (*IID*, 93)

Running away from his pursuers, O'Brien plunges into a forest and then makes his way up to the top of a mountain: 'I looked into the valley below me, and a carnival was there. A beautiful woman, covered with feathers and tan skin, was charming snakes. With her stick she prodded the creatures, making them dance and writhe and perform. I hollered down to her, "Which way to

---

21 T. J. Lustig, '"Which Way Home?" Tim O'Brien and the Question of Reference', *Textual Practice*, 18.3 (2004), pp. 395–414, p. 400.

freedom? Which way home?"' (*IID*, 93). The woman, configured as a dominating erotic figure, points him in the wrong direction; O'Brien meets her at the end of the road where she is laughing and embracing 'a swarthy, moustached captor' (*IID*, 94), whose weathered appearance and visible signs of sexual maturity add insult to the injury that is the young boy's crushed dreams of seduction and escape. In the gung-ho environment of active military service, and in the dangerous context of a night ambush in particular, O'Brien's adolescent fears make a predictable (tongue-in-cheek?) return to the surface of his consciousness.[22] This image of feminine treachery is the other side of Paul Berlin's equally naive projection of positive, caring, trustworthy qualities onto the figure of Sarkin Aung Wan.

Elsewhere the perception of a threat to masculinity and/or the expression of one's feelings of inadequacy is articulated in quite unsubtle terms as fear of castration. Thus in *Northern Lights* Harvey argues with Paul for the necessity of the bomb shelter on the grounds that a nuclear fallout would 'rot [a man's] testicles off' (*NL*, 68; see also page 20, where this belief is first mentioned). In *The Nuclear Age*, instead, William Cowling ends up with a 'mangled pecker', the result of the badly sutured 'huge gash' that he had suffered in a bicycle accident as a child (*NA*, 18, 19). In other cases, the male characters' unease with their gender identity is conveyed through a sense of inadequacy in relation to traditional masculine models. John Wade, for instance, is taunted for his chubbiness by his father, who also reproaches him for his unmanly hobby: 'That pansy magic crap. What's wrong with baseball, some regular exercise?' (*LW*, 67). This reminds us that O'Brien's male protagonists often grow up as lonely outsiders, emotionally stunted even before their involvement with the war or with other major traumatic events (such as Wade Senior's suicide in *Lake*, for example). In tune with these fears and insecurities are the characters' fantasies of return to the womb as to a place of safety and complete seamlessness. As a boy, William Cowling finds comfort in the kindness of a motherly librarian, 'all hips and breasts and brains', wishing 'to crawl into her lap and curl up for a long sleep, just the two of us, cuddling' (*NA*, 23, 24). John Wade's graphic dream of complete assimilation into his

---

22 On the other hand, the anxiety about masculinity in the sexual undercurrent of the dream effectively obscures O'Brien's awareness that in Vietnam he has become one of the captors, betraying his younger self who was running for freedom. Cf. Lustig's reading of O'Brien's dream in relation to its position in the narrative: 'in the light of basic training [where O'Brien declares his determination to resist the 'boors' that surround him and have effectively captured him in Fort Lewis], the invitation to produce a psychoanalytic reading of the dream becomes more clearly visible as defensive and compensatory. Set between an atrocity and an ambush, the memory of the 14-year-old's dream offers consolation in troubled times. But it also makes plain that the original identifications have been transformed and that the adult who remembers his childhood dream has become the figure that once he fled'; Lustig, '"Which Way Home?"', p. 410.

wife's body also blends images of infantilization – the crawling, the swimming, the pressing of his gums against her – with more disturbing material: '[he] wanted to open up Kathy's belly and crawl inside and stay there forever. He wanted to swim through her blood and climb up and down her spine and drink from her ovaries and press his gums against the firm red muscle of her heart. He wanted to suture their lives together' (*LW*, 70). And Wade's story, of course, is itself mediated by a damaged chronicler, the anonymous war veteran who has pieced together John and Kathy's mystery as a surrogate investigation for his own unspeakable secrets.

As far as Kathy's characterization is concerned, the novel quite openly signals its inability to fathom her complex personality and to provide a confident rendition not merely of her mysterious disappearance, but also of her past. While the narrator 'can at least depend on trying to understand himself in order to re-create Wade'[23] – and indeed, in the autobiographical references in his footnotes, he deliberately flaunts this connection – the apprehension of Kathy's story remains tantalizingly out of his reach. The narrator's speculations on Kathy's fate and on what might have led to her disappearance are presented in the 'Hypothesis' chapters, as if he 'were reflecting not only the absence of any witnesses to what happened to her but his own presumption in trying to read her mind'[24] – a presumption that Wade himself found difficult to cope with given his almost pathological desire to have full knowledge of his wife's actions and to rest secure in her loyalty and affection. In the end, the fact that Kathy's destiny remains more ambiguous than her husband's – of Wade we know that he sets off northwards into Lake of the Woods in one of Rasmussen's boats – gives her a lingering, fascinating quality that none of the other characters in the novel possesses. While the last image of Wade is that of a 'lost' man declaiming 'her name, his love' to the wind (*LW*, 306), cutting a rather pathetic figure, Kathy's final appearance is impressive and truly memorable: 'And here in a corner of John Wade's imagination, where things neither live nor die, Kathy stares up at him from beneath the surface of the silvered lake. Her eyes are brilliant green, her expression alert. She tries to speak but she can't. She belongs to the angle. Not quite present, not quite gone, she swims in the blending twilight of in between' (*LW*, 291). Forever haunting Wade's imagination, Kathy has become one with the impenetrable, dazzling wilderness, an image that recalls the characterization of Mary Anne Bell in 'Sweetheart of the Song Tra Bong', whose own disappearance marks her unavailability to her male admirers and chroniclers, while securing their enduring fascination with her mystery. In her association with the twilight, Kathy also deliberately resembles the 'wild and gorgeous appari-

23 Heberle, *A Trauma Artist*, p. 247.
24 Heberle, *A Trauma Artist*, p. 248.

tion of a woman'[25] in *Heart of Darkness* who, having struck Marlow with her silent, imposing presence, walks back into the forest with her self-possession intact and her story still unwritten but fully under her control.

On the opposite side of the spectrum from the self-aware narrators and wounded male characters is Paul Berlin, represented as a fundamentally innocent young man. As anticipated, Berlin naively subscribes to old-fashioned gender (and racial) stereotypes, but he too turns to an ideal of femininity for comfort, strength and inspiration. Sarkin Aung Wan is therefore quite clearly the product of a male imagination, the female mirror, as feminist critics have been quick to point out, reflecting the soldier's alienation back to him. Kalí Tal, for example, rightly suggests that in his confrontation with Sarkin Aung Wan, Berlin works out the opposition between masculine and feminine qualities within himself.[26] Taking a distance from Tal's position, I would argue that the transparency of this operation provides a constant reminder of the limitation of Berlin's perspective – a reminder that it is impossible to ignore. What Tal calls the novel's 'reactionary resolution', i.e. Berlin's final capitulation to the idea that 'the division between men and women [...] is unbreachable, and it is the male half which must triumph, even though that triumph will bring about the destruction of men and women alike' (78) is unmistakably the result of the solitary and private struggle of a character who is out of his depth, and it is not endorsed by the novel as a positive, desirable conclusion. The 'failure of imagination' is Berlin's failure, *not* the novel's failure and, sympathetic as readers will inevitably be to the plight of this insecure young soldier, whose good faith they have no reason to question, they will also remain aware of his shortcomings and mourn with him his inability to make the right decision.[27]

Bearing in mind this important distinction between the internal logic of individual texts and the gender politics of their author, a similar argument can be made in relation to the characterization of the female figures in *The Things They Carried*. At first glance, the female characters in *Things* do seem to exemplify the unavoidable remoteness of the civilian population from the soldiers' experience of Vietnam and, indeed, from any manifestation of evil. Reviving the old equation between femininity and innocence, purity and perfection, the four main female characters in the novel – the only female characters, in fact, to be identified by their name – share a virginal quality, for they are either prepubescent, or unsusceptible to male advances. These four

25 Conrad, *Heart of Darkness*, p. 99.
26 Kalí Tal, 'The Mind at War: Images of Women in Vietnam Novels by Combat Veterans', *Contemporary Literature*, 31.1 (1990), pp. 76–96, p. 77.
27 It goes without saying that I do not agree with Tal's argument that Berlin 'fails to undergo any kind of change' (78). As I explained in Chapter 2, Berlin might not find the strength to desert, but by the end of the novel he lets go of his self-delusion of innocence.

figures are arranged in two sets of opposite pairings: Martha and Mary Anne, and Kathleen and Linda. Martha, Lieutenant Jimmy Cross's love interest, remains clearly separate from the war and '[t]he things men do' (*TTC*, 26), while Mary Anne, the 'sweetheart' who follows her boyfriend 'in country', experiences the thrill of combat and embraces her fascination for the wilderness.[28] The two younger characters – uncorrupted and tame by definition – are set apart by their association with the future and the past, respectively: Kathleen, the daughter who questions O'Brien over his involvement with the war, and witnesses his attempts to learn to live with it, represents the promise of filial understanding (and, possibly, forgiveness?), while Linda, O'Brien's first, long-gone childhood love, becomes the narrator's muse for a fragile consolatory fantasy at the end of the novel. A closer look at these figures, however, reveals subtle nuances in their representation and in the gender dynamics that follow their appearance on the scene.

'The Things They Carried', the story that opens and gives its title to the entire book, introduces with Martha an early – and admittedly a gendered – example of the distance between the soldiers and the civilian population, uninitiated into the horror of war. However, together with its follow-up 'Love', this story also describes a poignant, unrequited passion, whose impasse – completely unrelated to the war – can equally account for the unbridgeable gap between the two protagonists. 'The Things They Carried' begins with a mention of the correspondence between Lieutenant Jimmy Cross and Martha, 'whose letters were mostly chatty, elusive on the matter of love' (*TTC*, 3). This epistolary interaction constitutes an early example in the novel of an exchange at cross-purposes. Martha's beautifully written letters, in which the girl describes her life as a student of English literature, are cherished by the lieutenant, who holds on to the fleeting, platonic connection they offer and to the promise of something deeper which he wilfully pretends to read between the lines, in spite of Martha's calculated detachment and of his own better judgement. At the end of each day, Cross retreats to his foxhole and escapes from the war, wondering whether Martha is a virgin and imagining that his love for her is requited. Blended with these fantasies are also the memories of how Martha had rejected his advances, when he had stroked her knee in a dark cinema, while they were watching *Bonnie and Clyde* (1967). Silent and stern, she had looked at him with her sad eyes and he had pulled his hand back: he would never forget 'the feel of the tweed skirt and the knee beneath it and the sound of the gunfire that killed Bonnie and Clyde, how embarrassing it was, how slow and oppressive' (*TTC*, 5). It is interesting that Jimmy Cross's anti-climactic, humiliating drama should unfold along-

---

28 Incidentally, notice how Mary Anne's extraordinary metamorphosis in Vietnam would appear to demonstrate, precisely because of its aberrant outcome, that a woman's natural state is rather one of innocuous domesticity.

side the projection of a film that celebrates a passionate relationship built on the strange combination of sex and violence with inexperience, or even with an intimation of innocence, as advertised by the slogan of the film trailer: 'They're young. They're in love. They kill people.' Bonnie and Clyde's deaths in an ambush, a bloodbath represented with graphic images in slow motion in the final scene of the film, makes an ironic contrast to Cross's awkward retreat, but it also establishes an early association between the recollection of his amorous failure and a violent killing.

In the course of his tour in Vietnam, Cross finds himself thinking about Martha more and more often, until her image begins to come to his mind even before the day's activities are over, quite independently from his conscious efforts to consign his fantasies to the safety of the foxhole. Critics have dwelt on one such spontaneous reverie in particular as symptomatic of the text's recurrent scapegoating of femininity, construed as hostile and alien to the soldiers' military pursuits. While the platoon are anxiously waiting for Lee Strunk to emerge from the search of an enemy tunnel, the lieutenant is seized by a worrying premonition:

> Trouble, he thought – a cave-in maybe. And then suddenly, without willing it, he was thinking about Martha. The stresses and fractures, the quick collapse, the two of them buried alive under all that weight. Dense, crushing love. Kneeling, watching the hole, he tried to concentrate on Lee Strunk and the war, all the dangers, but his love was too much for him, he felt paralyzed, he wanted to sleep inside her lungs and breathe her blood and be smothered. (*TTC*,10)[29]

Cross thinks of his love for Martha as an overwhelming experience: irresistible but also devastating, the communion of their bodies simultaneously desired and imagined as a bloody, suffocating experience – a not unlikely clash of emotions given the history of the lieutenant's courtship, and a not unlikely fantasy of self-annihilation as the ultimate escape from the war. Cross's ambivalence extends to the contradictory vision of Martha on which his love relies: 'He wanted her to be a virgin and not a virgin, all at once. He wanted to know her' (*TTC*, 10). The lieutenant's wish for Martha's impossible duality must be partly a reflection of the duality that he hopes to recognize within himself, as a fundamentally decent guy corrupted by circumstances beyond his control; through this double vision, Cross can hold on to a belief in his own essential innocence, while pragmatically acknowledging his part in the war. But contradiction is also a necessary element in his construction of Martha's idealized image as an object of desire. Cross needs

---

29 Notice how Jimmy Cross's fantasy about Martha is reminiscent of John Wade's wish about his wife Kathy in *In the Lake of the Woods*.

Martha to be distant and self-sufficient, for these are the qualities that make her a rarefied, unattainable creature to aspire to: 'Not lonely, just alone [...] and it was the aloneness that filled him with love' (*TTC*, 10), we are told as Cross's reverie progresses. At the same time, he also needs her to be approachable, earthly, knowable, for in her other guise she inevitably partakes of an innocence that makes it impossible for him to commune with her.

Martha's appeal to the lieutenant lies in a paradox, for the very qualities that make her desirable and worthy of his love also cause her to be forever unavailable. O'Brien is careful to present this unavailability as a quality in Martha that Cross is positively dependent on: without her mysterious distance she would not be the blank screen on which he projects his own fantasies, a dynamic articulated by Simone de Beauvoir and by many other feminist critics.[30] As the story comes to an end, it becomes clear that Jimmy Cross is caught up in a similar paradox, with the one difference that the inescapable contradictions of his role are inflected according to masculine, rather than feminine, standards. Soon after Lee Strunk has emerged safely from the tunnel, another soldier, Ted Lavender, 'is shot in the head on his way back from peeing' (*TTC*, 11). In what is undoubtedly a traumatized reaction to this unpredictable tragedy, the lieutenant's grief and sense of responsibility focus on his hopeless fantasies about Martha as a damaging distraction from his duties: Martha belongs 'elsewhere', to a world of 'pretty poems' and 'midterm exams' (*TTC*, 20), i.e. a place where people are allowed to pursue their own rarefied fancies while everyday life continues undisturbed – a world removed in two different ways from the soldiers' experience of Vietnam, where daydreams and trivial activities are equally dangerous. In the aftermath of Lavender's death, Cross burns Martha's photographs and letters, and decides to impose an absolute respect of standard operating procedures on his platoon: 'there would be grumbling, of course, and maybe worse, because their days would seem longer and their loads heavier, but Lieutenant Jimmy Cross reminded himself that his obligation was not to be loved but to lead. He would dispense with love [...]. And if anyone quarrelled

---

30 'Of all these *myths* [the binary oppositions – virgin vs. whore, angel of the hearth vs. demon, muse vs. preying mantis, woman Beatrix vs. temptress – that make up the 'Eternal Feminine'] none is more firmly anchored in masculine hearts than that of the feminine "mystery." [...] A heart smitten with love thus avoids many disappointments: if the loved one's behaviour is capricious, her remarks stupid, then the mystery serves to excuse it all. And finally, thanks again to the mystery, the negative relation is perpetuated which seemed to Kierkegaard infinitely preferable to positive possession: in the company of a living enigma man remains alone – alone with his dreams, his hopes, his fears, his love, his vanity'; Simone de Beauvoir, *The Second Sex* [1949], trans. Howard Madison Parshley (New York: Alfred A. Knopf, 1993), p. 270.

or complained, he would simply tighten his lips and arrange his shoulders in the correct command posture' (*TTC*, 21).

Cross's surrender to the rules of his military training – to what makes him an ideal leader, and what makes him a man – in fact drives him away from his men, not so much because of the rigidity of the newly enforced procedures, but because of the suppression of emotions that goes with this masculine role. We have been told earlier in the story that the lieutenant is admired precisely because of his ability to care, for his capacity for grief. Cross's striving for restraint, just like his fascination with Martha's unavailability, is shown to be a misguided acquiescence in familiar cultural notions, but in the end both the internalization of a severe masculine posturing and the desire for a model feminine composure turn out to be as sterile as they are equally grounded in old-fashioned gender ideals. All the same, this subtle critique of gender stereotypes does not extend to a condemnation of the young man who subscribes to them. Cross's characterization remains completely sympathetic: who could blame him for seeking refuge from the horror and the boredom of war in his imaginary romance with a sensitive, ethereal girl? And who could blame him for turning against her, when she seems so far away, both emotionally (in her rejection of his love) and intellectually (her letters never mention the war)? And yet, when, years after the war, the narrator O'Brien asks Jimmy Cross for permission to tell his story, the lieutenant's response reveals how his actions are still determined by a desire to impress the girl: 'Make me out to be a good guy, eh? Brave and handsome, all that stuff. Best platoon leader ever', so that the perfect woman will finally 'come begging' (*TTC*, 27).

While Jimmy Cross is constantly battling with the desire for acceptance and emotional validation, Martha is described as aloof, steely, autonomous, and distinctly uninspired by 'the things men do', which seem to be (violent) things done in order to impress or subjugate women, and affirm one's masculinity – unsurprisingly, the two things seem to go together. Martha, on her part, has called herself out of this game, never getting married, although the deliberateness of this move is definitely under question, giving rise to a host of hypotheses (is she sexually repressed? celibate for religious reasons? a lesbian? or – and why not? – simply not interested in romantic relationships?) and reiterating once again the point that her rejection of Jimmy Cross and of the masculine code of behaviour is not directly related to his participation to the war. It is easy to see why Martha's distant and censorious demeanour towards Cross – and, by extension, towards masculinity – should be viewed as problematic by feminist critics. They object to Martha's sketchy and unsympathetic characterization and resent the fact that the mode of Cross's initiation into his duty as a warrior, configured as a relinquishing of his feminine traits and presented as a sad, but nonetheless inevitable, consequence of the internalization of the army training and of the experience of combat, should not be criticized more openly.

On the other hand, Martha's naivety in her sweeping, and cryptic, condemnation of 'the things men do' finds its opposite number in the lieutenant's own belief in an ideal model of masculine behaviour that would lead to success in military and romantic conquests: the protagonists of this story are both prisoners of contrasting assumptions about what it is that men should or should not do (or even, what it is that men can or cannot get away with in the expression of their masculinity). And, in all fairness, Martha's scathing comment on masculine behaviour is a response to Cross's extraordinary confession that 'back in college he'd almost done something very brave. It was after seeing *Bonnie and Clyde*, he said, [...] he'd almost picked her up and carried her to his room and tied her to the bed and put his hand on her knee and just held it there all night long' (*TTC*, 26). Measured against this fantasy – which, quite apart from its 'move from chivalry to sado-masochistic erotica',[31] directly overrules Martha's express rejection of her suitor's hand on her knee – the lieutenant's understanding of bravery is clearly charged with a predatory and sinister intent. (It makes one wonder how Smith can argue that 'the violation and coercion' behind Cross's notion of gallantry are not considered in the story.) As I shall discuss in the final section of this chapter, the endless circle of male aggression and female passive resistance in which Jimmy Cross and Martha seem to have become locked is replicated, quite deliberately in all its shocking political incorrectness, in the interaction between other men and women in *Things* (see, for example, Rat Kiley and Curt Lemon's sister, or even the narrator Tim O'Brien and one of his listeners).

Martha's unwavering refusal to become implicated in 'the things men do' finds its opposite counterpart in the story of Mary Anne Bell in 'Sweetheart of the Song Tra Bong', a text geared to dispel the rigidity of gender stereotypes that are otherwise reinforced in time of war. In his gender-bending take on Conrad's classic tale of the journey into the wilderness, O'Brien openly contests the idea that women are naturally impervious to 'the fascination of the abomination',[32] without reducing Mary Anne either to a grotesque caricature, more manly than the men, or to a despicable and fearsome manifestation of a monstrous femininity. The success of this story relies in part on the rich web of intertextual references that O'Brien weaves between Mary Anne's

---

31 Smith, ""The Things Men Do"', p. 25. Lieutenant Cross is not the only character whose view of gallantry has violent undertones. This is how William Cowling describes his first, fleeting casual encounters with Sarah Strouch, before their relationship begins: 'Now and then, by chance, we brushed up against each other, and I could smell her skin, the skin itself, and there was that moment of hurt and panic, the urge to try something desperate, something gallant, like rape, a blow to the chin and then drag her off' (*NA*, 96).
32 Conrad, *Heart of Darkness*, p. 20.

adventure, and its convoluted history of transmission and reception, and Marlow's account of Kurtz's, and his own, remarkable voyage of self-discovery. An extensive comparative reading of the two texts will have to wait until Chapter 5, where we shall see how O'Brien's celebration of a character who transcends traditional gender roles is accomplished through a narrative strategy that embraces the challenges of *écriture féminine* to the phallogocentric discourse of patriarchy. For the purposes of the current discussion of the women in *Things*, suffice it to say that so keen is O'Brien to tell the story of a character who would disprove an essentialist view of gender that he abandons all the rules of plausibility to have the young Mary Anne join her soldier boyfriend in a small medical detachment near the village of Tra Bong. There Mary Anne becomes increasingly involved in military life, proving that the real divide between the soldiers and the people back home is not a matter of unbridgeable gender differences, but a question of exposure to the stress, as well as the thrill, of combat. In Vietnam, Mary Anne – who, unlike Martha, is introduced as gregarious and sexy in the wholesome manner that becomes an American sweetheart – finds an irresistible opportunity to follow her deepest and darkest instincts, losing her culturally determined sense of identity and entering into a space beyond the reach of language. Liberated from the patriarchal order, she is represented as a powerful figure who continues to haunt those who have witnessed her metamorphosis: her story remains a source of fascination, awe and curiosity to her 'fellow soldiers'. Crucially, in her journey from all-American girl to creature of the wilderness, Mary Anne not only disappoints all expectations of her, but ultimately breaks away from any attempt to rationalize or provide closure to her story. Her retreat into silence – the fact that, unlike other characters in *Things* (such as Mitchell Sanders, the platoon's self-appointed hermeneutist, and Tim O'Brien himself), she never gets to condense her experience into neat aphorisms, sardonic morals or paradoxical lessons – is a sign of her strength, as suggestive and awe-inspiring as Kurtz's final words.

Leaving intertextual considerations aside, for the time being, it is clear that Martha and Mary Anne are set on divergent narrative paths in order to represent, respectively, the self-perpetuating antagonism between gender roles posited in binary oppositions and the dissolution of these mutually defining bonds. The contrast between these two figures is further emphasized by the echo, in their names, of the biblical story of the two sisters in Luke 10:38-42, where Mary is shown listening to Jesus, while Martha preoccupies herself with the household arrangements – itself perhaps an allusion to Mary Anne's instinctive fascination with the soldiers' plight (Jimmy Cross shares the initials of Christ and is linked to the symbol of his passion) and to Martha's subservience to cultural conventions. Kathleen and Linda, on the other hand, fulfil a much more similar role in their representation of quintessential innocence, a quality which is reflected in their age and in the etymology of their names.[33] Significantly, the two girls are the only female characters to engage in direct interaction with O'Brien, for Martha and Mary Anne are known to him exclusively through the medium of somebody else's story-telling. (In fact, the other female character to interact with Tim O'Brien in *Things* is an older woman who is part of the audience at one of his readings, but their relationship is clearly confined within the bounds of a narrative exchange, much as it had been in the case of Martha and of Mary Anne.) With the presence of two prepubescent girls, one an uncomprehending witness, the other the necessary mediator in his quest for catharsis, O'Brien draws attention to a theme that he will later revisit and expand both in *In the Lake of the Woods* and in *Tomcat in Love*: the difficulty in establishing meaningful adult relationships as a result of traumatization. In *Things*, this difficulty is exemplified by the narrator's reliance on childhood innocence as an idealized backdrop against which it becomes possible – or even necessary – to play out a tentative search for signification and redemption.

Kathleen's blunt curiosity about whether her father has ever killed anybody takes us back to familiar territory, with O'Brien musing on the burden of guilt that comes with one's participation in the war, regardless of one's personal body count. O'Brien is in no doubt about his responsibility,[34] but he chooses to postpone the complex and painful explanation that such a question warrants until a time when his daughter is old enough to hear his full story. With a function not unlike Martha's in relation to Jimmy Cross, Kathleen represents the promise of future fulfilment, while – crucially – retaining her present innocence. In his daughter O'Brien finds the solace of an ingenuousness to be preserved for as long as possible while cultivating the potential for understanding which their close relationship undeniably possesses. The young child who is first introduced chiding her father for his obsession with the war and suggesting that he 'should write about a little girl who finds a million dollars and spends it all on a Shetland pony' (*TTC*, 33) makes her final appearance in the novel accompanying O'Brien on a 'field trip' to Vietnam, which includes a visit to the site of Kiowa's death and an elusive search for 'signs of forgiveness or personal grace or whatever else the land might offer' (*TTC*, 183). There, while Kathleen remains curious about the war and open with the locals, O'Brien is taken aback by how much things seem to have changed and how little trace of his past sorrow he can find, or indeed feel, in his exposure to once tragically familiar places. O'Brien's

---

33 Kathleen is a variation of Catherine, from the Greek for 'pure'. Linda stands for 'clean' in Italian, and 'pretty' in Spanish, while its Germanic root means 'yielding'.

34 Even so, it is in reply to Kathleen's demand for an honest answer that he articulates, for the reader, his distinction between 'story-truth' and 'happening-truth' (on this issue, see Chapter 5).

emotional numbness continues in his solitary performance of a brief remembrance ceremony for Kiowa, when he wades into the marshlands to return his friend's moccasins to the place of his drowning twenty years before. This private ritual, from which Kathleen remains markedly excluded (like the old Vietnamese farmer also present at the scene), is executed in silence, for the narrator struggles 'to think of something decent to say' (*TTC*, 187). The deluded investment in the possibility that this deed would provide some sense of closure, ratified by O'Brien's pithy 'There it is' (the refrain associated with the fatalistic, and ultimately meaningless, morals that Mitchell Sanders distils from the war), is further thrown into relief by Kathleen's defamiliarizing gaze, as she looks uncomprehendingly on at her father taking a swim in such an inopportune place. Kathleen's mundane protests at O'Brien's unexplained action add to the bathetic quality of his attempt to lay his ghosts to rest through anything other than the interweaving of memory and imagination and the endless refashioning of stories.

It is with Linda, through whom he first learnt the consolatory power of storytelling, that O'Brien gets closest to experiencing some kind of catharsis, although – as the paradoxical fragility of the title of her story, 'The Lives of the Dead', already seems to suggest – not even the endless possibilities opened up by a narrative act can yield lasting comfort and signification. This chapter, the last in the novel, envisages the possibility of superseding the irreversibility of death and grief through the most powerful secular grand narrative in the Western world, the notion of romantic love, which is found here in its most perfect manifestation: absolute, uncorrupted and eternal, it is the bond between the nine-year-old Timmy O'Brien and his school-mate Linda, a girl who dies soon afterwards of a brain tumour. O'Brien pointedly insists that his feelings for the girl, and vice versa, should not be dismissed as a childhood crush or a lesser form of love. On the contrary, this connection 'had all the shadings and complexities of mature adult love, and maybe more, because there were not yet words for it, and because it was not yet fixed to comparisons or chronologies or the ways by which adults measure things' (*TTC*, 223). Already grounded in an immediate and complete mutual understanding – itself made possible by the authenticity that is the prerogative of childhood – and crystallized in its perfection by its tragic curtailment, the love between Timmy and Linda is further elevated to the status of ennobling, pure passion by the reference to their precise age, which is the same as Dante's and Beatrice's at the time of their first, life-changing encounter, as described in the *Vita Nuova*.

Linda is thus set up to become the narrator's muse, a consolatory vision that Timmy first summons to his aid when trying to come to terms with her death. The nine-year-old's day-dreaming is the beginning of a lifelong faith in the ability of imaginative storytelling to offer a respite from sorrow and grief, a feeling of wholeness, even perhaps a glimpse of redemption:

> And then it becomes 1990. I'm forty-three years old, and a writer now, still dreaming Linda alive in exactly the same way. She's not the embodied Linda; she's mostly made up, with a new identity and a new name, like the man who never was. Her real name doesn't matter. She was nine years old. I loved her and then she died. And yet right here, in the spell of memory and imagination, I can still see her as if through ice, as if I'm gazing into some other world, a place where there are no brain tumors and no funeral homes, where there are no bodies at all. I can see Kiowa, too, and Ted Lavender and Curt Lemon, and sometimes I can even see Timmy skating with Linda under the yellow floodlights. I'm young and I'm happy. I'll never die. I'm skimming across the surface of my own history, moving fast, riding the melt between the blades, doing loops and spins, and when I take a high leap into the air and come down thirty years later, I realize it is as Tim trying to save Timmy's life with a story. (*TTC*, 236)

Following Linda, who by now has become fully transubstantiated into an incorporeal ideal, O'Brien accedes to a heavenly dimension where there is no death, no separation and no pain, where old friends are reunited and sorrows forgotten. The narrator's permanence in this 'other world', however, is described as fragile, particularly when it comes to his encounter with his younger, innocent self. In other words, O'Brien's imaginative leap is quite knowingly envisaged as a temporary fantasy, a willing suspension of disbelief aided by the mediation of an iconic figure who, for all her consolatory power, falls short (and how could she not!) of the beatific example on which she is modelled. In fact, the Dantesque allusion offers an ironic counterpoint to the scope of the narrator's journey, which is a quick, virtuoso 'skimming across the surface' of his personal history, an endless going around in circles, ultimately only amounting to an *attempt* to retrieve, fleetingly, a romanticized fragment of one's past.

With the creation of the two prepubescent characters, O'Brien avoids the undercurrent of male resentment against more mature female figures who, in the soldiers' eyes, are held responsible for their failure to understand the war, even when – as the careful reader is bound to acknowledge – the stories that they are asked to relate to and the attitudes that they are asked to condone contain a definite threat to femininity. Kathleen can suggest that her father should try to leave the war behind without incurring his wrath or sarcasm, unlike the elderly woman in the audience later in the narrative; on the other hand, her innocence precludes her father from truly opening up to her here and now. The possibility of understanding and forgiveness is thus available, but only through a story that has not yet been told, in a future conversation which, as O'Brien's evasiveness in 'Field Trip' seems to suggest, might never come. Linda, on her part, offers to the narrator the momentary chance to revive his childhood self through a vision – the two young sweethearts 'ice skating late at night, tracing loops and circles under yellow floodlights' (*TTC*, 235) – that was already at one remove from reality for Timmy: as we follow Tim dreaming of Timmy dreaming of himself and Linda, who appears 'as if through ice', visible yet separate, always on the other side of the mirror, O'Brien's return to innocence cannot but strike us as a mirage receding further and further away from view. With the significant exception of Mary Anne Bell, the main female figures in *Things* are all caught up in the male characters' attempt to come to terms with trauma, but the transparency of this operation, through which women are construed as the prototypical outsiders from the war, is such that the readers cannot be unaware of its tendentiousness – nor can they ignore the ensuing contradictions in the soldiers' expectations of their female interlocutors.

Bathos, caricatural excesses and the inaccessibility of love

The relationships between men and women analysed so far all illustrate a vulnerable, fraught masculinity, without condoning – rather, if anything, highlighting – the male characters' failure to envisage femininity in ways other than monstrous embodiments of one's anxieties or idealized projections of one's deepest desires. The moral strength and complexity of female figures such as Sarkin Aung Wan and Kathy Wade thus often end up being somewhat compromised by the male perspective that for the most part, in full view and with no pretence to objectivity, underpins O'Brien's narratives. In other words, we only get to see O'Brien's glorious, fascinating and at times downright powerful and mystifying heroines, and their less glamorous and positive counterparts, through damaged and/or unreliable male eyes, like Berlin's, Wade's or even the narrator's in *Lake*. Yet the deliberate partiality of the masculine perspective in O'Brien's works is not the only reason why some of his creations lack depth in their psychological characterization and development. On a few occasions, O'Brien's female figures, just like their male companions, appear underdeveloped or unconvincing because of a narrative heavy-handedness that relies on stark oppositions and larger-than-life protagonists. This is the case, for example, of the characters in *Northern Lights*, a text which, by the author's own admission, suffers from '[o]verwriting' and 'too much gamesmanship',[35] understandable flaws in a first creative effort. Having said that, the novel is not so overdetermined as to provide closure across a neat gendered divide: as we have seen, just to give an

---

35 Naparsteck, 'An Interview with Tim O'Brien', p. 2, p. 3.

obvious example, Grace is spared the role of beatific saviour that her name seems to promise. Like Addie, the other main female character in a novel that puts to the test Hemingway's model of masculinity, and like Paul and Harvey, the two male protagonists, she is a flawed human being, whose characterization is affected by the painting-by-numbers clumsiness of the narrative. O'Brien's calculated reliance on overstatement is particularly evident in his comic works, which tend to capitalize – with mixed results, it has to be said – on black humour and caricatural excesses. While O'Brien's first novel falls victim to its own attempt 'to parody Hemingway',[36] the three comic works in O'Brien's canon could all be described as novels of ideas, in which the narrative development and the psychological characterization of the central figures are subordinated to the illustration of one theme. *The Nuclear Age* is about nothing less than 'the safety of our own species, our survival'[37] and the need to take personal responsibility even for such a wide political issue as this one.[38] *Tomcat in Love* is a postmodern reflection on the subjective, slippery nature of language, told by an unreliable narrator, Thomas H. Chippering, Professor of Modern American Lexicology at the University of Minnesota. Chippering is a conceited, self-deluded womanizer, whose spectacular mid-life meltdown provides countless opportunities for O'Brien to emphasize the embarrassing gap between the unfolding events and the narrator's warped perception and rendition of them. Finally, *July, July* is about the collective fall from grace of the Vietnam war generation, captured thirty years after their turbulent halcyon days, at a time when their erstwhile antagonism in relation to their elders and the establishment – perfectly encapsulated in the provocative motto 'never trust anybody over thirty' – has backfired into a mocking self-indictment. These three comedies, and in particular the final two, all chart their characters' doomed quest for romantic love, outlining in the process the difficulty that traumatized subjects experience in opening up to other people and in establishing healthy, caring and enduring relationships.[39] Inevitably, these books invite a close scrutiny of O'Brien's representation of gender, and have often attracted criticism at the very least for their lack of subtlety on that front. While it is sometimes difficult to disagree with critics who think that these works are

36 Naparsteck, 'An Interview with Tim O'Brien', p. 3.
37 McCaffery, 'Interview with Tim O'Brien', p. 141.
38 The specific need to shake the American readers from their political torpor is reflected in the cover of the 1987 Flamingo edition of the book: under a heading, almost as big as the title, that reads 'This Novel Could Save Your Life', there is the image of Uncle Sam wearing a gas-mask and pointing to the reader with his finger in his usual 'The Country Needs YOU' recruitment pose.
39 Another common trait in O'Brien's three comedies is their treatment of the war, which is much more peripheral – although by no means unimportant both in plot and in character development – than in his other writing.

stunted by infelicitous narrative choices, clearly dictated by the pursuit of humorous effects, O'Brien's three novels of ideas do not deserve a cursory dismissal. Reading past their occasional mishandling of the comic register reveals perceptive insights on the nature of love, and the long-term effects of trauma, and introduces us to truly memorable figures.

The Nuclear Age, for example, offers us the portrait of Sarah Strouch, O'Brien's most developed and compelling female character, who more than makes up for the less than sympathetic characterization of Bobbi, William Cowling's later love interest. From the beginning of the narrative, the beautiful, unavailable Sarah Strouch strikes William as a cut above the rest of the high-school crowd. In his distrust of and contempt for the shallow life of his contemporaries – to whose company he opposes his 'affinity for rocks' (*NA*, 35), safe, silent, non-judgemental – William makes an exception for this vibrant, spirited cheerleader, with whom he entertains imaginary conversations on the phone, in his ploy to convince his parents that he is a regular teenager. At first glance, this would seem to be familiar territory, with the lead female character being introduced as a projection of the male protagonist. However, as the novel progresses, Sarah enters William's life for real, developing into a complex, rounded figure, often taking centre stage, and affecting the course of the events in a way that is not matched by anyone else in the story. When they eventually meet at university, Sarah is still a bright, attractive and popular student, while William has recently taken the momentous step of turning his private anxiety about the nuclear war into a public protest, brandishing a poster inscribed with 'THE BOMBS ARE REAL' in front of the student cafeteria and recruiting to the cause, amidst general indifference, a couple of misfits. The two outsiders who first join Cowling's crusade are Ollie Winkler, a short and stocky technological wizard, and Tina Roebuck, a home-economics major and a compulsive eater, who both immediately argue for the protest to become more incisive, perhaps even violent. Certain aspects of Ollie's description – the comparison to Friar Tuck in cowboy attire, to a gremlin, or the mention of 'obvious evidence of a misplaced chromosome' (*NA*, 75ff.) – are reminiscent of similar qualities in Cacciato; and, in a sense, with the fierceness of his commitment to raising the stakes, Ollie is showing William the way to put into action his long-cherished wishes.

However, it is only when Sarah joins this odd trio that William's small-scale and self-righteous protest acquires effectiveness and visibility. With her liveliness, fervour and temerity, Sarah seems to offer William a third possibility, beyond the impasse created by the dichotomy between 'screwball' and 'regular guy'. Sarah herself is full of contradictions, hiding behind the façade of good-looking exhibitionist, first-class student and popular girl a deep insecurity and an overwhelming need to feel alive and loved. If William's fears are crippling, Sarah's are the prime reason why she courts attention and why she throws herself into the anti-nuclear campaign, which becomes the centre both of her emotional life, through her relationship with William, and of her professional life, once she links up their amateurish college enterprise with an underground terrorist group. In love and war, Sarah quickly becomes William's guide and instigator, making things happen and taking to her role with natural aptitude:

> Cheerleader to rabble-rouser: It was a smooth, almost effortless transition. Surprising, maybe, and yet the impulse was there from the start. In a sense, I realized, cheerleaders *are* terrorists. All that zeal and commitment. A craving for control. A love of pageantry and slogans and swollen rhetoric. Power too. The hot, energizing rush of absolute authority: *Lean to the left, lean to the right.* And then finally that shrill imperative: *Fight – fight – fight!* [...] Her generalship was impeccable. Her demands were unqualified. In public, but also in bed, she was a born leader. (*NA*, 100)

And, of course, in the matter of another war, it is Sarah who turns into reality William's decision to dodge the draft call: '"Run," Sarah said. And I did. First by bus, then by plane, and by the second week in September I was deep underground' (*NA*, 121).

O'Brien's most fleshed out female character, Sarah Strouch is certainly the real heroine of the novel, the character who provides the moral centre of the narrative and who manages to turn her weakness (her craving for fame, love and recognition) into the fuel for her political battle. Half-way through the novel, as the group prepare for an escalation of their terrorist activities by going to Cuba for a gruelling quasi-military training at the hands of two Vietnam war veterans, Sarah issues one of her most exasperated demands to William, whom she has always jokingly accused of having a 'jellyfish mentality' (*NA*, 103). As the character with drive and backbone in the couple, Sarah urges William to 'crawl out of [his] goddamn hidey-hole' (*NA*, 162) – a metaphorical hidey-hole at this point in the narrative, but also clearly a foreshadowing of the climactic episode of the novel. To Sarah's reproach, William reacts with a silent admission of the fundamental difference which sets them apart: 'She was out to change the world, I was out to survive it. I couldn't summon the same moral resources' (*NA*, 163). For all her need for recognition, Sarah's investment in the outside world – through William and through her political campaigns – is at one with her deepest beliefs, be they the private dream of a passionate escape to Rio and of a large family, or the desire for success in getting America to stop and take notice of the dangers of the nuclear age. In Sarah's world, words immediately translate into actions, and William is quick to recognize this correspondence, in spite of Sarah's façade of bravado, flippancy, and sarcasm which acts 'as a kind of camouflage, like her cosmetics, the gaudy nail polish and lipstick and mascara. At times, I thought, it was as if she were hiding herself, or from herself' (*NA*, 103).

To William (and to Ned Rafferty, her other on-off boyfriend, who sticks with the group for love, rather than from deep political convictions), Sarah is a mesmerizing figure, to be held in awe, without full comprehension. She is a 'mystery' (*NA*, 107), intense and alluring, but also with a distinct affinity with danger. Her dark side is intimated by her relationship with death: the daughter of a mortician, she tries to shake off this association through her vitality and lust for life. She remains, however, a *femme fatale* in the literal sense of the word because of her 'fatal flaw' (*NA*, 103), a recurring fever blister on her lip. This cancerous mole eventually causes her death, thus marking her destiny as a tragic heroine; in a novel in which the larger-than-life nature of people's personality traits, quirks and obsessions typically has a dark comic (therefore laughable) undertone, Sarah's 'fatal flaw' – one might even say, the physical analogue of the Aristotelian *hamartia* of ancient Greek tragedy – and her ensuing, sombre demise bestow on her a distinct *gravitas* and single her out as the one character in the novel worthy of genuine pity and admiration. In this tragic solemnity – and other, more superficial, traits – Sarah Strouch anticipates Mary Anne Bell in 'Sweetheart of the Song Tra Bong' as a charismatic figure who, being true to herself, loses herself in the obscure meanders of her personality. Their similarity is hinted at in their fondness for culottes, which signal an active, athletic nature. They are part of Sarah's cheerleading outfit and associated with her rebellious spirit, as William's quip – 'Culottes to sansculottes – a radical realignment' (*NA*, 103) – indicates. Beside this small detail of her attire, Sarah shares with Mary Anne Bell an irresistible enthralment with war; true to her characterization, Sarah entertains strong, contradictory feelings about it: 'This goddamn war. I hate it, I *do* hate it, but it's what I'm here for. I hate it, but I love it' (*NA*, 171 – notice how there is ambiguity in the very reference to the war, which here stands for Sarah's political fight, but also inevitably alludes to the conflict in Vietnam). Of course, Sarah is a more realistic, more extensively developed version of Mary Anne, whose characterization is necessarily more vague than her predecessor's due to the obvious constraints of the short story genre. And yet Mary Anne's tale gains in evocative power, compared to the account of Sarah Strouch's life, because it is embedded within a legendary, even fantastic, logic, through the utter implausibility of its factual premises and the equally larger-than-life connotations derived from its intertextual dialogue with Conrad's *Heart of Darkness*.

In spite of her undeniable charisma, Sarah's repeated invitations to William to embrace their cause and join in the frontline of the terroristic network, like the other members of their original group, are ultimately to no avail. As his (always reluctant) involvement with the underground movement – which of course is tied in with his one-man campaign to avoid Vietnam – threatens to become more consuming and dangerous, William forgoes Sarah's guidance and, I would argue, full rights to the title of the only hero that O'Brien has ever written, bestowed on him by O'Brien himself in a 1991 interview with Martin Naparsteck.[40] However flawed and eccentric as a role model, it is Sarah who partakes of the defining quality of O'Brien's heroes, for her allegiance to her beliefs supersedes the desire to acquiesce to the rules of society. Unsurprisingly, William's reintegration into mainstream America must therefore begin with his departure from Sarah and the pursuit of a completely different companion. William's desires fix on Bobbi, a seductive air-stewardess-cum-poet met during one of his trips as a courier for the terrorist network, a woman in whose reassuring professional demeanour and lyrical sensitivity he is determined to see the possibility of a romantic happy ending. When Bobbi turns out to be on the verge of relocation to Germany with her new husband, William has no choice but to resort to a longer-term strategy. As already discussed, having put his romantic designs on Bobbi on hold for an indefinite period of time, he has a spectacular chance to resume them thanks to the proceeds of his uranium venture. The millionaire William and the now divorced Bobbi – who, it turns out, had walked out on her first husband only two months after their wedding – thus get married nearly a decade after their initial, casual encounter.

Rather underdeveloped as a character, depicted as something of a flirt and possibly a little too receptive to the lures of money, Bobbi functions in the novel as an antithesis to Sarah, particularly in her attitude to commitment and language. Sarah is loyal, Bobbi is a heart-breaker; Sarah lives intensely, underground, in the nitty-gritty world of Realpolitik; Bobbi inhabits a loftier realm with more rarefied feelings expressed in hermetic poems, such as her earliest offering to William (and, it turns out, to several other men) entitled 'Martian Travel', about 'flight and fantasy and pale green skin, which was hard to follow, but [...] seemed meaningful despite the absence of meaning' (*NA*, 152). Sarah is a woman for whom actions count more than words, Bobbi privileges words – and indirect communication at that – over any other form of expression; Sarah is riddled with contradictions and looks for the extraordinary, Bobbi settles for a quiet, comfortable, ordinary life. In accounting for his wife's and daughter's irritation about the sudden digging of the shelter, William points out his wife's meticulousness in keeping a tidy house and a tidy life: 'she's the poet, the creative type; she believes in clean metaphors and clean language; tidiness of structure, things neatly in place. Holes aren't clean. Safety can be very messy' (*NA*, 6). William's crisis and regression to

40 See n. 15 above.

his childhood fears of annihilation is partly a radical reaction to the possibility that Bobbi might abandon him, taking their daughter Melinda with her, partly also a rejection of Bobbi's world of neat metaphors. 'The world [...] is drugged on metaphor, the opiate of our age' (*NA*, 124), says William, while digging his hole. By contrast, as he had explained earlier on in the narrative, '[u]ranium is no figure of speech; it's a figure of nature. You can hold it in your hand. It has an atomic weight of 238.03; it melts at 1,132.30 degrees centigrade; it's hard and heavy and impregnable to metaphor. I should know, I made my fortune on the stuff' (*NA*, 65). William's alienation from his wife is as inevitable as his split from Sarah, whose example remains something for him to aspire to, and yet never to be reached.

Even if her story is subordinate to William's, Sarah Strouch remains a much more successful creation than he is, because her obsessions and insecurities have convincing, low-key explanations, and are conveyed without the frenzied quality that William otherwise uses in his self-analysis and in his relentless proselytizing. Paradoxically, Sarah's subsidiary role in the novel is in great part what safeguards her status as a more rounded and sympathetic character than William: as one of the subject matters in his life story, and not a narrator in her own right, Sarah is spared the negative connotations attached to the tone of his first-person narration (incidentally, getting the right narrative tone is a problem which *The Nuclear Age* definitely shares with O'Brien's other two comedies). The other major difference between the male narrator and the female heroine of this book is to do with their respective authenticity, to go back to what I have identified as the measure of true courage for O'Brien. William fails to be authentic – and therefore, to an extent, to command our sympathy in the same way that Sarah does – because, like Paul Perry, he mostly *re*acts to circumstances (hence, for example, his stint as an underground courier, his fortuitous career as an entrepreneur, and even his reinvention as a family man), instead of following his own inner dictates. Besides, like the protagonist of *If I Die* and Paul Berlin before him, he simply cares too much about what society thinks of him, and finally succumbs to the pressure of embarrassment and the fear of public censure. Even with all her insecurities Sarah, by contrast, is always fully committed to what she believes in. As William himself readily admits: 'She was *in* the world. I was *out* of it. [...] She wanted engagement, I did not' (*NA*, 258). The element of unthinking self-abandon in what Sarah does, with the potential dangers that such an instinctive reaction to things often comports, is aptly epitomized by her 'fatal flaw', the mark both of the character's tragic status, and of her innate truthfulness to her own nature.

Like *The Nuclear Age*, *Tomcat in Love* is characterized by the idiosyncratic voice of its unreliable, inauthentic protagonist. This time, however, the first-person narrator is fixated on self-promotion and justification, rather than on prophesies of doom: an incorrigible narcissist, Professor Chippering cannot but tell his tale through the constant aggrandizement of his achievements and the downplaying of his misdemeanours. Possibly because of the comparative lightness of the issues it deals with, and in spite of its frequent lapses into farcical tones, *Tomcat in Love* manages to let Chippering's fragility seep through his overwhelmingly boorish characterization. In a way, O'Brien adopts here – on a much larger scale, and for comic effects – the same technique that he had used to outline the protagonist of *If I Die*: the more mistakenly self-righteous the character, the greater the pathos in his demise when the reality behind his self-delusions eventually catches up with him. Chippering's narrative is prompted by the wish to account for and record his plans for revenge on his ex-wife Lorna Sue and her new husband. This desire for revenge is symptomatic, amongst other things, of his inability to acknowledge his responsibility in the disintegration of his marriage. In fact, Chippering is determined to settle the score with Lorna Sue's brother Herbie, whose overbearing protectiveness – construed by the narrator as patent evidence of incestuous feelings – has led him to expose Chippering's 'harmless' deceptions to his wife, thus causing an irreparable rift in the relationship. As in a bedroom farce, evidence of Chippering's final marital indiscretion is compromisingly found under his mattress; there Chippering has hidden several cheques to a fake psychiatrist, proof of his deceitful disregard for Lorna Sue's plea that he should seek medical support for his paranoia and for the other post-traumatic stress disorder symptoms that he has been suffering from for years. This betrayal is compounded by the discovery of another object hidden under the mattress: the ledger in which Chippering has been cataloguing with clinical precision all his sexual conquests, real and imagined. That Chippering should assume the moral high ground and plead for sympathy – the readers' and the narratee's, whom Chippering imagines in the guise of a woman abandoned by her husband for a sexier, younger lover – immediately gives us the measure of his effrontery and self-importance. Chippering, however, digs deep into his and his wife's past in order to explain their present circumstances.

The novel begins with the narrator's reminiscence of 'the ridiculous, in June 1952, middle-century Minnesota, on that silvery-hot morning when Herbie Zylstra and I nailed two plywood boards together and called it an airplane' (*TL*, 1). Unable to get the aeroplane to fly, Herbie decides to use it as a cross, and to re-enact the crucifixion, enlisting Lorna Sue in the role of Christ. This disturbing childhood tableau, predictably enough, leads to disaster, as the little girl ends up permanently scarred by a wound on her hand. The hole in Lorna Sue's hand – the tangible mark of the original trauma at the heart of the novel – raises once again, and more urgently perhaps than any analogous images in O'Brien's other books, the question of a possible gender bias in the author's depiction of distressful situations and shocking ordeals. We have already seen that, even when ambivalently caught between the promise of an (illusory) sense of security and wholeness and the reality of trauma, the holes and underground passages in O'Brien's other works offer an irresistible connection with psychoanalytic characterizations of the female body. After all, in psychoanalytic discourse the maternal body is cast as the site of pre-lapsarian stability and unity, while the female genitalia are the privileged signifier of lack and separation, and therefore, by extension, of post-lapsarian decay. So far I have suggested that we should resist the temptation to read O'Brien's topography of trauma as a gendered body, for O'Brien's most recurrent, deliberate anatomical allusions are to the organs of elimination, rather than to the female reproductive system, in a bid to make literal the waste of war. How should we read trauma, however, when its prime site is a penetrative wound inflicted on a female body, as appears to be the case in *Tomcat in Love*? What are the implications of the stigmata-like mark on Lorna Sue's hand?

With good reason, Chippering himself pinpoints Lorna Sue's immolation as the trigger of the dysfunctional triangular relationship between the two of them and Herbie, united as they all are in a strange bond of violence, complicity and guilt. Significantly, it is only by accident that the young Chippering does not take part in the crucifixion of Lorna Sue, with whom – it is worth remembering – he had already developed a mutual attraction. The boys' first attempt at nailing her hand to the makeshift cross is averted at the last minute by Chippering's mother, and later Herbie proceeds on his own. In a bout of characteristic self-righteousness, Chippering lists the eccentric motives as to why he feels cheated for not having been able to witness, let alone be actively involved in, this momentous event: 'It was my plywood. [...] Other reasons too: because at age sixteen I would make first love with Lorna Sue Zylstra on the hood of my father's Pontiac, and because ten years later we would be married, and because twenty-some years after that Lorna Sue would discover romance with another man, and betray me, and move to Tampa' (*TL*, 9). Chippering's regret for his exclusion from the wounding of Lorna Sue is dictated by his sense of entitlement over her and, one suspects, by his jealousy at the thought that he should have let Herbie 'penetrate' her first. For Chippering, Lorna Sue's crucifixion is the beginning of a lifelong obsession with issues of faith, in all the nuances of the word: the intimacy between lovers, the fidelity between spouses, the trust amongst friends, the support of one's family or even the bond between fellow soldiers, and the relationship with the divine.

His reaction to the pivotal, initial incident in the story is the disappointment of the worshipper who has been excluded from witnessing a mystery crucial to a cult; from this moment on, Chippering becomes convinced that

Lorna Sue's crucifixion has made her holy in the eyes of the Zylstras: 'it occurred to me that this entire family was in love with Lorna Sue, or obsessed by her, or caught up in some perverse form of idolatry. [...] The scar on her hand' (*TL*, 14). Clearly, Lorna Sue's alleged divine status amongst her kin reflects Chippering's own feelings for her: 'I told her she was sacred to me. I told her she was holy. I told her I had loved her before either of us had been born' (*TL*, 21). O'Brien continues to pursue these fanciful religious associations in the unfolding of the narrative, capitalizing on the ironic gap between Chippering's recourse to the language of spirituality and worship, and the man's much more mundane and self-serving preoccupations. (This move recalls the bathetic shift in the mention of O'Brien's musings about Canada and Sweden in the same breath as Socrates' refusal to leave Athens in *If I Die*). In punishment for his sister's martyrdom, Herbie is sent off to a Jesuit school, from which he returns a year later suitably repentant and withdrawn, but also possessed of a fanatic 'self-flagellating religiosity' (*TL*, 42). When in 1957 the local Catholic church is ravaged by fire, and four days later sexual graffiti appear on the ruins and a pair of female breasts are drawn with red lipstick on a statue of Christ, Chippering is convinced of Herbie's responsibility for these acts of vandalism. As the years go by, while Herbie seems to sink deeper into his strange moods and obsessive concern for his sister, Chippering flourishes – or so he would have us believe – into a devoted husband, an esteemed academic and a highly accomplished man whom 'women find [...] attractive beyond words' (*TL*, 29–30). So popular is he, particularly with his female students, that the jealousy of his colleagues is roused: Chippering is convinced of the existence of an academic plot against him, since he continues to be denied the prize for teaching excellence that is obviously, in his opinion, his due. Even his involvement in the conflict in Vietnam is a resounding triumph: the narrator proudly refers to himself as a 'war hero', the deserving 'recipient of the Silver Star for valor' (*TL*, 30).

In the course of the narrative, Chippering's boastful claims predictably turn out to be greatly exaggerated and to obscure terrible secrets. The professor's young conquests all see through his vanity and manipulate it to their advantage: when two students threaten to expose his advances, Chippering offers to ghostwrite their theses in exchange for their silence, but is forced into resigning from his job as soon as the entire arrangement becomes known to the academic authorities. More shocking still is the truth behind his service in Vietnam. Being an awards clerk, he manages to confer the Silver Star on himself, for what is really an act of revenge, and not of heroism. Chippering calls in an air-strike to spook the six Green Berets who, in a cruel prank, had abandoned him in the middle of the jungle; desire for retaliation for this terrible ordeal is compounded by further resentment because Chippering holds the Greenies responsible for having tainted his relationship with a beautiful Vietnamese girl. He had fallen for her, thinking her a model of purity and marvelling at her sexual prowess, only to realize that all along he had been sharing her with his six companions on their secluded military outpost. Years later, at the time when Chippering is telling us his story, the threat of the Green Berets' own revenge for the air-strike has become a further strain on the professor, the final straw that contributes to the definitive collapse of his plot against Lorna Sue.

Chippering's present-day progress thus unfolds through a series of humil-iating experiences: from a public spanking in front of his students, courtesy of Herbie and Lorna Sue's new husband, to his dishonourable dismissal from work, to a couple of pathetic attempts to start a new career. In a nursery school, he tries to teach Shakespeare to his charges and is apparently falsely accused of molesting the children; on live television, where he is competing to become the new 'Captain Nineteen', the superhero host of a children's show, he suffers a nervous breakdown. Unsurprisingly, instead of wreaking revenge on his ex-wife, Chippering ends up being institutionalized for post-traumatic stress disorder, before he decides to start a new life with the former Mrs Kooshof, the woman he has amazingly managed to conquer in spite of his pathological obsession with Lorna Sue and his disgraceful spiralling out of control. Of course, the endlessly accommodating and forgiving Mrs Kooshof is herself given a suitably dire background, in what looks like a dress rehearsal for the stories of incredible squalor of *July, July*: she is married to a fraudster who is serving time in prison and is evidently desperate enough for a fresh start to want to hook up with Thomas Chippering. In spite of this surprising happy ending, Chippering's redemption is far from assured: he may have taken up temporary residence with his new companion on a tropical island and, in view of his spectacular breakdown, he may be seeking to toe the line of domestic harmony but, as he readily admits, 'the proud, brawny tomcat still struts within [him]' (*TL*, 367), ogling every woman in sight, confident of his irresistible charms.

In Chippering O'Brien has created his most boorish character: preten-tious, sanctimonious, always on the defensive with embarrassingly transparent excuses. Chippering's rare glimpses of his true motives, though, are disarmingly honest, as this admission testifies: 'From childhood on, I had been consumed by an insatiable appetite for affection, hunger without limit, *a bottomless hole inside me*. I would (and I will) do virtually anything to acquire love, virtually anything to keep it. I would (and will) lie for love, cheat for love, beg for love, steal for love, ghostwrite for love, seek revenge for love, swim oceans for love, perhaps even kill for love' (*TL*, 168, my italics). Not content with the scope of this confession, which chimes with a conviction very dear to his author, Chippering draws us all in this desperate craving for love: 'Am I alone in this? Certainly not. Each of us, I firmly believe, is propelled through life by a restless, inexhaustible need for affection' (*TL*, 168). Chippering's moments of lucid self-analysis, however, never last long, and never lead to positive action and to attempts to mend his ways. Only his attitude to Lorna Sue changes radically at the end of the novel, and that is because of a dramatic twist in the plot: Chippering finally learns that Lorna Sue had been behind the acts of vandalism ascribed to Herbie. On his part, feeling responsible for his little sister's traumatization, Herbie had since then always been trying to take care of her and to hide her condition. The climactic showdown between the two ex-spouses occurs as a paradoxical reversal of Chippering's original plans for revenge, when one night Lorna Sue creeps into the house he shares with Mrs Kooshof, demanding unconditional adoration and threatening to blow up the entire place.

With its extravagant plot, overblown characters and insufferable narrator, *Tomcat in Love* has generally left critics indifferent or, at best, perplexed.[41] Yet the heavy-handed execution of the novel – misguided or otherwise – leaves readers with no doubts about O'Brien's position *vis-à-vis* his protagonist's misogynist arrogance: Chippering is a figure of fun, whether we can get over his unpleasantness or not. Still, unlike other authorial alter egos, whose pretensions to intellectual superiority and to a moral high ground are similarly, more or less explicitly, ridiculed – as in the case of the Tim O'Brien in *If I Die* – Chippering remains a particularly inauthentic character, undeserving of our sympathy. For the protagonist of *If I Die*, the act of railing against the 'jungle of robots' is, all in all, a rather uncharacteristic moment, since he is too busy scrutinizing his own failings, of which he is painfully aware. Chippering, instead, *never* appears to be even remotely willing to accept responsibility for his lot, and spends the best part of the novel fabricating one conspiracy theory after another. Always ready to claim agency if the outcome is positive (witness his confidence in his irresistibility to women, his academic brilliance, his valour as a soldier), he otherwise sees himself as an innocent victim of circumstances. Moreover, while readers might be inclined to forgive the young protagonist of *If I Die* his (occasionally) aggrandized sense of his own worth, they will not be so understanding with the self-delusions of a middle-aged man like Chippering who, having received more than his fair share of knocks from life, really ought to know better.

Worthy of more serious and careful consideration from the readers is Herbie and Lorna Sue's disturbing childhood prank, and the significance of what at the end of the narrative transpires to have been an act of protest on

41 See for example the two reviews of *Tomcat in Love*, published in the *New York Times* in September 1998: Michiko Kakutani's ferocious critique of the book was followed, a week later, by Jane Smiley's more appreciative response to O'Brien's change in style and direction, in spite of some reservations on his command of the comic register.

Lorna Sue's part, in her self-immolation. Herbie's long overdue account recasts their re-enactment of the crucifixion as a challenge to the patriarchal hierarchy of Christianity, prompted by Lorna Sue's desire for inclusion in a male-dominated world, and by his own curiosity: 'Wanted to see if she'd go to heaven. If I'd go to hell. If the skies would open. *Curious*' (*TL*, 341). The little girl is indeed eager to participate in her brother's 'experiment' because she wants to play Jesus, replacing a male divinity with a female one, as testified also by her defilement of religious images later on in the narrative. In significant contrast to what would have been Chippering's attitude in the same circumstance, and what has indeed been his attitude throughout the book, even after his shocking revelation, Herbie refuses to find excuses for his behaviour and to lay the blame on Lorna Sue as a victim colluding with her own torturer. Mark Heberle indeed goes as far as to suggest that Lorna Sue's characterization – her self-destructiveness, her aggression, her picking at the wound, effectively a form of self-mutilation – actually captures the post-traumatic symptoms of childhood sexual abuse.[42] Unfortunately, the narrow scope allowed by the first-person narration, and Chippering's own peculiar limitations as a narrator, prevent O'Brien from delving any deeper into the traumas represented – and possibly hidden – by Lorna Sue's wound. And yet, in spite of the final twist in the plot, Lorna Sue is not typecast as the villain of the piece, another aberrant (female) figure and a convenient scapegoat for the (male) protagonist's misadventures. On the contrary, her former husband's insensitivity and his track record of exploitative relationships highlight Lorna Sue's victimhood, even if the novel fails to provide a detailed explanation of its causes. For the readers, the hole in Lorna Sue's hand remains the most visible sign of Chippering's inability to fathom his ex-wife and of O'Brien's difficulty in finding the words to articulate the experience of a post-traumatic survivor. The scar on Lorna Sue's body is the physical correlative of the 'bottomless hole' inside the narrator, with both characters exemplifying the 'inexhaustible need for affection' that Chippering – convincingly for once – identifies as the common plight of mankind.

Unlike the previous two comedies, *July, July* does not suffer from the overbearing voice of a disturbed narrator; in his latest novel to date, O'Brien's gusto for the excessive has been channelled into the extravagant quantitative, as well as qualitative, permutations of the lonely, maladjusted anti-hero, a type that in its numerous reincarnations in the cast of *July, July* exemplifies the disillusionment and cynicism of a generation who, for all the inevitable distance from their youthful idealism, do not seem able to get over the rude awakening that time has in store for us all. In a standard narrative ploy for the exploration of nostalgic reminiscences, longstanding recriminations and

42 Heberle, *A Trauma Artist*, p. 268.

bittersweet self-reflections, O'Brien's Vietnam war generation is epitomized by the Class of '69 of Darton Hall College, gathered together for a belated thirtieth anniversary reunion in the summer of 2000, in all its textbook topical manifestations: the amputated veteran, the draft dodger who relocated to Canada, the women liberated by the sexual revolution but incapable of finding love or peace of mind, alongside characters who more generally exemplify middle-age frustrations, regrets and disillusionments. The chapters alternate between the account of the mawkish celebration, unfolding in the present time in the 'Class of '69' sequence, and individual vignettes each dealing with one of the main characters and focusing on a pivotal episode in his or her past. For the first time in O'Brien's work, the female protagonists outnumber the male ones, by a ratio of nearly two to one. Asked about the reason for his interest in the numerous female figures in *July, July*, O'Brien readily admits that this is a deliberate departure from his more usual focus on male experience:

> I suppose in part it was a technical challenge, to prove to myself that I could do it, that as a writer I could portray convincing, detailed, intelligent, compelling women. More important, it seemed to me that most of the fiction set in the watershed era of the late 1960s focuses on stories about men — the pressures of war, draft-dodging, and so on. But for every man who went to Vietnam, or for every man who went to Canada, there were countless sisters and girlfriends and wives and mothers, each of whom had her own fascinating story, her own tragedies and suffering, her own healing afterward. I mean, sure, the war was important back then, but Vietnam wasn't everything.[43]

O'Brien's success in this venture is only partial, compromised by the sheer scope of his self-imposed challenge: a three-hundred-page novel, covering a span of thirty years in the life of a dozen unique individuals, simply does not allow for the psychological depth and the detailed characterization that had prompted this enterprise in the first place. Perhaps as a result of this constraint, and more clearly as a result of the flattening fatalism with which the narrative is imbued, the eleven protagonists whose stories make up this 'ensemble novel'[44] all sound remarkably similar, each a slight modulation of a very specific type: the cynical anti-hero whose life has been marred by rejection or disappointment, particularly in matters of the heart. By contrast, *The Things They Carried*, O'Brien's only other novel with a substantial cast, is much more subtle in the characterization of the men of Alpha Company,

43 'Interview with Tim O'Brien', *Readers Read*, http://www.readersread.com/features/timobrien.htm (accessed 22 October 2008).
44 'Ensemble novel' is O'Brien's own definition, from an interview with Josh Karp for *The Atlantic*.

possibly because of its narrower thematic scope and of the unifying, moderating filter provided by the voice of a sympathetic intradiegetic narrator: with his relentless self-questioning and incessant tinkering with his stories, the fictional Tim O'Brien in *Things* prevents his co-protagonists from turning into larger-than-life but mono-dimensional figures.

Focused on distilling the essence of each character in turn, *July, July* instead provides an elaborate series of variations on the same topic, i.e. the extremes that people will go to in an effort to be loved, a theme that Heberle and other critics have identified as one of the recurrent preoccupations, if not *the* recurrent preoccupation, behind O'Brien's work. As in his other comedies, however, the main concern of the text is presented in its most overblown manifestations, for *July, July* concentrates with unremitting pessimism on the failures in the private lives of its protagonists. The body count for casualties of disastrous romantic liaisons is particularly disheartening – and I am afraid that the expression 'body count' is quite literal in a couple of cases: 'Loon Point', for example, is about an adultery that ends in tragedy, with the accidental drowning of one of the lovers. Overall, *July, July* describes several unsuccessful marriages and abusive relationships, as well as unrequited loves: 'Nogales' provides a particularly tragic study of emotional manipulation in the story of Karen Burns, the middle-aged, lonely director of a retirement community in Tucson, Arizona. Karen's infatuation for Darrell, one of her employees, a younger man who knows how to lead her on to his advantage, costs her her life and the lives of four elderly people in her care: the small party are left to die in the desert after they have ceased to be of use to Darrell as a cover for a drug deal.

Compared to the plight of other members of the Class of '69, Karen's story – dreadful as it is – is rather low-key, for the novel spans a range of ever darker and more bizarre amorous predicaments. In 'Well Married', we are told of Spook Spinelli and her two husbands, Lincoln and James: their bigamous arrangement finds itself under strain when the two men, after years of peaceful acceptance of the status quo, finally side together against their wife. In 'Little People', we learn about Jan Huebner, the class clown, and her double life as Veronica, the uninhibited model of salacious private photoshoots. Jan embarks on this brief, secret career when she acquiesces in the request of Andrew Wilton, 'a diminutive, large-headed young man with an offer of fifty easy dollars' (*JJ*, 62). The fact that her first, and main, client is a little person who manages to exploit Jan's own lack of conventional beauty is a further illustration of the unceasing, determinate focus on human misery in *July, July*. Jan eventually quits her seedy career and rejoins ordinary life; she even finds love and gets married to Andrew's brother. Needless to say, their marriage is not destined to last, and at the class reunion in the summer of 2000 she is just another bitter divorcée. To end the overview of O'Brien's grotesque turn in *July, July*, and lest readers should be under the impression that it is only the women who make spectacular mistakes in this novel, it is worth mentioning 'Too Skinny', another tale about how insecurity and self-hatred can cause people to plummet into unlikely double lives. This time the protagonist is a man, Marv Bertel. A mop manufacturer and an overweight, middle-aged widower, he gets caught up in a silly, unsustainable lie that he has impulsively spun to his secretary. In an attempt to impress the young, beautiful Sandra, in a moment of madness, Marv leads her to believe that he is the venerable Thomas Pierce, a famously reclusive and much celebrated postmodern author, clearly modelled by O'Brien on Thomas Pynchon. Sandra is suitably struck by Marv's revelation, and the two soon embark on a romance which culminates in an unsurprisingly resentful and short-lived marriage.

As this catalogue of wacky characters and extreme situations intimates, *July, July* does not tread softly on its subject matter. It would probably have worked better as a collection of short stories than it does as a novel: the attempt to bring together all these extraordinary characters – through the apt, but careworn, expedient of the class reunion – backfires, because it heightens the morbid, mock-cynical and self-pitying mood that already mars the premises of some of the individual vignettes. Again, as in *Tomcat in Love*, the narcissistic indulgences and commiserations that pervade *July, July* strike a false note both for quantitative and for qualitative reasons. What is forgivable in the characterization and the narrative voice of the young O'Brien in *If I Die* becomes much less understandable in the case of the eleven men and women who share the limelight in the later text. All in all, the protagonist of *If I Die* gives in to self-pity and dejection, and to lamenting the unfairness of his circumstances, with remarkable constraint, considering both his young age and the fact that he is faced with the prospect of death and with the painful awareness that he has betrayed his own ideals. By comparison, the lot of the class of '69, who are troubled, in most cases, by more mundane dilemmas and problems (lack of popularity, amorous frustrations, fear of solitude and, of course, middle-age disillusionments and disappointments) is vastly easier. O'Brien's self-imposed challenge thus fails primarily for technical reasons. In other words, my reservations about the overall success of the female characters in *July, July* are connected to O'Brien's failure to master the comedic mode rather than to his subscription to dubious gender politics: the female protagonists in *July, July* are as accomplished and as autonomous in the general economy of the narrative as their male counterparts. What they all suffer from is O'Brien's weak control of the satirical register, which here finds expression in monotone bleakness and excessive grotesqueness, products of the same tendency to go overboard that undermines the author's other comedies. Besides, the poignancy of the novel's main themes – the crumbling of illusions, the desperate quest for love and acceptance – is not particularly well-matched to the scathing style of comedy that O'Brien has chosen to write. In fact, the possibility of success in a dark comic novel lies in achieving a difficult balance between the unsparing criticism required of satire, paired with the irreverent, merciless wit of black humour, and the creation of a modicum of sympathy towards the main characters. Such sympathy is absolutely necessary for readers to get involved in the story.

In this and his other comic works, in trying to combine the denigrating spirit of black humour with the didacticism of the novel of ideas, which both require bold narrative strokes, O'Brien has often ended up alienating readers, by losing the measure of his caricatural exaggerations and therefore eliciting little or no compassion for his characters. In her *New York Times* review of *The Nuclear Age*, for example, Michiko Kakutani complains that, since '[p]eople do not normally spend every waking hour obsessing about abstractions like nuclear war or worldwide devastation', Cowling must 'strik[e] us as little more than an aberration – a kook, and a pretty boring kook at that'; and speaking of the 'cartoonish' characters in *Tomcat in Love*, she questions their actual success in making the narrator's desired point ('bullying, macho men and catty, calculating women; clownish figures, meant perhaps to underscore the comic similarities between "wartime combat and peacetime romance," in Tom's words').[45] In a ferocious review of *July, July*, David Gates also complains about the predictable, caricatural quality of the protagonists and situations depicted in the text:

> But this is only a novel, not reality. So O'Brien gives us capital-C Characters. A still-traumatized Vietnam veteran. (Here, you play novelist: Do you make him an amputee? A druggie? Have him hear a voice in his head?) An uptight Republican housewife. (Do you give her breast cancer? A husband who's 'a senior vice president'? Put her on a 30-years-too-late acid trip?) A draft dodger who split for Canada. (Did the Republican woman jilt him all those years ago?) If you correctly answered yes to each of those questions, you can imagine the other major characters for yourself – as long as you don't go hog-wild for diversity.[46]

---

45 Michiko Kakutani, 'Prophet of Doom', *The New York Times*, 28 September 1985, http://www.nytimes.com/1985/09/28/books/books-of-the-times-prophet-of-doom.html (accessed 20 October 2008). I agree with Kakutani's general critique of the limitations of *The Nuclear Age*: the dialogue is often 'leaden' and Cowling's characterization, after the 'pleasing specificity' of his childhood recollections, does 'grow increasingly vague and full of clichés'. Unsurprisingly, Kakutani is even more critical of the supporting characters in *The Nuclear Age*, and particularly of the women, whom she finds 'ridiculous in the extreme'. This is where my reading departs from hers, in the case of Sarah Strouch.

46 David Gates, 'Everybody Must Get Sloshed', *The New York Times*, 13 October 2002, http://www.nytimes.com/2002/10/13/books/everybody-must-get-sloshed.html (accessed 20 October 2008).

Of course, not all the reviews were so negative, and even the most critical ones tend to give O'Brien credit for setting himself the challenge to deliver comedy through deeply unsympathetic characters. Still, it is easy to see why these novels fail to draw readers in in quite the same way as O'Brien's most successful works, like *Cacciato* or *Things*. It is primarily the dedicated reader, interested in charting the development of O'Brien as a writer and his command of the comic register, who can summon the emotional and intellectual energy to follow to the end either Cowling's mad, monomaniacal adventure, Chippering's self-obsessed, justificatory ramblings, or the drunken, cynical reminiscences of the Class of '69. What these characters also lack, in comparison to O'Brien's more accomplished creations, is not so much the ability to be true to themselves – authenticity, as we have seen, is not achieved by any of O'Brien's protagonists – but the willingness to admit, or even the awareness of, their full responsibility for their actions, and their failures to act. In my opinion, the most revealing and compelling aspect of O'Brien's engagement with the comic mode is that it inevitably unfolds with the development of a series of pathetic men and women, who are incapable of meaningful adult relationships, tainted as they all are by past traumas and secrets. O'Brien's writing, and his characterization of male and female figures alike, are undoubtedly at their strongest in the adoption of more level tones and the cultivation of a poetics of ambiguity and uncertainty. On their part, with their unapologetic brashness, O'Brien's three comedies certainly bring the point home: nowhere is the connection between trauma and the inability to establish healthy emotional and sexual relationships articulated more openly than in *The Nuclear Age*, *Tomcat in Love* and *July, July*.

Ambiguity, ellipses and gut reactions

With the notable exception of Mary Anne Bell, the protagonist of a story in her own right, the female figures in *The Things They Carried* play several variations on the type of the distant and/or idealized addressee of tales of masculine traumas, or the wished-for purveyors of consolation and sympathy to the male traumatized subjects. In what is generally acknowledged as his best work, O'Brien describes several instances of failed communication: attempts to establish emotional connections that seem to fall on deaf ears or are met by inadequate, conventional reactions, tales that remain untold for fear that the intended listener will not want or will not be able to relate to them, even stories whose unfolding deliberately baffles and offends an audience looking for narrative precision and a sense of closure or moral progression. It is through the description of such failures that O'Brien outlines – by contrast – his vision of a model readership and of the ideal response that he wishes to bring about in his audience. O'Brien's is a poetics of reception that cuts across traditional gender divides and that explains his reliance on scatological references and images of the grotesque body. By drawing attention to this non-gender-specific physiognomy, once again I hope to redress the criticism that O'Brien has received for the inability – of his work in general but particularly of *Things* – to challenge 'a discourse of war in which apparently innocent American men are tragically wounded and women are objectified, excluded, and silenced'.[47] A closer look at the narrative exchanges and at the contextualization of the gender stereotypes that O'Brien uses reveals that the author is continuously at pains to show the constructed nature of the notions of masculinity and femininity, and that he ultimately supersedes them both in order to argue for – and ideally to ensure – a visceral reception to his stories.

As already mentioned, early on in the novel we are made privy to the exchange at cross-purposes between Jimmy Cross and Martha, whose reluctance to be drawn into the lieutenant's account of the war finds a plausible explanation in her desire to distance herself from his more violent, predatory side – a side of which she has had a brief intimation during their awkward courtship. Much more unsuccessful than this stunted correspondence, and infinitely more shocking in the violence of the male reaction to the lack of female response, is the failure of communication between Rat Kiley and the sister of a fellow soldier killed in Vietnam. Kiley pours his heart out in a letter of condolences to Curt Lemon's sister, singing the praises of his best friend and recalling his crazy deeds. With the letter remaining unanswered, Kiley feels provoked to brand the woman as a 'dumb cooze' (*TTC*, 68) – a insult whose misogynistic violence appears to be implicitly condoned by the narrative, given the seemingly inexplicable heartlessness of the woman in question and, conversely, the highly emotional state of the bereaved soldier. The key to understanding the woman's behaviour, however, lies in the exact content of the letter, as well as in the general characterization of her brother which, significantly, is developed here and in the rest of the novel in great part through Kiley's own perspective. In his exchange with Lemon's sister, for example, Kiley mentions admiringly Curt Lemon's unforgettable Halloween celebrations: with his body painted in several colours and a weird mask on his face, Curt 'hikes over to a ville and goes trick-or-treating almost stark naked, just boots and balls and an M-16' (*TTC*, 67–68). This preliminary conflation of sex and violence is later made much more explicit in Rat Kiley's 'spiced up' retelling of this anecdote:

See, what happens is, it's like four in the morning, and Lemon sneaks into a

47 Smith, "'The Things Men Do'", p. 17.

hootch with that weird mask on. Everybody's asleep, right? So he wakes up this cute little mama-san. 'Hey, Mama-san,' he goes, real soft like. 'Hey, Mama-san – trick or treat!' Should've seen her *face*. About freaks. I mean, there's this buck naked ghost standing there, and he's got this M-16 up against her ear and he whispers, 'Hey, Mama-san, trick or fuckin' treat!' Then he takes off her pj's. Strips her right down. Sticks the pajamas in his sack and tucks her into bed and heads for the next hootch. (*TTC*, 232)

Of course, no one knows or can know what really happened during Curt Lemon's solitary expedition, and the focus, anyway, is on the mythology created around the character's identity as a maverick. Rat Kiley, the enthusiastic custodian of Lemon's reckless exploits, relies on this particular anecdote as the linchpin of his tribute to his friend, while remaining completely oblivious to the offensive, humiliating aspects of his story. For the likes of Lemon and Kiley, the indulgence in some gratuitous violence – harmless pranks, such as going fishing 'with a whole damn crate of hand grenades [...] all that gore, about twenty zillion dead gook fish' or going trick-or-treating 'just boots and balls and an M-16' (*TTC*, 231) – is the mark of a humorous gutsiness, the confirmation – to be duly acclaimed – that boys will be boys. And, if this is what boys will do, the silence of Curt Lemon's sister in response to the letter where Rat Kiley mourns his friend's death and salutes the *joie de vivre* of his pranks should be read as something quite different from the sign of unconcern that provokes Kiley's anger against the 'dumb cooze' who never wrote back. He may not be aware of the threat of sexual violence underlying gestures that the soldiers regard as examples of fearlessness and heroic panache, but she is – and so are we. Elsewhere, the novel provides an incontrovertible critique of Curt Lemon's machismo; already dismissed by the narrator as a posturing that would often go too far and that would often be embellished with 'little flourishes that never happened', in an endless refashioning of the 'tough soldier' mythology (*TTC*, 83), Lemon's desire to live up to his ideal self-image is made the object of ridicule in 'The Dentist'. In this brief chapter Lemon proves his absolute fearlessness by having a perfectly good tooth removed by the army dentist on whose chair he had fainted earlier on the same day.

More generally, throughout the novel, and in spite of the frequent references to the soldiers' youth, O'Brien tries to instil in his readers a healthy scepticism towards the idea that age should be treated as an excuse for violent behaviour. In 'The Things They Carried' the identification of Jimmy Cross with 'just a kid at war, in love' (*TTC*, 11) hovers precariously between the character's free indirect speech and a comment from the narrator, but our temptation to take this statement at face value, whatever its source, is seriously undermined once it resurfaces as a justification mouthed by Azar, a particularly disagreeable and sadistic soldier, when he blows up a puppy, having strapped him to an antipersonnel mine: "'What's everybody so upset about? [...] I mean, Christ, I'm just a *boy*'" (*TTC*, 35). This episode foreshadows another act of cruelty against a harmless animal, Rat Kiley's slow killing of a baby water buffalo in the aftermath of Curt Lemon's death. This time the gory execution is witnessed silently by the platoon, who feel no pity for the mauled, dying creature, even though they are dumbstruck in amazement at Kiley's violent expression of grief. In spite of the obvious, if irrational, significance of Kiley's gesture as an act of retribution for Lemon's own dismemberment, the event remains not fully comprehensible, let alone definable: it is 'something essential, something brand new and profound, a piece of the world so startling there was not yet a name for it' (*TTC*, 76). An attempt at an explanation is provided, as is to be expected, by Mitchell Sanders, whose marked need to distil a moral from every story leads him to dispense one of his typical aphorisms in recognition of the iniquity of Kiley's act: 'Well, that's Nam. [...] Garden of Evil. Over here, man, every sin's real fresh and original' (*TTC*, 76). And yet, as we shall see later on, O'Brien's fashioning of his ideal reader, through metafictional reflections and negative examples, undermines this interpretative act which conveniently ascribes to the war all the blame for the soldiers' fall from grace.

Kiley's grieving, of course, continues in the penning of the unanswered letter to Lemon's sister, in which he gives full expression to his love for his dead friend and to his admiration for his daredevil personality. The threatening subtext of sexual violence in Kiley's tale of male camaraderie is an unlikely premise for a positive female response to what can be effectively viewed as an act of narrative seduction, much like the heroic tale of Jimmy Cross – to be written, in the lieutenant's wishes, by his friend Tim O'Brien – that will get Martha 'to come begging'.[48] The seductive intent of Kiley's glorification of masculinity is reiterated by his choice of words to qualify his interlocutor's silence – a choice disturbingly foregrounded by a gloss made in the narrator's voice: 'Listen to Rat Kiley. Cooze, he says. He does not say bitch. He certainly does not say woman, or girl. He says cooze. Then he spits and stares. He's nineteen years old – it's too much for him – so he looks at you with those big sad gentle killer eyes and says *cooze*, because his friend is dead, and because it's so incredibly sad and true: she never wrote back' (*TTC*, 68). The narrator's intervention rationalizes Kiley's misogynistic rage. At the

---

48 Cf. Pamela Smiley, 'The Role of the Ideal (Female) Reader in Tim O'Brien's *The Things They Carried*: Why Should Real Women Play?', *The Massachusetts Review*, 43.4 (2002), pp. 602–13. Incidentally, in *Going After Cacciato* – the only other fictional text in which O'Brien mentions a correspondence between a soldier and his buddy's sister – makes the narrative seduction explicit, when Stink Harris find out that his little sister has been sending naked photographs of herself to Bernie Lynn (*GAC*, 140).

same time, however, this unsavoury anecdote is inscribed within the narrator's attempt to corroborate his belief that a true war story is distinguished by an 'absolute and uncompromising allegiance to obscenity and evil. [...] You can tell a true war story if it embarrasses you. If you don't care for obscenity, you don't care for the truth; if you don't care for the truth, watch how you vote. Send guys to war, they come home talking dirty' (*TTC*, 68).

The obscene truths of a true war story – the blood, the filth, the explosions of physical and verbal violence – must cause *embarrassment*, a word that, with its social rather than private implications, draws attention to the relationship between the storyteller and his or her audience.[49] With his own personal allegiance to obscenity and evil in the metanarrative notations to Kiley's abusive reaction, O'Brien makes sure that the collapse of the norms of human decency caused by the war is replicated in the impropriety of the act of storytelling itself, which becomes a 'talking dirty' both in its content and in its delivery. Such a duality is already present in the ambivalence of the expression 'how to tell' which, alongside its most immediate meaning, in this context, as a guide to assess the veracity of a specific tale on the grounds of its realistic portrayal of the immorality of war, also works as a reminder of the qualities that the storyteller must put into his or her narrative in order to infuse it with some kind of truth. Thus, the novel's programmatic subscription to obscenity and evil continues in a shocking revelation of how the main storyteller in the book is also susceptible to its draw. In an unsettling metafictional coda to 'How to Tell a True War Story', the forty-three-year-old narrator Tim O'Brien – the same character who has set himself up as a self-aware intellectual, the draftee who was too good for the war, 'too smart, too compassionate, too everything. [...] A *liberal*, for Christ's sake' (*TTC*, 40-41), the protagonist and writer of *If I Die in a Combat Zone* and the acclaimed author of *Going After Cacciato* – sheds his carefully constructed politically correct persona to echo Rat Kiley's angry misogyny. O'Brien explains how occasionally, after he has told the story of Kiley's grief, a member of the audience – 'always a woman. Usually it's an older woman of kindly temperament and humane politics' (*TTC*, 80) – will approach him to share her appreciation of the tale and her concern for its teller's inability to move on to new, less painful material. This figure, who embodies a stereotypically feminine response to O'Brien's stories, becomes the object of the narrator's ridiculing scorn – 'The poor baby buffalo, it made her sad. Sometimes, even, there are little tears' (*TTC*, 80): the woman's emotional reaction is clearly inadequate – and is eventually dismissed as another, uncomprehending 'dumb cooze' (*TTC*, 80). This deliberately crude slip seals the narrator's

49 One cannot overemphasize here the crucial difference between *embarrassment* and *shame*: the former involves the humiliating exposure in the public sphere, while the latter can be experienced in relation to qualities or actions known only to oneself.

absolute allegiance to obscenity and evil, capitalizing on the gender divide, but also highlights, through shock tactics, the effect of the war on his own self-regarding humane politics. Much as the woman's response to the story might be belittled for its simplistic sentimentality, O'Brien's transformation into a foul-mouthed chauvinist is a long step away from the image of the pedigreed liberal – 'Phi Beta Kappa and summa cum laude and president of the student body and full-ride scholarship for grad studies at Harvard' (*TTC*, 41) – and sensitive writer on which his authority as a narrator has been built. Moreover, the confusion between the fictional character and the real-life author increases the shock experienced by readers in the verbal lashing-out against the older woman, who is effectively one of their number, an addressee of O'Brien's stories.

This coda is an expansion of the communicational dynamics that we have already seen at work between Jimmy Cross and Martha, and Kiley and Lemon's sister: men seeking for validation from an ideal female reader who is excluded *a priori* from the very narrative that she is asked to relate to. It is no wonder that the woman in O'Brien's audience is shown to comment only on the killing of the baby buffalo – the death of an innocent creature which, as Smith points out, echoes the death of the soldiers' innocence[50] – and not on those parts of the story that contain a more or less explicit sexual threat. While it is true that in *Things* women are often configured as distant, unini- tiated and unsympathetic readers, O'Brien does problematize this equation, which, it ought to be noted, typically arises when male narrators are telling particularly emotional and traumatic tales – a circumstance that possibly explains, but cannot excuse, their sexist implications. In the three above- mentioned encounters between men and women, O'Brien offers an unpalatable, but honest, representation of the gender divide in our culture – a divide that has traditionally been heightened by war (it is a fact that Martha and Lemon's sister would not have had to fear the draft call) and that is shown to have been further exasperated in the male veterans' processing of trauma and perception of their alienation from the uninitiated civilian population.[51] The 'woman of kindly temperament and humane politics', who explains that 'as a rule she hates war stories, she can't understand why people want to wallow in all the blood and gore' (*TTC*, 80), is singled out by the narrator O'Brien as a predictable epitome of that part of society which, by

50 Smith, '"The Things Men Do"', p. 30.
51 'The veteran is isolated not only by the images of the horror that he has witnessed and perpetrated but also by his special status as an initiate in the cult of war. He imagines that no civilian, certainly no woman or child, can comprehend his confrontation with evil and death. He views the civilian with a mixture of idealization and contempt: she is at once innocent and ignorant. He views himself, by contrast, as at once superior and defiled'; Judith Lewis Herman, *Trauma and Recovery: From Domestic Abuse to Political Terror* (London: Pandora, 1992), p. 66.

definition, has no connection to war. To his credit, though, O'Brien (the author) does not conceal the strand of sexual aggressiveness – in male behaviour and in male stories – that causes the various women in the narrative to maintain their distance from the men's appeals for sympathy.

Besides, the sketches about Mitchell Sanders' tale of the six-man patrol on an unlikely listening-post operation in 'How to Tell a True War Story' – whose episodic organization reproduces in small the structure of the entire book – focus on the failure of communication between the soldiers and their superiors. In this particular incident, the six men on patrol, who are themselves engaged in a frustrating attempt to listen, allegedly hear all sorts of strange sounds in the mountains: 'The place talks', explains Sanders (*TTC*, 72). Finally, unable to cope, they call in the artillery and 'make jungle juice' (*TTC*, 72–73). Upon their return from this unsettling mission, the soldiers lock horns with a colonel over his request to be told the reason for the employment of firepower on the listening post. The story emphasizes the unbridgeable gap between the soldiers, whose spooky experiences are impossible to articulate, and the officer, who must demand objective reports and rational accounts for the strategic decisions made by his men in the field. Sanders' sympathy is all with his fellow soldiers, of course, and his outrage at this (all-male) breakdown in communication finds expression through gendered terms of abuse that are on a par with Kiley's and O'Brien's outbursts against their own (female) obtuse listeners. In Sanders' words,

> 'this fatass colonel wants answers [...]. But the guys don't say zip. They just look at him for a while, sort of funny like, sort of amazed, and the whole war is right there in that stare. It says everything you can't ever say. It says, man, you got *wax* in your ears. It says, poor bastard, you'll never know – wrong frequency – you don't even want to hear this. Then they salute the fucker and walk away, because certain stories you don't ever tell.' (*TTC*, 73)

Lack of understanding, therefore, is not to be found exclusively on one side of the gender divide, and is met once more with unspoken invectives and with a categorical refusal to engage in explanations. Admittedly, in drawing the moral of the story, Sanders once more identifies virginal young women as the epitome of the character who will not listen,[52] but by now it is clear that the real divide is between those who have experienced the same things together (and a colonel's experience of the war will be significantly different from a grunt's), and those who have not. In fact, O'Brien takes things one step further when in 'Notes' he talks about the genesis of 'Speaking of Courage',

52 '"Just came to me," [Sanders] whispered. "The moral, I mean. Nobody listens. Nobody hears nothin'. Like that fatass colonel. The politicians, all the civilian types. Your girlfriend. My girlfriend. Everybody's sweet little virgin girlfriend"' (*TTC*, 74).

and his failure to get it right the first time. The idea to write about the terrible events that had taken place in the thick muck caused by the overflowing of the Song Tra Bong had been originally prompted by Norman Bowker's poignant request to his writer friend: 'What you should do, Tim, is write a story about a guy who feels like he got zapped over in that shithole' (*TTC*, 156). Bowker, however, is disappointed by the award-winning first draft of the story, and complains to O'Brien that he has 'left out Vietnam. Where's Kiowa? Where's the shit?' (*TTC*, 158). And, one might add, where is Bowker, given that O'Brien initially chose to fictionalize his experience in the story of Paul Berlin, the (patently invented) protagonist of *Going After Cacciato*? O'Brien's failure to tell fully the story of the shit field first time round is a failure to follow Bowker's instructions, and '[t]hat is the tragedy of the first version of "Courage": no one listens – not even the author/narrator "O'Brien," who is ostensibly telling Bowker's story.'[53]

Where does this leave us, though, with the gender oppositions that *are* perpetuated in the narrative? In particular, how should we respond to the misogyny that surfaces in the text, especially when it is voiced by the narrator, who otherwise provides the intellectual and moral compass of the story? Is his aggressive streak against the 'dumb cooze' the ultimate legitimization – disguised under the pretence of a necessary 'allegiance to obscenity and evil' – of a pervasive disparagement of women for which the traumatized soldiers cannot be held fully accountable? I think that it would be unfair – and, frankly, mistaken – to draw such a conclusion from the representation of gender relations in *Things*. After all, O'Brien's aggressive outburst against the older woman, as we have seen, is part of a larger sequence of irrational, incommensurate acts of violence against female and/or innocent targets, like Cross's burning of Martha's mementos or Kiley's killing of the water buffalo. These events – memorable because of the narrative space which they are given as well as for their attribution to individualized characters – displace the full horror of the military retaliations that would often follow the deaths of American soldiers, as O'Brien reminds us at the very beginning of his book: 'After the chopper took Lavender away, Lieutenant Jimmy Cross led his men into the village of Than Khe. They burned everything. They shot chickens and dogs, they trashed the village well, they called in artillery and watched the wreckage, then they marched for several hours through the hot afternoon, and then at dusk, while Kiowa explained how Lavender died, Lieutenant Cross found himself trembling' (*TTC*, 14). (Of course, the trembling is a first, physical symptom of the shame and sense of

---

53 Kaufmann, 'The Solace of Bad Form', p. 336. Kaufmann glosses this observation with a fine footnote: 'O'Brien shows through his [eponymous] narrator that even having the same experience does not guarantee one will listen and be able to understand' (p. 342).

responsibility which Cross will later transfer to his love for Martha.) While *Things* may encourage us to pity the perpetrators of these acts, the gratuitousness of their violent reactions remains painfully clear.

To the reader already acquainted with the character 'Tim O'Brien' from the pages of *If I Die*, the narrator's misogynist cry against the 'dumb cooze' and, by extension, against all the women who will not listen, sounds even more like an about turn, the veteran's delayed giving-in to the indoctrination that he had resisted during his army training. The marching songs reported in the memoirs configure the soldiers' relationship with women only in debased sexual terms, with references to sex as a commodity that is sold and bought and with the metonymical identification of women with their genitalia (*IID*, 50–51). The army lesson on gender relations is summarized by O'Brien in a few lines: 'There is no thing named love in the world. Women are dinks. Women are villains. They are creatures akin to Communists and yellow-skinned people and hippies' (*IID*, 51). The word 'love', clearly meant here in the sense of a romantic relationship between a man and a woman, has no referent in reality. In order to counteract this lesson, as 'a way to remain a stranger, only a visitor at Fort Lewis' (*IID*, 41), O'Brien would turn to the image of a girl. Like Jimmy Cross, he would rely on a mix of memory and imagination in order to create a secret refuge from military life: 'I spent hours comparing her hair to the colour of sand just at dusk. That sort of thing' (*IID*, 41). In time, however, this strategy becomes less and less successful, until one day in Vietnam O'Brien finds out that the girl has receded away from his thoughts to become virtually unavailable: 'It was hopeless, of course, but I tried to visualize her face. Only words would come in my mind. One word was "smile", and I tacked on the adjective "intriguing" to make it more personal. I thought of the word "hair", and modified it with the words "thick" and "sandy", not sure if they were accurate anymore, and then a whole string of words popped in – "mysterious", "Magdalene", "Eternal" as a modifier' (*IID*, 96–97). O'Brien cannot imagine the girl other than in pieces, through details that remain vague in spite of his efforts to qualify them; even when 'a whole string of words' finally comes to mind to define her, the description unfolds paratactically, along the axis of combination, for the three final attributes, which appear to gesture towards transcendence, are brought down to earth by their status as 'modifiers'. According to T. J. Lustig, whose argument I am borrowing here, O'Brien's failure to recall the image of the girl is the result of a type of linguistic impairment – what Roman Jakobson would call 'similarity disorder' – brought about by the experience of conflict in Vietnam: '[a]s the code of "culture" gives way to the obscene speech of war, contexts are deprived of sense and the heightened reactiveness of combat turns life into a series of reflex responses to urgent situational clues. Whilst metaphor connects, introduces similarity and comparison,

Vietnam happens metonymically, in terms of fact, detail, and a crushing horizontality'.[54] The soldiers' relationship with women in *Things* can also be read as an instance of this linguistic reduction, whereby, on some telling occasions, the metonym standing in for the loved one continues to be valued even when the emotional connection that was its ultimate frame of reference is definitely over (see, for example, the unnamed soldier's desperate search for Billie's photograph in the aftermath of Kiowa's death or Henry Dobbins' trust in his girlfriend's stockings as a lucky charm: both objects retain their importance even after the girls they represent have rejected their respective boyfriends.)

O'Brien's move away from the totalizing drive of metaphor does not stop at the 'crushing horizontality' of metonymy, but continues with the narrator's tantalizing insistence on the presence of unbridgeable gaps in his narratives, ellipses which cannot be filled in by any one interpretative act. One such gap that resists closure is the account of Kiowa's death: as we have seen, the tripartite sequence of stories about this event – 'Speaking of Courage', 'Notes' and 'In the Field' – produces a proliferation of hypotheses, instead of delivering the clarifications that it purports to offer through metanarrative explanations and the revisiting of material already covered. Thus, besides its metonymical representation of utter abjection through 'death by waste' and its factual depiction of war as filth, the shit field lends itself to a further *literal* reading as a hole in the narrative, a segment of the story that can never be fully articulated and understood. It is this literal image of the hole as an obscene void in the narrative, as something definitely left unsaid and located in the centre of a tale, that O'Brien ultimately exploits in his poetics of reception, whereby he posits an equally physical and inarticulate response to the elusive core of meaning conveyed by truthful storytelling. This physical reaction, I would argue, is defined in contrast to the behaviour of the two main intradiegetic listeners in *Things*: the 'older woman of kindly temperament and humane politics' in 'How to Tell a True War Story', who, as we have seen, stands in for a more generally feminine way of reading war stories, and Mitchell Sanders in 'Sweetheart of the Song Tra Bong', who occupies a diametrically opposite position, for his direct involvement in the conflict and for his markedly unemotional, rationalizing attitude towards the war.

The older woman responds emotionally and sympathetically to the tale of Kiley's grief. In addition, she clearly invests in the uplifting power of story-

---

54 T. J. Lustig, '"Moments of Punctuation": Metonymy and Ellipsis in Tim O'Brien', *The Yearbook of English Studies*, 31 (2001), pp. 74–92, p. 80. For Roman Jakobson's work on metaphor and metonymy, see 'Two Aspects of Language and Two Types of Aphasic Disturbances', in Roman Jakobson, *Language in Literature*, eds. and trans. Krystyna Pomorska and Stephen Rudy (Cambridge, MA: Belknap, 1987), pp. 95–114.

telling: 'What I should do, she'll say, is put it all behind me. Find new stories to tell' (*TTC*, 80). But O'Brien, of course, does not believe that he is on a path towards redemption, nor indeed that war stories should suggest the possibility of catharsis or closure: the stereotypically feminine response is at fault for sublimating the horror of war into a meaningful, affecting experience (and for sidestepping the obscenity of the conflict, as the narrator provocatively reminds us with his invective against the 'dumb cooze'). Sanders, on his part, is characterized throughout the novel as a relentless hermeneutist, quick to isolate catchy anecdotes and sententious lessons from the war, always in search for some kind of moral, even if the moral amounts to nothing more than the empty deictic affirmation 'there it is', which masks the tautological logic behind his truisms. Kiley's convoluted and impassioned tale about Mary Anne is therefore met with mounting frustration by Sanders, whose 'inner ear' is just as offended by the lack of closure in Mary Anne's story as it is by the lack of direction in Kiley's storytelling.[55] Inscribed in a tale whose structure recalls the expansiveness and superabundance of *écriture féminine*, Sanders' demands for linearity and consistency, not to mention his desire for a clear meaning to be deduced from the tale, perhaps typify a stereotypical masculine stance towards storytelling, which is expected to be punchy and trustworthy, and to yield memorable lessons. However, as the narrator reminds us in 'How to Tell a True War Story', 'True war stories do not generalize. They do not indulge in abstraction or analysis. For example: War is hell. As a moral declaration the old truism seems perfectly true, and yet because it abstracts, because it generalizes I can't believe it in my stomach. Nothing turns inside. It comes down to gut instinct. A true war story, if truly told, makes the stomach believe' (*TTC*, 75).

What O'Brien is positing here, as the proper response to a true war story, is something radically different from either the woman's display of compassion or Sanders' analytical drive. These two stances are themselves comparable to metaphorical and metonymical operations respectively: the sympathetic identification with another relies on recognizing a relationship of similarity between people belonging to different worlds, whereas the rationalizing processes wished for by Sanders rest very much on a relationship of contiguity, with the soldiers-witnesses-storytellers drawing general lessons from their first-hand experience of the war.[56] The problem with the above-

---

55 Piqued, Kiley interrupts his account to boil it down, in Sanders' manner, to the inevitable moral: 'The girl joined the zoo. One more animal – end of story.' 'Yeah, fine. But tell it right' is Sanders' own retort (*TTC*, 100).

56 This belief in the didactic power of storytelling, and indeed in the moral authority of the witness, had already been openly criticized in *If I Die*, where – as if his structural and thematic departure from the soldier's-loss-of-innocence *Bildungsroman* model were not evident enough – O'Brien declares: 'Can the foot soldier teach anything important about war, merely for having been there? I think not. He can tell war stories' (*IID*, 32).

mentioned attitudes is that they both manage to retrieve meaning from the storytelling act, thus endowing war with the status of a significant experience. A true war story, instead, should hit us in the stomach and leave us speechless, much as its truth resists a final verbal articulation, dwelling as it does in the gaps and the aporias of the endless modulations of the same stories, slightly different with each obsessive retelling. Unsurprisingly, this bodily response is not located in the heart, nor in the brain, but rather in the guts: once again, with the image of an immediate, *visceral* reaction, we are drawn back to that scatological dimension so stubbornly present in O'Brien's topography of trauma and most clearly epitomized by the shit hole lying at the centre of *The Things They Carried*.

5

The Power of Storytelling

Tim O'Brien's writing is characterized by structural complexity and literary and linguistic self-awareness. Yet formal reflections and experimentations may also be regarded as one of the recurrent thematic concerns of his work, particularly when we consider that his attention to questions of style and structure is connected with the investigation into the power of storytelling as a viable epistemological tool, an effective means of communication and, even, as a source and a conduit for compassion and catharsis. The most obvious structural feature common to O'Brien's books is the rejection of a linear narrative development, often accompanied by an explicit foregrounding – through chapter and section titles, or through metafictional notations – of the alternative organizing principles of the text in question. Whether only a few pages long or spanning an entire book, his stories frequently unfold through multiple, interweaving narrative strands, each covering a different temporal dimension or exploring the relationship between facts, memory and imagination, or even providing various perspectives on the same theme and separate accounts of the same events. At other times, O'Brien relies on the juxtaposition of self-contained, and occasionally overlapping, vignettes, whose deep connection readers are invited to work out by themselves. Whatever the narrative strategy, at the heart of O'Brien's emphasis on the artistry of storytelling lie questions about the nature of truth and the possibility of its apprehension and representation. This issue is clearly behind the generic hybridity of texts such as *If I Die in a Combat Zone* and *The Things They Carried*, which deliberately blur the boundary between autobiography and fiction, and *In the Lake of the Woods*, an example of historiographic metafiction, the postmodern take on that already cross-breed genre, the historical novel. The investigation into the availability and communication of truth also underpins the intertextual connections in 'Sweetheart of the Song Tra Bong'.

Since the beginning of his career, O'Brien has carefully arranged his material in such a way as to highlight or mirror the plight of his protagonists, and the central themes of his novels. In his less accomplished works, while clearly meant to guide the reader through the development of the story, the narrative organization can feel a little laboured and obscure: such is the case of *Northern Lights*, whose evocative list of section titles gestures to the cyclical nature of the plot punctuated by the rising and setting of the 'Black Sun' and of the 'Blood Moon' (the masculine and feminine principles embodied by Harvey's lust for adventure and Grace's domesticity, respectively).[1] Definitely more complex, but similarly strained (a fact that perhaps accounts for the reviewers' failure to comment on it, much to O'Brien's disappointment), is the tripartite division – 'Fission', 'Fusion' and 'Critical Mass', terms connected with the idea of explosive reactions – of *The Nuclear Age*, whose 'Quantum Jumps' chapters, which constitute the narrative strand set in the present, about William Cowling's building of the shelter, replicate with their varying length 'the progression of a release of nuclear energy'.[2]

Tomcat in Love and *July, July*, O'Brien's other two novels of ideas, adopt simpler organizing principles, which are for this reason more effective in emphasizing the central theme of their respective narratives. Most chapters in *Tomcat* are titled by a single word amongst the many in Chippering's personal dictionary of trauma, a collection of (mainly) nouns whose idiosyncratic connotations are explained by the protagonist's reminiscences and self-justifications. The Professor's private re-definition of these terms immediately alerts the readers to the subjective, slippery nature of language: Chippering is indeed proof that there is no such thing as a neutral utterance, that even common words – such as 'tulip', 'cat' or 'ledger' – trigger the most diverse associations of ideas in each individual. Of course, given Chippering's self-serving attitude, what is exposed is above all the negative side of the protean quality of language: particular words may summon unpleasant memories in the novel's protagonist, but he is certainly not averse to tweaking these very terms, and their accompanying anecdotes, in order to distort the narrative of his life and to quibble with its critics. The theme of *Tomcat* is that language can be a dangerous weapon in the hands of private prevaricators and public demagogues. *July, July* instead focuses unambiguously on the passage of time, with chapters on the thirtieth anniversary reunion of the Class of '69 at Darton Hall College alternating with self-contained sketches each dealing with a pivotal moment in the life of one of the book's main eleven characters. The disillusionment of the Baby Boomers in the years between graduation and the present is thus charted discontinuously, with an emphasis on the defining episodes of eleven different narratives that are otherwise left undeveloped. The result is a deliberately incomplete mosaic, with only a handful of very vivid – perhaps too flamboyant – tesserae.

1   *Northern Lights* is divided in two parts: 'One' comprises 'Heat Storm', 'Elements', 'Shelter' and 'Black Sun'; 'Two' begins with the pivotal 'Blizzard' (with the two brothers getting lost in the woods) and then repeats the sequence of 'Heat Storm', 'Elements' and 'Shelter' to culminate with 'Blood Moon'.
2   Heberle, *A Trauma Artist*, p. 157.

O'Brien's more interesting formal experimentations, however, all draw attention to the generic classification and to the claim to truth of the narratives which they shape. In Chapter 2, we have seen how the episodic structure of *If I Die*, paired with the overt references to the wide literary and philosophical context of O'Brien's first-person account, prevents the memoirs from reading as a straightforward anti-military story of innocence lost in the madness of war. In subverting the *Bildungsroman* conventions of autobiography, and of anti-war literature, O'Brien also raises interesting questions about the exact status of his tale which, factual in its content, deploys strategies – the jumbled chronology, the montage of self-contained vignettes, the vivid dialogue and characterization in the creation of dramatic scenes – that give it a distinctly fictional feel.[3] An opposite impulse instead governs the three narrative levels in *Going After Cacciato*: Paul Berlin's solitary reflections while on duty on the observation post, the flashback chapters about his tour of duty and finally the company's fantastic pursuit of Cacciato all the way to Paris. Contrary to what might be expected, Berlin's indirect interior monologues and the account of the chase after Cacciato, i.e. the two most properly subjective and fictive strands in the novel, develop with much greater adherence to mimetic techniques – as defined by Ian Watts's seminal analysis of the traits of 'formal realism' – than the series of factual chapters about the war. The latter strand, in fact, beginning *in medias res* and proceeding in a random sequence of isolated episodes, provides fewer details of time, place, action or character than Berlin's meditations or the fantastic picaresque journey from Vietnam to Paris.[4] It would seem that the techniques of formal realism are inadequate for an accurate representation of the soldiers' perception of the terrifying absurdity of their military experience.

In the Lake of the Woods continues to blur the distinction between mimetic and imaginative drives, while also shifting the focus from a private, unremarkable individual like Berlin to a story with a much wider resonance, given its protagonist's political ambitions and, above all, his involvement in the My Lai massacre. In *In the Lake of the Woods* John Wade's personal tale is played out against a major, and shameful, historical event, but O'Brien's intermingling of the factual and the fictional goes beyond the blending of different ontological levels typical of the historical novel. The book is divided in four sets of chapters, whose labels prove to be rather elastic and unreliable, so that they end up highlighting their common textual – and, to an extent, subjective and fanciful – nature. The 'Evidence' chapters, for example, do

---

3 Schroeder begins his interview with O'Brien precisely with the issue of the interplay of fiction and non-fiction in Vietnam war writing, and O'Brien answers with an interesting and enlightening discussion of the history of *If I Die*.
4 On this issue see, amongst others, Michael Raymond, Robert M. Slabey and Dennis Vannatta.

contain references to the actual material evidence from the inquest on Kathy's disappearance (photographs, descriptions of places, etc.), and report real and fictional excerpts from the court martial following the exposure of the My Lai massacre. At the same time, though, they also include people's testimonies and opinions on the main characters, and passages from various real texts: historical documents, psychological studies, the magician's handbook used by Wade, or even literary classics such as Dostoevsky's *Notes from the Underground* (1864). This hotchpotch of sources is underpinned by and, in turn, exposes several different ways of interpreting the word 'evidence', from its rigorous legal definition to a much looser sense, hinting perhaps at the idiosyncrasy of the narrator's *modus operandi* and at his invested interest in throwing light on Wade's story as a surrogate way of dealing with his own painful past.

The remaining chapters of *Lake* are categorized under three different kinds of heading: besides the self-explanatory 'Hypothesis', there is a group of what appear to be more general reflections on 'The Nature of...' disparate concepts and, finally, a series of ostensibly more factual chapters which promise to tell us the 'What...', 'How...' and 'Where...' of the Wades' story.[5] And yet, not only is the distinction between these categories less than airtight (after all, the visible presence of an intradiegetic narrator guarantees that we are aware that the entire novel is the product of a mixture of rigorous research and necessary speculations, the work of one man, who is also not an impartial storyteller), but as in *Cacciato*, the 'Hypothesis' strand, that is the more overtly fictional section of the narrative, is possibly the most coherent and linear sequence of chapters in the novel. The Wades' past, by contrast, is pieced together much more sketchily, the absence of a clear chronology and the frequent recurrence of particularly traumatic events, such as the killing of PFC Weatherby, perhaps mimicking the incoherent, obsessive memories of a post-traumatic stress disorder sufferer. The narrator in *Lake*, an anonymous Vietnam veteran who intervenes in the reconstruction of the Wades' story with a number of autobiographical and metafictional footnotes, flags up the fragmentation and the generic instability of his account, but he also expresses an unequivocal epistemological scepticism that turns out to be rooted primarily in the belief in the mysteriousness of 'human motive and human desire' (*LW*, 30, n. 21) and the impenetrability of the 'human soul' (*LW*, 103, n. 36). Against these unknowable subjects, even the most rigorous factual research must in the end give way to a leap into the realm of imagina-

---

5 See Heberle, *A Trauma Artist*, p. 220: '"The Nature of..." chapters describe significant events in Wade's past life and his relationship with Kathy before her disappearance; the title of each is a formulaic phrase that gives Wade's story figural significance.' The remaining factual chapters cover the period since the Wades' arrival in Lake of the Woods; their titles 'parody the headings of an official investigation'.

tion, as the anonymous narrator is only too happy to admit on several occasions.[6]

The recourse to imaginative resources in order to try to accede to 'some hidden truth' (*LW*, 298, n. 124), and the relative validity of fictional truth *vis-à-vis* factually accurate mimetic representations is explored in *The Things They Carried*, O'Brien's most accomplished work to date and, predictably, the one text from his entire output most frequently under critical scrutiny. Together with *Cacciato* and, to a lesser extent, with *If I Die*, the book has acquired canonical status in the field of Vietnam war literature. The chaos and gruesomeness of the conflict are depicted more vividly and continuously here than in the previous narratives, which are both dominated by the inquiry into the ethical quandary of their protagonists. As we have seen, the account of the soldiers' experience in Vietnam and the horror of the battlefield are accompanied – even, one might say, interrupted – by O'Brien's philosophical speculations in *If I Die* and by Berlin's imaginary journey in *Cacciato*. In *Things* O'Brien develops the non-linear, discontinuous structure of his previous works to such an extent that the resulting sequence of interconnected tales about the war – unified by the recurrent presence of the same members of Alpha Company, as well as by an intradiegetic narrator named 'Tim O'Brien' – reads both like a novel with a jumbled chronology and like a collection of short stories.[7] In fact, '[m]ore than a collection of stories, *The Things They Carried* is a book about the need to tell stories, the ways to tell

6 See for example the following self-reflective notations: 'Biographer, historian, medium – call me what you want – but even after four years of hard labor I'm left with little more than supposition and possibility. John Wade was a magician; he did not give away many tricks. Moreover there are certain mysteries that weave through life itself, human motive and human desire. Even much of what might appear to be fact in this narrative – action, word, thought – must ultimately be viewed as diligent but still imaginative reconstruction of events. Yet evidence is not truth. It is only evident. In any case, Kathy Wade is forever missing, and if you require solutions, you will have to look beyond these pages. Or read a different book' (*LW*, 30, n. 21). Cf. also: 'Aren't we all [others]? John Wade – he's beyond knowing. He's an other. For all my years of struggle with this depressing record, for all the travel and interviews and musty libraries, the man's soul remains for me an absolute and impenetrable unknown, a nametag drifting willy-nilly on oceans of hapless fact' (*LW*, 103, n. 36). Again: 'But there is also the craving to know what cannot be known. Our own children, our fathers, our wives and husbands: Do we truly know them? How much is camouflage? How much is guessed at? How many lies get told, and when, and about what? How often do we say, or think, God, I never *knew* her? How often do we lie awake speculating – seeking some hidden truth? Oh, yes, it gnaws at me. I have my own secrets, my own trapdoors. I know something about deceit. Far too much. How it corrodes and corrupts. […] We find truth inside, or not at all.' (*LW*, 298, n. 124).

7 O'Brien himself explains that it 'is sort of half novel, half group of stories. It's part nonfiction too: some of the stuff is commentary on the stories, talking about where a particular one came from'; Naparsteck, 'An Interview with Tim O'Brien', p. 7. As a matter of fact, several of its chapters were originally published in various journals as self-contained short stories (although the same is true of excerpts from O'Brien's other works).

stories, and the reasons for telling stories'.[8] Of course, *Things* is also the book in which O'Brien performs his most evident, thought-provoking and accomplished act of intertextual engagement, rewriting in 'Sweetheart of the Song Tra Bong' the Conradian journey into the heart of darkness, and revising the poetics and politics of Conrad's early modernist novella in line with postmodern concerns. This study of Tim O'Brien's place on the literary scene at the turn from the twentieth to the twenty-first century cannot but end with a focus on his reflections on the writer's craft, and on his abilities and moral responsibilities.

Conradian echoes in 'Sweetheart of the Song Tra Bong'

Heart of Darkness provides an excellent template for the literature of the Vietnam war not only on a thematic level, with its deconstruction of the wilderness/civilization dichotomy and its critique of Western ideology, but also in its technical and self-reflexive aspects. The suggestiveness of the language, the surrealism of the imagery and the endorsement of the poetics of modernism are all part of the stylistic legacy of Conrad's novella, whose narrative structure directs the reader's attention onto the nature and the challenges of storytelling. It is indeed the metafictional sphere that is immediately given emphasis by O'Brien's engagement with *Heart of Darkness* in 'Sweetheart of the Song Tra Bong'. The allusion to Conrad's work foregrounds first of all the literariness of the later narrative and opens up the range and depth of available interpretations. Ultimately, the intertextual dialogue with *Heart of Darkness* amplifies the large symbolic scope of 'Sweetheart': from a military tall-tale and an indictment of the psychological wreckage caused by the war, the story turns into a universal parable about the reservoir of savagery and desire for transgression lurking in every human being and waiting to be released. On a more superficial level, of course, the modes of such a terrible liberation are recounted in keeping with O'Brien's personal knowledge and condemnation of the war: it is exactly in this oscillation between an appeal to a universal condition and a contingent comment on Vietnam that O'Brien's short story most resembles Conrad's novella, whose sharp critique of European colonialism reaches out to expose the obscure depths of the human predicament.[9]

---

8 Tina Chen, '"Unraveling the Deeper Meaning": Exile and the Embodied Poetics of Displacement in Tim O'Brien's *The Things They Carried*, *Contemporary Literature*, 39.1 (1998), pp. 77–98, p. 94.
9 Conrad also had first-hand experience of travelling in Congo in 1890. 'The Congo Diary' provides a record of that trip.

The most striking discrepancy between the two texts is the identity of the character who undergoes the journey into the heart of darkness. In O'Brien's short story the protagonist is the young Mary Anne Bell on an improbable visit to her boyfriend Mark Fossie, an equally young medic assigned to a military detachment on the mountains to the west of Chu Lai. This time the spell of the wilderness does not capture an uncommon, charismatic man, betrayed by a 'singleness of intention'[10] despite his 'noble', philanthropic instincts; in 'Sweetheart' the 'fascination of the abomination' seizes a girl who embodies the very ideals of white American suburban femininity. While archetypically innocent and demure, Mary Anne is the ultimate male fantasy: 'This cute blonde – just a kid, just barely out of high school – she shows up with a suitcase and one of those plastic cosmetic bags. Comes right out to the boonies. I swear to God, man, she's got on culottes. White culottes and this sexy pink sweater' (*TTC*, 88). Mary Anne hears the call of savagery and gets drawn into it, leaving the boundaries of civilization behind and surrendering to the seductiveness of the jungle and of a life of ambushes. 'Vietnam had the effect of a powerful drug; that mix of unnamed terror and unnamed pleasure that comes as the needle slips in and you know you're risking something' (*TTC*, 105).[11] The ineffable combination of dread and delight that lures Mary Anne into the uncharted reality of the war is reminiscent of 'the spell – the heavy, mute spell of the wilderness – that seemed to draw [Kurtz] to its pitiless breast by the awakening of forgotten and brutal instincts, by the memory of gratified and monstrous passions' (*HD*, 106–107). As the reader already knows at this stage in the narrative, Kurtz has answered the silent incantation of the jungle with his very own 'unspeakable rites' at the inner station on the Congo river (83). This image of speechless horror is one of the elements of Kurtz's degradation that O'Brien reworks towards the end of his short story, as we shall see later; yet the essential equivalence between Mary Anne's and Kurtz's psychological journey is immediately conveyed through the recurrence of numerous terms in the semantic areas of 'wilderness' and 'darkness' in both texts.

The Vietnamese landscape is a disturbing and oppressive presence, covered in vegetation so luxurious that it may well be described as baroque:

> To the north and *west* the country rose up in thick walls of *wilderness*, triple-canopied jungle, mountains unfolding into higher mountains, ravines and gorges and fast-moving rivers and waterfalls and exotic

---

10 *Heart of Darkness*, p. 65, henceforward referred to as *HD*.

11 The analogy suggested by this passage works on several levels: it recalls the psychedelic nature of the conflict, marked by the American soldiers' widespread use of drugs as an escape from reality, but it also signals the paradoxical addictiveness of combat, while hinting at the unspeakable nature of the experience of transgression.

butterflies and steep cliffs and smoky little hamlets and great valleys of bamboo and elephant grass. (*TTC*, 89, my italics)

O'Brien's stylistic choices emphasize the sense of exuberance of the environment: the initial asyndeton escalates into the reiterative crescendo of the 'mountains unfolding into higher mountains' and the quick sequence of 'and's', with the sentence dissolving into a long catalogue of natural excesses.[12] This passage provides more than the physical coordinates of the place: the association between wilderness and the west – a subtle leitmotif in the whole narrative – begins to sketch the moral geography of the tale, disrupting the easy equation that would pair off the Western world with the idea of civilization. The same strategy is adopted to similar effect in the opening of *Heart of Darkness*, where Conrad peppers his description of London with allusions to its 'gloom to the west' (see, for example, *HD*, 15, 16 and 18), an 'ominous' (to use another recurrent term) reminder that the trite colonial self-identification with the 'bearers of the spark of the sacred fire' should not be taken for granted.

Mary Anne has no such prejudices; her main psychological trait, we are told, is a great curiosity; open and determined to learn from her peculiar experience, the girl shows a keen interest in the soldiers' tasks, the natives' predicament and the routine of war but, most of all, the secrets of the Vietnamese landscape: 'What was behind those scary *green* mountains to the *west*? [...] The war intrigued her. The land, too, and the mystery' (*TTC*, 91–92, my italics). Soon enough the land responds to Mary Anne's fascination by exacting a radical change from her; in her effortless adjustment to the demands of life on the compound, Mary Anne unlearns her superfluous (feminine) cares, discarding her jewels, her make-up and her girly attire. The 'white culottes' and the 'sexy pink sweater' are replaced by 'green fatigues' and a 'dark green bandana' to wrap her hair, which has been cut short as if to suggest the girl's claim to a military status. Neither her original outfit nor her military gear are mere realistic details, of course: the former hints at a now receding ingenuous coquettishness, while the latter unveils Mary Anne's latent affinity with the Green Berets and, more crucially, her chameleon–like assimilation into the jungle. It is only a matter of time until Mary Anne loosens her ties from her boyfriend and his comrades to take part in an ambush with the six Greenies who preside over the compound. Mark's reaction to Mary Anne's clandestine escapade is a rather weak call to order, through a desperate enforcement of 'some new rules. Mary Anne's hair was freshly shampooed. She wore a white blouse, a navy blue skirt, a pair of plain

---

12 Other terms connected with the wilderness will be 'green' and 'edge', which are also immediately associated with the exceptional status of the Special Forces.

black flats. Over dinner she kept her eyes down, poking at her food, subdued to the point of silence' (*TTC*, 97). This is clearly an appeal to the most superficial attributes of the Western ideal of femininity (prettiness, cleanliness, docility); within this cultural context, Mark's trump card in his attempt to reverse the progress of Mary Anne's metamorphosis is a marriage proposal. Needless to say, this gesture proves totally ineffective as a reminder of the patriarchal rules of 'the world', for the girl is so far gone into her solitary journey that she is cut off from her old cultural coordinates.[13] Thus, Mary Anne's strained return to normality is as short-lived as the engagement, which succumbs to the girl's disdain for the only role that Mark can envisage for her: that of sweetheart/fiancée and ultimately, one presumes, wife and mother. The apathy with which Mary Anne embraces her 'Intended' destiny is soon replaced by an ever-growing fascination with the unknown territory unfolding under her eyes:

> after a day or two she fell into a restless *gloom*, sitting off by herself at the *edge* of the perimeter. [...] Mary Anne just stared out at the dark *green* mountains to the *west. The wilderness seemed to draw her in.* A haunted look, Rat said, – partly terror, partly rapture. *It was as if she had come up on the edge of something,* as if she were caught in that no-man's land between Cleveland Heights and deep jungle. (*TTC*, 98–99, my italics)

Prey to the Conradian gloom, Mary Anne has moved into a liminal space – the mythical 'middle landscape' (to use Leo Marx's expression) between savagery and civilization, which American military strategists envisioned as the Special Forces' domain.

The Special Forces are introduced by O'Brien as a different species from the regular soldiers:

> The Greenies were not social animals. Animals, Rat said, but far from social. They had their own hootch at the *edge* of the perimeter [...]. Secretive and suspicious, loners by nature, the six Greenies would sometimes vanish for days at a time, or

---

13 Mark's stubborn adherence to a mentality now completely alien to Mary Anne's logic recalls the short-sighted strategy for petty survival and self-possession of the Chief Accountant in *Heart of Darkness*. Conrad's character cherishes the illusion of his superior integrity by behaving in the heart of Africa as if he were in the City; inevitably, he cuts a pathetic figure, hiding behind his 'high starched collar' and 'white cuffs' in the oppressive heat of the jungle. Oblivious to the suffering and the inhumane material conditions of the natives, he remains nonetheless a minuscule, ridiculous villain, keeping up the appearance of civilization with his impeccable European dress sense and his books in 'apple pie order' (36–37). This vignette is underscored by the cruel irony of the Chief Accountant's dependence on the natives for his own semblance of Western refinement: it is in fact his black mistress who irons his shirts, in spite of her understandable 'distaste for the work'.

even weeks, then late in the night they would magically reappear, *moving like shadows* through the moonlight, filing in silently from the dense rain forest *off to the west*. (*TTC*, 89, my italics)[14]

The Special Forces' ghost-like apparitions and their isolation at the margin of the compound emphasize their dark and beastly side: they literally exist *in extremis*, leading a life out of bounds in every sense. Present-day Charons, the Greenies ferry Mary Anne into their underworld, until she is a shadow amongst shadows, alienated from the medical staff, often alone at the edge of the perimeter, caught up in a limbo, 'that no-man's-land between Cleveland Heights and deep jungle' (*TTC*, 99). In this metaphorical space, hovering – like Leatherstocking, the western hero – in a precarious balance between the rules of society and an amoral chaos, the hootch of the Green Berets represents the physical correlative to an ongoing struggle with the 'fascination of the abomination', much as Kurtz's stakes decorated with human heads confirm his crossing-over to a realm of transgression. Inevitably, O'Brien's description of this 'middle landscape' is cast in shady hues; Mary Anne's retreat into the Greenies' quarters marks the first step in her irreversible drifting away from civilization: the characteristic seclusion and obscurity of the Special Forces' hut sanctions the girl's willingness to belong to a nocturnal, subversive dimension.[15] In the end, Mary Anne will sever this mediated connection to the world, leaving even the Special Forces behind:

'Lost', [Mark] kept whispering. (*TTC*, 99)

'Do something', [Mark] whispered. 'I can't just let her go like that.' Rat listened for a time, then shook his head. 'Man, you must be deaf. She's already gone.' (*TTC*, 104)

She was lost inside herself. (*TTC*, 106)

Mary Anne is 'lost' even before her final disappearing act into the jungle; the geographical and the inner journey are a reflection of each other, as well as an echo of Kurtz's own tale of perdition:

14 See also the description of their return from the first mission with Mary Anne: 'then off to the *west* a column of *silhouettes* appeared as if by magic at the *edge* of the jungle. At first he [Rat] didn't recognise her [Mary Anne] – a small soft, *shadow* among six other *shadows*' (*TTC*, 99, my italics).
15 See, for example, 'Off in the gloom a few dim figures lounged in hammocks', or 'In the shadow there was a laughter', and the suggestive 'she [Mary Anne] turned and moved back into the gloom' (*TTC*, 102, 103 and 104).

'You will be lost,' [Marlow] said – 'utterly lost.' [...] I did say the right thing, though indeed he could not have been more irretrievably lost than he was at this very moment, when the foundations of our intimacy were being laid... (*HD*, 106)

What makes the account of Mary Anne's inexorable descent different from that of Kurtz's degradation is mainly a matter of the nature and timing of the revelations concerning their respective character development. In this sense, O'Brien's narrative can be said to fill in the gaps in Conrad's story, in which Marlow (and the reader) only ever meet Kurtz when he is already near the end of his journey. The several proleptic passages in *Heart of Darkness* – a host of rumours surrounding Kurtz (who is primarily referred to as a nameless voice) – create an atmosphere of anticipation and suspense for the reader; these are the same feelings that have obviously fed Marlow's instinctive fascination with and sympathy for the man, and that underlie Marlow's determination to save 'the gifted Mr Kurtz from his fate' (*HD*, 81). Conversely, the mythical plot of 'search and deliverance' – i.e. the hero's quest and victorious fight against evil – is impossible in 'Sweetheart'; Mark Fossie is no knight-in-shining-armour, and no Marlow either, lacking the psychological subtlety and self-awareness of the modernist (anti)hero. For its part, Marlow's mission retains a mythical flair; it can be envisaged as a catabasis, the descent into the abode of the shades of the dead, which in the best classical tradition (see Odysseus, Aeneas or, even more appropriately, Orpheus) is doomed from the start: Kurtz cannot be brought back to the world, because he always already belongs to the heart of darkness, a voice rather than a body, 'that Shadow – this wandering and tormented thing' (*HD*, 106).[16] Still, Marlow's quest is a success of sorts; like his epic predecessors, what he has really undertaken is a journey of self-discovery (fruitful in so far as he survives to tell, and muse about, the tale) – albeit under the guise of a mission to retrieve a lost soul. Of course, if only in retrospect (see *HD*, 106 quoted above), Marlow acknowledges the hopelessness of his attempt to reach out to Kurtz. Mark Fossie, by contrast, can never comprehend, let alone come to terms with, his loss of Mary Anne: the shock of this discovery will drive him insane.

16 Odysseus and Aeneas both descend into the underworld (Hades/Dis) in order to question the dead (the soothsayer Tiresias and Anchises, Aeneas's father, respectively) about their destiny and ask for advice: theirs is a journey of self-discovery, made poignant by the two heroes' impossible desire to embrace their deceased beloved (see Homer, *Odyssey*, Book XI and Virgil, *Aeneid*, Book VI). Orpheus's mission into the underworld is the rescue of his dead wife Eurydice, who disappears forever into the realm of the dead when Orpheus breaks his promise not to turn around and check that she is following him back to the world (see Ovid, *Metamorphoses*, Book X). These are easily the three best known secular epic examples of catabasis, and they all make quite clear that the inhabitants of the underworld are insubstantial shadows, who can never get back to the world. The shadow's doom is also Kurtz's destiny, although Conrad's narrative is no epic tale, but rather a modernist epic reversal.

One observation to be made about the web of character associations and narrative functions that I have just outlined concerns the doubling up of Marlow's position in 'Sweetheart'. In O'Brien's tale there are two counterparts to the two roles invested in Marlow in *Heart of Darkness*, where Marlow is both the (anti)hero of his own journey to Africa and of his doomed attempt to rescue Kurtz *and* the narrator of these complex, intertwined events. The combined functions of would-be saviour and self-conscious narrator are split up by O'Brien and assigned to Mark Fossie and Rat Kiley respectively.

O'Brien's choice to have two characters share Marlow's legacy does not extend to his treatment of Kurtz, whose heavy literary inheritance is taken up solely by Mary Anne: the parallelisms between the two figures go well beyond their common solitude and ghostliness.[17] An interesting shared trait, particularly in the light of Conrad's and O'Brien's own evocative writing, is the oneiric quality of Mary Anne's and Kurtz's speech: the two characters develop their own idiosyncratic language and are susceptible to the influence of vernacular forms of communication. Kurtz's utterances are cryptic and contradictory, the ravings of a lunatic or perhaps a seer, and resist all attempts at a rational paraphrase. As Marlow admits, 'They were common everyday words [...] [but t]hey had behind them, to my mind, the terrific suggestiveness of words heard in dreams, of phrases spoken in nightmares' (*HD*, 107). Mary Anne, on her part, gradually abandons language for music – and non-Western music at that. The tune coming from the Green Berets' hootch 'had a chaotic, almost unmusical sound, without rhythm or form or progression, like the noise of nature [...] In the background, just audible, a woman's voice was half-singing, half-chanting, but the lyrics seemed to be in a foreign tongue' (*TTC*, 110).[18] O'Brien insists on the savage dimension of the sound: 'The place seemed to echo with a weird deep-wilderness sound – tribal music' (*TTC*, 102), and later, 'In the darkness there was that weird tribal music, which seemed to come from the earth itself, from the deep rain forest, and a woman's voice rising up in a language beyond translation' (*TTC*, 104).[19]

17 Kurtz's own literary ancestry of course places him in the Romantic tradition of the great transgressors or overreachers, the monomaniacal figures consumed by an obsession and betrayed by their *hubris*. 'The charismatic Kurtz, brilliant yet depraved, corrupt yet fascinating, descends from the "hero-villains" of Gothic fiction, the most notable of these being Emily Brontë's Heathcliff (who, like Ann Radcliffe's Montoni, is in turn a literary descendant of Milton's Satan, regarded by the Romantics as a sublime rebel). Furthermore, the tale's imagery suggests, Kurtz is a modern Faust, who has sold his soul for power and gratification; so perhaps Charlie Marlow owes a debt to Christopher Marlowe'; Cedric Watts, '"Heart of Darkness"', in *The Cambridge Companion to Joseph Conrad*, ed. John H. Stape (Cambridge: Cambridge University Press, 1996), pp. 45–62, p. 47.

18 Interestingly, Marlow is made to understand that 'Kurtz had been essentially a great musician' (*HD*, 115).

19 As already hinted, Kurtz's and Mary Anne's language take to an extreme the non-linearity and opacity of the texture of *Heart of Darkness* and 'Sweetheart', and of their several narra-

The untranslatable quality of Mary Anne's chant brings to mind the African natives' cries to mourn Kurtz's departure, 'strings of amazing words that resembled no sounds of human language; [...] the deep murmurs of the crowd [...] were like the responses of some satanic litany' (although O'Brien understandably avoids any suggestion of hell in his description of an *other* form of speech: as already pointed out, 'Sweetheart' plays down the catabatic element of the tale, perhaps reflecting a more or less conscious postcolonial political correctness).

Mary Anne's and Kurtz's oral relationship with the wilderness eventually takes a grotesque, horrific turn in their cannibalistic desire for the land; Mary Anne is so enthralled by her surroundings that she wants to make them part of herself: 'Sometimes I want to *eat* this place. Vietnam. I want to swallow the whole country – the dirt, the death – I just want to eat it and have it there inside me. That's how I feel. It's like ... this appetite' (*TTC*, 103). Mary Anne spells out what is only implicit in Marlow's first impression of Kurtz as an image of greed: 'I saw him open his mouth wide – it gave him a weirdly voracious aspect, as though he wanted to swallow all the air, all the earth, all the men before him' (*HD*, 97) and, in a later passage,

> I had a vision of him on the stretcher, opening his mouth voraciously, as if to devour all the earth with all its mankind. He lived then before me; he lived as much as he had ever lived – a shadow insatiable of splendid appearances, of frightful realities; a shadow darker than the shadow of the night, and draped nobly in the folds of a gorgeous eloquence. (*HD*, 117)

Devouring the land does signal an extreme yearning for its possession, but it also flags up the need for a selfless sense of belonging, the ultimate merging of subject and object. It is in the fulfilment of this complete assimilation that Mary Anne's destiny differs from Kurtz's. After all, Kurtz's journey comes to an abrupt halt with his death well within the boundaries of the narration,

---

tors' storytelling style. This highlights a profound analogy between the creative/narrative act and an existential journey, a point which Conrad theorizes in his 'Preface' to *The Nigger of the "Narcissus"* (1897): it is in the exploration of the self that the writer must seek the realization of his claim to truth. Unlike the thinker and the scientist, who pursue this same quest in their respective engagement with the world of ideas and of facts, 'the artist descends within himself and, in that lonely region of stress and strife, if he be deserving and fortunate, he finds the terms of his appeal. His appeal is made to our less obvious capacities; to that part of our nature which, because of the warlike conditions of existence, is necessarily kept out of sight within the most resisting and hard qualities – like the vulnerable body within a steel armour'; Conrad, *The Nigger of the "Narcissus"* [1897], ed. Robert Kimbrough (New York: Norton, 1979), p. 145. The passage sets up a dichotomy between inside and outside, but it also posits the idea that both regions of human existence involve struggle and conflict. The inside/outside opposition appears, in a different guise, at the beginning of *Heart of Darkness* too.

which means that at the most superficial level of the plot, we do get some answers: "'Mistah Kurtz – he dead'" (*HD*, 112). The ambiguity in the story lies not so much in ascertaining the circumstances of Kurtz's demise (although even these are deliberately obscured by Marlow's lie to the Intended), but in the difficulty of penetrating the true nature and the deeper meaning of his experience. The challenge of such an interpretative task is neatly exemplified in the ambiguity of Kurtz's last words, 'The horror! The horror!' (*HD*, 112). We cannot know whether this is an admission of depravity, or a condemnation of the African 'savagery' akin to his earlier call to 'Exterminate all the brutes!' (*HD*, 84). Moreover, the interpretative challenge is made even harder for the reader by Marlow's tentative, ambiguous mediation of the story. In other words, the facts being clear (clearer than in 'Sweetheart' at least), the lack of closure in *Heart of Darkness* lies at a hermeneutical level and, to a large extent, it is a function of the inconclusiveness of Marlow's storytelling and of Conrad's modernist poetics. At the end of the tale, when it is once more apparent that the story is as much – if not more – about Marlow as it is about Kurtz, both characters remain equally impenetrable ciphers. This is in tune with Conrad's appeal in the 'Preface' to "*Narcissus*" that each individual must embark on his or her own quest for signification: as we shall see later, the (partial, evanescent) truth is illuminated on the outside, by the mood of the writing, while the story itself reveals an empty core. The only certainty yielded by *Heart of Darkness* is a revelation into the thought-provoking nature of Conrad's – and Marlow's – narrative (possibly to be adopted by the reader as a model of self-reflection), while the sequence of embedded tales seemingly stages the infinite regress of the final truth away from our firm grasp.

For his part, O'Brien refuses to provide his readers with even a factual ending. The story is inconclusive at the most basic level: there is no way of knowing what has really happened to Mary Anne, other than that she has disappeared into the jungle. In this respect, the girl recalls Kurtz's native lover, the memorable incarnation of the African charm:

> a wild and gorgeous apparition of a woman. She walked with measured steps, draped in striped and fringed cloths, treading the earth proudly, with a slight jingle and flash of barbarous ornaments [...] bizarre things, charms, gifts of witchmen, that hung about her, glittered and trembled at every step. [...] She was savage and superb, wild-eyed and magnificent; there was something ominous and stately in her deliberate progress. And in the hush that had fallen suddenly upon the whole sorrowful land, the immense wilderness, the colossal body of the fecund and mysterious life seemed to look at her, pensive, as though it had been looking at the image of its own tenebrous and passionate soul. (*HD*, 99)

This 'wild and gorgeous apparition of a woman' enters the scene as a direct emanation of the jungle, which she immediately returns to – her uncharted story a symbol of the mystery of the heart of darkness.[20] Mary Anne resembles the embodiment of the Conradian wilderness in her sinister gaze and her barbarous ornaments and poise, the signs of her own consubstantiality with the earth: it is no surprise that she finally becomes 'part of the land'.[21] Never a corpse, Mary Anne remains an enigmatic story, always eluding death (and a narrative conclusion) in the sequence of speculations that make up her tale. Moreover, as my analysis of the textual challenges to conventional gender roles will make clear, Mary Anne's trajectory can be traced as a transformation from a readerly text (in her initial conformity to a predictable feminine plot) to a writerly one (in her ultimate resistance to fixed interpretations: her parable gets written anew with every reading, a fact that O'Brien highlights in the complex structure of his narrative). This journey progressively takes Mary Anne away from a patriarchal terrain, as the girl, once the perfect object of male desire, rejects Mark's domestic idyll to inhabit the androgynous 'no-man's-land between Cleveland Heights and the deep jungle' (*TTC*, 99) and eventually metamorphoses into a wilderness that we might want to characterize as *féminine*: abundant, powerful, alluring and incontainable. This non-phallocentric stance, voiced with great gusto by French feminist theory, defuses the derogatory association of the wilderness with femininity typical of the repressive and self-defensive strategies of patriarchal colonial ideology: viewed as weak, savage and amoral, the feminized and/or emasculated foreign land demands Western mastery and control.[22] Taking their cue from

---

20 The woman's exit is as memorable as her entrance onto the scene, and confirms her identification with the jungle: 'She looked at us all as if her life had depended on the steadiness of her glance. Suddenly she opened her bared arms and threw them up rigid above her head, as though in an uncontrollable desire to touch the sky, and at the same time the swift shadows darted out on the earth, swept around on the river, gathering the steamer in a shadowy embrace. [...] Once only her eyes gleamed back at us in the dusk of the thickets before she disappeared' (*HD*, 99–100).

21 See her physical assimilation to the wilderness: 'Her eyes seemed to shine in the dark – not blue, though, but a bright glowing jungle green' (*TTC*, 99); her vacuous gaze and barbarous ornaments: 'Quietly then, she stepped out of the shadows. [...] For a long while the girl gazed down at Fossie, almost blankly, and in the candlelight her face had the composure of someone perfectly at peace with herself. [...] At the girl's throat was a necklace of human tongues. Elongated and narrow, like pieces of blackened leather, the tongues were threaded along a length of copper wire, one overlapping the next, the tips curled upward as if caught in a final horrified syllable' (*TTC*, 103).

22 This feminization of the exotic, languid, seductive Orient has long underpinned the imperialist ideology of the West; see, for example, Edward Said, who sees in Flaubert's relationship with the Egyptian courtesan Kuchuk Hanem a paradigm for 'the pattern of relative strength between East and West'; *Orientalism* [1978] (London: Penguin, 1995), p. 6. This patriarchal, Orientalist stance is replicated by Conrad, with ironic distance, in his

– and challenging – the oppressive reduction of femininity to the realms of nature, passivity and obscurity, critics such as Hélène Cixous celebrate the feminine 'pleasure in being boundless, outside self, outside same, far from a "center," from any capital of her "dark continent," very far from the "hearth" to which man brings her so that she will tend his fire, which always threatens to go out'.[23] It is to the energy, freedom, plenitude and fulfilling quality of this vision that Mary Anne responds in her merging with the jungle, an awe-inspiring and empowering image magnified by the rippling away, in several directions, of O'Brien's decentred narrative. But before moving to the analysis of the conclusion and the general structure of O'Brien's story, it is worth dwelling on Conrad's own representation of female characters and on his narrative technique.

The final impossibility of pinning down Mary Anne, who has shown a dangerous degree of adaptability, being equally credible as the American sweetheart and as a creature of the wilderness, differs greatly from what appears to be an unbridgeable dichotomy in the feminine roles in *Heart of Darkness*. At a first glance, Conrad's representation of women sways between two antithetic stereotypes, the savagery of the 'wild and gorgeous apparition' and the innocence of the Intended, firmly grounded in a patriarchal discourse which would, in Peter Hyland's words,

> locate women away from the active but corrupting world of work and commerce to protect the superior morality they were supposed to embody. A woman defined in this way could have no interest in 'truth' as it relates to the confrontation with the reality of the outside world, which is represented in its purest form by the wilderness, the savage frontier.[24]

representation of the jungle (see the early episode of the shelling of the continent by the French man-of-war, which reads like an absurd and unsuccessful sexual assault (*HD*, 30ff.); or also revealing choices of words, as in the description of the silent wilderness taking a native 'into its bosom again' (*HD*, 45) and the isolated stations on the river bank 'clinging to the skirts of the unknown' (*HD*, 61)). In time of war, in particular, the demeaning feminization of the Other/the enemy/the oppressed is the obvious counterpart of the celebration of male bonding and of the masculine virtues of courage, strength and fortitude. Interestingly, the feminization of Vietnam comes through also in the best known image of the war, Pulizer Prize-winner Huyng Cong Nick Ut's iconic photograph of Kim Phuc, a little girl running away, naked, from a napalm attack on the village of Trang Bang in June 1972. On this issue, see Marita Sturken, *Tangled Memories: The Vietnam War, the AIDS Epidemic, and the Politics of Remembering* (Berkeley and London: University of California Press, 1997), p. 93.

23 Hélène Cixous, 'Sorties: Out and Out: Attacks/Ways Out/Forays', in Hélène Cixous and Catherine Clément, *The Newly Born Woman* [1975], trans. Betsy Wing [1986] (London: I.B. Tauris Publishers, 1996), pp. 63–132, p. 91.

24 Peter Hyland, 'The Little Woman in the *Heart of Darkness*', *Conradiana*, 20.1 (1988), pp. 3–11, p. 5. On the patriarchal rationale of the lie to the Intended, see also Susan Jones,

Hyland sees a perfect justification for Marlow's lie to the Intended in the patriarchal desire to preserve the woman's natural innocence, and retain an image of feminine virtue to counterbalance the disturbing figure of Kurtz's native mistress: rarefied perfection in opposition to earthly abasement, the Intended must be a Madonna to the barbarous woman's whore. The reason for Marlow's disingenuous behaviour is one final mystery to be unravelled by the reader, who should have no difficulty in seeing through the self-deception at work in Marlow's patronizing manipulation of the truth. In order to reveal the latent misogyny in this ostensibly sympathetic gesture, it is enough to follow the main hermeneutical example within the text, which is paradoxically provided by Marlow's discerning and cynical attitude towards the ideological flaws of the colonial enterprise.

It is in fact Marlow's ironic narrative stance that provides a model for a sharp critical response, quick to spot the 'redeeming ideas' behind Western culture; of course, the necessity of a disenchanted, inquiring interpretative mood becomes much more pressing when Marlow fails us, having internalized (for once) the patriarchal bias. At this point it falls to the reader to adopt an ironic attitude in his or her interpretation of *Heart of Darkness*: in this sense, the text can be said to have created its own ideal audience, and I would argue that this training cuts across gender distinctions, in spite of the much debated fact that the intradiegetic addressees of Marlow's story are all men.[25] Marlow's companions on board the *Nellie*, including the nameless character who opens and closes the novella, framing Kurtz's story with the account of its telling, provide not so much a model of a reader's response as a background to highlight the peculiar qualities of Marlow's tale and narrative technique. In fact, the only – anonymous – remark directly elicited by Marlow's storytelling is a request for civility in mock outrage at the suggestion that life is but a series of 'monkey tricks' (*HD*, 60); for the rest, the intradiegetic narrator intervenes only twice to interrupt the story,

---

Conrad and Women (Oxford and New York: Oxford University Press, 1999), pp. 171–72: 'Conrad remarks on the fundamental importance of the role of Kurtz's fiancée, where, "in the light of the final incident", the whole story gains its real significance: "the last pages of Heart of Darkness where the interview of the man and the girl locks in … makes of that story something quite on another plane than an anecdote of a man who went mad in the Centre of Africa." By having Marlow protect her from the truth, Conrad exposes the patriarchal strategy that has traditionally excluded women from knowledge in male affairs.' For an opposite view of the function of Marlow's lie – seen as an act of collusion with the male ideology of the Empire – see Joanna M. Smith, '"Too Beautiful Altogether:" Patriarchal Ideology in *Heart of Darkness*', in *Heart of Darkness: A Case Study in Contemporary Criticism*, ed. Ross C. Murfin (New York: St. Martin's Press, 1989), pp. 179–95.

25 For a different position, see the feminist thesis about Conrad's naturalization of the reader's role as a privileged white European male position argued by Nina Pelikan Straus in 'The Exclusion of the Intended from Secret Sharing in Conrad's *Heart of Darkness*', *Novel*, 20.2 (1987), pp. 123–37, and reprised in Jones, *Conrad and Women*, p. 172.

commenting on its eerie progress.[26] Even at the very end, following a brief reminder of Marlow's Buddha-like posture and indistinctness in the dark, the story is met with a prolonged silence, eventually broken by a matter-of-fact remark about the ebbing of the tide. While the narrator expresses our yearning for signification, the audience on the *Nellie* mirror our bewilderment with the story; it is only Marlow who fully embodies the figure of the active listener/reader within the text, in his reaction to the rumours surrounding Kurtz and indeed in his attempt to decipher, in its telling, his whole experience of this encounter. If anything, the masculine, nautical bond that pervades the narrative frame draws attention to the eccentricity of Marlow's tale, by measuring it up against the 'direct simplicity' of seamen's yarns,

> the whole meaning of which lies within the shell of a cracked nut. But Marlow was not typical (if his propensity to spin yarns be excepted), and to him the meaning of an episode was not inside like a kernel but outside, enveloping the tale which brought it out only as a glow brings out a haze, in the likeness of one of those misty halos that sometimes are made visible by the spectral illumination of moonshine. (*HD*, 18)

At odds with the unwritten rules of the bond of the sea, Marlow's storytelling style has been seen to correspond to Cixous's definition of *écriture féminine*.[27] The passage quoted above seems to endorse this critical position. Marlow does not tell straightforward stories: rather he *spins* yarns, whose pursuit of signification is characterized by the rejection of a forceful, intrusive prying, so that any apprehended truth remains glowing – evasively, bathed in lunar radiance – on the surface. Besides, the (traditionally feminine) figure of the moon is summoned to officiate over what could be described as the celebration of female, non-penetrative, polymorphous sexuality, which is reflected in the digressive, evocative quality of Marlow's narrative. Marlow's complicity with a feminine realm does not end here: in fact, his journey to the Congo is made possible by the intercession of his 'excellent aunt'; ironically,

---

26 'It had become so pitch dark that we listeners could hardly see one another. For a long time already he [i.e. Marlow], sitting apart, had been no more to us than a voice. There was not a word from anybody. The others might have been asleep, but I was awake. I listened, I listened on the watch for the sentence, for the word, that would give me the clue to the faint uneasiness inspired by this narrative that seemed to shape itself without human lips in the heavy night-air of the river' (*HD*, 50). Here Marlow has become a voice, like Kurtz, while his narrative seems almost non-human: the witness/teller of the story of transgression undergoes his or her own journey into the heart of darkness. The other brief interruption to Marlow's storytelling occurs on page 80.

27 See footnote in Jones, *Conrad and Women*, pp. 20–21, where the problematic intermittent essentialism of Cixous's position is also acknowledged.

this character's unwavering faith in the civilizing mission of the colonial venture causes her nephew to muse on how 'out of touch with truth' women are (*HD*, 28). The African expedition is therefore bracketed within two mirror-like female encounters, during which Marlow is the recipient first and the perpetrator later of an ideological lie: for all his disparagement of his aunt's misguided piety, Marlow chooses not to tamper with the Intended's illusions. In this way, men and women are ultimately shown to inhabit the same world and, if women often remain at the 'door of Darkness', it is because of the role that patriarchy has reserved for them, rather than the result of an essential difference.[28] While it is true that the portrayal of women in *Heart of Darkness* is often underdeveloped and caricatural (and yet the same could be said of every character in that story, with the exception of Marlow and – possibly – Kurtz),[29] the Manichaean stereotyping of femininity is only true of those figures who represent a potential or an actual sexual object, that is the Intended and the 'superb and barbarous woman', Kurtz's sweethearts.[30]

The construction of the female objects of male desire according to the opposite stereotypes of the angel of the hearth and the untamed fiend – the one function usually sought after in legitimate, the other in illegitimate relationships – is part of the patriarchal discourse on women, which O'Brien immediately addresses in making his female protagonist somebody's sweet-

28 The 'door of Darkness', in the headquarters of the Belgian company who commission Marlow to undertake his journey, is presided over by two ladies knitting black wool. Marlow encounters them on the eve of his appointment and will later think about them in Africa. These memorable figures are traditionally identified with the Greek Fates, the mythical weavers responsible for the span of each individual's life. They are a symbolic, extreme illustration of women's ability to play an active role in the realm of brute reality, much as Marlow's aunt is invested with that function on a realistic level. Joanna Smith also points out that Marlow's aunt's naive colonial attitude (her belief in 'weaning those ignorant millions') is ultimately 'a variant of the masculine imperialism in Kurtz's "we can exert a power for good practically unbounded"'; '"Too Beautiful Altogether"', p. 190); in other words, the 'redeeming' idea is neither an exclusively masculine nor a feminine fabrication. For further comments on female agency in the novel and Marlow's patriarchal double standards, see also Watts, '"Heart of Darkness"', p. 56.

29 A small detail in support of the shared caricatural quality of both male and female minor characters in *Heart of Darkness* is the 'starched white affair' (*HD*, 26) on the knitting lady's head, which reminds us of the Chief Accountant's 'high starched collar' (*HD*, 36). These are all empty, puppet-like figures, anticipating Eliot's hollow men (see also Marlow's description of one of the agents at the Central Station as a 'papier-mâché Mephistopheles', *HD*, 48). On the lack of depth of most characters in *Heart of Darkness*, see also Gabrielle McIntire, 'The Women Do Not Travel: Gender, Difference, and Incommensurability in Conrad's *Heart of Darkness*', *Modern Fiction Studies*, 48.2 (2002), pp. 257–84.

30 Watts points out that Marlow himself is infatuated with the Intended, a detail which contributes to the explanation of the lie as a chivalrous (i.e. patriarchal) gesture; see '"Heart of Darkness"', p. 49.

heart.[31] Not a nurse, nor a journalist, let alone a soldier, Mary Anne, a recent high-school graduate, is in Vietnam as Mark's girlfriend, a status which in itself authenticates her innocence and propriety. Even her flirtatiousness is all for Mark's benefit, 'the sort of show that a girl will sometimes put on for her boyfriend's entertainment and education' (*TTC*, 91). In line with the standards of late-twentieth-century Western culture, the figure of Mark's 'Intended' is allowed, indeed required, to be more sexually explicit than in Conrad's time, and yet the goal of this performance is always the same: the fulfilment of a male fantasy. Mary Anne's transformation exposes the artificiality of this eternal myth of femininity, which turns out to be as easily disposable as a sexy pink sweater. The essentialist view of the notions of masculinity and femininity is expressly refuted by Rat Kiley, the eye-witness and original narrator of Mary Anne's story, who makes a passionate oration against our cultural resistance to the idea that America's sweetheart might accomplish the ultimate transgression.[32] Rat's argument is further corroborated by the physical and emotional likeness between the early Mary Anne (a 'cute blonde – just a kid', 'a tall, big-boned blonde', 'just a child, blond and innocent', *TTC*, 88, 90, 99) and Mark ('just a boy – eighteen years old. Tall and blond. [...] A nice kid, too, polite and good-hearted', *TTC*, 95). In the end, it is only Mark, still innocent, who persists in the gender fallacy, holding on to such traditional conventions as the engagement and refusing to acknowledge the radical changes in his girlfriend. In a significant reversal of stereotypical gender roles, Mark is exposed as more naive and fragile than Mary Anne: while his drama is played out on a small, bureaucratic scale, with his demotion and medical discharge from the army, Mary Anne's story

31 After making the point that in *Heart of Darkness*, with the exceptions of Marlow and Kurtz, 'characters are known by function rather than by proper name', Gabrielle McIntire adds that women in particular are defined 'in terms of their relation to men': the aunt, the mother, the laundress, the mistress, the Intended, etc. ('The Women Do Not Travel', p. 281). With similar polemic intent, Joanna Smith argues that Marlow – and Conrad – ultimately collude with patriarchy in their silencing and symbolic reduction of women, to whom the male rationality and articulacy, and the ability to engage with truth, are not made available. It seems to me that both critics underplay the fact that Marlow's own storytelling practice contravenes the very masculine rules, standards and goals that he can otherwise be seen occasionally to endorse in his treatment of women.

32 This is a particularly convincing argument, since it is voiced by a speaker who cannot be accused of political correctness: 'She was a girl, that's all. I mean, if it was a guy, anybody'd say, Hey, no big deal, he got caught up in the Nam shit, he got seduced by the Greenies. See what I mean? You got these blinders on about women. How gentle and peaceful they are. All that crap about how if we had a pussy for president there wouldn't be no more wars. Pure garbage. You got to get rid of that sexist attitude' (*TTC*, 100). See also, earlier in the narration: '"She *wasn't* dumb," [Rat]'d snap. "I never said that. Young, that's all I said. Like you and me. A *girl*, that's the only difference, and I'll tell you something. It didn't amount to jack. I mean, when we first got here – all of us – we were real young and innocent, full of romantic bullshit, but we learned pretty damn quick. And so did Mary Anne"' (*TTC*, 93).

unfolds in an awe-inspiring tragedy, with her transfiguration into a legendary figure, a grand personification of the jungle and its unyielding mystery.[33] The powerful image of the woman lurking in the wilderness is a clever, subtle critique both of the myth of masculinity and of the American expectation of a moral renaissance in the conquest of the Vietnamese 'frontier': 'What happened to her, Rat said, was what happened to all of them. You come over clean and you get dirty and then afterward it's never the same. A question of degree. Some make it intact, some don't make it at all' (*TTC*, 105).[34] The self-reliance, resilience and entrepreneurial spirit embodied by the pioneers of the American west could not be further away from the simple lesson learnt by the soldiers in Vietnam, as the powerful epigrammatic statement from 'How to Tell a True War Story' explains: 'Send guys to war, they come home talking dirty' (*TTC*, 68). If they come home at all.

'Sweetheart' shows that there is an irreconcilable difference not between the sexes, but between those who are, or have been, 'in country' and those who have remained 'in the world' (as we have seen, the latter is a thesis common to most war literature). In this respect, the intradiegetic audience of Rat's narrative – an all-male group of soldiers united by the 'bond of war' much as the people on the *Nellie* shared 'the bond of the sea' (*HD*, 15) – functions as a reminder of the insurmountable challenges in trying to represent the alterity of the conflict, rather than as the example of an unbridgeable

33 Mary Anne's tragic – and unspeakable – sublimation makes her akin to the mythical figures (such as Medusa or Penthesileia) reclaimed by Cixous as strong, empowering models of femininity. I do not agree with Lorrie N. Smith, who thinks that O'Brien's deconstruction of gender difference in this story is only a token gesture ('as if he's read plenty of French feminism') and that 'Sweetheart' is only superficially 'a feminist assertion of semiotic power disrupting patriarchal symbolic order'; '"The Things Men Do"', p. 36, p. 35. According to Smith, the complexity and inconclusiveness of the story's ending would mask the author's inability to dispose of his monstrous female creation, who 'remains a sort of macabre, B-movie "joke," good for a nervous laugh among men', p. 36. This position strikes me as rather ungenerous towards O'Brien and his text – while perhaps also indicative of the 'no-win' situation in which attempts to reconfigure gender relations can often get caught: surely, the silence around Mary Anne's end can be interpreted as a sign of her successful escape both from a patriarchal world and from a narrative told by and for men. Moreover, while it is true that, in perfect tune with their gung-ho mentality, the Green Berets immortalize the wildest, deadliest aspect of the girl's mythical transfiguration, Mary Anne is remembered and/or encountered with wonder and admiration, even with love, by tellers and listeners of her story alike. In the end, to her male audience, she is no laughing matter, nor (on the other end of the scale) a frightening, emasculating figure: an awe-inspiring, self-possessed, mysterious creature, 'she seemed to flow like water through the dark, without sound or center. She went barefoot. She stopped carrying a weapon. [...] It was as if she were taunting some wild creature out in the bush, or in her head' (*TTC*, 106).

34 It is worth pointing out again that Rat's anticlimactic moral to Mary Anne's story, which exposes the corrupting effect on war on all people, regardless of gender, is later somewhat superseded by the much more compelling and lingering impression that Mary Anne makes on the witnesses, listeners and readers of her tale. She is both the contingent proof of the evil of war *and* a larger-than-life, tantalizing mythical creation.

gender divide. As the story repeatedly makes clear, Mary Anne is not
precluded a priori from entering the war enclave: it is only a cultural prejudice that makes it out of bounds for women (hence their typical absence from
gatherings such as the one in which Rat's storytelling takes place). O'Brien
exploits the uniformity and exclusiveness of the 'bond of war' so as to raise
metanarrative rather than gender issues. The listeners' incredulity towards
Rat's tale reiterates the incommunicability of the experience of Vietnam: if
Rat's fellow soldiers will not believe his story – O'Brien seems to say – then
who will? At the same time, Rat's presence complicates the narrative structure of 'Sweetheart', which, like *Heart of Darkness*, contains a frame to
introduce and accompany the telling of the core episode. In Conrad's text,
however, the degree of interference between the two narrative levels is
minimal: the narrator's longest intervention is at the very beginning of the
novella, when the reader is warned of the complexity and inconclusiveness of
Marlow's yarns. Not so in 'Sweetheart', where Rat's tale about Mary Anne is
interwoven with the account of its telling, in a much bolder metafictional
gesture, whose narcissism is further highlighted by the fact that the narrator
of the frame, and indeed of the entire book, is a character called 'Tim
O'Brien'. At the intradiegetic level, as it is perhaps to be expected, Rat's
storytelling style is very similar to Marlow's: they both take a tortuous route
in unravelling the plot, which is constantly interrupted by assiduous clarifications of the events in question, as well as by a running metanarrative
commentary. If the crew on the *Nellie* face Marlow's meanderings with good-
natured resignation, Rat's self-reflective interludes trigger the vocal
remonstrations of one of his listeners, Mitchell Sanders, who clings to the
idea that stories should have a 'direct simplicity'. What matters to Sanders is
the 'raw material' (*TTC*, 117), and Rat is accordingly urged on several
occasions to stick to the facts (yet, ironically, Sanders' unsuccessful objections impede the flow of Rat's story, increasing its inconclusiveness). What,
if anything, can possibly justify such persistent artfulness in O'Brien's storytelling?

Complementing the suggestiveness of the image of Mary Anne's union
with the jungle, the intricacy and the eccentricity of 'Sweetheart' work as an
enactment of a *féminine* mode of storytelling, and constitute a tireless and
open narrative attempt to *relate* (with) the other. Finally 'Sweetheart' is a love
story, a passionate celebration of Mary Anne, which does 'take the risk of
other, of difference, without feeling threatened by the existence of an otherness, rather, delighting to increase through the unknown that is there to
discover, to respect, to favour, to cherish'.[35] As we shall see in the conclusion
of the tale, Mary Anne's charismatic presence is neither excised from the

35 Cixous, 'Sorties', p. 78.

story, nor is it reduced to a terrible yet intelligible victim of 'The Nam' (in spite of Rat's epigrammatic pronouncement), nor even to a feared female monster. The convoluted and centrifugal structure of the narrative inevitably also proves to be a challenge to a straightforward claim to truth. In fact, the fictional 'O'Brien' jeopardizes the entire credibility of Mary Anne's story very openly and from the beginning:

> I heard it from Rat Kiley, who swore up and down to its truth, although in the end, I'll admit, that doesn't amount to much of a warranty. Among the men in Alpha Company, Rat had a reputation for exaggeration and overstatement, a compulsion to rev up the facts [...] It wasn't a question of deceit. Just the opposite: he wanted to heat up the truth, to make it burn so hot that you would feel exactly what he felt. (*TTC*, 87)

Adopting a technique endorsed by O'Brien, both in his fictional persona and in his prolific writing career,[36] Rat is an odd kind of unreliable narrator, who chooses to exaggerate and embellish the bare facts in order to provoke a reaction in his audience as similar as possible to the emotions experienced by the protagonists of his stories. This unorthodox strategy would have Conrad's approval, judging from his 1917 'Author's Note' to *Youth: A Narrative; and Two Other Stories* (first published in 1902): '[*Heart of Darkness*] is experience pushed a little (and only very little) beyond the actual facts of the case for the perfectly legitimate, I believe, purpose of bringing it home to the minds and bosoms of the readers' (*HD*, 11).

O'Brien's storytelling differs in degree, not in kind, from Conrad's, a fact witnessed by the subtle variation in the narrative structure between *Heart of Darkness* and 'Sweetheart'. Marlow's yarn is embedded in the anonymous narration of one of the characters on the *Nellie*, i.e. a member of the original audience of the intradiegetic tale. This 'Russian dolls' structure is supplanted by an *alternation* of two stories (Mary Anne's adventure and Rat's narrative feat) in 'Sweetheart', as opposed to the insertion of the one tale within the other. The narration of the act of narration, comparable in significance to a frame, does not envelop the account of Mary Anne's journey, which, dotted with expressions such as 'Rat said', or 'As Rat described it', is evidently

---

36 See, for example, 'Good Form' with its proclamation of the supremacy of 'story-truth' over 'happening-truth', or the already mentioned 'How to Tell a True War Story', in which the programmatic inconclusiveness of true stories is also theorized. Sanders' rage at the inconclusiveness of Rat's narrative (and conversely, his perceptive guess that Mary Anne must end at some point with the Greenies, otherwise there would have been no reason to mention them in the story) provides a witty comment on narrative conventions and the expectations that they engender ('"Jesus Christ, it's against the *rules*," Sanders said. "Against human *nature*. This elaborate story, you can't say, Hey, by the way, I don't know the *ending*. I mean, you got certain obligations"', *TTC*, 104).

indirect speech, reported by a character called Tim O'Brien.[37] This fictional 'O'Brien' is therefore responsible for both narratives but, while he can personally vouch for Rat's performance, of which he was a witness, he must rely on Rat as a source for Mary Anne's tale. Interestingly, even Rat is only a *partial* eye-witness, having left the medical compound a few days after Mary Anne had moved to the Greenies' hut: by his own admission (mediated, of course, by 'O'Brien''s voice), the conclusion of Mary Anne's story has reached Rat via a circuitous route, so that his authority on the matter is 'secondhand. Thirdhand, actually' (*TTC*, 104). Always at the risk of losing the thread of the rumours and voices that overlap and follow each other, the reader might be forgiven for thinking that this proliferation of narrative levels is a gratuitous, narcissistic game. Still, O'Brien is merely putting into practice the lesson underlying his whole oeuvre: 'You can tell a true war story by the way it never seems to end' (*TTC*, 73) or even 'You can tell a true war story if you just keep on telling it' (*TTC*, 80). O'Brien makes sure that this one keeps on being told, over and over, one more time: by the O'Brien-author of *The Things They Carried*, by the fictional character of the same name, by Rat Kiley, even by the Special Forces. The multiple performances, evidenced by the presence of parallel and interlinking narrative strands in 'Sweetheart', are what puts the truth into the story. This may be regarded as a narrative strategy typical of postmodernity, within which truth is judged for its relative, and contingent, effectiveness rather than in absolute terms of faithfulness to the facts.

A similar conclusion can be reached from the analysis of the implications of Conrad's embedded sequence of eye-witness accounts: each successive narrator relies on an authority made progressively weaker by the increased distance from the original events, until the whole process becomes a game of Chinese whispers, with the truth receding further and further away from view. The O'Brien-narrator instead has taken it upon himself to mediate *simultaneously* Mary Anne's story and the debate on Rat's narrative performance: this latter subplot prompts metafictional reflections, which are ultimately subsumed within the practice of O'Brien (both the real and the fictional one). Mary Anne's tale has never been a question of eye-witness account, but survives on the strength of its symbolic, suggestive status: it is a timeless story, handed over from one teller to the next for its sheer narrative charm, prompting continuous tellings and retellings in each speaker's hope of getting somewhat closer to the truth. Interestingly, 'Sweetheart' ends with a short paragraph from the (always mediated) perspective of the Special

37 At the risk of stretching the point, I would argue that this form of narrative, with multiple strands and a collaborative conclusion, has a much more open-ended, plural and dispersive (hence *féminine*) structure than Conrad's Russian dolls series of tales which, while lacking a basic linearity, each *sequentially* contains another.

Forces who, like a Greek chorus, consecrate the appeal of Mary Anne's story to a collective, mythical imaginary:

> But the story did not end there [i.e. in an enquiry and Mark's dismissal from the army]. If you believed the Greenies, Rat said, Mary Anne was still somewhere out there in the dark. Odd movements, odd shapes. Late at night, when the Greenies were out on ambush, the rain forest seemed to stare in at them – a watched feeling – and a couple of times they almost saw her sliding through the shadows. Not quite, but almost. She had crossed to the other side. She was part of the land. She was wearing her culottes, her pink sweater, and a necklace of human tongues. She was dangerous. She was ready for the kill. (*TTC*, 106–107)

The final image of Mary Anne with her necklace of human tongues, earlier described with 'the tips curled upward as if caught in a final horrified syllable' (*TTC*, 103), locks her within a silence that is as tantalizing as it is shocking and impenetrable. Like the Conradian Intended, whose (unspoken) name is ironically declared by Marlow to have been the last word uttered by Kurtz, the figure of Mary Anne is collapsed with an unspeakable, elusive truth, and finally with 'The horror! The horror!', an ambiguous, haunting cry still echoing in our culture.[38] Indeed, Mary Anne's story does not end here, in the final page of 'Sweetheart of the Song Tra Bong', as it did not begin on the mountains to the west of Chu Lai: we have all heard it before (in *Heart of Darkness*, but also in every other tale of transgression and perdition) and we will hear it again, for as long as we will feel the need to try to cast light on the truth about that part of human nature 'still somewhere out there in the dark'.

O'Brien's intertextual dialogue with the Conradian model offers a clear example of the process of invention, that is of the discovery (from the Latin *inventio*, meaning 'to find out') and creation of 'truth' in the mirror-like acts of translation and mythopoesis of something 'original'. As we have seen, in the first instance the elusive meaning of O'Brien's 'Sweetheart of the Song Tra Bong' comes out of the incessant tweaking of a story – Mary Anne Bell's story – that is both private and collective, both personal anecdote and collective myth (once again, 'original' in the present *and* the etymological sense of the word). At the most superficial level, 'Sweetheart of the Song Tra Bong' disputes the (male) myths of progress and heroism – the pillars of the grand

---

38 An actual example of the intriguing persistence of this cry in our culture is offered by Coppola's *Apocalypse Now*, in which the memorable line 'The horror! The horror!' is uttered twice by Marlon Brando (Kurtz) in a spine-chilling whisper, the laconic voiceover that accompanies the departure of Captain Willard (the Marlow figure, played by Martin Sheen) from Kurtz's compound and his return to 'civilization'. Kurtz's final words are thus the last line in the film (and their delivery is extremely faithful to Conrad's text, where they are described as 'a cry that was no more than a breath'; *HD*, 112).

American narratives of the frontier and of Manifest Destiny – in an obvious counterpart to Conrad's critique of the white man's burden and the imperialist mission. In the eyes of the discerning reader, however, O'Brien's powerful rewriting of Kurtz's voyage into 'The horror!' adds a further layer of signification and literariness to his project: if nothing else, by drawing inspiration from Conrad's challenge to the dichotomy between wilderness and civilization, and the subsequent exposure of the lies that underpin the patriarchal, colonial enterprise, O'Brien appears to claim a similar critical scope for his narrative, which thus becomes a parable not merely for the iniquity of the Vietnam war, but for the absurdity of a Manichaean, clear-cut opposition between good and evil, or feminine innocence and masculine experience. Inevitably, both texts end up posing more questions than they solve: yet a reading of 'Sweetheart of the Song Tra Bong' against the grain of *Heart of Darkness* throws into relief the strength of O'Brien's commitment to the notion that fictional truth is truer than factual truth, particularly when the truth in question must try to do justice to an event that demands and resists comprehension – let alone an adequate, literal translation into words. O'Brien's solution to this narrative conundrum is the development of the modernist premises of Conrad's novella within a postmodern sensitivity: the disclosure of the problematic patriarchal view of women in *Heart of Darkness* is revisited in O'Brien's provocative characterization of his protagonists, which challenges the very naturalness of the notions of masculinity and femininity, and gives birth in Mary Anne to a memorable evocation of the ambivalent and undefinable energy that fuels all human existence.[39] Similarly, the modernist disillusionment with the idea of meaning, portrayed in its elusiveness and frailty in *Heart of Darkness*, becomes a profession of faith in the performativity of truth in the telling of 'Sweetheart of the Song Tra Bong'. A fleeting sense of signification occasionally reveals itself in the act of (compulsive) storytelling; truth is in the self-evident success of the performance, rather than in its content: 'A true war story, if truly told, makes the stomach believe' (*TTC*, 75). And if that does not happen, 'All you can do is tell it one more time, patiently, adding and subtracting, making up a few things to get at the real truth' (*TTC*, 80). As the entirety of O'Brien's writing testifies, this quest is an ongoing process.

---

39 On the other hand, as I have shown with my references to a possible interpretation of the two texts as examples of writing akin to Cixous's definition of *écriture féminine*, both *Heart of Darkness* and 'Sweetheart' challenge conventional boundaries between the masculine and the feminine at the level of the narrative structure.

The life of imagination and story-truth

The Third Squad's fantastic journey in pursuit of Cacciato is the result of Paul Berlin's book-length reflection on his comrade's chances of success, as well as an exploration of, or even an indulgence in, his own wish for desertion. In following Berlin's flight of fancy, *Cacciato* presents the individual's reliance on his or her own imaginative powers as an important route towards self-knowledge and as a crucial way of testing one's relationship with reality. This issue is tied in with the novel's structural and thematic emphasis on the epistemological confusion that surrounds the experience of modern war and its extraordinary technological power, with the soldiers' perceptions impaired or twisted by their constant proximity to death and the strain of combat. This uncertainty is heightened by O'Brien's choice of protagonist, a naive draftee who does not share the self-awareness, the intellectual convictions and the moral high ground ironically ascribed to the narrator of *If I Die*. To a certain extent, the novel's main point about the importance of imagination is made possible precisely through Berlin's naivety and through his ensuing need to figure out the implications of his presence in Vietnam against Cacciato's 'separate peace': self-analysis is a new exercise for this young recruit, and the exploration of the options available to him is not merely a rhetorical operation, but rather leads to a genuine development.

In the first of the 'Observation Post' chapters, Berlin reflects on the reality and plausibility of the events that have followed the explosion of Cacciato's booby trap, securing the latter's escape, while triggering his own attack of the biles, as readers later discover:

> Time to consider the possibilities. Had it ended there on Cacciato's grassy hill, flares coloring the morning sky? Had it ended in tragedy with a jerking, shaking feeling – noise and confusion? Or had it ended farther along the trail west? Had it ever ended? What, in fact, had become of Cacciato? More precisely – as Doc Peret would insist it be phrased – more precisely, what part was fact and what part was the extension of fact? And how were facts separated from possibilities? What had really happened and what merely might have happened? How did it end? (*GAC*, 34)

The entire novel is an elaborate attempt to answer these questions, showing how the difference between facts and their extension is not as clear-cut as their neat division into three separate narrative strands might initially lead us to assume: Berlin's imaginary journey to Paris is increasingly shaped as a re-elaboration of his recollections of the war, some of which, in turn, are finally brought to the surface of the protagonist's consciousness in the course of his fantasizing. As Dean McWilliams points out, the most surreal parts of the flight from Vietnam – the fall into the hole in the ground *à la* Alice in Wonderland and the escape from Tehran, as in a cartoonish action movie, with the explosion of the prison and the garish getaway car – 'occur as responses to obstacles posed by Berlin's two most traumatic memories: the tunnels and Lt. Martin'.[40] Berlin perceives his failure to volunteer to retrieve Frenchie Tucker from a dangerous enemy tunnel as the moment that confirms his inability to live up to the military ideal, even if this rescue operation, significantly carried out by his near-homonymous comrade *Ber*nie *Lyn*n, ends up with a double death. This is a crucial episode not merely for Berlin's realization that he is not Silver Star material, but also because it triggers the soldiers' plotting against Lieutenant Martin, whose own attitude towards discipline and military regulations will later be echoed by Captain Rhallon, the *Savak* officer who arrests the squad in Iran. Berlin might be trying to leave Vietnam behind, but its two most traumatic memories resurface on the road to Paris in the guise of forbidding complications – the surreal tunnel and Lieutenant Martin's revenant – which force the narrative to take its most bizarre and tortuous turns.

The influence of memory on the imagination becomes gradually more explicit, with direct intrusions of anecdotes from the war or brief references to Berlin's past, in chapters otherwise devoted to the pursuit of Cacciato.[41] The novel shows how this is a two-way influence: the traces of traumatic events that emerge in the unfolding of the imaginary flight to Paris eventually enable Berlin to face the actual incidents to which they allude. The confrontation with Captain Rhallon in Chapter 33, for example, precedes the two consecutive chapters about 'Lake Country', where Berlin manages at last to recall the plot against Lieutenant Martin, the pivotal, shameful event whose memory he had until then tried to avoid – hence the jumbled-up chronology of the early vignettes about the war. Even if the 'Lake Country' chapters end before reaching the moment of the lieutenant's death, Berlin's ability to get close to this unspeakable incident represents a significant breakthrough: once the block created by the repression of his complicity in an act of murder is removed, 'the remaining events prior to Cacciato's departure

---

40 Dean McWilliams, 'Time in O'Brien's *Going After Cacciato*', *Critique*, 29.4 (1988), pp. 245–55, p. 253.

41 In Chapter 21, for example, Berlin searches people on a Burmese train, in what is a clear displacement of the frisking of Vietnamese villagers; the mountains of Afghanistan bring to his mind the Vietnamese landscape of Lake Country in Chapter 27; Berlin's musings about the role of imagination in his journey to Paris lead to a comparison with more mundane uses of the imaginative faculty, exemplified by the memory of his younger self working out the possibility of making it into professional football (*GAC*, 217). Last but not least, the beheading of a deserter in Tehran is an expression of Berlin's anxieties about his own imagined desertion to Paris and, more disturbingly, about his role in the fragging of Lieutenant Martin. For a more extensive discussion of these points, see McWilliams, 'Time in O'Brien's *Going After Cacciato*'.

can be narrated in their natural sequence'.[42] The dynamic outlined by
McWilliams explains the subconscious drives at play in the interconnections
between mimetic and fantastic strands in the narrative but, as we have seen
in Chapter 2, Berlin's quest for Cacciato is more than a spontaneous, oneiric
reverie. It is true that the beginning of the squad's adventure with Cacciato's
disappearance across the border into Laos coincides with Berlin's fainting fit,
which might suggest that the soldiers' march continues as part of a delirious
vision, another effect of an excess of the fear biles. This hypothesis is then
complemented, and perhaps even superseded, by a compelling alternative
interpretation, initially articulated in the first 'Observation Post': 'Doc was
wrong when he called it dreaming. Biles or no biles, it wasn't dreaming – it
wasn't even pretending, not in the strict sense. It was an idea. It was a
working out of the possibilities. [...] It was a way of asking questions. What
became of Cacciato? Where did he go, and why? What were his motives, or
did he have motives, and did motives matter?' (*GAC*, 35–36).

In denying the oneiric, fanciful quality of his experience, Berlin emphasizes his active role in developing this journey into an adventure of epic
proportions and with a definite mission. Three hours, and three Observation
Posts, later, in the dead of night, Berlin chooses not to wake Stink Harris,
who is scheduled to relieve him of his guard duties, so as to continue the story
of the squad's pursuit at a point in the narrative where the first major obstacle
– Li Van Hgoc's tunnel – has just been overcome thanks to Sarkin's provi-
dential intervention. In other words, Berlin deliberately cultivates and, to an
extent, pilots his fantasy so as to try to envisage an alternative future, and
measure its viability and appeal. Interestingly, he is aware of the implausibility of his subject matter which, he is nonetheless convinced, 'would made
[*sic*] a fine war story' (*GAC*, 123), but he pointedly dismisses as trivial what
he imagines to be the sceptics' objections to the far-fetched development of
his fantastic plot. (Compare, for example, the overlooked practical details,
such as the soldiers' lack of money and passports, and the missing psychological considerations, such as their awareness of the illegality of their actions,
that would make their adventure realistic, both in terms of feasibility and in
terms of its adherence to mimetic narrative conventions.) Berlin's nonchalant
attitude towards these 'petty details' leads, by contrast, to the revelation of
what is really important to him as a storyteller:

> Money could be earned. Or stolen or begged or borrowed. Passports could be
> forged, lies could be told, cops could be bribed. [...] If pressed he could make up
> the solutions – good, convincing solutions. But his imagination worked faster than
> that. Speed, momentum. Since means could be found, since answers were

---

42 McWilliams, 'Time in O'Brien's *Going After Cacciato*', p. 249.

possible, his imagination went racing toward more important matters: Cacciato, the feel of the journey, what was seen along the way, what was learned, colors and motion and people and finally Paris. It could be done. Wasn't that the critical point? It could truly be done. (*GAC*, 123)

Unconcerned with the observance of the rules of formal realism, Berlin is instead interested in 'the feel of the journey', in what will be 'learned' from following its trajectory all the way to the final destination. O'Brien develops this point in an interview where he talks of the imagination as 'a way of goal-setting, or objective-setting, of figuring out purposes':

> The imagined journey after Cacciato isn't just a way of escaping from the war in his head – it's that, too, I'm sure – but it's also a way of asking the questions, 'should I go after Cacciato, *really*? should I follow him off into the jungle toward Paris? could I live with myself doing that?' See what I'm getting at? How the imagination is a heuristic tool that we can use to help ourselves set goals. We use the outcomes of our imaginings. We do this all the time in the real world. You imagine yourself picking up the phone to call this girl. You imagine yourself dialing. What will you say? What will she say? Okay, you'll say this, and she'll say that. What if she says no? What shall I do? What if you start sweating? What if she says *yes*? [...] Somehow the outcome of that long mental process will determine whether you're going to pick the phone up and actually make the call. The central theme of the novel has to do with how we use our imaginations to deal with situations around us, not just to cope with them psychologically but, most importantly, to deal with them philosophically and morally.[43]

Last but not least, there is a third, elemental reason why Berlin's flight of imagination deserves to be given such ample space, and such a realistic treatment, in the novel. In the final chapter of the book, as the picaresque narrative comes to an end, we are taken back to the moment when Berlin recovers from his fainting fit and Cacciato vanishes for good. The novel's conclusion confirms in no uncertain terms what we have known all along: the squad's journey to Paris only happened in Berlin's mind. Yet O'Brien insists on the reality of this mental dimension and claims that *Cacciato* abides to a 'strict realism' in its accurate recording of Berlin's daydreams:

> Things actually happen in daydreams. There's a reality you can't deny. It's not happening in the physical world, but it's certainly happening in the sense data of the brain. There's a reality to imaginative experience that's critical to the book. The life of imagination is half of war, half of *any* kind of experience. We live in our

43 Schroeder, 'Two Interviews', p. 139.

heads a lot, but especially during situations of stress and great peril. It's a means of escape in part, but it's also a means of dealing with the real world – not just escaping it, but dealing with it. And so I chose to render about half of the book in a naturalistic mode, but I also treated fantasy as fully real.[44]

O'Brien's belief in the importance of the life of the mind is reflected in the novel by the closing exchange between Berlin and Lieutenant Corson, who remain hopeful in spite of Cacciato's 'miserable odds' of success: having just brought to an end the fantastic pursuit, O'Brien takes leave of his readers by inviting them to go back to the realm of the imagination and join in his characters' speculations. Conversely, Cacciato's actual disappearance and the squad's short-lived, ineffective pursuit of the deserter suddenly appear to the soldiers as an implausible tale that people at home will find ridiculous and hard to believe; the real events fleetingly present themselves to their protagonists as the stuff of fiction: 'It would become a war story. People would laugh and shake their heads, nobody would believe a word. Just one more war story' (GAC, 316–17). This self-reflective comment, which narcissistically hints at the composition of Going After Cacciato, confirms once more the proximity of fact and fiction, this time drawing our attention to the ways in which even real perceptions and events – no matter how correctly recorded – are ultimately channelled into narratives and are transformed by this process into textual artefacts, whose truthfulness will not – and *should* not – necessarily be gauged on the basis of their adherence to historical reality. The elaborations on this theme in *The Things They Carried* prove indeed that true (war) stories, according to O'Brien, should claim a different kind of truth from the factual accuracy of historical writing.

The previous chapter mentioned O'Brien's proposition that a true war story should induce a visceral response in the audience. More specifically, the occurrence of this bodily reaction is one of the requisites of 'telling' a true war story – and the double meaning of this expression suggests that gut instinct is required both to recognize a true story and to spin one. In *Things* O'Brien outlines the unorthodox technique of a couple of narrators who are at pains to recreate in the audience the 'quick truth goose' (*TTC*, 34) that their stories provoke in them. In 'How to Tell a True War Story', for example, Mitchell Sanders concocts a meticulous, sustained – and, ultimately, *imaginative* – description of the mysterious sounds that had spooked a patrol conducting a listening-post operation in the mountains. The noise of a cocktail party, a glee club, opera music, Buddhist chanting, even the land, the animals and the vegetation talking: these are clearly hyperbolic embellishments that Sanders, as he later confesses to a receptive O'Brien, has to make up in order to convey

44 Schroeder, 'Two Interviews', p. 138.

the incredible truth of his story, i.e. the fact that the patrol 'heard sound you just plain won't believe' (*TTC*, 74), which in turn suggests the scary, ineffable otherness of Vietnam as perceived by the American soldiers. At the beginning of 'Sweetheart of the Song Tra Bong', O'Brien reiterates his comprehension and, implicitly, his endorsement of Sanders' narrative strategy in his comments on Rat Kiley's 'reputation for exaggeration and overstatement, a compulsion to rev up the facts' (*TTC*, 87). As we have already seen, O'Brien explains that, rather than being motivated by the intent to deceive, Kiley is moved by the opposite desire, a hankering to recreate in the listeners the same sensations that his material engenders in him: 'he wanted to heat up the truth, to make it burn so hot that you would feel exactly what he felt' (*TTC*, 87).

This choice of words and the imagery of the burning truth recall Nathaniel Hawthorne's characterization of the power of the scarlet letter in 'The Custom House'. In this introductory sketch to *The Scarlet Letter* (1850), Hawthorne writes of the clash between what we might want to call an empirical interpretative act, which ends in the failure to unveil the truth of the enigmatic piece of red cloth representing Hester Prynne's story, and the immediacy and efficacy of an empathic approach to the mysterious text, which instead produces an instantaneous physical reaction in its 'reader'. Hawthorne's description of his attempt to decode that 'certain affair of fine red cloth' found by chance in the archives of the Custom House in Salem illustrates – appropriately through fiction, rather than fact – the evanescent truth conveyed by the text (Hester's scarlet letter and his *Scarlet Letter*) and the way in which such truth is imparted to those who want to receive it. 'Careful examination' and 'accurate measurement' of the red cloth do not yield the deep meaning which Hawthorne senses 'streaming forth' from the letter, 'subtly communicating itself to [his] sensibilities, but evading the analysis of [his] mind'.[45] Having thus dismissed the empirical dissection of the object as a viable interpretative option, the passage discloses how the letter offers itself as a completely different kind of reading to its now captive audience:

> While thus perplexed, – and cogitating, among other hypotheses, whether the letter might not have been one of those decorations which the white men used to contrive, in order to take the eyes of the Indians, – I happened to place it on my breast. It seemed to me, – the reader may smile, but must not doubt my word, – it seemed to me, then, that I experienced a sensation not altogether similar, yet almost so, as of burning heat; as if the letter were not of red cloth, but red-hot iron. I shuddered, and involuntarily let it fall upon the floor.[46]

45 Nathaniel Hawthorne, *The Scarlet Letter* [1850] (Oxford: Oxford University Press, 1962), p. 31.
46 Hawthorne, *The Scarlet Letter*, pp. 31–32.

The letter asserts its intense grip on Hawthorne even before he has had a chance to consult the papers that accompany his strange discovery; this purely physical response seizes a reader extraneous to the secret of the text and yet characterized by an unprejudiced openness towards it: both his successful approach to the letter and his reaction to its 'burning heat' are described as uncalculated actions.

Hawthorne also places great emphasis on the impossibility of explaining in a rational way, other than through a personal guarantee, the peculiarity of the phenomenon that he has just experienced. He forestalls, tongue-in-cheek, the predictable scepticism in his readers, pleading with them to believe in the truth of what he is saying – and, consequently, of the story that he is about to tell – on the strength of an *individual sensation* of his. This attitude runs counter to the conventional disclaimers to be found in the novelistic tradition of formal realism where, in the face of the apparent implausibility of the events (to be) described, the author refers to the genuineness and trustworthiness of his or her sources, and in some cases takes on the dependable role of eye-witness to the story, always appealing to the reliability of actual facts rather than to the dubious authority of personal impressions and intuitions. Hawthorne instead asserts the special nature of the truth of the scarlet letter (that it is not susceptible to rational verification, let alone accountable for by objective evidence) and declares his faith in its power to affect the receptive reader (himself in this case) in a physical, instinctive way. Having done so, he proceeds to claim for himself, as the mediator of such a peculiar truth, what he would elsewhere call 'a certain latitude'[47] in his storytelling, that is a margin of imaginative freedom with the documentary sources that accompany Hester Prynne's remarkable embroidery. The letter, in fact, has been preserved together with the old surveyor's record of Hester's story and of the origin of her flamboyant artefact.

The 'small roll of dingy paper' is indeed mentioned by Hawthorne as the source of the narration that he is about to begin; however, this reference to the traditional realist device of the retrieved manuscript as a guarantee of authenticity is made only to be immediately overturned, since in the same breath Hawthorne admits to having adapted the original text to such an extent that the resulting story is now for the most part the product of his imagination.

> The original papers, together with the scarlet letter itself, – a most curious relic, – are still in my possession, and shall be freely exhibited to whomsoever, induced by the great interest of the narrative, may desire a sight of them. I must not be under-

47 Nathaniel Hawthorne, *The House of the Seven Gables* [1851] (London: The Penguin American Library, 1981), p. 1.

stood as affirming, that, in the dressing up of the tale, and imagining the motives
and modes of passion that influenced the characters who figure in it, I have invari-
ably confined myself within the limits of the old Surveyor's half a dozen of
foolscap. On the contrary, I have allowed myself, as to such points, nearly or
altogether as much licence as if the facts had been entirely of my own invention.
What I contend for is the authenticity of the outline.[48]

Hawthorne is effectively saying that, so long as the 'dressed up' tale abides by
an emotional verisimilitude, which has its roots in the *authorial knowledge and
interpretation* of a distant extratextual reality (the 'motives and modes of
passion' that characterize human beings under certain circumstances), the
storyteller need not concern himself with the material and empirically
measurable aspect of human experience. Hawthorne's contention is a
redrafting of the pact between the author and his audience: moving away
from the realist expectation that the reader should be in a position to verify,
or judge, the veracity of the tale in terms of its actual occurrence or plausibility, he gestures us towards the definition of 'Romance' – and of the genre's
claim, and responsibility, to capture the 'truth of the human heart' – that he
will elaborate more fully in his 'Preface' to *The House of the Seven Gables*
(1851).[49] Within this framework, the issue of the factuality of the narrative is
completely beyond the point, for it is the storyteller's personal guarantee,
through his or her individual sensitivity to the human condition, that
provides the only relevant proof of the truthfulness of his or her tale.

O'Brien too makes a claim for 'a certain latitude' in his storytelling: calling
upon a degree of imaginative freedom is a necessity, rather than a privilege or
a whim, linked to the narrator's task and to his desire to approximate – and
communicate to his readership – a particularly elusive truth. In these circumstances, the author's right to creative licence is tied in to the development of
a new mode of writing: much as Hawthorne was concerned with redefining
the genre of romance, O'Brien configures his inventiveness as an integral part
of his quest for a new way of telling stories – a narrative strategy whose origi-

48 Hawthorne, *The Scarlet Letter*, pp. 32–33.
49 'When a writer calls his work a Romance, it need hardly be observed that he wishes to claim
   a certain latitude, both as to its fashion and material, which he would not have felt himself
   entitled to assume, had he professed to be writing a Novel. The latter form of composition
   is presumed to aim at a very minute fidelity, not merely to the possible, but to the probable
   and ordinary course of man's experience. The former – while as a work of art, it must
   rigidly subject itself to laws, and while it sins unpardonably so far as it may swerve aside
   from the truth of the human heart – has fairly a right to present that truth under circumstances, to a great extent, of the writer's own choosing or creation. [...] The point of view
   in which this tale comes under the Romantic definition lies in the attempt to connect a
   bygone time with the very present that is flitting away from us'; Hawthorne, 'Preface' to
   The House of the Seven Gables, pp. 1–2.

nality is not a question of style or authorial self-indulgence, but rather something deeply connected with the apprehension and articulation of truths that would otherwise be impossible to come to terms with and elaborate. This issue is the subject-matter of one of the briefest sketches in *Things*, 'Good Form', which opens with the blunt declaration that, apart from O'Brien's age, his profession as a writer and the fact that he served as a foot soldier in the Quang Ngai Province, 'almost everything else [in the book] is invented' (*TTC*, 179). Nonetheless, as O'Brien proceeds to explain,

> it's not a game. It's a form. Right here, now, as I invent myself, I'm thinking of all I want to tell you about why this book is written as it is. For instance, I want to tell you this: twenty years ago I watched a man die on a trail near the village of My Khe. I did not kill him. But I was present, you see, and my presence was guilt enough. [...] But listen. Even *that* story is made up. I want you to feel what I felt. I want you to know why story-truth is truer sometimes than happening-truth. (*TTC*, 179)

These self-reflective comments, with their frequent direct addresses to the reader and their reference to the thoughts engendered by the act of story-telling, at the very moment of composition ('Right here, now, as I invent myself...'), convey the urgency and the commitment behind O'Brien's unorthodox narrative choices. This attitude is compounded by the obvious sense of personal accountability that transpires from the anecdote mentioned to exemplify the difference between story-truth and happening-truth. The latter, in this sketch as in the rest of the book, is left significantly vague, when not continuously redefined: in the passage just quoted, O'Brien insists that he did not physically kill the man on the trail, but that his own presence in the war has made him complicit in this and other murders. Immediately afterwards, having admitted that the initial story is made up, O'Brien reiterates the happening-truth that provides the inspiration for the creation of (the different versions of) the man on the trail: as a soldier in Vietnam, O'Brien was exposed to death on a large scale, to many 'real bodies with real faces', but he was young and did not have the courage to look, so that twenty years on, he is left with 'faceless responsibility and faceless grief' (*TTC*, 179). The story-truth relating to the emotional core of this happening-truth (and to the initial confession at the beginning of the sketch) is a portrait in quick, broad strokes of the young Vietnamese soldier already described by O'Brien as his victim in 'The Man I Killed': 'He was a slim, dead, almost dainty young man of about twenty. He lay in the center of a red clay trail near the village of My Khe. His jaw was in his throat. His one eye was shut, the other eye was a star-shaped hole. I killed him. What stories can do, I guess, is make things present', O'Brien concludes. 'I can look at things I never looked at. I can attach faces to grief and love and pity and God' (*TTC*, 179–80).

The power of storytelling to 'make things present' clearly does not rely on the evocation of actual events, but on the imaginative re-elaboration of a particularly haunting experience or of something elemental in the human condition, like grief, love, pity and the quest for signification. (Interestingly, in this specific example, with his emphasis on the face-to-face encounter with the other, O'Brien draws our attention to his attempt to recuperate, through his narrative act, the fundamental ethical relationship obliterated by the perverse logic of war.) O'Brien's story-truth, like Hawthorne's 'truth of the human heart', thus corresponds to what Tzvetan Todorov calls 'truth-disclosure' (*la verité de dévoilement*) in opposition to 'truth-adequation' (*la verité d'adequation*). While truth-adequation can be measured 'only against all or nothing', since it rests on a verifiable adherence to empirical evidence, truth-disclosure should be measured 'against more or less' because it endeavours 'to reveal the essence of a phenomenon, not to establish facts. Novelists aim only for this latter type of truth; nor do they have to teach historians anything about the former'.[50] In other words, Todorov's *verité de dévoilement* is the truth of fiction, and it is for this reason that O'Brien can legitimately get away from the either/or logic of *la verité d'adequation* and make instead the 'both...and' claim of the paradox that concludes 'Good Form': '"Daddy, tell the truth," Kathleen can say, "did you ever kill anybody?" and I can say, honestly, "Of course not." Or I can say, honestly, "Yes"' (*TTC*, 180).

In the course of defining story-truth in opposition to the rigorous philosophical standard of logic, where the truth of speech is configured as *adequatio intellectus ad rem* (adequation of the intellect to the thing or, in Gadamer's words, 'adequation of the presentation through speech to the presented thing'[51]), O'Brien makes a further important distinction between different kinds of tales whose meaningfulness and reliability do not hinge on adherence to actual facts. In 'How to Tell a True War Story', he recounts an anecdote that 'we've all heard', the heartbreaking tale of a self-sacrificing soldier who deliberately takes the blast of an explosion in order to save the life of his comrades. As O'Brien maintains, it is natural to wonder about the veracity of such a story: 'Is it true? The answer matters. You'd feel cheated if it never happened. Without the grounding reality, it's just a trite bit of puffery, pure Hollywood, untrue in the way all such stories are untrue' (*TTC*, 79). The factuality of this episode is not beside the point: without it, the story becomes nothing but a variation on an old cliché, a feel-good narrative based on the archetypal figure of the selfless hero. In the continuation of the same

---

50 Tzvetan Todorov, *The Morals of History* [1991], trans. Alyson Waters (Minneapolis: University of Minnesota Press, 1995), p. 90.
51 Hans-Georg Gadamer, 'What Is Truth?', in *Hermeneutics and Truth*, ed. Brice R. Wachterhauser (Evanston, IL: Northwestern University Press, 1994), pp. 33–46, p. 36.

passage, O'Brien provocatively disputes that the factuality of this event would turn its account into a 'true war story':

> Yet even if it did happen – and maybe it did, anything's possible – even then you know it can't be true, because a true war story does not depend upon that kind of truth. Absolute occurrence is irrelevant. A thing may happen and be a total lie, another thing may not happen and be truer than the truth. For example: Four guys go down a trail. A grenade sails out. One guy jumps on it and takes the blast, but it's a killer grenade and everybody dies anyway. Before they die, though, one of the dead guys says, 'The fuck you do *that* for?' and the jumper says, 'Story of my life, man,' and the other guy starts to smile but he's dead. That's a true story that never happened. (*TTC*, 79)

The anecdote of the selfless hero who succeeds in saving his friends' lives is not a 'true war story' in either case, whether the event it describes is factual or not. If it is, then the account should clearly be viewed as a piece of documentary evidence, an act of testimony – in other words, a statement whose validity relies on the propositional truth of logic, rather than on the story-truth claimed by O'Brien for his narrative. If the same anecdote had no basis in reality, then its profession of truth ought to be seen as pertaining to the self-evident, indisputable authoritativeness of myth, firmly grounded in the circular logic of the *a priori* social consensus that distinguishes sacred from secular writing. As Northrop Frye discusses in *The Secular Scripture* (1976), the appeal of the mythical text to its audience, in terms of the truth it purports to convey, is a question of cultural relevance rather than of factual accuracy.[52] The claim to truth of myth follows as a consequence of the social bearing of the text and not the other way round, as it would happen within a secular framework in which credence must be earned and is not accorded unconditionally. The hold of myth on its audience is inscribed within a tautological, circular temporality, for in this case the interpretative act is caught within the time-warp of sacred culture: the addressees of mythical stories are, by definition, insiders to the civilization whose very *Weltanschauung* these narratives have contributed to shape. In other words, the community's

---

52 'Myths are usually assumed to be true, stories about what really happened. But truth is not the central basis for distinguishing the mythical from the fabulous: it is a certain quality of importance or authority for the community that marks the myth, not truth as such. The anxiety of society, when it urges the authority of a myth and the necessity of believing it, seems to be less to proclaim its truth than to prevent anyone from questioning it. It aims at consent, including the consent of silence, rather than conviction. Thus the Christian myth of providence, *after* a battle, is often invoked by the winning side in a way which makes its truth of secondary importance'; Northrop Frye, *The Secular Scripture: A Study of the Structure of the Romance* (Cambridge, MA, and London: Harvard University Press, 1976), p. 16, my italics.

perception of itself is simultaneously reflected in and created by its own mythical tradition.[53] It is not for its propositional truth that we are asked to engage with and trust the anecdote of the selfless, heroic soldier; on the contrary, as a myth, this story demands our unquestioning subscription because it is always already validated by the deep-rooted investment of our culture in the belief that *dulce et decorum est pro patria mori.*

O'Brien's 'true story that never happened' by contrast, while flying in the face of plausibility ('Before they die, though, one of the dead guys says…') and therefore renouncing any claim to factuality, demystifies the ideal of heroism propounded by its mythical counterpart, rejecting in the process the consolatory function implicit in the reiteration of a valued communal message. Thus O'Brien does not define the scope of his narratives through their ability to communicate a definite truth, either grounded in reality or in shared principles; rather, he configures the storytelling act as an ongoing, endless process of exploration and quest for (provisional) meaning. His juxtaposition between the 'Hollywood' version of the anecdote and the 'true story that never happened' encapsulates the different attitudes towards sensemaking of mythical and fictional narratives respectively:

> Myth operates within the diagrams of ritual, which presupposes total and adequate explanation of things as they are and were; it is a sequence of radically unchangeable gestures. Fictions are for finding things out, and they change as the needs of sense-making change. Myths are the agents of stability, fictions the agents of change. Myths call for absolute, fictions for conditional assent. Myths make sense in terms of a lost order of time, *illud tempus* as Eliade calls it; fictions, if successful, make sense of the here and now, *hoc tempus.*[54]

It is clear that O'Brien claims for his writing the drive of fiction towards 'finding things out' and making sense of the contingent, without ever uttering the last word on any particular subject – especially a thorny one such as the war in Vietnam, and the epistemological and ethical questions triggered by it. Talking about his approach to the definition of courage in a 1991 interview with Martin Naparsteck, O'Brien openly asserts his belief that '[t]he best literature is always explorative. It's searching for answers and never finding them. It's almost like Platonic dialogue. If you knew what courage is, if you had a really wonderful, philosophical explanation of courage, you would do it as philosophy, as explication: you wouldn't write fiction. Fiction is a way of

---

53 See Alasdair MacIntyre's *Three Rival Versions of Moral Enquiry: Encyclopaedia, Genealogy, and Tradition*, for an extensive analysis of this tautological temporality.

54 Frank Kermode, *The Sense of an Ending: Studies in the Theory of Fiction* [1966] (Oxford: Oxford University Press, 1970), p. 39.

testing possibilities and testing hypotheses, and not defining...'.[55] In positing the exploratory function of fiction and circumscribing its claim to truth to *la verité de dévoilement*, O'Brien outlines a view of storytelling as an ongoing project with limited epistemological aims: the emphasis is on the process, which is open-ended, and not on its results, which are at best tentative and provisional, as we shall see in the final section of this chapter.

The ethics of fiction

At the beginning of *If I Die in a Combat Zone*, the most overtly autobiographical of his narratives, O'Brien expresses in no uncertain terms his scepticism towards the testimonial and moral authority of experience: 'Can the foot soldier teach anything important about war, merely for having been there? I think not. He can tell war stories' (*IID*, 32). And, as we have seen, the truthfulness of these stories does not depend on their factuality – guaranteed by the eye-witness status of the soldier-narrator – but on something much less tangible and yet self-evident, because its effects are written on the body, in the 'quick truth goose' that comes when a tale, however implausible or even patently fictional, still manages to offer us a brief, partial and provisional glimpse of what we instinctively recognize as belonging to a fundamentally human sphere. In denying the authority associated with a first-person involvement in an event, O'Brien reiterates the point made in 'The Storyteller' (1935) by Walter Benjamin, who argues that 'the art of storytelling is coming to an end'[56] because of the devaluation of experience – the raw material of the tales exchanged between the storyteller, their occasional sources and their audience – in the modern world. Interestingly, Benjamin maintains that this phenomenon, clearly related to the ever-increasing reliance on technology started by the industrial revolution, has become particularly apparent in the aftermath of the Great War, when 'men returned from the battlefield grown silent – not richer, but poorer in communicable experience'.[57]

The alienating, fragmented reality of modern existence – and what, indeed, is more alienating and traumatic than technological warfare? – is such that it is no longer possible for the individual to translate his or her own *Erlebnis* ('experience' in the sense of something that has been lived through, in a passing moment, and remains unprocessed) into *Erfahrung* ('experience'

---

55 Naparsteck, 'An Interview with Tim O'Brien', p. 5.
56 Walter Benjamin, 'The Storyteller: Reflections on the Works of Nikolai Leskov', in *Illuminations* [1955], trans. Harry Zohn, ed. Hannah Arendt (London: Fontana, 1973), pp. 83–109, p. 83.
57 Benjamin, 'The Storyteller', p. 84.

as something that accrues, and can be reflected upon and communicated to others). *Erfahrung* is also difficult to attain because the rise of the novel and, more generally, the modern decline of oral forms of storytelling in favour of written narratives, have brought about, in the face of the devaluation of the direct communication of experience, the privileging of the more pragmatic category of information, that is a description of things always already 'shot through with explanation'[58] but disconnected from the subjective understanding and the personal guarantee of the storyteller. According to Benjamin, in the modern world we no longer exchange stories, but rather trade in information, whose value does not outlive the moment when the piece of news is first communicated. By contrast, '[a] story is different. It does not expend itself. It preserves and concentrates its strength and is capable of releasing it even after a long time'.[59] Today we know about things, but this knowledge is no longer rooted in either our own, or the storyteller's, experience of them. For this reason, the figure of the storyteller as a dispenser of wisdom or counsel for his audience has become an anachronism – an idea that O'Brien endorses in his refusal to endow his tales with any didactic or testimonial scope.

On the other hand, however, it seems to me that O'Brien still claims for the storyteller an important role as providing a (limited) guarantee of signification, not because of his or her direct engagement with the events at the root of his or her tales (i.e. not because of his or her 'experience' of things), but on the basis of his or her commitment (however idiosyncratic) to the relevance, and to the performative potential, of his or her storytelling activity, regardless of the verifiability of its sources. Following on from Benjamin's diagnosis of the '"poverty of experience" of the modern age', and having remarked on how it was the everyday, and not the unusual, that made up the stuff of experience in pre-modern times, Giorgio Agamben articulates the self-fulfilling connection between authorial trustworthiness and a belief in the power of storytelling:

> [f]or experience has its necessary correlation not in knowledge but in authority – that is the power of words and narration; and no one now seems to wield sufficient authority to guarantee the truth of an experience, and if they do, it does not in the least occur to them that their own authority has its roots in an experience. On the contrary, it is the character of the present time that all authority is founded on what cannot be experienced, and nobody would be inclined to accept the validity of an authority whose sole claim to legitimation was experience.[60]

58 Benjamin, 'The Storyteller', p. 89.
59 Benjamin, 'The Storyteller', p. 90.
60 Giorgio Agamben, *Infancy and History: Essays on the Destruction of Experience* [1978], trans. Liz Heron (London and New York: Verso, 1993), pp. 13, 14.

In O'Brien, too, the notion of authority is detached from the verifiable, and related instead to the storyteller's personal investment in the tales that he or she chooses to tell (in the case of *Things*, and indeed most of O'Brien's other works, these tales are grounded in the unexperienceable reality of war) and to a pressing desire to communicate what resists communication. Obviously, this is an urge that can never be fully satisfied, and is often met at the cost of abandoning factuality and sacrificing the plausibility of the story. Even Mitchell Sanders, the one character who is constantly associated with the need for a moral and who, as a listener to the story of Mary Anne's disappearance into the jungle, demands narrative linearity and plausibility, complaining about Rat Kiley's distant, third-hand connection with the events, feels entitled to embroider his own second-hand account of the listening patrol's mission to the 'talking jungle' ("'Last night, man, I had to make up a few things'", he explains to O'Brien, *TTC*, 74) while insisting on the truthfulness of his tale precisely because of the incredible nature of the incident that it chronicles: "'Yeah, but listen, it's still true. Those six guys, they heard wicked sound out there. They heard sound you just plain won't believe'", *TTC*, 74). The same is true for the O'Brien-narrator of 'How to Tell a True War Story' and, by implication, of the general scope of *Things*, where the fictional and the factual, the imaginary and the autobiographical, are deliberately confused in a never-ending attempt to capture something that approximates the incommunicable *Erlebnis* of war. Faced with his failure to get through to 'the older woman of kindly temperament and humane politics' with his story about Rat Kiley and Curt Lemon's sister, O'Brien acknowledges that his only option is to tell his tale

> one more time, patiently, adding and subtracting, making up a few things to get at the real truth. No Mitchell Sanders, you tell her. No Lemon, no Rat Kiley. No trail junction. No baby buffalo. No vines or moss or white blossoms. Beginning to end, you tell her, it's all made up. Every goddamn detail – the mountains and the river and especially the poor dumb baby buffalo. None of it happened. *None* of it. And even if it did happen, it didn't happen in the mountains, it happened in this little village on the Batangan Peninsula, and it was raining like crazy, and one night a guy named Stink Harris woke up screaming with a leech on his tongue. You can tell a true war story if you just keep on telling it. (*TTC*, 80)

The connection between the truthfulness of a story and its susceptibility to being constantly reshaped and honed, in an endless sequence of retellings, is a question that we will return to later on in this chapter. Before we do that, I would like to reprise O'Brien's general take on the ethics of war narratives; the contention that not even those who have been to Vietnam can draw lessons from the experience of war is in fact a corollary of O'Brien's wider scepticism about any account of the conflict to claim a didactic and/or cathartic function:

> A true war story is never moral. It does not instruct, nor encourage virtue, nor suggest proper models of human behaviour, nor restrain men from doing the things men have always done. If a story seems moral, do not believe it. If at the end of a war story you feel uplifted, or if you feel that a small bit of rectitude has been salvaged from the larger waste, then you have been made victim of a very old and terrible lie. There is no rectitude whatsoever. There is no virtue. As a first rule of thumb, therefore, you can tell a true war story by its absolute and uncompromising allegiance to obscenity and evil. (*TTC*, 68)

This categorical denial of the moral scope of war narratives is predicated on an *ethical* need to avoid any reference to decency and any investment in the possibility of rescuing some kind of signification out of an event whose meaninglessness seems to be the only certainty that modern and contemporary war writers hold on to. Ironically, for somebody so keen to emphasise the amorality of true war stories, O'Brien thus adopts a position that is inherently moral in positing the unredeemable horror of war as an undisputable *a priori*.

In arguing against any attempt to rationalize, and therefore to an extent justify, the conflict, O'Brien is also caught up in another paradox, given how the impulse towards sense-making underscores – more or less explicitly – any narrative act. In selecting, ordering and verbalizing their material, storytellers shape, however loosely, and create connections in what was previously inchoate and unstructured; in Jean-François Lyotard's words, 'narratives are like temporal filters whose function is to transform the emotive charge linked to the event into sequences of units of information capable of giving rise to something like meaning'.[61] In this sense, even the true war stories distinguished by their 'absolute and uncompromising allegiance to obscenity and evil' will inevitably be endowed with some kind of signification by the reader's engagement with them. As Giorgio Mariani points out, O'Brien's refusal to endorse an explicitly didactic stance in storytelling eventually must come up against the fact that 'lessons are not simply encoded in a text by the author. They are the result of textual interpretation and, unless a text goes unread, it cannot escape interpretation; it cannot escape being turned into a "moral"'.[62] O'Brien's response to this objection comes with a remark that openly contradicts (or does it?) his previous point about the amorality of true

61 Jean-François Lyotard, *The Inhuman: Reflections on Time* [1988], trans. Geoffrey Bennington and Rachel Bowlby (Cambridge: Polity Press, 1993), p. 63.
62 Giorgio Mariani, 'Of War, Fiction and Truth: Some Notes on Tim O'Brien's "How To Tell a True War Story"', publication of the Università degli Studi di Salerno, n.d., pp. 223–38, pp. 225–26.

war stories: 'In a true war story, if there's a moral at all, it's like the thread that makes the cloth. You can't tease it out. You can't extract the meaning without unraveling the deeper meaning. And in the end, really, there's nothing much to say about a true war story, except maybe "Oh"' (*TTC*, 75). The acknowledgement of the possibility that a true war story might have a lesson to yield is made simultaneously with a disclaimer of the actual availability of such meaning to those who are looking for it; having declared his aversion to facile didacticisms, O'Brien is careful not to let the investment in moral lessons in through the back door.

The elusive significance of a true war story is reiterated once more in a later section of 'How to Tell' which extends O'Brien's nihilistic hermeneutical attitude from the realm of conscious interpretative acts to that of sudden, unsought epiphanies – delayed revelations that hit us when we least expect them, only to leave us again as soon as we think that we have finally grasped them:

> Often in a true war story there is not even a point, or else the point doesn't hit you until twenty years later, in your sleep, and you wake up and shake your wife and start telling the story to her, except when you get to the end you've forgotten the point again. And then for a long time you lie there watching the story happen in your head. You listen to your wife's breathing. The war's over. You close your eyes. You smile and think, Christ, what's the *point*? (*TTC*, 78)

Apart from the tantalizing futility of the quest for meaning outlined here, this vignette is fundamentally in line with the idea that stories do not expend themselves immediately, but rather resonate with us for a long time and are capable of releasing their strength after years, as Benjamin argued. This point, in turn, leads us back to the consideration of the only way out of the postmodern impasse that O'Brien's utopian rejection of signification brings about.

If the possibility of signification is inherent in any interpretative attempt, then a true war story will defer the production of meaning – and its own reduction to a moral lesson – for as long as it can escape becoming the object of a conclusive hermeneutical act, that is for as long as it remains fluid, ever-changing, liable to infinite performances. 'The endless retelling of a war story will ensure its eternal openness: at any new telling, as oral historians have taught us, a more or less different story will be produced so that the story will never deliver any final truth, but only provisional, precarious, local *truths*'.[63] Interestingly, 'How to Tell' follows the observation that '[y]ou can tell a true war story if you just keep on telling it' with a closing remark which expands

---

63 Mariani, 'Of War, Fiction and Truth', pp. 226–27.

the narrow definition of the genre, refusing a rigid, mimetic subscription to its military subject in order to claim much greater emotional latitude instead:

> And in the end, of course, a true war story is never about war. It's about sunlight. It's about the special way the dawn spreads out on a river when you know you must cross the river and march into the mountains and do things you are afraid to do. It's about love and memory. It's about sorrow. It's about sisters who never write back and people who never listen. (*TTC*, 80)

A true war story is about life and death, about fear, grief and love, about trauma and our inability to process and talk about certain things. This is a point that O'Brien makes implicitly as soon as he lists the first example of what war stories are really about, for the sunlight is a reference to the narrator's recollection – mentioned in the previous page – of the death of Curt Lemon. Blown up by a 'rigged 105 round', Lemon is lifted into the air in the glaring light, thus appearing to have been killed by the sun, an image that O'Brien shares with his readers while confessing that he can never really get it right. If only he could do so, 'then you would believe the last thing Curt Lemon believed, which for him must've been the final truth' (*TTC*, 79). Yet the narrator's effort is doomed. In the end, then, a true war story is about the difficulty of writing true war stories, and about the storyteller's stubborn determination to work in the face of this challenge and in spite of the futility of trying to establish a complete connection with one's audience.

Viewed from this perspective, O'Brien's literary manifesto in 'How to Tell' is reminiscent of John Barth's argument in 'The Literature of Exhaustion' (1967), in which the contemporary artist is configured as someone who may, or rather has no option but to, 'paradoxically turn the felt ultimacies of our time into material and means for his work – *paradoxically* because by doing so he transcends what had appeared to be his refutation, in the same way that the mystic who transcends finitude is said to be enabled to live, spiritually and physically, in the finite world'.[64] In O'Brien's case, of course, the felt ultimacies of postmodernity and the epistemological limitations of a 'literature of exhausted possibilities'[65] are further exacerbated by having war – and the Vietnam war, at that – as subject matter.

Does this mean then that O'Brien sees his writing as ultimately caught up in an endless, narcissistic loop? Do the ontological self-reflections and the epistemological scepticism of postmodern literature, paired with a declared – if provocatively utopian – anti-didactic stance leave no room for an ethical

64 John Barth, 'The Literature of Exhaustion' [1967], in *The Novel Today: Contemporary Writers on Modern Fiction*, ed. Malcolm Bradbury (Manchester: Manchester University Press, 1977), pp. 70–83, p. 78.
65 Barth, 'The Literature of Exhaustion', p. 70.

commitment? O'Brien addresses this issue with a poignant narrative gesture, exploring the possibility of representing the point of view of the dead enemy in 'The Man I Killed'. This is clearly a radical proposition, for, as argued by Roland Barthes, the perspective of the dead is truly unrepresentable, and marks the limit of our capacity for empathy.[66] The latter, in this particular case, is already being tested by the extreme alterity of the subject in question, whose Otherness, predicated in the first instance on ontological or existential grounds and accentuated by his cultural difference from the narrator, is further intensified by his status as a military opponent and purveyor of death. Nevertheless, the confrontation with the dead enemy becomes one of the key moments of *Things*, signalled as it is by the centrality of 'The Man I Killed' in the text, as well as by the insistent focus on this episode throughout the entire narrative, much as in the case of the traumatic deaths of Kiowa and Curt Lemon. The portrait of this nameless casualty of war begins in a factual manner, with a very meticulous, graphic description of the man's body, his disfigured face and his empty gaze; while it is clearly pervaded by the desire to give an accurate, individual identity to its subject, this account cannot but mention, as the character's distinctive traits, details which highlight his sudden, violent departure from the realm of the living, his gruesome trans-formation from a human being into a catalogue of monstrous images – or even of shocking absences – of body parts: 'His jaw was in his throat, his upper lip and teeth were gone, his one eye was shut, his other eye was a star-shaped hole' (*TTC*, 121). After this opening onto a gritty reality, the narrative then soars into an imaginative dimension, as the fictional Tim O'Brien traces the dead man's story from his birth in 1946 in a village of the Quang Ngai Province to his somewhat tentative enlistment with the 48th Vietcong Battalion and his demise at the hands of a young American soldier whose own participation in the war had been dictated by the desire not to let his community down. The dead man's identity is thus configured with obvious echoes of (the fictional and the real) O'Brien's past, with particular emphasis on their common studious, intellectual nature, their aversion to conflict, and their fear of the military enterprise in the face of a legacy of heroism, both in their family's and in their country's history.

The similarities in the two men's backgrounds – all related to biographical elements that have marked O'Brien's reluctant engagement with the war, so as to place emphasis on the fact that both killer and dead man are victims, albeit in dramatically different ways – are overt enough to make clear that the identity of the Vietnamese soldier is an invention of O'Brien's and indeed a

---

66 See Roland Barthes, 'Diderot, Brecht, Eisenstein', in *Image, Music, Text*, trans. Stephen Heath (London: Fontana, 1977), pp. 69–78, p. 77. I am indebted for this reading to the work of Giorgio Mariani and Stefano Rosso, who have both repeatedly dwelt on 'The Man I Killed' as a key text in O'Brien's oeuvre.

projection of his own life. Because it is so transparent and urgent, this strikes me as an honest and necessary gesture of empathy, an attempt to achieve an ideal reconciliation in the understandable effort to assuage one's guilt, no matter how ultimately powerless O'Brien is in undoing the terrible deed that he once committed, and no matter how fraught with neo-colonizing impulses his narrative act will inevitably be: the points of contact between the dead Vietnamese's (imagined) life and O'Brien's own background highlight the two characters' fundamental common humanity, as well as their accidental similarities, but, without spelling it out, they also draw attention to the American soldier's inability to conceive of the enemy in any way other than in his own image. At the same time, however, the story of the dead man contains minute details – his passion for maths rather than literature and philosophy, or the presence of a young wife, for example – that prevent what would be a complete, and therefore patently inappropriate, flattening of the one character onto the other. And, significantly, O'Brien's reconstruction of his victim's identity does not stretch to the invention of a name, or a ventriloquizing of his voice.

The outline of the dead soldier's past and the imaginative adoption of the dead man's perspective, all in all, cultivate and indeed flag up the precarious balance between the factual and the fictional, the desire to find or establish sympathetic connections and the obvious one-sidedness of this process, which must necessarily teeter on the brink of hijacking the story of the man who has been condemned to silence, even as it tries to redress, in the only way it can, the taking of his life. Interestingly, while the story of the dead soldier is, of necessity, an imaginative creation, it unfolds in the indicative mode, with only the occasional 'maybe' to signal its speculative nature. O'Brien continues to demand that the reader should pause to take stock of the narrative strategies (and the implications thereof) in place in this unlikely story by multiplying its strands and layers. As we have come to expect from the wider structure of *Things* and from O'Brien's general writing practice, 'The Man I Killed' contains two interweaving tales: the (re)construction of the dead man's past and an account of the immediate aftermath of his death. More than showing us the perspective of the killer side by side with that of his victim, the description of O'Brien's reaction to his first casualty offers an opportunity to portray this character too as someone who is simultaneously silent and being spoken for, as he is both the speechless recipient and the exemplary subject of a well-meaning and pious narrative (while of course also being the fictional narrator of *Things* and of 'The Man I Killed', and an overt reference to the extratextual author and war veteran).

On one hand, the story of the intradiegetic O'Brien's wordless traumatization following the death of the Vietnamese soldier is a perfect complement, and corrective, to the story of the O'Brien-narrator who, years after the incident, can talk to us about what happened and try to bring the past back to life, while laying old ghosts to rest. On the other hand, the intradiegetic O'Brien, silent addressee of the consolatory, if perfectly reasonable, platitudes uttered by Kiowa ('Tim, it's a *war*. The guy wasn't Heidi – he had a weapon, right?', *TTC*, 123) provides something of a mirror to our position as recipients of 'The Man I Killed', which is itself partly moved by and therefore mired in an inescapable, and inevitably flawed, cathartic drive. Through this reverberation of points of view and narrative positions, the readers are effectively being asked to identify with the killer in the story who, in turn, tries to identify with his victim, while also having been shown to have failed to find any redemptive power in the early sense-making narrative attempts addressed to him by his fellow soldier Kiowa. In reading 'The Man I Killed', we therefore both witness *and* become implicated in a desperate effort to face up to and process feelings of guilt and responsibility, in a doomed experiment to achieve some kind of redemption and signification through a view of the events which aspires to open up to opposite perspectives, even when these perspectives are obviously unavailable and unrepresentable. This story is O'Brien's attempt to articulate – and enact, for as much (or as little) as it is possible – the only truly ethical position available to the war writer. As Stefano Rosso argues,

> 'The Man I Killed' puts forth the idea that writing should try and avoid the monologism and the 'panopticism' typical of so much literature still centred on a simplified idea of meaning and narrator, while at the same time acknowledging that this is an impossible task. It is perhaps for this reason that the story closes with Kiowa's desperate plea ['Talk to me, Kiowa said', *TTC*, 125] left unanswered by Tim […]. The O'Brien-narrator, who continues to multiply the points of view, is determined to contradict the O'Brien-character, who remains absolutely silent. And this seems to me a potentially productive contradiction – maybe the only available chance – for a kind of writing that is trying to break out of the silence in which those who have experienced the war are inevitably driven to seek shelter.[67]

This is a move that, quite apart from trying to recuperate an ethical dimension to the saturated representational power of postmodernity, perhaps also enables O'Brien to bypass the paradox created by his call for an uncompromising allegiance to evil in war stories. Such an allegiance, spurred by what Mariani calls the 'anti-war impulse' of modern war literature, is completely

---

67 Stefano Rosso, 'Narrativa statunitense e guerra del Vietnam: un'introduzione' [US Fiction and the Vietnam War: An Introduction], in *Vietnam e ritorno. La 'guerra sporca' nel cinema, nella letteratura e nel teatro* [*Vietnam and Back: The 'Dirty War' in Cinema, Literature and Theatre*], eds. Stefano Ghislotti and Stefano Rosso (Milan: Marcos y Marcos, 1996), pp. 107–38, p. 129, my translation.

impracticable for narrative, if not moral, reasons, since it 'conflicts power-fully and unpredictably with the writer's need for a plot that will draw the reader's interest and attention'.[68] First of all, allegiance to evil implies a writer and a reader capable of distinguishing between right and wrong, and there-fore the possibility of inscribing the story in question within an ethical interpretative horizon. Concomitantly, an uncompromising allegiance to evil would alienate the reader from the story, causing him/her to withhold sympathy and recoil in horror in the face of what would presumably be an unbearable and unacceptable burden. If a true war story really ought to be nothing more than a representation of pure evil, then how can the writer hope to capture readers' interest and appeal to their understanding and compas-sion? If one were to go for this approach to storytelling – if it were indeed feasible to avoid the very possibility of generating comprehension and sympathy – war would be turned into pure Otherness, whereas O'Brien wants his audience to feel implicated and to participate in his, and his charac-ters', inconclusive attempts to come to terms with difficult moral choices, traumatic memories and unspeakable experiences.[69] O'Brien himself has explained the limitations of a merely mimetic conception of the task of story-telling with his reflections on how to convey the boredom of war:

> …fiction – good writing of *any* kind – can't employ this imitative fallacy. You don't try to get at boredom by being boring in your writing. […] So you compress the monotony down. In a way, of course, it's a kind of lie, a kind of embellishing, but you're trying to get at a deeper truth. Truth does not reside on the surface of events. Truth resides in those deeper moments of punctuation, when things explode. So you compress the boredom down, hinting at it but always going for drama – because the essence of the experience was dramatic. You tell lies to get at the truth.[70]

O'Brien's writing is all about these 'moments of punctuation, when things explode': unresolved tensions and dilemmas, inconclusive stories, compul-sive tellings and retellings that erase one another, fail to gather narrative threads and instead let meaning disperse in opposite directions, because it is the sense-making process itself – the author's as well as the reader's – and not the end result, which is always inadequate and untrustworthy, that really matters. Whether the overt artistry, moral ambiguity and self-contradictori-ness of texts such as 'The Man I Killed' and *The Things They Carried* are more than postmodern gimmickry and manage, with their moments of

---

68 Mariani, 'Of War, Fiction and Truth', p. 227.
69 Remember his endorsement of Rat Kiley's narrative strategy, his 'heat[ing] up the truth, to make it burn so hot that you would feel exactly what he felt' (*TTC*, 87).
70 Schroeder, 'Two Interviews', p. 141.

punctuation, to achieve that fleeting 'quick truth goose' (*TTC*, 34), touch the audience and resonate with them through time, it is for the individual reader to judge. At the time of writing, on the twentieth anniversary of the publication of *Things*, aged sixty-three, O'Brien continues to proclaim his suspicion of absolutism and certainty, his scepticism towards 'what's declared to be true'.[71] In the same interview, asked about his opinion on the current American military engagement in the Middle East, while not shrinking from a clear attack on George W. Bush's foreign politics and its legacy, O'Brien identifies the main source of his frustration in the lack of a general critical perspective, in the absence of a desire to ask difficult questions even when these are likely to remain unanswered. Can the foot soldier teach anything important about war, merely for having been there then? No. But he can tell war stories, and hope that they will prompt some uncomfortable questions.

---

71 'Interview with Tim O'Brien', http://bigthink.com/timobrien, 15 April 2010 (accessed 10 July 2010).

Bibliography

Works by Tim O'Brien

Books

If I Die in a Combat Zone. [1973] London: Harper Perennial, 2006.
Northern Lights. [1975] London: Flamingo, 1998.
Going After Cacciato. [1978] London: Flamingo, 1988.
The Nuclear Age. [1985] London: Collins, 1986.
The Things They Carried. [1990] London: Flamingo, 1991.
In the Lake of the Woods. [1994] London: Flamingo, 1995.
Tomcat in Love. [1998] London: Flamingo, 2000.
July, July. London: Flamingo, 2002.

Interviews

Bourne, Daniel. 'A Conversation with Tim O'Brien'. *Artful Dodge.* 2 October 1991, http://www3.wooster.edu/ artfuldodge/interviews/obrien.htm (accessed 10 July 2010).

Elborough, Travis. 'Relying on Memory and Imagination: Travis Elborough Talks to Tim O'Brien'. Tim O'Brien. *If I Die in a Combat Zone.* [1973]. London: Harper Perennial, 2006. 2–9.

Karp, Josh. 'The "What If?" Game'. *The Atlantic.* 30 October 2002. http://www.theatlantic.com/unbound/interviews/int2002-10-30.htm (accessed 22 October 2008).

'Interview with Tim O'Brien'. *Readers Read.* http://www.readersread.com/features/timobrien.htm (accessed 22 October 2008).

'Interview with Tim O'Brien'. http://bigthink.com/timobrien. 15 April 2010 (accessed 10 July 2010).

McCaffery, Larry. 'Interview with Tim O'Brien'. *Chicago Review.* 33.2 (1982), 129–49.

McNerney, Brian C. 'Responsibly Inventing History: An Interview with Tim O'Brien'. *War, Literature, and the Arts: An International Journal of the Humanities.* 6.2 (1994), 1–26.

Naparsteck, Martin. 'An Interview with Tim O'Brien'. *Contemporary Literature.* 32.1 (1991), 1–11.

Schroeder, Eric James. 'Two Interviews: Talks with Tim O'Brien and Robert Stone'. *Modern Fiction Studies.* 30.1 (1984), 135–64.

Secondary works on Tim O'Brien

Books

Heberle, Mark A. *A Trauma Artist: Tim O'Brien and the Fiction of Vietnam*. Iowa City: University of Iowa Press, 2001.

Herzog, Tobey C. *Tim O'Brien*. New York: Twayne Publishers, 1997.

Kaplan, Steven. *Understanding Tim O'Brien*. Columbia, SC: University of South Carolina Press, 1994.

Vernon, Alex. *Soldiers Once and Still: Ernest Hemingway, James Salter and Tim O'Brien*. Iowa City: University of Iowa Press, 2004.

Journal articles and chapters in books

Bates, Milton J. 'Tim O'Brien's Myth of Courage'. *Modern Fiction Studies*. 33.2 (1987), 263–79.

Bonn, Maria S. 'Can Stories Save Us? Tim O'Brien and the Efficacy of the Text'. *Critique*. 36.1 (1994), 2–15.

Chen, Tina. '"Unraveling the Deeper Meaning": Exile and the Embodied Poetics of Displacement in Tim O'Brien's *The Things They Carried*'. *Contemporary Literature*. 39.1 (1998), 77–98.

Jarraway, David R. '"Excremental Assault" in Tim O'Brien: Trauma and Recovery in Vietnam War Literature'. *Modern Fiction Studies*. 44.3 (1998), 695–711.

Jarvis, Brian. 'Skating on a Shit Field: Tim O'Brien and the Topography of Trauma'. *American Fiction of the 1990s: Reflections of History and Culture*. Ed. Jay Prosser. London and New York: Routledge, 2008, 134–47.

Kaufmann, Michael. 'The Solace of Bad Form: Tim O'Brien's Postmodernist Revisions of Vietnam in "Speaking of Courage"'. *Critique*. 46.4 (2005), 333–43.

Lustig, T. J. '"Moments of Punctuation": Metonymy and Ellipsis in Tim O'Brien'. *The Yearbook of English Studies*. 31 (2001), 74–92.

Lustig, T. J. '"Which Way Home?" Tim O'Brien and the Question of Reference'. *Textual Practice*. 18.3 (2004), 395–414.

Mariani, Giorgio. 'Of War, Fiction and Truth: Some Notes on Tim O'Brien's "How To Tell a True War Story"', publication of the Università degli Studi di Salerno, n.d., 223–38.

McWilliams, Dean. 'Time in O'Brien's *Going After Cacciato*'. *Critique*. 29.4 (1988), 245–55.

Piwinski, David J. 'My Lai, Flies, Beelzebub in Tim O'Brien's *In the Lake of the Woods*'. *War, Literature and the Arts*. 12.2 (2000), 196–202.

Raymond, Michael. 'Imagined Responses to Vietnam: Tim O'Brien's *Going After Cacciato*'. *Critique: Studies in Contemporary Fiction*. 24.2 (1983), 97–104.

Rosso, Stefano. 'La mascolinità problematica nella narrativa di guerra di Tim O'Brien'. *Methodologies of Gender*. Eds. Mario Corona and Giuseppe Lombardo. Rome: Herder, 1993, 493–504.

Slabey, Robert M. '*Going After Cacciato*: Tim O'Brien "Separate Peace"'. *America Rediscovered: Critical Essays on Literature and Film on the Vietnam War*. Eds. Owen W. Gilman, Jr and Lorrie Smith. New York and London: Garland

Publishing Inc., 1990, 205–24.

Smiley, Pamela. 'The Role of the Ideal (Female) Reader in Tim O'Brien's *The Things They Carried*: Why Should Real Women Play?'. *The Massachusetts Review*. 43.4 (2002), 602–13.

Smith, Lorrie N. '"The Things Men Do": The Gendered Subtext in Tim O'Brien's Esquire Stories'. *Critique*. 36.1 (1994), 16–39.

Vannatta, Dennis. 'Theme and Structure in Tim O'Brien's *Going After Cacciato*'. *Modern Fiction Studies*. 28.2 (1982), 242–46.

Vernon, Alex. 'O'Brien in an American War Literature Class'. *Approaches to Teaching the Works of Tim O'Brien*. Eds. Alex Vernon and Catherine Calloway. New York: The Modern Language Association of America, 2010, 103–10.

Book reviews

Freedman, Richard. 'A Separate Peace'. *The New York Times*. 12 February 1978. http://www.nytimes.com/books/98/09/20/specials/obrien-cacciato.html (accessed 21 July 2010).

Gates, David. 'Everybody Must Get Sloshed'. *The New York Times*. 13 October 2002. http://www.nytimes.com/2002/10/13/books/everybody-must-get-sloshed.html (accessed 20 October 2008).

Hodara, Susan. 'Asking the Whole Country to Embrace a War Story'. *The New York Times*. 29 January 2010. http://www.nytimes.com/2010/01/31/nyregion/31bookwe.html (accessed 25 November 2010).

Kakutani, Michiko. 'Prophet of Doom'. *The New York Times*. 28 September 1985. http://www.nytimes.com/1985/09/28/books/books-of-the-times-prophet-of-doom.html (accessed 20 October 2008).

Kakutani, Michiko. '*Tomcat in Love*: Shell Shock on the Battlefields of a Messy Love Life'. *The New York Times*. 15 September 1998. http://www.nytimes.com/books/98/09/13/daily/tomcat-book-review.html (accessed 12 October 2008).

Peschel, Joseph. 'Tim O'Brien's *The Things They Carried*, released in 20th anniversary edition, renews war's ambiguity'. Steven Levingston. 'Political Bookworm. Where Tomorrow's Must-read Political Books Are Discovered Today'. *The Washington Post*. 24 March 2010. http://voices.washingtonpost.com/political-bookworm/2010/03/tim_obriens_the_things_they_ca.html (accessed 25 November 2010).

Smiley, Jane. 'Catting Around'. *The New York Times*. 20 September 1998. http://www.nytimes.com/books/98/09/20/reviews/980920.20smiley.html (accessed 12 October 2008).

Other Primary Sources

Baker, Mark. *Nam: The Vietnam War in the Words of the Men and Women Who Fought There*. [1981] London: Abacus, 1982.

Caputo, Philip. *A Rumor of War*. [1977] London: Pimlico, 1999.

Conrad, Joseph. *Heart of Darkness*. [1899] Ed. Robert Hampson. London: Penguin, 1995.

Conrad, Joseph. *The Nigger of the "Narcissus"*. [1897] Ed. Robert Kimbrough. New York: Norton, 1979.

Conrad, Joseph. 'Youth: A Narrative'. [1902] *Selected Short Stories*. Ed. Keith Carabine. London: Wordsworth, 1997, 69–94.

Cooper, James Fenimore. *The Last of the Mohicans*. [1926] Ed. John McWilliams. Oxford: Oxford World Classics, 1990.

Crane, Stephen. *The Red Badge of Courage*. [1895] *The Red Badge of Courage and Other Stories*. Ed. Pascal Covici, Jr. London: Penguin, 1991.

Emerson, Ralph Waldo. *Essays and Poems by Ralph Waldo Emerson*. Ed. Peter Norberg. New York: Barnes and Noble, 2004.

Hawthorne, Nathaniel. *The Scarlet Letter*. [1850] Oxford: Oxford University Press, 1962.

Hawthorne, Nathaniel. *The House of the Seven Gables*. [1851] London: The Penguin American Library, 1981.

Hemingway, Ernest. *Fiesta: The Sun Also Rises*. [1927] London: Arrow Books, 2004.

Hemingway, Ernest. *A Farewell to Arms*. [1929] London: Arrow Books, 1994.

Herr, Michael. *Dispatches*. [1977] London: Picador, 1978.

Melville, Herman. 'Billy Budd, Sailor'. *Billy Budd, Sailor and Other Stories*. Ed. Harold Beaver. London: Penguin, 1985, 317–409.

Sassoon, Siegfried. *Memoirs of an Infantry Officer*. [1930] London: Faber & Faber, 2000.

Spencer, Ernest. *Welcome to Vietnam, Macho Man: Reflections of a Khe San Vet*. [1987] New York: Bantam, 1991.

General

Achebe, Chinua. 'An Image of Africa'. *Research in African Literatures*. 9.1 (1978), 1–15.

Addington, Larry H. *America's War in Vietnam: A Short Narrative History*. Bloomington and Indianapolis: Indiana University Press, 2000.

Agamben, Giorgio. *Infancy and History: Essays on the Destruction of Experience*. [1978] Trans. Liz Heron. London New York, Verso, 1993.

Amato, Joseph A. and Anthony Amato, 'Minnesota, Real and Imagined: A View from the Countryside'. *Daedalus*. 129.3 (2000), 55–80.

Bakhtin, Mikhail. *Rabelais and his World*. [1965] Trans. Hélène Iswolsky. Bloomington: Indiana University Press, 1984.

Barth, John. 'The Literature of Exhaustion'. [1967] *The Novel Today: Contemporary Writers on Modern Fiction*. Ed. Malcolm Bradbury. Manchester: Manchester University Press, 1977, 70–83.

Barthes, Roland. 'Diderot, Brecht, Eisenstein'. *Image, Music, Text*. Trans. Stephen Heath. London: Fontana, 1977, 69–78.

Bates, Milton J. *The Wars We Took to Vietnam: Cultural Conflict and Storytelling*.

Berkeley and Los Angeles: University of California Press, 1996.

Beidler, Philip D. *American Literature and the Experience of Vietnam*. Athens, GA: The University of Georgia Press, 1982.

Beidler, Philip D. *Re-Writing America: Vietnam Authors in their Generation*. Athens, GA: The University of Georgia Press, 1991.

Benjamin, Walter. 'The Storyteller: Reflections on the Works of Nikolai Leskov'. *Illuminations*. [1955] Ed. Hannah Arendt. Trans. Harry Zohn. London: Fontana, 1973, 83–109.

Booth, Wayne C. *The Rhetoric of Fiction*. Chicago: University of Chicago Press, 1961.

Cixous, Hélène. 'Sorties: Out and Out: Attacks/Ways Out/Forays'. Hélène Cixous and Catherine Clément. *The Newly Born Woman*. [1975] Trans. Betsy Wing. [1986] London: I. B. Tauris Publishers, 1996, 63–132.

Connell, Evan S. *Son of the Morning Star: General Custer and the Battle of the Little Bighorn*. [1984] London: Picador, 1985.

de Beauvoir, Simone. *The Second Sex*. [1949] Trans. Howard Madison Parshley. New York: Alfred A. Knopf, 1993.

Eliade, Mircea. *The Myth of the Eternal Return or, Cosmos and History*. [1949] Trans. Willard R. Trask. Princeton: Princeton University Press, 1974.

Fiedler, Leslie. *Love and Death in the American Novel*. [1960] Champaign, IL, and London: Dalkey Archive Press, 2003.

Forter, Greg. 'Melancholy Modernism: Gender and the Politics of Mourning in *The Sun Also Rises*'. *The Hemingway Review*. 21.1 (2001), 22–37.

Frye, Northrop. *The Secular Scripture: A Study of the Structure of the Romance*. Cambridge, MA, and London: Harvard University Press, 1976.

Fussell, Paul. *The Great War and Modern Memory*. [1975] Oxford: Oxford University Press, 2000.

Gadamer, Hans-Georg. 'What Is Truth?'. *Hermeneutics and Truth*. Ed. Brice R. Wachterhauser. Evanston, IL: Northwestern University Press, 1994, 33–46.

Genette, Gérard. *Narrative Discourse: An Essay in Method*. [1972] Trans. Jane E. Lewin. Ithaca, NY: Cornell University Press, 1980.

Gibson, James William. *Warrior Dreams: Violence and Manhood in Post-Vietnam America*. New York: Hill and Wang, 1994.

Golomb, Jacob. *In Search of Authenticity: From Kierkegaard to Camus*. London and New York: Routledge, 1995.

Hables Gray, Chris. 'Postmodernism with a Vengeance: The Vietnam War'. *The Vietnam War and Postmodernity*. Ed. Michael Bibby. Boston: University of Massachusetts, 2000, 173–97.

John Hellman, *American Myth and the Legacy of Vietnam* (New York: Columbia University Press, 1986).

Herman, Judith Lewis. *Trauma and Recovery: From Domestic Abuse to Political Terror*. London: Pandora, 1992.

Herzog, Tobey C. *Vietnam War Stories: Innocence Lost*. London and New York: Routledge, 1992.

Hutcheon, Linda. *A Poetics of Postmodernism: History, Theory, Fiction*. New York and London: Routledge, 1988.

Hutcheon, Linda. *The Politics of Postmodernism.* New York: Routledge, 1989.

Hyland, Peter. 'The Little Woman in the *Heart of Darkness*'. *Conradiana.* 20.1 (1988), 3–11.

Jakobson, Roman. 'Two Aspects of Language and Two Types of Aphasic Disturbances'. *Language in Literature.* Eds. and trans. Krystyna Pomorska and Stephen Rudy. Cambridge, MA: Belknap, 1987, 95–114.

Jameson, Fredric. 'Postmodernism, or the Cultural Logic of Late Capitalism'. *New Left Review*, 146 (1984), 53–92.

Jeffords, Susan. *The Remasculinization of America: Gender and the Vietnam War*, Bloomington and Indianapolis: Indiana University Press, 1989.

Johnson, Barbara. 'Melville's Fist: The Execution of *Billy Budd*'. *Studies in Romanticism.* 18.4 (1979), 567–99.

Johnson, Kermit D. *Realism and Hope in a Nuclear Age.* Louisville, KY: John Knox Press, 1988.

Jones, Susan. *Conrad and Women.* Oxford and New York: Oxford University Press, 1999.

Kermode, Frank. *The Sense of an Ending: Studies in the Theory of Fiction.* [1966] Oxford and New York: Oxford University Press, 1970.

Lewis, Lloyd B. *The Tainted War: Culture and Identity in Vietnam War Narratives.* Westport, CT: Greenwood Press, 1985.

Lyotard, Jean-François. *The Inhuman. Reflections on Time.* [1988] Trans. Geoffrey Bennington and Rachel Bowlby. Cambridge: Polity Press, 1993.

MacIntyre, Alasdair. *Three Rival Versions of Moral Enquiry: Encyclopaedia, Genealogy, and Tradition.* Notre Dame, IN: University of Notre Dame Press, 1990.

Martin, Andrew. *Receptions of War: Vietnam in American Culture.* [1993] Norman, OK, and London: University of Oklahoma Press, 1994.

McIntire, Gabrielle. 'The Women Do Not Travel: Gender, Difference, and Incommensurability in Conrad's *Heart of Darkness*'. *Modern Fiction Studies*, 48.2 (2002), 257–84.

Melling, Philip. *Vietnam in American Literature.* Boston: G. K. Hall, 1990.

Newman, John. *Vietnam War Literature: An Annotated Bibliography of Imaginative Works About Americans Fighting in Vietnam.* Metuchen, NJ: Scarecrow Press, 1988.

Rosso, Stefano. 'Narrativa statunitense e guerra del Vietnam: un canone in formazione'. *Acoma.* 4 (1995), 73–85.

Rosso, Stefano. 'Narrativa statunitense e guerra del Vietnam: un'introduzione'. *Vietnam e ritorno. La 'guerra sporca' nel cinema, nella letteratura e nel teatro.* Eds. Stefano Ghislotti and Stefano Rosso. Milan: Marcos y Marcos, 1996, 107–38.

Rosso, Stefano. *Musi gialli e Berretti verdi. Narrazioni USA sulla Guerra del Vietnam.* Bergamo: Bergamo University Press, 2003.

Ruane, Kevin. *The Vietnam Wars.* Manchester and New York: Manchester University Press, 2000.

Said, Edward. *Orientalism.* [1978] London: Penguin, 1995.

Slotkin, Richard. *Regeneration Through Violence: The Mythology of the American*

Frontier 1600–1860. [1973] Norman, OK: University of Oklahoma Press, 2000.

Slotkin, Richard. *Gunfighter Nation: The Myth of the Frontier in Twentieth-Century America.* [1992] New York: HarperCollins, 1993.

Smith, Joanna M. '"Too Beautiful Altogether:" Patriarchal Ideology in *Heart of Darkness'. Heart of Darkness: A Case Study in Contemporary Criticism.* Ed. Ross C. Murfin. New York: St. Martin's Press, 1989, 179–95.

Straus, Nina Pelikan. 'The Exclusion of the Intended from Secret Sharing in Conrad's *Heart of Darkness'. Novel.* 20.2 (1987), 123–37.

Sturken, Marita. *Tangled Memories: The Vietnam War, the AIDS Epidemic, and the Politics of Remembering.* Berkeley and London: University of California Press, 1997.

Tal, Kalí. 'The Mind at War: Images of Women in Vietnam Novels by Combat Veterans'. *Contemporary Literature.* 31.1 (1990), 76–96.

Taylor, Mark. *The Vietnam War in History, Literature and Film.* Edinburgh: Edinburgh University Press, 2003.

Trilling, Lionel. *Sincerity and Authenticity.* [1971] Oxford: Oxford University Press, 1972.

Todorov, Tzvetan. *Facing the Extreme: Moral Life in the Concentration Camps.* [1996] Trans. Arthur Denner and Abigail Pollack. London: Phoenix, 2000.

Todorov, Tzvetan. *The Morals of History.* [1991] Trans. Alyson Waters. Minneapolis: University of Minnesota Press, 1995.

Watt, Ian. *The Rise of the Novel: Studies in Defoe, Richardson and Fielding.* [1957] London: Chatto & Windus, 1963.

Watts, Cedric. '"Heart of Darkness"'. *The Cambridge Companion to Joseph Conrad.* Ed. John H. Stape. Cambridge: Cambridge University Press, 1996, 45–62.

Wintle, Justin. *The Viet Nam Wars.* London: Weidenfeld & Nicolson, 1991.

Young, Marilyn B. *The Vietnam Wars, 1945–1990.* New York: HarperCollins, 1991.

Index

Printed and bound by CPI Group (UK) Ltd, Croydon, CR0 4YY

13/04/2025

14656593-0005